To Judge Andree Roaf:
    A good friend a
judge who has given so much
time to the legal profession.
            Best regards,
            Robert R. Wright
    4/13/02

OLD SEEDS IN THE NEW LAND

HISTORY AND REMINISCENCES
OF THE BAR OF ARKANSAS

Robert Ross Wright

Donaghey Distinguished Professor of Law Emeritus

University of Arkansas at Little Rock

PRESS

FAYETTEVILLE ARKANSAS

ISBN 0-943099-25-0

m & m Press
P.O. Box 338
Fayetteville, AR 72702

Printed on recycled paper

Let us now praise famous men, and our fathers in their generations. The Lord apportioned to them great glory, his majesty from the beginning. There were those who ruled in their kingdoms, and were men renowned for their power, giving counsel by their understanding, and proclaiming prophecies; leaders of the people in their deliberations and in understanding of learning for the people, wise in their words of instruction—all these were honored in their generations, and were the glory of their times. There are some of them who have left a name, so that men declare their praise. And there are some who have no memorial, who have perished as though they had not lived; they have become as though they had not been born, and so have their children after them. But these were men of mercy, whose righteous deeds have not been forgotten; their posterity will continue forever, and their glory will not be blotted out. Their bodies were buried in peace, and their names live to all generations.

—Ecclesiasticus

DONORS

The following attorneys and firms contributed financial support to this History of the Bar project and made its completion possible.

Charles W. Baker

Brazil, Clawson &
  Adlong

Charles A. Brown

Ruth H. Brunson

John C. Calhoun, Jr.

Maurice Cathey

W. Dane Clay

Howard Cockrill

Ben Core

Jack C. Deacon

E. Charles
  Eichenbaum

Eldridge & Eldridge

Robert R. Estes

Oscar Fendler

John C. Finley III

John A. Fogleman

James M. Gardner

Charles R. Garner

Greg Giles

Jeffrey M. Graham

Albert Graves

J. W. Green, Jr.

Steven D. Gunderson

Mark K. Halter

Ralph C. Hamner

Hubbard Patton Peek

Haltom & Roberts

Horace Jewell

David J. Lach

Robert A. Leflar

Chester C. Lowe, Jr.

William A. Martin

Susan Fox Martin

S. Hubert Mayes, Jr.

A. D. McAllister, Jr.

Andre McNeil

H. Maurice Mitchell

Ralph C. Murray

Pettus Law Firm

John B. Plegge

Louis L. Ramsay, Jr.

Murray O. Reed

Kirby Riffel

Ramona Roe

Louis Rosen

Scheiffler Law Firm

Mary Davies Scott

Shackleford, Shackle-
  ford & Phillips

Stephen M. Sharum

J. Michael Shaw

George Rose Smith

William J. Smith

John F. Stroud, Jr.

Winfred A. Trafford

Otis H. Turner

Col. John Norman
  Warnock

Franklin Wilder

Richard A. Williams

J. Gaston Williamson

Roxanne T. Wilson

Wm. R. Wilson, Jr.

Henry Woods

Truman E. Yancy

†

PREFACE

The title to this book is taken from a statement of Sir Edward Coke in Coke's Reports that "out of the old fields" will spring and grow new corn. He was not discussing agriculture, but the English common law and how precedent affects it. Because we received the common law and certain acts of Parliament into our law and because our Bar is the product of that system, I thought it was a fitting title for the history of the Bar. The old seeds were represented by the law that we received, and the new land was ours.

This book does not purport to be a history of Arkansas. It is a history of the organized bar and certain segments of the bar such as women lawyers and African-American lawyers or particular aspects of the profession such as legal education. The book also discusses some of the leading judges in Arkansas over the years taking into account as may be appropriate the setting in which they served. It begins with a chronological development of Arkansas, prominent lawyers and the events that they were involved in, and carries that theme to the end of the 19th Century when the organized bar developed on a permanent basis. The events that affected practicing lawyers and the organized bar during the 20th Century are covered in that context. At the end of the book, in the last chapter, there is a lengthy discussion of different lawyers of the 20th Century with a particular emphasis on those of the last sixty years. This is a long chapter about their reminiscences and recollections along with some stories they told.

One disappointment was that I had much more material than I could get into this book. Another was that I did not have the opportunity to tell more about some lawyers who were not mentioned or mentioned only in passing. Finally, I was disappointed that I could not finish this book a couple of years earlier, so that it would be in print in 1998, the year that the Bar Association views as its centennial anniversary. (Was 1998 or 1999 the centennial of the Arkansas Bar Association? See the chapter on the organized Bar and make up your own mind.)

There are some fascinating life stories in this book. U. M. Rose is a figure larger than life, one of the founders of the American Bar Association, and the founder (after one attempt failed) of the Arkansas Bar Association. Augustus H. Garland was a towering figure in the late 19th Century. Albert Pike, Chester Ashley, and Robert Crittenden, among many others, are fascinating figures in their time. Judge Isaac Parker, the hanging judge in Fort Smith, with his unparalleled jurisdiction and non-appealable judgments, has been the subject of numerous articles and was the backdrop to an award-winning movie.

One thing I should say concerns political figures who are or were lawyers. This book tells what they did in connection with the organized Bar, but it does not get into an evaluation of their political activities or legal problems. You will not find anything in the book about Bill or Hillary Clinton in connection with "Whitewater" or about Kenneth Starr, the independent prosecutor or his associates, or about the Paula Jones case. There was no attempt made to evaluate the conduct of anyone, nor should there be. That was not the purpose of the book.

I want to express appreciation for the work of Cathy Underwood who assisted me in putting together the final manuscript in a form that would suit the requirements of M & M Press. I want to express appreciation also for the lawyers who served on the Arkansas Bar Association committee, especially John Fogleman, the Chair. I tried their patience more than I like to think.

This book is for the Bar and for the lawyers who love the profession. Contrary to popular opinion, we lawyers are few in number. But we can be powerful when we set our mind to it because the profession has provided the leadership for Arkansas from the beginning. And when the people have listened to us, the state has progressed. We have been more progressive at many times than the ordinary citizen. But we can be proud of what we have been able to achieve. Arkansas is a better state because of the Arkansas Bar Association and its leaders.

Robert Ross Wright

Little Rock, Arkansas
November 1, 1999

DEDICATION

To George Rose Smith and Peg Newton Smith and

To John A. Fogleman and Annis Fogleman.

Friends in the law and contributors to the

worthy history of the legal profession in

Arkansas.

TABLE OF CONTENTS

PART I. HISTORY OF THE BAR

Chapter I

THE NEW LAND

The first statute in the old Arkansas Statutes Annotated, the compilation of legislative enactments used by lawyers until 1987, was Section 1-101, under which Arkansas adopted the common law of England and all statutes of the British Parliament in aid of the common law which were applicable to our form of government and not inconsistent with our Constitutions unless repealed by the General Assembly. Unfortunately, the compilers of the Arkansas Code relegated this to Section 1-2-119. It should still be the first statute because, second only to the federal and state Constitutions, it is the basis of Arkansas law. Similar "reception" statutes exist in other states.

In adopting the common law of England as it existed before the fourth year of the reign of King James I, Arkansas incorporated into its legal system an already developed body of law that was familiar to most of the people who settled the United States and this State after the Louisiana Purchase. The legal principles which provided the foundation for the law of property had largely been developed by the early seventeenth century, and had been summarized by Sir Edward Coke in his writing, although the influence of Lord Coke in that period of time continued to shape it somewhat. The great undergirding principles of constitutional rights, as we know them today, had already been introduced through the Magna Carta and shaped by subsequent documents and events in English history. The rise of equity had taken place, and the criminal system (although it would be subject to substantial change in the years that followed) already existed in basic form. The law of contracts had developed in its essentials.

The English colonies in the New World developed in accord with what laws, customs and practices their settlers had known before. Considerable study has gone into the composition and mores of the Englishmen who came here, and there is substantial evidence that the various geographical sections of this country reflected in large measure the parts of England from which the predominant number of their citizens migrated.[1] Virginia was settled in large measure by people from the southeastern counties of England, and the colonial society which resulted was a substantial reflection of the ways that they had known before.[2] The same could be said for the coastal sections of the Carolinas. The hill country or back country of the southern colonies were settled to a substantial extent by the residents of the northern English counties and the lowlands of Scotland.[3] Their customs were adapted from a somewhat different background. There was more homogeneity in certain regions of England in that period of time than in the country as a whole.

New England's settlers came largely from English counties in the eastern and central parts of England, with East Anglia supplying a goodly number.[4] Differences in the puritan customs and mores of New England when compared to those of the coastal regions of the South result from the somewhat differing cultures of the areas from which they came. The middle colonies, although later influenced heavily by settlers from areas other than England, were originally settled with English from the west and central sections of the mother country.[5]

Arkansas was influenced heavily, particularly in the uplands, by the hill people of the Southern highlands who came from the western portions of Virginia and North Carolina and from Tennessee and Kentucky. The laws, customs and practices of those people were brought with them to Arkansas just as they had been brought to those places earlier by their ancestors from the north of England, from the lowlands of Scotland, and from Northern Ireland through the Scots-Irish. The low country of Arkansas—the delta in particular—was the product in part of the people who had come to the coastal and Piedmont regions of Virginia and the Carolinas and had eventually made their way westward through the deep South. South Arkansas was also settled in large measure by people of similar origins but with greater influence from the hill people in the outer reaches of that area.

This situation is still manifested today in differences in dialect and customs, although differences in dialect are rapidly vanishing due to the impact of modern transportation and the movement of people from place to place and, most of all, due to the obsessive and consuming intrusion of modern communication with particular regard to television. It may not be long before everyone in Arkansas will utter much the same vocal sounds as people in the Midwest. Law itself has increasingly become homogeneous in the United States through uniform laws adopted by the various states, the tendency of state courts to give increasing weight to decisions on the same subject from other jurisdictions, and the intrusion of federal statutes and case law as Congress persistently extends the scope and power of the federal government.

With these general observations as background, it is useful to consider very briefly the early history of Arkansas, since the law and the early lawyers were a reflection of that situation.

Explorers, the First Settlements, and the Louisiana Territory

The early explorers were Spaniards, and the first of them was Hernando DeSoto in 1541, a well-educated nobleman who had served in expeditions in South America under Pizarro. After roaming for two years through the swamps and wilderness of what is today Florida, Georgia, Alabama and Mississippi, suffering hardship, disease and Indian attacks, and preying upon the Indians themselves, DeSoto and his soldiers came upon and eventually crossed near what is now Memphis the largest river they had ever seen, which the Indians called the "Mes-cha-ce-be" and the Spaniards called the Rio Grande. It took about a month of preparation of flatboats and barges for them to cross the Mississippi.

The records or diaries of the travels of DeSoto in Arkansas are sparse and incomplete. References to rivers, mountains and other landmarks are unclear. It does appear that he and his band likely encountered the White and Arkansas rivers, mountainous areas in lower reaches of the Ozark and Ouachita ranges including Hot Springs and the Ouachita River, and eventually traveled to the southwest encountering the Red River.

The DeSoto expedition was a failure. Not only did they fail to discover gold or other precious metals, but DeSoto died toward the end of it, near the Mississippi River. Not until 1673 with the expedition of Father Jacques Marquette and Louis Joliet did any further exploration take place. This was largely a river exploration of the Mississippi and its tributaries, including the Arkansas, in which the Frenchmen were hosted by the Quapaw Indians.[6]

Subsequently, in 1682, Robert Chevelier, Sieur de La Salle, claimed the entire Mississippi River valley for France, naming it Louisiana in honor of the French King, Louis XIV. LaSalle's lieutenant, Henri de Tonti, founded Arkansas Post in 1686 near the mouth of the Arkansas River, which was the first permanent European settlement west of the Mississippi.[7] Subsequently, in 1762, France ceded Louisiana to Spain, as a result of the Treaty of Fontainbleau, which ended the French and Indian (or Seven Years) War.[8] Under the treaty, France ceded to England what is now Canada, as well as the Great Lakes region, and land east of the Mississippi which had been considered part of Louisiana. The Louisiana territory west of the Mississippi was ceded to Spain to keep it out of British hands, this being viewed as "a gift which Spain neither coveted nor appreciated."[9] The Treaty of Paris confirmed this settlement on February 10, 1763.

The main significance that this early history has is with regard to Spanish land grants made by Baron de Carondelet, the sixth governor of Louisiana to be appointed by Spain. He took office on December 30, 1791, and made a number of land grants in Arkansas. He continued to make them after the Treaty of St. Ildefonso on October 1, 1800, under which Spain ceded Louisiana back to France.[10] The treaty was confirmed by the Treaty of Madrid on March 21, 1801, but Spanish land grants continued until around the end of 1803.[11] Yet all land grants after the Treaty of St. Ildefonso were held to be void.[12] Thus, even though title could stem from a foreign land grant issued by a sovereign, the validity of these grants would depend on whether that sovereign state owned Arkansas at the time.

The fact that France now owned the Louisiana territory presented a major problem to President Thomas Jefferson and the country in general. Jefferson's dilemma was that, on the one hand, he was a strict constructionist when it came to the U. S. Constitution. There was nothing in that fundamental document that gave him the power to purchase the area. On the other hand, he was concerned about navigation of the Mississippi by Americans and about the power that this gave the French at the immediate borders of the young country. Moreover, westward expansion beyond the Mississippi was effectively stifled. Pragmatism, as it usually is, was the winner. Jefferson approached the French government through Robert Livingston, our minister to France, and Talleyrand, the French foreign minister, offered to sell the entire Louisiana Territory. James Monroe was sent to France as minister plenipotentiary to effect the agreement, and 900,000 square miles including Arkansas were purchased in the Treaty of Paris of April 30, 1803.[13]

After the purchase, what we today know as Louisiana was designated as the "Territory of Orleans." Arkansas originally was in what was called the "District of Louisiana," which was headquartered from St. Louis. This district was soon subdivided, however, on June 27, 1806, and an act of the territorial legislature created the District of Arkansas.[14] When "Orleans" was admitted to the Union in 1812 as the State of Louisiana, Congress changed the name of the area above it to the "Territory of Missouri." After the residents of what is now Missouri petitioned for statehood in 1818, Congress changed the name of the District of Arkansas to the "Arkansas Territory" on March 2, 1819.[15]

Judge Morris S. Arnold has written extensively on European legal traditions in Arkansas covering the period from the settlement of Arkansas Post up to the time of statehood in 1836.[16] Since the original settlers were French and the land was subsequently ceded to Spain, the original law was the civil law of France and Spain.

Legal matters at Arkansas Post under the French and Spanish had largely been handled by the commandant. When the Louisiana Territory became a part of the United States, there was a considerable backlog of cases, and magistrates were appointed for the outlying districts giving them the same powers in civil matters that had been exercised by the Spanish commandant.[17] Some of the Spanish laws were considered still to be in effect, but not the law of property and obligations, tort and contract.[18] Over and over, the Governor of the Territory, W. C. C. Claiborne, told the magistrates simply to act as they thought proper and as justice required.[19] For some years, at Arkansas Post, the residents submitted their disputes to the American commandant, Lt. James B. Many, in much the way it had been done under the Spanish.[20]

When the boundary line between the Orleans Territory and the Territory of Louisiana was set at the current Arkansas-Louisiana line, it determined the future Arkansas legal system.[21] In 1805, Congress passed a second organic act for Louisiana (Arkansas and northward) that required "judicial proceedings according to the course of the common law" (as had the Northwest Ordinance of 1787).[22] This was controversial in the Orleans Territory, with a judge declaring that it must mean the law common to that area, which was the civil law.[23] After several efforts by the territorial legislature to comply met with stiff opposition, the Orleans legislature in 1808 essentially promulgated the civil law in private law for what would become the present State of Louisiana.[24]

The act creating the District of Louisiana placed the upper territory, including Arkansas, under the government of the Indiana Territory, which then passed some basic laws that became effective on October 1, 1804.[25] These incorporated wholesale the common law of crimes. An elaborate court system was created, but much of the private law remained that observed under the Spanish.[26] While the local inhabitants were not happy with the change in regime, their opposition to the common law was mild compared to that in Orleans. Arnold notes that the absence of a professional lawyer class may have made it easier to effect change.[27] Moreover, while the French remained overwhelmingly predominant in Orleans, a considerable influx of Americans in the latter part of the eighteenth century was narrowing the gap in the upper territory and diluting the French influence.[28]

The settlement at Arkansas Post was little more than a trading post in the early years and for most of the time was controlled by and governed from New Madrid, Missouri. It had military commanders who recorded deeds and performed functions similar to the Spanish commandants.[29] Frederick Bates, the Acting Governor for the territory and member of the Board of Land Commissioners, traveled to Arkansas in that early period and found the people to be unacquainted with the manner of asserting claims or with "every kind of business" and thought that "affairs requiring method, order and an observance of legal forms should be totally unintelligible to them."[30] Bates appointed Benjamin Fooy and George Armistead as Justices of the Peace, and Governor Meriwether Lewis on August 20, 1808, separated the District of Arkansas and began to appoint other judges and civil officials.[31] In late 1808, the first court sat in Arkansas since its acquisition by the United States. Charles Refeld, Benjamin Fooy, Francis Vaugine and Joseph Stilwell were appointed as judges, although they were only lay people of some prominence.[32] Not much activity ensued. Court was held sparingly, usually with a bare quorum, and sometimes did not meet at all.

Some revamping of the courts took place, but in late 1812, the District of Arkansas was again abolished. Ultimately, Congress would have to provide for a stable legal system.[33]

A man named Perly Wallace [Wallis] is credited by Judge Arnold with being the first professional lawyer in Arkansas.[34] He was admitted, probably illegally, in Arkansas in 1808, but was legally admitted by the General Court of Louisiana in 1809. Three others from the Territory of Orleans came to Arkansas in 1809-10 and were admitted—Patrick Darby, Hezekiah Kirkpatrick, and J. L. Henderson. They often worked together. Anthony Haden had been a lawyer in the Missouri bootheel since 1805, and he came late in 1811 and was referred to as "the first truly regular practitioner."[35]

In civil cases in those territorial years, about half of the litigation involved debt, although covenant, replevin, false imprisonment, slander, defamation, and trespass *vi et armis* also were actions that were filed. Eighty percent of the criminal work involved assault and battery cases, although there were other cases as well.[36]

In 1812, the Territory of Louisiana [Arkansas and Missouri] became the Territory of Missouri, and a court system revolving around a Superior Court was created. Inferior courts could be established by the legislature.[37] Arkansas became, briefly, the County of Arkansas. A lawyer from Ste. Genevieve, Missouri, George C. Bullitt, became the first professional lawyer ever to serve on the bench in Arkansas, becoming the judge of a new Court of Common Pleas in 1814.[38] A new County of Lawrence was formed in north Arkansas, and the circuit court from southern Missouri began sitting there.[39]

The old Spanish legal practices and the civil law in general rapidly gave way to the common law. This was largely complete by 1810, but in any event in 1816, the Territory of Missouri legislature adopted a statute almost exactly like the one found in Arkansas law today, adopting the English common law and acts of Parliament as they existed prior to the fourth year of the reign of James the First.[40] A wave of American immigration into Arkansas from about 1815 to 1820 solidified and coincided with this transformation.[41]

It is noted that the Americanization of Arkansas under the English common law created hostility among the French settlers of the Territory, which also seems to have been aggravated by the exclusion of the French from juries.[42] These new inhabitants were described by a naturalist, Henry R. Schoolcraft, as being crude people dependent largely on hunting for survival. He viewed them as having suffered societal retrogression with their dependence on hunting being a prime example of their near-savage situation.[43] These people seemed to have been located along the rivers, principally the Arkansas, the White and the Red, and in what is now North Arkansas and Southern Missouri. Arkansas Post and environs appeared to be more civilized with many of the people engaged in agriculture. The wave of American frontier immigration into Arkansas, however, was rapidly dwarfing the small Arkansas Post settlement and those of French extraction. Even the Arkansas Post settlement and the French who were there did not impress the English naturalist, Thomas Nuttall, who was most critical of it after a visit in 1819.[44] However, he was more impressed with it when he came back shortly thereafter because of changes that had resulted from the establishment of the Territory of Arkansas and from an influx of American settlers, noting that a weekly newspaper, the *Arkansas Gazette*, had been established there. This did not impress James J. Audubon, however, who visited there in 1820.[45]

Washington Irving, visiting the Post in 1832, noted the impact of the influx of Americans and changes in the legal system as working a transformation in the small village. The French by then had somewhat isolated themselves from the Americans, whom they did not like, retaining their own language and habits. Irving contrasted this with Little Rock, which was by then active and growing.[46]

The Arkansas Territory and Territorial Cases

When the Missouri Territory was created in 1812, it was divided into five counties by gubernatorial proclamation, and the old District of Arkansas was placed in New Madrid County. A year later, Arkansas County was separated from the south end of New Madrid County, with Arkansas Post as the county seat. Then, in 1815, the northern part of Arkansas was separated and designated as Lawrence County, all of this being done by the Missouri territorial legislature. In 1818, counties named Pulaski, Clark and Hempstead were carved out of Arkansas County.[47] None of these counties had boundaries remotely relating to those of today, except that some portions of the current counties were included within them.

By early 1818, several petitions for statehood or territorial status had been presented to Congress. Contemporaneously, the upper Missouri Territory [Missouri] was seeking statehood. To achieve it, they found it expedient to sever the lower portion of the Missouri Territory [Arkansas], regarding in particular Arkansas County as being in something of a state of anarchy.[48]

This effort soon collided with the problem of slavery. There was substantial objection by a large number of Northern congressman to introducing slavery into Missouri. The Southerners barely won in the House, and when the bill went to the Senate, the House took up the establishment of the Arkansas Territory. The slavery issue was raised again, and an effort was made to prohibit it in the new territory. After heated debate and some very close votes, slavery was eventually permitted—with some of the votes being by a margin of one, two or four. In the Senate, the same firestorm over slavery eventuated, but eventually the bill passed by 19-14, with the two senators from Illinois and one each from Indiana and Ohio voting with the South.[49]

The debate over slavery in the Arkansas Territory mirrored many of the arguments that led to the Missouri Compromise of 1820. As a part of the Arkansas slavery debate, there was strong support for drawing a line at 36 degrees 30 minutes latitude (the northern border of Arkansas) as far as western territories were concerned and not permitting slavery north of that line.

Under the Act, the judiciary was to consist of a superior court, inferior courts as might be established, and justices of the peace. The President would appoint three justices for four year terms for the superior court, and the court would have jurisdiction in criminal cases, exclusive jurisdiction in capital cases, and concurrent jurisdiction and appellate jurisdiction in civil cases amounting to more than $100.00. The law of the Missouri Territory was essentially incorporated, until changed by the legislature.[50]

Being a territorial court, the superior court was the Superior Court of the United States for the Territory of Arkansas. In *Hempstead's Arkansas Reports* 1 (1859), the first case decided was a rape case decided in January, 1820. There was a trial by jury before Judge Andrew Scott in Arkansas County, and the jury found the Defendant, Thomas Dickinson, guilty.[51] Dickinson had four lawyers, including Perly Wallis, earlier mentioned. He asserted ten different grounds for reasons to set aside the verdict, including the argument that since his victim had become pregnant, it had to be consensual. The Court viewed that argument as "quite exploded,"

citing various treatises. The defendant was sentenced to be cas-
trated by a skilful physician directed by the sheriff. (Of course, the
castration of a person by a "skilful physician" under the direction of
the Sheriff in 1820 was quite possibly a death sentence. Anesthesia
was not used at all until 1846, according to 11 Encyclopedia Bri-
tannica, "Surgery" 406 (1993), and probably not in Arkansas until
much later. There were no sulfa drugs or antibiotics for infection.
The surgical instruments were cruder than what might be picked
up in a large hardware or drug store today, much less a physician's
supply service. Death from shock, bleeding or infection would have
been common.)

Hempstead's Reports reveal the rather basic form of law practice
in the Arkansas Territory. Some of the types of lawsuits found in
these reports are forcible entry and detainer actions, procedural
questions, replevin suits, actions of trover, appeals, damages, pleas,
crimes, trespass, writs of execution, attachment, assumpsit, statutes
of limitation, land sales contracts, assignments, promissory notes,
domestic relations, parol contracts, venue, ejectment, mandamus,
detinue, chancery jurisdiction, juries, bona fide purchasers, bonds,
slaves and Indians. Some of the law applied in these cases is obso-
lete, often due to more modern statutes. A number of the early
cases had to do with the common law forms of action which were
ultimately replaced by code pleading (although the common law
causes of action are still sometimes referred to in modern cases).

Some of these territorial decisions, however, are still the law
today. For example, an appeal will not lie except from a final decision or judgment (which is, generally speaking, still the law with
some exceptions in the federal courts).[52] Also, a gambling contract
is "immoral in its tendency" and will not be enforced.[53] Further,
where there is a plain and adequate remedy at law, a court of equity
has no jurisdiction.[54]

One case of note in the territorial period was *Grande v. Foy*,
Hempstead's Arkansas Reports 105 (1831), which apparently was

the first case to recognize that Arkansas followed the English common law and acts of Parliament which had not been changed by our legislature and were not contrary to our form of government. The opinion by Judge Edward Cross on the subject of ejectment rambles somewhat through English law and territorial precedent including the territorial act of 1816 to conclude that ejectment actions formed a part of our common law inheritance.

Early Lawyers, Judges, Laws and Politics

Among the early Arkansas lawyers and judges, some of whom made their names more in politics than in lawyering, were some who merit particular mention. The lawyer population began to increase when Arkansas became a territory, and some of these individuals were still around when the territory became a state. Some of them played prominent roles in the early history of the State of Arkansas as well as during territorial days.

Although many of these people came to Arkansas from Kentucky or Tennessee, the first territorial governor was a New Hampshireman, Brigadier General James Miller, who had been admitted to the Bar there in 1803 and had practiced law until he entered the army in 1808. His outstanding service in the War of 1812, in addition to leading to his generalship, resulted in a gold medal being awarded him by Congress. He resigned from the army after his appointment as Governor.[55] The first territorial Secretary was Robert Crittenden of Kentucky, the younger brother of Senator John J. Crittenden of that State. He had entered the army in 1814 and had fought as a Captain in the Seminole War of 1817-18. Admitted to the Bar in 1818, he was referred to by Albert Pike as a "well-bred Kentucky gentleman," "sagacious and well informed."[56]

The appointed judges of the Superior Court were Andrew Scott of the Missouri Territory, Charles Jouett of the Michigan

Territory, and Robert P. Letcher of Kentucky—all of whom were Virginia natives. All had either practiced law or held minor political posts or both.[57] Governor Miller had not yet arrived in Arkansas, and so Crittenden called the Superior Court into session, where they adopted the laws of a general effect of the Missouri Territory and formed two judicial circuits.[58] Crittenden subsequently appointed James Woodson Bates and Neil McLane to be circuit judges and Henry Cassidy and William Trimble to be circuit attorneys. Later that year, Judge Bates was elected as territorial delegate to Congress defeating several opponents, including runner-up Stephen F. Austin. Bates was a Virginian, who had practiced law there after attending Yale and graduating from Princeton.[59] Albert Pike referred to Bates as a "genius" who was a "polished, keen, brilliant writer" but a poor orator.[60]

After Governor Miller finally arrived in Arkansas in late December of 1819, he questioned in February, 1820, some of the actions taken by Crittenden. At stake was the law that applied in the election of the legislative council. There was a division of views, even among the superior court judges. Nonetheless, Miller commended Crittenden before the Assembly for his work. The matter was eventually solved by an Act of Congress deciding the matter as the Arkansas legislature had wished.[61]

Another problem was that Judges Letcher and Jouett were not in residence and were not performing their duties. Letcher eventually resigned, and President James Monroe in May, 1820, appointed an army officer, Joseph Selden, a Virginian, to take his place. Jouett resigned shortly thereafter, and Monroe first appointed an Ohioan, who returned home after he had gotten as far as Missouri, and then appointed a former Kentucky circuit judge, Benjamin Johnson.[62] There were numerous other appointments made by President Monroe, many of them lawyers, including Samuel C. Roane as U. S. Attorney. There was a dominance of

Kentuckians among the appointments, even though most of the white migrants came from Tennessee.[63]

The territorial legislature of October, 1820, dealt with some familiar matters. As recommended by the Governor, taxes were raised to cover the value of scrip issued to pay public creditors; provision was made for more jails; and horse-trading with the Indians was prohibited. The legislature on its own declared death from a duel to be murder where death resulted, and imposed a heavy fine on anyone making such a challenge; the circuit court system was replaced by a court of common pleas with three judges in each county; and the Territory was divided into three superior court districts, with each to be presided over by a superior judge.[64]

Many of the early territorial events involved politics or the basic necessities of organizing a civilized, democratic society. Much of it pertained to finance, although all of it related in one way or another to providing basic government services. Lawyers were heavily involved in much of this, although they were involved more in a public than in a legal capacity.

In 1824, one event that combined politics and two judges was a duel between Superior Court Judges Andrew Scott and Joseph Selden. Apparently, this came about as the result of a game of cards in which Selden refused a demand by Scott that he apologize to one of the ladies present. Although Selden apologized later, the quarrel remained, and ultimately Scott challenged Selden to a duel. The duel actually took place in Mississippi, across from Helena, presumably due to the Arkansas dueling law mentioned earlier, and the result was that Selden was shot through the heart by Scott and died almost immediately.[65]

Presaging its later controversial stances, the *Arkansas Gazette*, in a blistering editorial by editor and publisher William E. Woodruff, denounced both this duel and the practice generally. He was denounced in turn by James Woodson Bates and Robert C.

Oden, both of whom appear to have been involved in some capacity.[66]

Selden was replaced as Superior Court judge by President Monroe's appointment of Circuit Judge William Trimble, then of Arkansas County and formerly of Kentucky.[67]

Another event of significance in 1824 was the resignation and departure of Governor Miller, who was replaced as Governor by George Izard, who came from a prominent South Carolina family. Izard was born in England, the origin of his family, which had held lands in the counties of Middlesex and Surrey. His background was in the military, not in law, and he served for only three and one-half years, dying of a protracted illness.[68] His remains lie in the burial plot of the Chester Ashley family in Mount Holly Cemetery in Little Rock.

It is interesting to consider the subsequent events in the lives of those involved in the Scott-Selden duel. James Woodson Bates sought re-election as Delegate to Congress. He was opposed by Henry W. Conway, a Tennessee native with an army background who had also served in the Treasury Department in Washington, who defeated Bates. He became the leader of the Democrats in Arkansas, while Robert Crittenden was the leader of the Whigs. Conway served a couple of terms in Congress and was candidate for a third against Robert C. Oden, who was backed by Crittenden, when the ferocity of politics led to Crittenden challenging Conway to a duel (to take place in Mississippi, of course). Conway was killed in the duel, and a monument to him was erected at Arkansas Post by his brother, James S. Conway, who was to become first Governor of the State.[69]

In the case of Judge Andrew Scott, his nomination for reappointment was rejected by the United States Senate because of his duel with Selden, and President John Quincy Adams appointed Circuit Judge Thomas P. Eskridge, a Virginia native, to replace him.[70]

The dueling law itself was severely crippled in the 1827 legislature by an act introduced by Speaker of the House Ambrose H. Sevier which repealed that part of it disqualifying from office anyone issuing, delivering or accepting a challenge and also eliminated the requirement that all officeholders swear that the act had not been violated.[71] Arkansas duels had become a matter of attention beyond our borders. The death of Conway led a Kentucky paper "to say bitterly that down in Arkansas when a man couldn't be gotten rid of at the polls he was immediately killed off in a duel."[72]

Sevier is a lawyer of particular note. A native of Tennessee, Sevier had a great uncle called Nolachucky Jack, a celebrated Indian fighter, who had moved from western Virginia to western North Carolina and had founded the "State of Franklin," of which he was governor. Sevier served several terms in the Arkansas legislature and as prosecuting attorney of Pulaski County in 1824. He later served four terms as Delegate to Congress, and was elected U. S. Senator from Arkansas after statehood, serving until 1847, when he became Minister to Mexico. He was a participant in fashioning the Treaty of Guadaloupe Hidalgo, which ended the Mexican War and added California and New Mexico to our country. When he died on December 31, 1848, he was barely 48 years old.[73]

Sevier's father-in-law, Judge Benjamin Johnson, was also a distinguished lawyer of that period. He was one of the first judges of the Superior Court of the Territory, and when Arkansas became a State, he was appointed United States District Judge and served until his death in October, 1849. His son, Robert W. Johnson, served as a U. S. Senator for many years, and his grandson, Benjamin S. Johnson, served for many years as General Attorney for the Missouri Pacific Railway.[74]

Politically—and politics often intermingled with the law in this and in subsequent periods in Arkansas history—the 1820's were somewhat turbulent, as illustrated by the duels mentioned previously. These times are discussed in greater detail in other books cited in this text. There seemed, however, to be a thrashing around to determine who would be the biggest of the frogs in a rather small, thinly populated pond. This can be illustrated to some extent by a summary of the events surrounding the case of *Hightower v. Hawthorn*, Hempstead's Arkansas Rep. 42 (1826). The background is more important than the little two-page opinion.

Both Governor Izard and Secretary Crittenden (who would have been acting Governor) were absent from the State. A vacancy had arisen in the office of sheriff of Independence County which could not be filled. A series of letters from people calling themselves "A Citizen of Independence," "A Citizen of Pulaski," "Conservator," "Junius," and "Tuckahoe" were printed in the *Arkansas Gazette* arguing essentially whether Izard or Crittenden were to blame for this sorry state of affairs. "Tuckahoe" intimated that "A Citizen of Independence" was Circuit Judge James Woodson Bates, as designated by Crittenden's defenders. He then proceeded to trash Crittenden. A week later, "Junius" addressed a letter to Bates as being the same as "A Citizen of Independence." "Junius" castigated Bates for his lack of knowledge and disregard of the law, with particular reference to Bates' decision in *Hawthorn v. Hightower*, which had been reversed by the Superior Court (with the parties' names reversed). Crittenden returned to the State, but the newspaper letter-writing controversy continued, with "Tuckahoe" denying the allegations of "Junius."

At that point, Thomas W. Newton, who was reading law under Crittenden and living in his home, identified himself as "Junius" and published a letter to Bates as being "Tuckahoe." He asserted that Bates had been disgraced by gross ignorance and by "a visible intoxication on the bench."[75] Other lawyers joined in the fray against Bates. Richard Searcy, the lawyer who had apparently been victimized by him in the case but redeemed on appeal, and William Quarles, who had signed bills of exceptions in the case and thought he had been impugned as being the disreputable lawyer referred to in the letter by "Tuckahoe" (Bates), lambasted him. Searcy stated that Bates had improperly tried the case since Bates had been the original attorney for the defendant. Searcy inquired as to how anyone could "have respect for a Court, when they see the Judge of that Court intoxicated on the bench and rioting with the crowd in the grog-shops and court-yards?"[76] Crittenden entered the fray by assailing Bates also.

Bates responded under his own name in October, 1827, by attempting to justify what he had done and by assailing Searcy's ability and qualifications, stating that Searcy lacked education exceeding that required for apprentices and was ignorant even of terms of the legal profession. He never admitted to being the anonymous author of the letters assailing Crittenden.[77]

The matter ended, surprisingly, without a duel. It may be presumed that Crittenden could as easily have shot Bates as Conway. In *Hightower v. Hawthorn*, incidentally, the Superior Court held that it was completely improper to deny a party the right to appear by attorney, thus holding for Searcy and reversing Bates in no uncertain terms.

At a special session of the legislature in 1828, after some jousting between that body and Governor Izard, the assembly repealed the Judiciary Act of 1827 and divided the Territory into four circuits presided over by judges of the Superior Court, and the Superior Court was required to hold two terms annually at the state capital.[78] (By this time, the Superior Court had become largely an appellate body, similar to what the Supreme Court of Arkansas would become, and the Circuit Courts had become the trial courts of general jurisdiction.) This and other legislative sessions also took up questions that are not discussed, since they involve matters other than lawyers, judges, the courts, and the legal structure. This session, for example, dealt with land acquired from the Cherokees, as earlier sessions had dealt with the Choctaws or other Indian tribes; and it also created new counties, which was an ongoing process. A fourth Superior Court judgeship, incidentally, had been created by Congress in 1827, and it went to James Woodson Bates, who had managed to survive both physically and politically (the latter through his support of Ambrose H. Sevier).

When Governor Izard died shortly after that legislative session, Acting Governor Crittenden applied for the job, as did Judge Andrew Scott. Congressional Delegate Ambrose H. Sevier stated to the Congress that he wanted "a man unconnected with any of our quarrels," adding that "I have an unconquerable hatred for *Mr. Crittenden*, and the same aversion exists with two thirds of our citizens." He gave Crittenden "the credit of having caused nearly every duel that has taken place in Arkansas."[79]

Outgoing President John Quincy Adams nominated Hutchins G. Burton, former Governor of North Carolina, but this nomination was not confirmed by the Senate, presumably in deference to incoming President Andrew Jackson. Jackson appointed John Pope of Kentucky, who was approved. Interestingly enough, Pope was John Quincy Adams' brother-in-law, but they had had a permanent falling out in 1825 when Adams chose Pope's political enemy, Henry Clay, to be Secretary of State. Pope became an avid Jackson supporter and helped swing Kentucky to Old Hickory in the 1828 election.

Pope himself was angling for bigger fish, such as Attorney General or a seat in Congress, but he reluctantly accepted. He was highly qualified, having practiced law in Kentucky, served in the legislature, in the U. S. Senate, and as Kentucky Secretary of State.

Jackson then removed Crittenden from his office and commissioned William S. Fulton of Alabama as Secretary. Fulton had served in the War of 1812, had practiced law briefly, had served in the Alabama legislature and as a county judge and as editor of a newspaper.

The selection of Pope and Fulton, and the removal of Crittenden from office along with the re-election of Sevier as Delegate to

Congress (a role in which he had been unusually successful and productive) brought relative quietude to the young Territory in the last couple of years of the 1820's. The legislative session of 1829 was quite productive, resulting in seventy acts and twenty-four resolutions to the Congress. One of these acts established county courts.

In 1830, an occurrence took place which is evocative of the recent Arkansas past of the 1980's—there was a newspaper war. A man named Charles P. Bertrand, a New Yorker, who had worked on the *Gazette* for Woodruff and had read law with Robert Crittenden (and would later marry Crittenden's wife's sister), established the *Arkansas Advocate*. Shortly thereafter, a fuss ensued between the two editors which manifested itself, as in the Bates-Searcy matter, in anonymous letters printed in each paper. The dispute purported to brand Woodruff as an "Adams editor" and Bertrand as a "Jackson editor," an issue disputed by Woodruff.[80] The fight escalated with an attack on Secretary Fulton, who was defended in the *Gazette* by "Jaw-Bone," who also strongly attacked Fulton's predecessor, Crittenden, along with Bertrand. "Jaw-Bone," although it was never established, apparently was Woodruff's good friend, Chester Ashley—who, according to Bertrand, wrote what was provided to him by "his jackal and pimp, Wm. E. Woodruff."[81]

Ashley is a particularly important figure in Arkansas legal history. A native of Massachusetts, he graduated from Williams College and studied law at Litchfield in Connecticut, which was actually the first law school in the United States, although it was not operated as are law schools of today. Another Litchfield student, although probably not at the same time, was John C. Calhoun. Ashley made his way to Little Rock in 1820, having acquired an interest in the New Madrid claims to the townsite. He served as attorney for the New Madrid proprietors and seems to have played an important role in the removal of the capital from Arkansas Post to Little Rock. At one time, he and Crittenden were law partners. A land speculator, he was regarded as a "cunning" attorney, "perhaps the most able attorney" in early Arkansas.[82] A Conway supporter, a powerful member of the Sevier faction, he was regarded by his enemies as a modern "Tallyrand," who served as "prime minister" to Governors Izard and Pope.[83]

The newspaper vituperation waxed hot and heavy, including attacks and defenses relative to Governor Pope, who was in Washington much of the time attempting, said his supporters, to advance the interests of the Territory in concert with Delegate Sevier, or attempting, said his detractors, to advance his own career through some other federal position. Eventually, it was all but certain to culminate in a duel or two.

The first duel took place as the result of alleged toasts at the country home of Dr. John H. Cocke questioning the character of Governor Pope. The toasts had actually been read by Sevier, but Sevier said that he did so on behalf of the presiding officer at the meeting, who was temporarily absent, and that he had no hand in writing them. The newspaper fulminations that followed heightened the incident. Cocke was charged with duplicity in attempting to increase a supposed breach between Pope and Sevier and inviting Pope's friends to dinner to attack his feelings. The anonymous author of this letter was revealed to Cocke by Editor Woodruff to be William Fontaine Pope, private secretary and nephew of Governor Pope. Cocke challenged him to a duel.[84]

In accord with what seemed almost tradition by now in the young Territory, the duel took place in Mississippi, this one opposite the mouth of the White River. The combatants shot at each other three times each and missed. They then reconciled and the duel ended.[85]

Young Pope should have by now been aware that his marksmanship left something to be desired. However, shortly thereafter, after "Devereux" had accused Governor Pope with retailing liquor to become even more wealthy, the younger Pope challenged "Devereux" to a duel. The latter turned out to be Charles F. M. Noland, a young Virginian who had been dismissed from West Point. Breaking with tradition, the duel took place south of the Red River in Miller County. Noland's first shot severely wounded Pope in the hip. Pope never fully recovered and died some months later.[86]

Although the younger Pope, Noland and Dr. Cocke were not lawyers, their activities as fueled by the newspapers commingled with politics and politics in turn commingled with the law. It is difficult to segregate fully these activities in that time period. It is interesting to observe that, then as now, the catalyst and to some extent progenitor of so much civil debate and disturbance was the news media.

By this time, discussion of statehood had become common in the Arkansas Territory. Before turning to that important legal event, however, notice should be taken of the fact that the old State House construction was begun in territorial days, in March, 1833. The initial money came from the sale of one thousand acres and from private subscriptions from Chester Ashley, Joseph Anderson, Richard C. Byrd, William E. Woodruff and Ambrose H. Sevier. The current site was selected by Governor Pope, and the architectural design was that of Gideon Shryock, who had designed the Kentucky state capitol. It was not completed during territorial times. The first session of the state legislature was held in it beginning on September 12, 1836, but the building was not actually completed until 1840.[87]

Entry Into the Union: Statehood

The question of statehood for Arkansas broke out into the open in the election of a Delegate to Congress in 1831. Sevier, who sought reelection, advised caution. The Territory had, for those times, a substantial territorial debt and would have the additional expense of providing for the cost of government and paying for the construction of government buildings.[88]

Sevier was opposed by the Crittenden faction, specifically by Benjamin Desha, who was not a lawyer and whose background was in the military, in farming, in the Kentucky legislature, and as a receiver of the Arkansas land district. He favored statehood when Arkansas had enough population to apply for it, but would not act until the Territory petitioned Congress. The Crittenden-Desha alliance was strange in the sense that Desha was a supporter of Jackson while Crittenden favored Clay. Their friendship came from army days. After a heated campaign, in which the *Gazette* favored Sevier and the *Advocate* favored Desha, Sevier was elected. He won by 447 votes out of less than 5,000 cast.[89] No duels were fought, although Crittenden suggested one time in a Little Rock "coffee-house" that Sevier could get a "fight" (duel) out of him although he would not seek one. A Crittenden partisan later denied the statement.[90]

In Governor Pope's address to the territorial legislature in October, 1831, he stated that the time was "at hand when the people may rightfully claim to be admitted into the Union as a State."[91] This was due to the rapid increase in territorial population and what he regarded as the improvement and prosperity of the territory. In this same address, he noted that Congress had given ten sections of land to the territory for erection of public buildings, and this was the land that was used in connection with the construction of the State House. The territorial legislature had been meeting in a two room log house with no fireplace and a leaky roof. What ensued, however, in the legislature was a deadlock over three proposals regarding the purchase of the ten sections—one from Ashley, one from Crittenden, and one from William McK. Ball. Ultimately, no decision was reached, and in 1832, Sevier obtained the approval of Congress to permit the governor to dispose of the ten sections, and the governor ultimately sold the sections for much more than the government price for public land.[92]

The competition between Sevier and Crittenden continued in the territorial election of 1833. The same day that Sevier announced that he would seek a fourth term as Congressional Delegate, Crittenden also announced. Both called attention to their accomplishments in public life, Sevier in the Congress and Crittenden as territorial Secretary.[93]

Before the campaign began, William Cummins, a Pulaski County attorney and former Kentuckian, sought the impeachment by Congress of Judge Benjamin Johnson of the Superior Court, who as previously mentioned was Sevier's father-in-law. He accused Judge Johnson of partiality in a trial, threatening to cut a person's throat, drinking on the bench, deciding cases before submission, rendering contradictory decisions, taking advantage of a fellow judge in a faro game, deciding a circuit court case contrary to precedent, and failing to punish someone who twice tried to kill another at a circuit court proceeding presided over by Johnson. In the House of Representatives, Sevier gave a long, eloquent speech in defense of Johnson, along with supporting letters from Governor Pope, Secretary Fulton, Superior Court Judges Cross and Eskridge and District Attorney Roane.[94] The Speaker referred it to the Judiciary Committee, as Sevier had requested, and when the Committee reported in favor of Johnson, the House killed the charges against Johnson by a motion to table. In Arkansas, Cummins denied that politics were involved.[95]

Without going into the details of the political campaign, which others have done extensively,[96] one of the issues involved Governor Pope's actions relating to the ten government sections and their sale and the location of the State House. The furor over the State House did not subside until after the bitter election had been concluded, and while the campaign went on, the Crittenden followers made all sorts of assertions of wrongdoing against the Sevier faction and against Pope, Woodruff and Ashley, among others. National politics intruded, with Crittenden being generally branded as a Clay supporter and the Sevier camp as Jackson men. Neither one was actually that pure in his support. The Crittenden-Conway duel was resurrected. Desha's removal as a federal tax receiver at Little Rock was said to have been the work of Sevier, although Desha was actually removed due to a deficiency of $6,432.62. There was vacillation, back-stabbing, and two-faced conduct. Judge James Woodson Bates, now a Crittenden man, had said a few years earlier that Crittenden would join forces with "Old Nick himself to accomplish his purposes." Oddly enough, the two candidates often traveled together in the western and northern sections of the territory, where a substantial number of the inhabitants lived, spoke at the same places, and managed to avoid a duel. Nonetheless, politics were primitive and many stories involved whiskey, knives, pistols and fights.

When the election finally came, Sevier won decisively with 4,476 votes to Crittenden's 2,520. Sevier carried eighteen of the twenty-three counties, losing Monroe and Arkansas counties in the east and Lafayette, Miller and Sevier county (which was named for him) in southwest Arkansas.

Two duels, oddly enough for that time, never took place. Bad blood had developed during the campaign between Superior Court Judge Thomas P. Eskridge and Crittenden, who challenged Eskridge to a duel because of remarks made by him in the *Gazette*, accusing Crittenden among other things of having been "the *curse* and *scourge*" of the territory. Eskridge declined on religious grounds.[97] Sevier's old tormentor, William Cummins, challenged him because of expressions and insinuations made by Sevier against his character. Sevier refused because of his obligations as congressional delegate and the difficulty of scheduling it, although he indicated that after he left office, he might view it differently.[98]

Although Sevier had earlier feared that Arkansas' financial condition and insufficient population presented a problem as to statehood, he now altered his view as a result of the application of the Michigan Territory for admission to the union. On December 17, 1833, he offered a resolution in the House of Representatives requesting that the Committee on Territories consider allowing the people of Arkansas to form a constitution in preparation for statehood. A major problem presented by the Michigan petition was that Michigan would come in as a free state, adversely affecting the political balance in the U. S. Senate. If Florida were to come in as a sister state with Michigan, he thought it would delay Arkansas' admission until the Wisconsin Territory petitioned some quarter of a century later. (As it turned out, it would not have been that long of a delay because Wisconsin petitioned earlier.)[99]

Editor Woodruff of the *Gazette* had opposed statehood, but the changed attitude of his ally, Sevier, caused him to take a neutral stance, and numerous writers in the *Gazette* advocated statehood. The rival newspaper, the *Advocate*, favored statehood believing that Arkansas' debt situation would be cured by the population increase that would result. It questioned Sevier's motives, however.[100]

In Congress, in late January of 1833, Representative John Tipton of Indiana introduced bills to permit Michigan and Arkansas to form state constitutions. The committee to which the bills were referred wanted to take censuses in each territory, which would delay things. (At that time, to become a state, each territory had to have 47,700 inhabitants.) Action was delayed by very close votes in Congress, and ultimately Congress adjourned for the summer without taking any action.

In the meantime, in Arkansas, the Sevier machine had begun to show signs of friction. Governor Pope and Secretary Fulton had had a falling out over the building of the State House and the disposition of the ten section lands. Editor Woodruff had supported

Pope. However, in July, 1834, John Steele, founder of the relatively recent Helena *Herald* had formed a new paper in Little Rock which had been blessed by Governor Pope with funds provided by Congress to digest and print the territorial statutes. This led to the disaffection of Woodruff with Pope, since Woodruff thought that the job should have gone to him. Pope and Woodruff actually began to quarrel over who was the closest friend to Sevier. The Crittenden camp debated how to exploit this divisiveness and contemplated some ultimate alliance with Sevier, but it all became moot when Robert Crittenden died on December 18, 1834.[101]

Secretary Fulton, about this time, began to express his strong support of Jackson to the President himself as well as to Jackson's friends and advisors, particularly William B. Lewis of Tennessee. The basic thought was that Jackson should not reappoint Pope as Governor and should instead appoint Fulton. Jackson nominated Fulton as Governor and Lewis Randolph of Virginia as Secretary, to the extreme disappointment of Pope.[102] Pope blamed Sevier for his misfortune and returned to Kentucky.

The statehood question had remained dormant during this period, but Michigan revived it in 1835 by calling for election of delegates to a constitutional convention. Sevier, in a circular addressed to the people of Arkansas, warned that if Michigan were admitted without Arkansas, then Arkansas would be at the mercy of Congress in the matter of slavery. Alarmed by growing abolitionist activity in the Northeast, Woodruff called for immediate admission, and Sevier favored emulating Michigan in having a constitutional convention. The *Advocate*, which had favored statehood for some time, went along, although it chided the vacillation of Woodruff and Sevier. The *Advocate*, as of January, 1835, belonged to and was edited by Albert Pike, one of Arkansas' great leaders of the nineteenth century. The same position was adopted by the *Times*, which was the successor publication to the one founded by Steele.[103] There was some opposition, and some pointed out that slavery in Arkansas was protected under the Missouri Compromise of 1820, but statehood had overwhelming support. Moreover, a new census showed the Arkansas population in summer, 1835, at 52,240, which was more than the required amount.

Governor Fulton did not believe that he had the power to call a constitutional convention in the absence of a congressional enabling act. Because of the popular disagreement with his view, he wrote President Jackson about the problem, and Jackson in turn requested an opinion from Attorney General Benjamin F. Butler. Butler agreed with Fulton's conclusion, but stated that the people could convene peaceably for the purpose of petitioning Congress for admission to the union, and if the petition happened to be accompanied by a constitution framed by delegates to such an assembly, there was no legal reason for not accepting the petition with such an appendage.

The matter came before the legislature in October, 1835, and sentiment was overwhelming for having a constitutional convention. Disagreement ensued, however, over representation from the south and east of the territory as opposed to the north and west. This divisiveness in Arkansas politics, presenting regional conflicts within Arkansas, has reoccurred consistently in various periods of our history. Slavery was at the root of the problem in 1835, as it was later in the debate over secession from the union. As has been stated:

> The difficulty rose from Arkansas' being divided geographically into two major regions—the highlands of the north and west and the lowlands of the south and east. In 1835 about 46 per cent of the total population and about 66 per cent of the slaves lived in the seventeen lowland counties of the south and east, the remainder in the seventeen highland counties of the north and west. This disparity in

total and slave populations between the two regions is also evident in later censuses.[104]

Some of the principal combatants in this legislative struggle appear to have been William Cummins of Pulaski County and James H. Walker of Hempstead County for the south and east, and David Walker and Abraham Whinnery of Washington County for the north and west. Ultimately, a compromise proposal by David Walker prevailed, and the convention had fifty-two delegates, with twenty-seven from the north and west and twenty-five from the south and east. The main difficulty was how to count the slaves, and the legislators from the south and east wanted to count each slaves as three-fifths of a person (based on the three-fifths compromise in the U. S. Constitution), while the north and west wanted to base the representation on the free white population. Some commentators at the time denied that the real desire of the south and east was to follow the three-fifths formula—they simply did not want to be dominated by what was then the more populous north and west.

Governor Fulton did not sign the bill which passed the legislature on the constitutional convention, and it became law without his signature.

The delegates assembled on January 4, 1836, in Little Rock in the Baptist Meeting House, elected officers and voted to write a constitution, and then moved the next day to the Presbyterian Church, which had better facilities. Committees on various areas of the constitution were organized and prepared reports that were well-received.

What plagued the convention as it had the legislature were the sectional differences over slaves. Fifty-eight per cent of the whites but only thirty-four per cent of the slaves lived in the north and west. Consequently, as in the earlier Mississippi and Alabama constitutional conventions, how slaves were counted in the apportionment of representation made a difference. By way of contrast, in 1835, there were 6,724 people in Washington County (the largest county by far), but only 508 blacks. But in Lafayette County, there were 1,446 people, of whom 1,032 were blacks, and in Chicot County, there were 2,471 people, of whom 1,364 were blacks.[105]

The early harmony of the convention gave way to disagreement over this problem. A number of proposals were floated and failed, often by very close votes. A final compromise put forth by a select committee provided for representation on the basis of the free white male population, but the method of apportionment favored the south and east to the point that its senators represented a much smaller number of whites. After this compromise was approved, the constitution was adopted by a vote of 46 to 4 on January 30.[106]

This first constitution provided for a governor elected for a four-year term with a provision that he could not serve more than eight years over a twelve year period. Next in line of succession were the president of the senate and the speaker of the house. A secretary of state was to be selected by the legislature for a four-year term, and there was to be an auditor, a treasurer, and circuit attorneys for two-year terms. The judicial power was vested in a supreme court, circuit courts, county courts, and justices of the peace, and the legislature could establish chancery and corporation courts. The supreme court would have a chief justice and two other justices selected by the legislature for eight-year terms and have only appellate jurisdiction. Circuit judges would be selected for four-year terms. Representatives would have two-year terms and senators four-year terms, and the legislature would meet biennially. Without going into any more detail, the Arkansas constitution was similar to other Southern state constitutions of that time period.

Gaining the approval of Congress for Arkansas' entry into the nation as a sister state of Michigan, however, was not that simple. Charles F. M. Noland was sent out from Little Rock to take the ordinance and the constitution to Washington. He was delayed, and although he left on February 5, he did not show up until March 8. In the meantime copies of the constitution printed in the *Gazette* had arrived in Washington. The Committee on Territories, which had already reported out a bill to admit Michigan, refused to report out a bill on Arkansas until the official copy arrived. Noland brought only one copy of the constitution, when more were needed, but Sevier had by that time gotten the committee to agree to report the bill out without an official copy of the constitution. The constitution was acceptable, but the ordinance had to be pruned "with a heavy hand" or it would not pass.[107]

One interesting aspect of the senatorial debate over the admission of Arkansas and Michigan to the union was that Michigan had chosen Senator Thomas Hart Benton of Missouri as its advocate, the representative of a slave state. Arkansas' case was put in the hands of Senator James Buchanan of Pennsylvania, the representative of a non-slave state who would later become President of the United States immediately prior to the War Between the States.

Although the debate in both houses of Congress sometimes revolved around issues other than slavery, the major issue with regard to Arkansas was that its constitution provided that slavery would be "perpetual." Moreover, a substantial amount of politics entered in, other than that involving slavery. Arkansas supported Andrew Jackson and would almost certainly support Martin Van Buren, who would be his chosen successor. Woodruff reprinted in the *Gazette* an article from the Washington *Globe* stating that opposition to admission of Arkansas and Michigan stemmed from the knowledge that their admission would weaken the Whigs in the next election.[108]

After much maneuvering, the Michigan bill passed the Senate on April 2, 1836, and the Arkansas bill passed two days later on the 4th of April by a vote of 31-6. In opposition were the four senators from Vermont and Rhode Island, Alexander Porter of Louisiana and Henry Clay of Kentucky, the latter being the leader of the Whigs. The bills then went to the House where much of the same debate and bickering reoccurred. Most of the fight against Arkansas' admission was over slavery, and the opposition was led by congressmen from Massachusetts. Senator Thomas Hart Benton, however, viewed the real basis for the opposition as political—the knowledge that Arkansas and Michigan would support the candidacy of Van Buren, the Democrat.[109]

The Michigan bill stalled in the House, and Michigan did not become a state until January, 1837. But on June 15, 1836, by a vote of 143-50, Arkansas was admitted to the union. On June 23, the Congress passed a "supplementary act" which substituted five propositions for those that had been put forward by the state constitutional convention. These five propositions (1) gave to Arkansas every sixteenth section of land for use by the public schools; (2) granted all publicly owned salt springs, not exceeding twelve, together with six sections of land adjoining each spring; (3) gave the state five per cent of the net proceeds from the sale of public lands in Arkansas for internal improvements; (4) gave the state five sections of land for completing the State House; and (5) vested and confirmed in the state for a seminary of learning two townships of land previously granted to the territory. The supplementary act was accepted by the first state legislature in October, 1836.[110]

It was important not only to Arkansas, but also to the slaveholding South that Arkansas be admitted ahead of Michigan. One Alabama congressman stated that this was because the Arkansas constitution provided for slavery. It was important, he said, that the South have "a hostage" to protect its interests, and Michigan was that hostage. Other than the fact that Michigan would support the Jacksonian Democrats, as would Arkansas, the arguments over the admission of Michigan were technical in nature. But the controversy over Arkansas brought to the forefront the issue of slavery and what would come to be an increase in sectional hostility during the two decades that would follow.

A state government had to be organized before statehood became reality. In August, 1836, James S. Conway defeated Absolom Fowler and Alexander S. Walker to become the first Governor of the State of Arkansas. Archibald Yell was elected to Congress defeating William Cummins. Subsequently, the legislature selected Ambrose H. Sevier and William S. Fulton as the first two U. S. Senators. Robert A. Watkins was named Secretary of State, Elias N. Conway, Auditor, and William E. Woodruff, Treasurer. The legislature also chose Townshend Dickinson, Thomas J. Lacy and Daniel Ringo as the first Supreme Court justices, with Ringo becoming the first Chief Justice. Benjamin Johnson was appointed federal judge by the President, along with Elias Rector as marshal, and Thomas J. Lacy as district attorney.[111]

Legally, although not certainly in any other way, statehood was a watershed event in the sense that it put Arkansas in the same category as the original states of the Eastern seaboard. But it was simply a continuum of the basically frontier society that prevailed at that time. One thing, however, that it had in common with the older Southern states to its east was that it had already begun to experience the influence of certain families, often interrelated or at least interconnected, in the life and politics of the state. To be sure, these were not families with names as ancient as those in Virginia, but this minor happening is at least mildly noteworthy.

Ambrose H. Sevier at the time of statehood was unquestionably the most powerful figure in Arkansas. Although he apparently never capitalized upon it, his late great uncle, John Sevier of Tennessee, had been a power in that state. From 1834 to 1850, Tennessee had by far provided more white migrants to Arkansas than any other state. Kentucky had not provided all that many, although many appointees to office in the Arkansas Territory came from Kentucky. Sevier's father-in-law was Superior Court Judge Benjamin Johnson, formerly of Kentucky, whose brother was the prominent Richard M. Johnson of that state. Sevier's cousin was Henry W. Conway, who was his predecessor as Delegate to Congress, and who was killed in the duel with Robert Crittenden. Henry's brother, James S. Conway, became the first Governor of the State of Arkansas. Another brother, Elias Conway, served in public office. Judge Johnson, who became U. S. District Judge with statehood, had a son, Robert W. Johnson, who served during early statehood in both houses of Congress. The Conways in turn were related to the Rectors. William Rector was Henry Conway's uncle, and he served as surveyor general of Missouri, Illinois and the Arkansas Territory. Henry Conway's cousins, Elias and Wharton Rector, held minor offices and were supporters of Conway and Sevier. Another cousin, Henry M. Rector, became Governor later on. Along with their friends and supporters, Ashley and Woodruff, Governors Pope and Fulton, they ran things.[112]

It was a young dynasty, to say the least, established in a very short time. It was less dependent on family than in Virginia or Massachusetts, and more on the personalities involved. But for the short run, in the quarter-century from about 1825 to 1850, it was a dominant feature of Arkansas politics, and as such, of Arkansas law. Law, lawyers, judges and politics were inextricably intertwined in the early years of Arkansas, and that would not change appreciably even up to the present day.

Notes

1. A recent study of considerable note is David Hackett Fischer, *Albion's Seed* (New York, 1989). Professor Fischer's work examined numerous sources extensively and also resulted from in depth research of records in Great Britain. Many of the observations and citations in this book are based on Fischer's studies.

2. Fischer, *Albion's Seed*, *supra* note 1, 236, observes that while immigrants to Virginia came from every county in England, a majority of both the Virginia elite and indentured servants came from sixteen counties in the southeast and southwest of England. He states that in the mid-seventeenth century, the origin of the vast majority of Virginia settlers could be located by drawing two great circles of a radius of about sixty miles around the cities of London and Bristol, excluding East Anglia in southeastern England and Cornwall in the southwest. *Id*. at 237.

3. Fischer, *id*. at 621, quotes an immigrant to the highlands of the South as saying, "We are mixed people." He writes that they mixed in many ways—in social rank, religious denominations and ancestry, which was Celtic, Roman, German, English, Scandinavian, Irish and Scottish in varying proportions. They came largely from the border region of the north of England (particularly the six counties of Cumberland, Westmoreland, Northumberland, Durham and parts of Lancashire and Yorkshire), from the Scottish lowlands (although a good many were highland Scots also) and from Northern Ireland (probably most of whom were of Scottish origin rather than Irish). Five counties of southern Scotland (Ayr, Dumfries, Wigtown, Roxburgh and Berwick) and five counties of Ulster (Derry, Down, Armagh, Antrim and Tyrone) were heavy contributors. *Id*. at 621-622.

4. To account for a majority of the founders of Massachusetts, Fischer states that you may take the geographic center in England to be the market town of Haverhill, near where the three counties of Suffolk, Essex and Cambridge come together, draw a circle with a radius of sixty miles, and (eliminating the North Sea part of it), circumscribe the area from which most New England families came. This roughly encompassed an area defined in England in 1643 as the Eastern Association—Norfolk, Suffolk, Essex, Hertfordshire, Cambridgeshire, Huntingdonshire and Lincolnshire —plus parts of Kent and Bedfordshire. Fischer, *id*. at 31. A secon-

dary center of migration came from the southwest of England near where Dorset, Wiltshire and Somerset came together. *Id*. at 34.

5. Fischer writes: "The Quaker founders of Pennsylvania and West Jersey came from every part of England. But one English region stood out above the rest. The Friends' migration drew heavily upon the North Midlands, and especially the counties of Cheshire, Lancashire, Yorkshire, Derbyshire and Nottinghamshire. ... Only a few came from the south and west, and none were from East Anglia." *Id*. at 438. He makes other references to the Welsh Quakers to the later, mid-eighteenth century influx of Scots and Irish. *Id*. at 436, 444-445.

6. C. Bolton, C. Ledbetter and G. Hanson, *Arkansas Becomes a State* 4 (1985).

7. *Id*., at 5.

8. *Ibid*.; *Jones on Ark. Titles*, p. 14.

9. Jones, *ibid*.

10. *Id*. at 14-16.

11. *Ibid*.

12. *Id*. at 16.

13. *Ibid*.

14. *Id*. at 18-19.

15. *Id*. at 19-20.

16. M. Arnold, *Unequal Laws Unto A Savage Race: European Legal Traditions in Arkansas*, 1686-1836 (1985).

17. *Id*. at 131.

18. *Id*. at 134.

19. *Id*. at 135.

20. *Id*. at 139.

21. *Id*. at 138.

22. *Id*. at 140.

23. *Ibid*.

24. *Id*. at 142.

25. *Id*. at 143.

26. *Id.* at 144-146.
27. *Id.* at 148.
28. *Id.* at 148-149.
29. *Id.* at 149-151.
30. *Id.* at 154-155.
31. *Id.* at 155-156.
32. *Id.* at 156-57.
33. *Id.* at 160.
34. *Id.* at 166.
35. *Id.* at 168-169.
36. *Id.* at 170-171.
37. 2 Stats. at Large 74.
38. *Id.* at 174-175.
39. *Id.* at 176.
40. Laws of a General and Public Nature of the District of Louisiana ch. 154 (1842), cited in Arnold, *supra* n. 17 at 180-181.
41. D. Herndon, *The Centennial History of Arkansas* 995 (1922).
42. Arnold, *supra* n. 17 at 181-182.
43. H. Schoolcraft, *A View of the Lead Mines of Missouri* 175 (1819), as quoted in Arnold, *supra* n. 17 at 183-184.
44. T. Nuttall, *A Journal of Travels into the Arkansas Territory During the Year 1819* (Lottinville, ed. 1980), as quoted in Arnold, *supra* n. 17 at 187-190.
45. Arnold, *supra* n. 17 at 190-191.
46. *Id.* at 192-93, quoting from *The Western Journals of Washington Irving* 166-68 (McDermott, ed., 1944).
47. L. White, *Politics of the Southwestern Frontier: Arkansas Territory, 1819-1836* 4 (1964).
48. *Id.* at 5-7.
49. *Id.* at 8-16.
50. Id. at 16-17. There is a concise discussion of the territorial period, and its politics, in C. Bolton, C. Ledbetter, and G. Hanson, *Arkansas Becomes a State* 15-29 (1985).

51. *U. S. v. Dickinson*, Hempstead's Arkansas Reports 1 (1820).

52. *Blakely v. Fish*, Hempstead's Arkansas Reports 11 (1822).

53. *Lemmons v. Flanakin*, Hempstead's Arkansas Reports 32 (1825) and *Harding v. Walker*, Hempstead's Arkansas Reports 53 (1828).

54. *Blakeley v. Biscoe, id.* at 114 (1831), and other cases.

55. White, *supra* n. 47 at 18-19.

56. *Id.* at 19, quoting from a biographical and pictorial history of Arkansas, of which only one volume was ever published.

57. White, *supra* n. 47 at 20.

58. *Ark. Acts*, 1819, at 70-82.

59. White *supra* n. 47 at 22.

60. *Id.* at 23, quoting from Hallum, *History of Arkansas* 85.

61. White, *supra* n. 47 at 23-25.

62. *Id.* at 26-27.

63. *Id.* at 28.

64. *Id.* at 29-30.

65. *Id.* at 48.

66. *Id.* at 49.

67. *Ibid.*

68. F. Hempstead, *1 Historical Review of Arkansas* 103-105 (1911).

69. *Id.* at 107-108.

70. White, *supra* n. 47 at 50.

71. *Id.* at 57.

72. Hempstead, *supra* n. 68 at 108.

73. *Id.* at 109.

74. *Id.* at 109-110.

75. White, *supra* n. 47 at 63-64.

76. *Id.* at 64, quoting from the *Arkansas Gazette*, June 4 and June 12, 1827.

77. *Id.* at 64-65.

78. *Id.* at 89.

79. *Id.* at 90.

80. *Id.* at 99-100.

81. *Id.* at 102-105.

82. *Id.* at 105-106.

83. *Id.* at 106. (His modern counterpart might have been William J. Smith.)

84. *Id.* at 111-112.

85. *Id.* at 112.

86. *Id.* at 113-114.

87. Hempstead, *supra* n. 68 at 117-118.

88. White, *supra* n. 47 at 115.

89. *Id.* at 113-125.

90. *Id.* at 117-118.

91. *Id.* at 126.

92. *Id.* at 138, 140.

93. *Id.* at 141-142.

94. *Id.* at 142-143.

95. *Id.* at 143-144.

96. *Id.* at 146-157.

97. *Id.* at 155-58.

98. *Ibid.*

99. *Id.* at 164-65.

100. *Id.* at 165-66.

101. *Id.* at 159, 168-170.

102. *Id.* at 171-172.

103. *Id.* at 172-173.

104. *Id.* at 178, quoting from a book and an article in the *Arkansas Historical Quarterly*.

105. *Id.* at 185-86.

106. *Id.* at 188-89.

107. *Id.* at 192.

108. *Id.* at 195, citing *Arkansas Gazette*, April 26, 1836.

109. *Id.* at 198, quoting from Thomas Hart Benton, *Thirty Years'
View; or, A History of the Working of the American Government for
Thirty Years, from 1820 to 1850* (2 vols., New York, 1854).
110. *Id.* at 199.
111. D. Thomas, *I Arkansas and Its People* 93 (1930).
112. White, *supra* n. 47 at 201-203.

Chapter II

FROM STATEHOOD TO THE CIVIL WAR

When Arkansas became a state in 1836, there was no sudden transformation other than from a strictly legal and political standpoint. It was still a sparsely populated frontier society that acquired no sudden glisten as if tarnished silver had just been polished.

The period from roughly 1830 to 1850, however, was a rapidly evolving period in American life and legal institutions—one that has been referred to as a "take-off" period in American history. In the same year that Arkansas was moving from territorial status into statehood, our neighbors to the southwest were evolving from what had been a Mexican possession into what would be on a short-term basis a separate nation with few people but a broad expanse. The events that transpired in Texas in 1836 could not help but touch Arkansas. In 1821, Stephen F. Austin had left Arkansas and established a small colony on the Brazos River. The oppression of the Mexican government combined with its fear of the influx of Americans led to revolution, the Alamo, the "take no prisoners" slaughter of the Texans at Goliad, and the ultimate triumph of General Sam Houston in the Battle of San Jacinto. The Texas Republic was quickly recognized by the United States, England and France, and during 1835 and 1836, the Little Rock newspapers were filled with letters and reports from Sam Houston and Stephen F. Austin. Many Arkansawyers fought with the Texans in their battles, and many more of the people who fought and died for Texas were Tennesseans. Enlistment in the Texas cause was particularly high in Lafayette and Miller counties, and many went from counties as far away as Pulaski. Colonel Benjamin E. Milam of Long Prairie, Lafayette County, died in the Battle of San Antonio; Charles E. Rice, one of the publishers of the *Advocate* in Little

Rock, fell in another battle; Arkansawyers died at the Alamo, as did Jim Bowie, whose brother, Rezin P. Bowie, lived in Lafayette County. Jim Bowie is reputed to have invented the Bowie knife at old Washington in Hempstead County, and both Davy Crockett and Austin spent much time there before going to Texas.[1] The victory in Texas was a comfort to the people of the southwest Arkansas counties, since the Mexicans prior to that time seemed to claim everything south of the Red River, and under an Act of Congress, an Arkansas militia existed in the area even after statehood "for service against the depredations of Mexicans and 'Cumanches,' as it was then spelled."[2]

As Texas developed for a short time as a Republic and later was admitted to statehood, that element of the frontier rapidly stabilized. But what was to become Oklahoma remained on the western edge of Arkansas and what would be for some time the Indian Territory kept this state on the edge of the frontier. This will be covered later in connection with the law pertaining to the Indian Territory and the powers and activities of Judge Isaac Parker and his deputy U. S. marshals.

The last cases to come before the Superior Court of the Territory of Arkansas, as reported in *Hempstead's Arkansas Reports*, were decided in February, 1836, before Judges Benjamin Johnson, Edward Cross, and Archibald Yell (or before two of the three). In *United States v. Town-Maker, an Indian*, Hemp. Ark. Rep. 299, the full Court held the indictment of the defendant for murder to be faulty, but remanded him to custody upon testimony of a witness "who proved that the defendant had been guilty of the homicide of a citizen . . . in the district of country occupied by the Osage nation. . . ." In a case before Judges Johnson and Yell, *Marshall v. Jeffries*, Hemp. Ark. Rep. 299, the Court reversed an assault and battery judgment on the basis that the plaintiff was known as "Jesse Jeffery" and not "Jesse Jeffries," a rather peculiar problem which would be cured easily today. *Fletcher v. Ellis*, Hemp. Ark. Rep.

300, appeared to be an action of maintenance which failed to allege the pendency of a suit or the court in which it was pending or any of the circumstances, and was dismissed in an opinion by Judge Cross who determined the case along with Judge Yell. Another case involving civil procedure was *Leadbetter v. Kendall*, Hemp. Ark. Rep. 302, in which Judge Cross for himself and Judge Yell invalidated the process of a justice of the peace extending beyond the limits of his jurisdiction.

Judge Johnson, as earlier mentioned, became U. S. District Judge for the new State of Arkansas. Judge Archibald Yell was elected to Congress. Judge Edward Cross was appointed surveyor-general of the U. S. public lands in Arkansas in 1836 and in 1838 was elected to Congress. Judge Cross had a distinguished career in Arkansas. A native of Virginia who was reared in Kentucky, he came to the territory in 1824 at the age of 26 and began his law practice in old Washington, which was then the county seat of Hempstead County. In addition to serving on the Superior Court and subsequently serving as surveyor-general in Arkansas and for three terms in Congress, he served as Associate Justice of the Supreme Court from 1845 to 1855, when he became president of the Cairo and Fulton Railroad. He was assistant to the Confederate Secretary of the Treasury during the War Between the States, and in 1874 "assisted in the restoration of constitutional government in Arkansas after the overthrow of the mob law of the carpetbaggers."[3]

It was not unusual in the early history of the United States for us to draw upon the impressions of Europeans, such as Alexis de Toqueville, for uncommonly perceptive views of our new Republic. One such person, a German named Friedrich Gerstaecker, traveled through Arkansas beginning in January, 1838. He kept detailed notebooks on his journeys. In one excerpt he described a court session in Perryville where lawyers from Little Rock and elsewhere were "put up" at various farmhouses. The convening of court, he wrote, brought "new life" to this "quiet village" and the "entire surrounding territory was visibly stirred." There being no courthouse, half of the postmaster's house was used as a court. He continues:

> The judge who travelled this circuit had come from Little Rock with four lawyers. Seated in the cane-bottom rocker near the fireplace, he solemnly announced the opening of court. In the center of the room and directly in front of the fireplace had been placed two tables at which the lawyers and the court clerks were seated. The first case to be tried was one growing out of a fist-fight. ... According to legal practice either of the parties involved had the right to reject six of the suggested twelve jurors without giving any special reason. ... Once the oath is taken the members of the jury are seated on a long bench against the wall. The prosecuting attorney opens the trial by setting forth the complaint and explaining the law as it bears upon the particular case. After this the prosecutor calls his witnesses. After the state's attorney has finished, the defendant's lawyer calls his witnesses and ends his presentation of the case with a long speech to the jurors in which he flatters them upon their sound and conscientious judgment. The prosecuting attorney's turn is next. He makes a speech ridiculing the statements made by the defense lawyer and urges the jury to give the defendant a severe sentence. To listen to the prosecuting attorney's summation, one would think this particular case to be the worst the prosecutor had ever encountered in all his practice.
>
> Now the judge rises, delivers his charge to the jury and closes with the remarkable statement of principles which the jury must keep in mind—"If any doubt arises in your

hearts which would affect in any way your decision, the law says this is to be in favor of the accused." Having said this he sat down. To decide upon a verdict the jury was supposed to file into another room. Since the verdict must be unanimous, a single juror can hang the jury. In the present case, however, there was no room available for the deliberations, for the court assembly had already taken up roughly one-fourth of the available space in the village. The weather was too disagreeable to permit the jurors to deliberate out of doors. So two horses were driven out of the stable and the twelve jurors waded through deep mud into the barn where they debated the guilt or innocence of the accused.[4]

In another case described by Gerstaecker, a respected farmer had shot and killed a neighbor's cow some years before and had taken its carcass home and consumed it. The legal punishment at the time of the event was lashing and imprisonment. After much deliberation, the jury found him not guilty. The jury apparently applied its own statute of limitations unless it exonerated the farmer for accidentally or mistakenly killing the cow. That is unclear, but Gerstaecker pointed out that court sessions "create considerable excitement, but by and by conditions return to normal."

Scholars have noted this phenomenon in American life which persisted throughout the nineteenth century. Court sessions and trials were a form of societal interest and entertainment in a time that pre-dated radio and television.

In this period of time, the U. S. Supreme Court Justices had circuits and held court sessions in the assigned circuits. This was a duty that most of them abhorred, even if the circuit happened to be some place like North Carolina. We do not have to imagine how the unlucky fellow felt who was assigned Arkansas because the Honorable Peter Daniel, Associate Justice of the Supreme Court,

revealed his thoughts upon visiting Arkansas in 1851. He viewed
the place as primitive in letters to his daughter and was critical of
travel difficulties, poor accommodations, the character of the people, and the bad climate. From Napoleon (no longer in existence)
at the point where the Arkansas River entered into the Mississippi,
he wrote to his daughter, Elizabeth Randolph Daniel, in his native
Virginia that he had "reached this delepidated [sic] and most
wretched of wretched place[s] . . . & am compelled to remain until
2 p.m. tomorrow for the mail Boat to little Rock [sic]." "But
nothing," he wrote, "can surpass, if indeed it can equal, the false-
hood of the Steam Boat Captains; they lie without hesitation &
without remorse—promise you the greatest expedition & deligence
[sic], and then put in at every point which holds out the least
promise of freight & remain as long as there is the smallest hope of
success."[5]

Justice Daniel described Napoleon as a "miserable place" consisting of "a few slightly built wood houses, hastily erected no
doubt under some scheme of speculation, and which are tumbling
down without ever having been finished—and those which are
standing are some of them without doors or windows." In his
quarters in an old steamboat, he was "serenaded by muschetos
[mosquitoes], who are not deterred from their attack [by] the motion of my fingers, on which they constantly fasten; whilst out of
doors, they are joined by clouds of what in this region is called the
Buffalo Gnat; an insect so fierce & so insatiate, that it kills the
horses & mules bleeding them to death. ... But in spite of them,
the Yankees flock hither as numerously almost as the insects, &
flourish & fatten amongst them."[6] A subsequent trip to Little Rock
in 1853 led to complaints only about the trip, and the small and
unsafe filthy boats "crowded with rude dirty people."[7]

Despite these probably accurate views on the lowly state of society in ante-bellum Arkansas, the fact is that population was rapidly increasing. The 1830 census count of 30,388 grew to 97,574

by 1840 and to 209,897 by 1850. Little Rock had only about 1,500 inhabitants in 1835, but to John Gould Fletcher in his book *Arkansas*, "it was a city nevertheless."[8] He refers to the fine houses that had been built, particularly "[Chester] Ashley's magnificent mansion which faced the steamboat wharf and the river" on the southern edge of town which was "in keeping with the Southern aristocratic tradition of Natchez and elsewhere."[9] Fletcher points to the existence of a theater, two or three churches, a visiting circus, a federal arsenal, horse-racing, and occasional fireworks displays as evidence of civility. Stagecoaches ran fairly regularly. The Anthony House, a fine two-story, twenty-eight room hotel, with various conveniences had been built.[10] Compared with Reconstruction, Fletcher viewed this as "the golden age in Arkansas" although he admits that few who survived both "the War and Reconstruction would, probably, have really cared to live in it."[11]

Within this setting, the new State of Arkansas set about to govern itself, and aside from appointments to office and some political activities, an initial legal problem involved the creation of capital and credit in a land-rich, capital-poor society. The same problem confronted the United States as an infant nation, and it was guided in no small measure by Alexander Hamilton, the first Secretary of the Treasury, and his "Report on Manufactures," which advocated the need for balancing an agricultural economy with manufacturing. That particular document was a seedbed of economic development suggesting in many of its aspects the "multiplier factor" which is basic to many economists. Hamilton, moreover, was in essence the progenitor of the Bank of the United States, which eventually was killed by Andrew Jackson's veto of the continuation of it through the congressional act on the Second Bank of the United States.

Arkansas was about as Jacksonian as a state could get. Its leaders were Jackson followers, and whether it was Jackson himself or his selected successor, Van Buren, or Ambrose H. Sevier, the former Delegate and now U. S. Senator from Arkansas, the Jacksonians won. Nonetheless, one of the first legal steps taken by the legislature was to establish two banks, known as the State Bank and the Real Estate Bank. It was thought that since almost everyone had land, but few had ready money, these banks would create a credit economy and remedy that problem (in what, although they never apparently thought about it, would be in the best Hamiltonian and non-Jacksonian tradition).

The banks both failed within a few years. The State Bank had no stockholders, was owned by the state, and its officers were appointed by the legislature. Through the influence of Chester Ashley, the selection for bank president was army Major Jacob Brown, who was well-liked and "urbane," but whose principal encounter with financial matters was to disburse funds for the U. S. Army post in Little Rock. He resigned after a year and a half and was replaced by Major William Field. The capital stock was one million dollars, and to raise that amount in capital, the bank sold one thousand $1,000 bonds issued by the state. In 1842, after five years of operation, the bank was put into liquidation with liabilities of almost two million dollars and with assets of about the same on the face of things, but with one and one-half million in its assets owed by individuals, about half of which was uncollectible. The state was left with a debt of about one million three hundred thousand dollars of principal and interest due on the bonds secured by the full faith and credit of the state. By 1858, after extensive efforts to recover from debtors, the state still had a deficiency of about $1,200,000.

The Real Estate Bank had a capital stock of two million dollars, for which the state had delivered to it two thousand of the $1,000 bonds to be sold at par and constitute the capital. It differed somewhat, however. A bond purchaser became a stockholder who could obtain credit to the extent of one-half of his stock. Anyone could borrow money from the bank by giving a ten-year mortgage on his land as collateral. The bank sold five hundred of the bonds to the U. S. Treasury to support the Smithsonian Institution and one thousand to the North American Trust and Banking Company of New York. Soon, they had loaned out all of the funds with mortgages on land as security. Before the bank ultimately failed, it borrowed money from North American using the five hundred unsold bonds as security. It expected to receive $250,000 for the loan, but only received about half of that. North American was by then in trouble, and it sold the bonds to James Holford, a London banker, for $325,000. North American then failed, but made a little over $200,000 on the transaction.

After the Real Estate Bank was assigned to trustees, its effort to recover debts to it was no more successful than the State Bank. Much land was forfeited with thousands of people suffering disaster as a result. The bonds which Holford bought became known as the Holford Bonds and were the subject of considerable concern in the years that followed. The Real Estate Bank suffered an ultimate loss by 1858 of about the same as the State Bank, with the result that Arkansas was burdened with a debt of over $2,500,000. Efforts to collect the money ran on for years. In 1855, a separate chancery court was created in Pulaski County to deal with lawsuits involving this situation. Hulburt F. Fairchild was the chancellor, and upon his retirement he was replaced by U. M. Rose, of whom much will subsequently be written. C. F. M. Noland was named receiver and was replaced by Gordon N. Peay when he died.

In 1869, the legislature passed an act under which all bonds, including the Holford Bonds, could be exchanged for new twenty-five year bonds bearing six per cent interest. However, with regard to the Holford Bonds, an amendment to the Constitution of 1874 proposed by William M. Fishback of Fort Smith prohibited their payment. Voted down in one election, it was presented again in 1884 and was adopted by an overwhelming vote. It was originally Amendment 1 to the Constitution and is now shown as Article 20.

The discussion of the financial problems of Arkansas in its early days has carried us far beyond that period and into the latter part of the nineteenth century. (It was thought that the matter should be covered completely in a single discussion.) It is discussed at length in 1 F. Hempstead, *Historical Review of Arkansas* 142-146 (1911). While Hempstead seems to take the Jacksonian approach to banks, *i.e.* that they are somehow inherently evil and bear the seeds of mischief, the truth probably is that no one in Arkansas was qualified to operate a bank when these were created, which was true generally in the banking business in the United States prior to the formation of the federal reserve system in the twentieth century. Banking in that period was a risky business and the notes or bonds issued by small banks were often worth far less than the face value. The fact of the matter is that the Jacksonian elimination of a central bank created a boom and bust situation in this country, which in turn produced periods of inflation and recession, or mini-depression, throughout the nineteenth century and early part of the twentieth century.

Arkansas politics after statehood still involved lawyers and still involved occasional violence. A prime example was the knife fight in the legislature between J. J. Anthony of Jackson County and John Wilson, Speaker of the House from Clark County. Both were prominent men, Anthony being also a director of the new State Bank, and Wilson having served as president of the constitutional convention and also being president of the Real Estate Bank.

Wilson arrived at the House chamber in a bad mood as the result of disparaging remarks made about his being president of the Real Estate Bank. A bill was being considered involving the payment of a bounty on wolves to be awarded by a magistrate out of the county treasury. After several proposed amendments, Anthony proposed that "president of the Real Estate Bank" be substituted for "magistrate." Wilson viewed this as a continuation of the previous unpleasantness and became angry. As Speaker, he ordered

Anthony to take his seat, but Anthony refused. Wilson then said he would make him do it, and each man drew a Bowie knife. In the ensuing fight, Anthony slashed the left wrist of Wilson, almost severing it from his hand. Anthony then threw his knife at Wilson's chest, but the knife did not penetrate him and fell to the floor. Wilson then plunged his knife in Anthony's abdomen up to the hilt, and Anthony died in a few minutes. Wilson was arrested, indicted in Pulaski County, but tried in Saline County on a change of venue. The Saline jury acquitted him based on self-defense. Wilson moved to Pike County, was re-elected to the legislature, but never got over the emotional effect of the deadly struggle. He moved to Texas not long thereafter and died there in 1865.[12]

By 1840, Arkansas was both growing and prosperous. Governor Conway, in his message to the legislature, emphasized this. The source of this prosperity was an abundance of money produced in large part by the two state banks which made borrowing easy and postponed the day to pay the piper. The State House had been built and a new penitentiary was being erected. Federal arsenals were being constructed in Little Rock and Fort Smith. There were no educational institutions within the state, except for public schools which were inadequately supported. The boundary line between Arkansas and Texas was surveyed and set—with Arkansas losing about ten miles of Miller County to Texas. Considering the false prosperity based on the spendthrift liberality of the banks and the absence of educational institutions, things were not as rosy as they were pictured by Governor Conway and the general public.

When Governor Conway decided not to seek a second term, former Judge and now Congressman Archibald Yell successfully sought the position. A native of North Carolina, Yell had come to Arkansas from Tennessee as a receiver of public money for the Little Rock Land District. He resigned from that post and practiced law for a couple of years before becoming a Superior Judge, and then the first Congressman. He served only one term as Governor before being re-elected to Congress in 1844. He resigned from Congress to fight in the Mexican War and was killed in the Battle of Buena Vista in 1847. Buried on the battlefield, his body was later disinterred and put to rest in Fayetteville, his home.

As governor, Yell inherited the Bank mess. He engaged in lengthy correspondence with Holford, who had improperly received the North American bonds as far as the state was concerned. The legislative session of 1842 was largely concerned with numerous matters relating to the affairs of the Real Estate Bank. The state treasury by 1840 was running a deficit. Yell's legislative address in 1840 emphasized the need for better schools teaching literature, science and practical farming, along with the need for public improvements, but the leaders of the state could educate their children in private academies and seemed to have little interest in schools, railroads and turnpikes. There were some internal improvements during Yell's gubernatorial tenure because of congressional concern over levees along the rivers. Congress gave Arkansas 500,000 acres of land in 1841 to be sold and the proceeds applied to road construction, improvement of navigable streams and levee work.[13]

It seems safe to say, however, that serving as governor had less attraction to Yell than he may have imagined, and he resigned in April, 1844, to be a candidate for another term in Congress. The president of the state senate, Samuel Adams of Johnson County, succeeded him under the state constitution. He served only until November, when he was replaced by Thomas S. Drew, who had been elected governor in August.[14] During the same time period, U. S. Senator William S. Fulton died in August, 1844, and was replaced in November by Chester Ashley, who was chosen by the legislature.

Chester Ashley has been mentioned a great deal previously. When he became U. S. Senator, he had developed a rather large law practice with an emphasis on real estate matters. In what would be unheard of today, while still a new senator, he was named Chairman of the Judiciary Committee. He made noteworthy speeches in the Senate on the Oregon boundary question and the annexation of Texas. When his appointed term ended, he was re-elected for a full term and was serving in the Senate when he died at age 57 on April 29, 1848.

Ashley was in many ways much like prominent Arkansas lawyers of later years, even though the time in which he labored was much different. He was like a modern lawyer in the sense that, first and foremost, he was a lawyer who practiced law successfully. Until he entered the U. S. Senate, his public life was more that of a public spirited individual who influenced political or societal decisions as opposed to an office-holder. When he came to Little Rock in 1820, it was only a village where the way to Missouri crossed the Arkansas River at the place where the "little rock" was located as opposed to the "big rock" upstream. There were only two houses. Ashley was involved for the next few decades in creating the foundation of a territory and then a state. He was one of the foundation builders of the state.

In writing about leading figures of the early Arkansas bench and bar in Hempstead's *Historical Review of Arkansas*, George B. Rose described Ashley as "a typical son of New England, shrewd, thrifty, laborious, ambitious, determined to grasp both wealth and power, and with a physical strength and mental vigor that insured success."[15] George Rose describes him as "a powerful debater and until his death . . . the foremost trial lawyer of the state."[16] Ashley built on Markham Street "the handsomest home then in the state," lived in a princely style and had a host of slaves to look after his needs and those of his friends. In this material by George Rose may be found written accolades to Ashley's qualities from several people including Judge U. M. Rose in a paper delivered to the Arkansas Bar Association in 1909.

It is interesting to observe that this newly admitted, obscure State of Arkansas, in addition to having Chester Ashley as Chairman of the Senate Judiciary Committee, had Ambrose H. Sevier as Chairman of the Senate Foreign Relations Committee. These were two of the principal committees of the United States Senate at that time.

In addition to Ashley, Crittenden, Sevier, and the various judges previously discussed, several other individuals deserve particular mention for their activities during this general period of time. Archibald Yell, a native of North Carolina, emigrated first to Tennessee and served with General Andrew Jackson in the Seminole War. As President, Jackson appointed him a territorial judge of the Superior Court, and Yell settled in Fayetteville. One time, a notorious bandit was indicted, but although the defendant was in town, the sheriff was unable to persuade people to join a posse and apprehend the desperado. Yell adjourned court, located the accused, grabbed him by the throat and shouted: "Come into court, d__n you, and answer to the indictment against you." The man surrendered to the judge and was put in jail.

Yell wanted to be the first governor of Arkansas, but his opponents put a four-year residency requirement in the constitution which he barely missed meeting. He contented himself with being the state's first congressman and second governor. When Yell and Judge David Walker were both running for Congress, they would travel together. Once they came to a place where some men were gambling for beef by shooting at a target. Yell took his rifle and hit the bull's-eye on the first shot. Having won the beef, he sent it to the poorest widow in the area with his compliments. Then, he ordered a jug of whiskey, drank with his competitors, and rode off as their hero. Walker, a pious man, neither gambled nor drank. Next, they came to a camp meeting, where Walker thought that he would surely have the best of it. Yell changed at an inn to some elegant clothes, went to the camp meeting, and led the hymn singing in a rich, strong voice. Walker saw the handwriting on the wall.[17]

Another remarkable lawyer-leader of his time was Albert Pike who, like Ashley, was a native of Massachusetts. Pike was unable to enter Harvard because he would have to pay two years tuition in advance, which he could not afford. He taught school, wandered out west with a trading party headed for Santa Fe, and came back by way of Arkansas where he opened a school near Van Buren. Like Crittenden, Pike was a Whig and Crittenden induced him to come to Little Rock and help edit the *Advocate*. He began to study law and was admitted to the bar in 1834. It is said that when Arkansas became a state and the first Revised Statutes were enacted, Pike had much to do with their preparation. After the Mexican War, in which he fought, he criticized the career of Governor Samuel Roane in the war, which resulted in a duel in the Indian Territory near Fort Smith. After an exchange of shots that did not find the target, a reconciliation was arranged by their seconds.

After a sojourn in New Orleans and Washington, Pike returned to Arkansas and practiced law until the war broke out in 1861. He tried to develop an Indian force in the Indian Territory, but they could not conform to the white man's way of fighting. After the war he edited the Memphis *Appeal*, and then moved first to Alexandria, Virginia, and then to Washington in 1870, where he lived until his death in 1891. Pike is remembered principally for his study, research and writing relating to Masonry. He attained the highest rank as a Mason, and the Albert Pike Masonic Temple in Little Rock is named for him.

One lawyer who rose to prominence but is not described in sunny terms as a hale-fellow-well-met whom people loved and admired is Absolom Fowler. He grew up in poverty in Tennessee and made some bad investments which saddled him with a huge debt that he paid back in full with considerable toil and effort. Fowler became bitter and soured and in law practice was a remorseless, take-no-prisoners type of practitioner. He honed his knowledge of the common law forms of action and took advantage of technicalities. He was bold, defiant, resolute and aggressive in his practice and devoted his solitude to study. He was sarcastic and bitter in debate, had few friends, and loved no one. The voters elected him to the legislature several times, but he held no other office. He died with considerable wealth in 1859, leaving a widow. No stone was erected to his memory in Mount Holly Cemetery, but George Rose caused the grave to be marked with a marble slab.[18]

A contrast to Fowler was Frederick W. Trapnall, "the beau-ideal of the perfect gentleman, with the dignified, courtly manners of the old school."[19] He was concerned with legal principles rather than minute points of procedure and sought to persuade rather than demolish his opposition. An eloquent orator, he was kind and urbane and socially active. Trapnall was born in Kentucky and died at 46 years of age while campaigning as a Whig nominee for Congress at Monticello on July 4, 1853.

Another earlier lawyer of note was George C. Watkins, a Kentucky native who came to Arkansas with his family at the age of six. He graduated from the Litchfield Law School in Connecticut, previously mentioned as the one attended by Chester Ashley, and upon his return to Arkansas in 1837 went into practice with Ashley. The accounts reflect that Watkins was not an advocate but a legal scholar "quiet, wary; skilled in forensic fence, never exposing the weak points of his case, and always ready to take advantage of any slip of his adversary; equally a master of technical procedure and of the broad principles of the law."[20] Watkins was very highly thought of and accumulated substantial wealth through investments. He served on the Supreme Court as Chief Justice for a period of slightly over two years from 1852 to the end of 1854, and his opinions were well-received. He returned to private practice after that and died in 1872.

Before turning to the Arkansas Supreme Court and some of its judges of that period, mention should be made of a lawyer who was something of a bridge between the bar and the bench of that period. Samuel H. Hempstead came to Little Rock from St. Louis in 1836, having read law in Missouri and having been admitted to the bar there. He held office as prosecuting attorney in 1842 and as U. S. district attorney in 1856. We owe to him the publication of the reports of the Superior Court, which have been referred to previously. Hempstead's *Reports* are confined solely to those cases and to the cases of the successor court, the United States District Court. In 1858, he served as "solicitor general," which was an office to look after the state's interest in the Real Estate Bank situation. Moreover, as Special Chief Justice of the Arkansas Supreme Court, he wrote the opinion in the important case of *Kelly's Heirs v. McGuire*, 15 Ark. 555, which set out the law of descent and distribution and remained of influence in probate law down to the time of the Inheritance Act of 1969. He died in 1862.[21]

Considering in particular the frontier nature of Arkansas in its early statehood, the people were generally fortunate with respect to those chosen to serve on the Supreme Court. Daniel Ringo, the first Chief Justice, was a Kentuckian who came to Arkadelphia in 1820 and served first as deputy clerk and then as clerk of the circuit court. In 1830, he began practicing law at Washington, in Hempstead County, and moved his practice to Little Rock three years later. In 1836, he was elected to the Supreme Court, drawing a long term of eight years, but was defeated for re-election in 1844. He returned to practice and was made U. S. District Judge in 1849 upon the death of Judge Johnson. He died in 1873. He was considered to be incorruptible, wise and courteous, but also dry and dull. His main interest was in common law pleading and its technicalities or fine points as opposed to broad principles of the law.[22]

Chief Justice Ringo's two Associate Justices on the first Arkansas Supreme Court were Justice Townsend Dickinson and Justice Thomas J. Lacy. Justice Dickinson was a New Yorker who settled in Batesville in 1821, became a legislator and was appointed by the legislature as prosecuting attorney of his district. The legislature also elected him to the Supreme Court. He was a small red-haired man "bright and shrewd, quick to comprehend a case and a fluent speaker."[23] He rendered opinions that were viewed as quite credible, clear and to the point. Joining him was Thomas J. Lacy, a North Carolina native and the "most esteemed" of the three.[24] He had served on the territorial court and, along with Dickinson, in the constitutional convention. His opinions were considered to be among the best of the day, and he commanded the respect of the bar. After being re-elected to his position, he resigned in 1845 to try to find a more congenial climate, moving to New Orleans where he later died.

Justice Lacy rendered two opinions of note during his time on the Court—one that was notable only in the political context of the time and the other that was notable because of its effect on Arkansas property law. The first one was *Conway et al., ex parte*, 4 Ark. 302 (1842), in which the Real Estate Bank had been compelled to make an assignment which preferred certain creditors. In a long opinion by Justice Lacy, concurred in by Justice Dickinson, with Chief Justice Ringo dissenting, the assignment was sustained. There was a hue and cry for the impeachment of the judges, but Albert Pike, who had drawn the assignment, had sent copies of it to both Justice Story (of Story's *Commentaries on American Law*) and Chancellor Kent (of Kent's *Commentaries on American Law*), probably the two leading legal scholars of the day, and both had pronounced the assignment to be valid. That ended the cry for impeachment.

But the opinion of Lacy which most influenced the law was *Moody v. Walker*, 3 Ark. 147 (1840), which was a literal seedbed of Arkansas property law. "Seedbed" is perhaps an erroneous term because the seeds came from English common law, as expounded principally by Lord Coke, and this opinion was the fruition of those seeds in the legal soil of Arkansas.[25]

After the short term of George C. Watkins as Chief Justice of the Arkansas Supreme Court, he was succeeded by Elbert H. English who was considered to be "one of the best judges that we ever had."[26] English was thorough, sometimes too detailed, and followed *stare decisis* to a fault. Changes in the law were to be left to the legislature. A native Alabaman, he was admitted to that Bar, served two terms in the Alabama legislature, and came to Little Rock in 1844. He had served as reporter for the Supreme Court, had revised the statutes, and served as Chief Justice from 1854 until forced out of office after the Civil War during the reconstruction era. At the end of reconstruction in 1874, he was elected Chief Justice by popular vote, was re-elected in 1882, and served until his death in 1884.

In volume one of *Historical Review of Arkansas* by Fay Hempstead, published in 1911, there are brief sketches on numerous other judges who apparently are viewed as less notable than the foregoing. They are mentioned only in passing.

Justice Dickinson was succeeded by George W. Paschal, who resigned shortly thereafter, went to Texas, and prepared *Paschal's Digest of the Texas Reports*. William K. Sebastian was appointed to replace Paschal. He had come to Helena from Tennessee and had served as prosecuting attorney and circuit judge prior to his appointment. After about five years on the Supreme Court, he was selected as U. S. Senator upon the death of Chester Ashley. He did not support secession by the South in 1861, but remained in the Senate along with Andrew Johnson of Tennessee. His attitude toward the war was passive, however, and the Senate expelled him. He returned to Helena and took no part in the war.[27]

Justice Lacy was succeeded by Justice Edward Cross, who has been mentioned previously and held many positions with honor. Chief Justice Ringo's term expired in 1840, and he was replaced by

Thomas Johnson, a Maryland native, from Batesville who served until 1852.

Justice Cross was followed by William Conway, B. That is not a misprint—Justice Conway put a "B" at the end of his name to distinguish him from another William Conway who kept getting his mail. Williamson S. Oldham, a native Tennessean living in Fayetteville, succeeded Judge Lacy. He resigned in 1848 to run for Congress and upon being defeated, moved to Austin, Texas, where he became quite prominent. He was replaced by Christopher C. Scott, who served for eleven years until his death. He had been a circuit judge at Camden.[28]

William Conway B. was succeeded by David Walker, a native Kentuckian from Fayetteville. He was surprised to be chosen by a Democratic Senate because he was a faithful Whig, but he accepted and served for seven years until he resigned. An antisecessionist, he was named Chief Justice in 1866, but was ousted in 1868 by the reconstruction government. He was elected to the Court again in 1874, serving until 1878.[29]

Justice Hulbert Fairchild, "one of the finest characters that we have had upon our bench,"[30] a New Yorker educated at Williams College who studied law in Louisville, was elevated from the Pulaski Chancery Court to the supreme bench in 1860. He only served until 1864. Judge Walker was replaced by Thomas B. Hanley, a native Kentuckian from Helena, who had previously been in both houses of the legislature and served as a circuit judge. He only served a few years, resigning in 1859. Justice Freeman W. Compton was elected in 1856 and again in 1866, but was displaced by the reconstructionists in 1868. He is described as "a powerful lawyer when aroused," but very slow and tedious in his work, although his writing is described as "remarkably terse and clear."[31]

In discussing the lawyers and judges of this period, an effort has been made not to go beyond 1860, although the careers of many of these men extended beyond that time.

Notes

1. F. Hempstead, 1 *Historical Review of Arkansas*, 127-28 (1911).
2. *Id.* at 128.
3. D. Herndon, "A Little of What Arkansas Was Like a Hundred Years Ago," *3 Ark. Hist. Q.* 97 (1944).
4. F. Gerstaecker (translated by C. Evans and L. Albrecht), 5 *Ark. Hist. Q.* 39 (1946).
5. W. Hoyt, "Justice Daniel in Arkansas, 1851 and 1853," 1 *Ark. Hist. Q.* 158 (1942).
6. *Id.* at 160.
7. *Id.* at 162.
8. J. Fletcher, *Arkansas* at 108 (1947).
9. *Ibid.*
10. *Id.* at 109.
11. *Id.* at 111.
12. 1 Hempstead, *supra* n. 1 at 146-149.
13. D. Thomas, 1 *Arkansas and its People*, 98 (1930).
14. 1 Hempstead, *supra* at 159-160.
15. *Id.* at 429.
16. *Id.* at 430.
17. The foregoing is from G. Rose, in 1 Hempstead, *Historical Review of Arkansas supra* n. 1 at 434-435.
18. *Id.* at 439-440. For Pike, *id.* at 436-438.
19. Rose, *id.* at 440.
20. Rose, *id.* at 438.
21. Rose, *id.* at 441-443.
22. *Id.* at 443-444.
23. Rose, *id.* at 444.
24. Rose, *id.* at 444.
25. In the case itself, after reproduction of thirty-seven pages of arguments by Pike for the appellant and by Fowler, Trapnall and

Cocke to the contrary (all previously mentioned), Lacy stated what appears to be a very simple question: "[W]hat interest or estate did Nancy Walker take in the slave, Sarah, by the will of William Walker, deceased?" But to arrive at the answer to this simple inquiry, Justice Lacy stated the following rules of property or of construction:

(1) The object in the construction of wills is to arrive at the true intention of the testator. [A black-letter rule today.]

(2) If a legacy is to be paid to a devisee upon his attaining a certain age, only payment is postponed, and it vests subject to divestment upon his failure to obtain that age.

(3) If there is an absolute gift in the first taker of property, then a limitation over by way of executory devise would be invalid. (Note: In the case, Nancy Walker was held to have received an absolute gift of the slave, Sarah.)

(4) Restraints on alienation and the creation of perpetuities were abhorred by the common law. The principles of our revolution swept away the doctrine of primogeniture and that of the entailed estate and left the citizen in free enjoyment of his property.

(5) An executory devise is a disposition of a future interest in land or chattels to arise at some future contingency, but must vest within the period of the rule against perpetuities.

(6) Thus, an executory devise dependent for vesting on a period beyond that permitted, such as indefinite failure of issue, would be void by reason of remoteness of vesting.

(7) Under the rule against perpetuities, it is of no importance how the fact turns out to be; it is void at the commencement if the event on which its existence depends may, by possibility, extend beyond the duration of the period prescribed.

(8) A fee simple [absolute] is a pure inheritance, clear of any qualification or condition, which is the greatest estate that person can have in lands or tenements and it is freely alienable.

(9) A qualified, base or determinable fee is an interest which may continue indefinitely but which may be determined by some act or event circumscribing its continuance or extent.

(10) The fee simple conditional was eliminated by the statute *De Donis* [Conditionalibus in the 13th century].

(11) Executory devises are valid, assuming there is no violation of the rule against perpetuities.

(12) Executory devises differ from contingent remainders [explaining the differences].

(13) A devise "with remainder over" (by which he meant a devise in which there was a shifting executory interest) if the devisee died without issue surviving him is valid. (Although his definition of definite and indefinite failure of issue is correct, some of what he says has been affected by subsequent law in Arkansas or in the United States.)

26. Rose, *id.* at 449.

27. 1 Hempstead, *supra* n. 1 at 451-452.

28. *Id.* at 452-453.

29. *Id.* at 453-454.

30. *Id.* at 454.

31. *Id.* at 455-456.

Chapter III

THE CIVIL WAR AND RECONSTRUCTION

The Civil War, as it is commonly known, was generally referred to in the South as the War Between the States. In this book, both terms are used at different times. The terms themselves reveal the differing views of the two sides. To the North, it was a war involving civil insurrection. But to the South, which believed that the states were independent, sovereign entities whose powers were limited only by the grant of authority specifically given to the Union in the Constitution, it was a war between the states of the South and those of the North. Arkansas, of course, had people who fought on both sides, and there was internal divisiveness over secession between the hill country of northern and western Arkansas and those who resided in the delta and prairie land of eastern Arkansas and in the rolling forest land of southern Arkansas. But Arkansas eventually seceded, and most of its sons who went to war wore the gray of the South.

Arkansas is essentially a Southern state although it combines some of the deep South and some of the hills of Tennessee. In the hills of North Arkansas, you essentially have a Southern highlands situation not unlike that in east Tennessee, combined somewhat with a lower middle west influence.

This chapter, unlike the preceding one, will deal largely with events and their effect upon the law and legal institutions during the Civil War rather than with personalities. The discussion of personalities largely relates to their involvement with events or legal institutions.

It is difficult to shortchange an event as significant in Arkansas and American history as the Civil War. But this is not a history of that war. Economically, it is well known that its consequences were devastating to the South, including Arkansas. Prior to its onset, in the quarter century preceding it, the Arkansas population had grown from around 51,000 to 435,000, and it had more than doubled in the decade preceding the war. Of that population, about 111,000 were slaves at the outset of the war, concentrated largely in Eastern and Southern Arkansas. Arkansas had an estimated $77,780,500 invested in slaves in 1860, which was obviously a large part of the wealth of the State.[1] Because slaves were considered chattels, the Southern states, including Arkansas, were among the wealthiest in the nation at the outset of the war, although there were obviously great disparities in wealth among whites. There can be no question that the war was a tragedy for Arkansas—one from which it took much longer to recover than some of the other states of the South.

In the late 1850's events rushed toward the possibility of secession and civil war. The escalation of abolition sentiment in New England, the *Dred Scott* case in 1857, John Brown's raid on Harper's Ferry, and the election of Lincoln in 1860 were all part of the rapid rush of events. In 1860 in Arkansas, Justice Henry M. Rector resigned from the Supreme Court to run for governor against the Democratic nominee, Col. Richard H. Johnson and the Whig candidate, Circuit Judge Thomas Hubbard. Rector won and became a major player in the question of Arkansas' secession.

After Lincoln's election, South Carolina seceded in December, 1860, to be followed by Mississippi, Florida, Alabama, Georgia and Louisiana in January, and Texas on February 1, 1861. Other Southern states were more cautious. North Carolina voted against holding a convention on secession. Virginia held one but voted against secession and then called a convention to promote peace. In Arkansas anti-union sentiment was growing. Governor Rector's inaugural address had called for secession, and in early February of 1861, under pressure from hundreds of people who had come to Little Rock from Helena, and upon demand of the governor, Captain James Totten surrendered the Little Rock arsenal and marched his troops away. This was a very peaceful and cordial surrender—the correspondence from Governor Rector had been quite gentlemanly, and the people of Little Rock raised some money and presented Captain Totten with a handsome sword upon his departure.[2] Not long after, by a 4-1 margin, the people voted to call a convention to consider secession.[3]

Judge David Walker of Fayetteville, an anti-secessionist and prominent lawyer, was elected president of the convention which seemed to indicate a preference for remaining in the union. Governor Rector, however, sent a message to the convention arguing for the right of secession and for slavery. He viewed the union as already severed and the question only one of which part Arkansas chose to join.[4] However, unionist sympathy was strong, and the convention did not vote to secede and adjourned to meet again in August or on call of the president. Less than a month after adjournment, Fort Sumter was fired upon and captured and Lincoln issued a proclamation calling for 75,000 men to put down the rebellion. The die was cast for Arkansas and its upper South sister states of Tennessee, North Carolina and Virginia. Judge Walker called the Arkansas convention back into session on May 6, 1861, and by that afternoon a secession resolution had been introduced and adopted, 65-5 (with four of the dissenters changing their votes to join the majority, leaving only Isaac Murphy of Madison County in the negative).[5]

Governor Henry Massie Rector, a lawyer and native of St. Louis, in addition to spending much of his professional career looking after his inherited land and litigating over property in Hot Springs, served as U. S. Marshal for several years in the 1840's and as state Supreme Court Justice from 1859 to 1860. His views were generally representative of those who lived in Eastern, Southern, and most of Central Arkansas. David Walker, on the other hand, was an example of the substantial anti-secessionist views existing in the hill country of North Arkansas.

Although numerous Arkansas lawyers participated in the war in one way or another, one of the most distinguished generals—one of seven from Helena—was General Patrick Ronayne Cleburne, a native of County Cork, Ireland. Cleburne had "read law in his spare time and was admitted to the bar in 1856."[6] Like many people of the South, he hoped "to see the Union preserved by granting to the South the full measure of her constitutional rights" and if that could not be done, "I hope to see all Southern states united in a new confederation and that we can effect a peaceable separation."[7] When war came, he had obviously not made his mark as a lawyer. He enlisted as a private, but soon was elevated to captain of a company, and then colonel of a regiment, the First Arkansas State Troops (later the Fifteenth Arkansas). He later became a general and participated in numerous engagements, including the protection of General Braxton Bragg's army after the disastrous defeat at Missionary Ridge. His division "was considered invincible"[8] until Cleburne's death in the Battle of Franklin, Tennessee, in late 1864. History buffs have shown a fondness for Cleburne's exploits, particularly Judge Henry Woods of Little Rock, who has studied, written and delivered lectures about him.

The passage of the war and the armies across Arkansas provided a disruptive situation to all people and institutions, but particularly to government and law. The federal forces captured Little Rock on September 10, 1863, and Governor Harris Flanagin, who had defeated Governor Rector, moved the government to the old town of Washington in Hempstead County. It was difficult to have a quorum of the legislature at its new Capitol. The legislature's last session during the war was held in September 1864.[9]

Our mission in the context of history during this period is not to revisit the war itself but to determine the status of law and law practice during the war years and immediately thereafter. It is obvious that it was a period of political disarray and upheaval and all civil institutions were disturbed including the courts and the practice of law.

An excellent introduction to what occurred is found in *Rebellion and Realignment* by James M. Woods. He describes in some detail the Arkansas situation as blended into the events elsewhere in the South and nationally. Basically, the secessionist convention in the spring of 1861 was affected to a large degree by events in the states of the upper South—Tennessee, North Carolina and Kentucky—since fifty-one of the seventy-seven delegates to that convention were natives of those states, while twenty-two others came from states of the lower South—Georgia, Alabama and South Carolina.[10] When it appeared that the upper South and border states would likely secede and go with the Confederacy, that had a substantial influence on the Arkansas delegates.[11] The tide of events, including Fort Sumter and the decision to secede among states of the upper South, provided the impetus that converted the upper South portion of Arkansas to go along with the deep South area of Southern and Eastern Arkansas.[12]

Secession brought with it a new basic document, the Constitution of 1861. It declared the State of Arkansas to be "a free and independent State." In Article II, its declaration of rights, it restated basic American principles as embodied in the United States Constitution and in the constitutional and legal thought of the time. Several times in the declaration these rights were said to belong to "free white men," as in Section one, or to "free white men and Indians."[13] Section sixteen, probably inadvertently, gave Indians a new status by declaring that "all white persons, Indians included" would be entitled to bail with certain limitations. Section twenty-one gave "free white men and Indians" the right to keep and bear arms, which suggests how little threat Indians were viewed in Arkansas in 1861.

The 1861 document was careful to refer to citizenship within the Confederate States of America.[14] Interestingly enough, it was provided that the General Assembly not only could exclude from Arkansas slaves who had committed "any high crime" elsewhere, but also could prohibit the slave trade entirely.[15] It established a position of Governor with few powers. The Judicial article provided for a Supreme Court appointed by the Governor subject to Senate approval. The Circuit Court judges were to be elected. All officials had to swear or affirm allegiance to the Confederate States of America.

It is apparent in the light of the subsequent history of the war in Arkansas as to why the 1861 Constitution would present problems. This document was adopted in response to secession and to becoming part of the Confederacy. As parts of Arkansas became occupied by the federal forces, a document of that nature would not be applied or viewed with favor by the union. Since the philosophy of the North, as expressed by Abraham Lincoln, was that the nation was not subject to dissolution or secession, then the 1861 Constitution could not be viewed by the United States as having been legally adopted. Presumably, in those federally occupied areas of Arkansas, the 1836 Constitution was still in effect. Moreover, who were the judges?—those elected under the 1836 Constitution by the legislature, as provided in Article VI, Section seven, or those appointed by the Governor to the Supreme Court or elected by the people to the Circuit Courts?

The Arkansas Reports for the terms of the court in 1861 do not reveal any appreciable change in "business as usual."[16] Such is not the case with the following volume of the Arkansas Reports. Volume 24 begins with this Reporter's Note:

> The cases reported from page 371 to 477, were pending, before the ratification of the constitution of 1864, and opinions were delivered, afterwards, by the judges of the supreme court elected under the constitution of 1836 and continuing to act as such. The cases having been re-

docketed and considered, the opinions then delivered were adopted, and ordered to be recorded as the opinions of this court, but are credited to the gentlemen who prepared them.

There follow cases "at the June and December terms, 1862 and 1863." The officers of the Supreme Court are interesting in this context. The Reports state at the very beginning that E. H. English, Chief Justice, and F. W. Compton and H. F. Fairchild, Associate Justices, were "elected under the constitution of 1836, and office vacated by the constitution of 1864." T. D. W. Yonley, Chief Justice, and Elisha Baxter and C. A. Harper, Associate Justices, were elected under the 1864 Constitution but "resigned." David Walker, Chief Justice, and F. W. Compton and J. J. Clendenin, Associate Justices, were "elected in August, 1866."

The 1861 Constitution was not without its impact, however. The first case in these Arkansas Reports was *Danley and Johnson, Ex Parte*, 24 Ark. 1 (1861) involving the constitutional provision relating to the office of Governor. Justice Fairchild wrestled with the question of the power of the Court, which had been chosen under the 1836 Constitution. He said that if the Court "were sitting under the constitution of 1836, and the question was whether the constitution of 1861, proposed by the convention, had been ratified by the state and adopted . . . and the decision should affirm the validity of the new constitution, the decision would be made by a tribunal not authorized to exercise judicial authority: for, upon the principle of the decision, no pretended court would be a court unless constituted by, and acting under, the new constitution." However, "as a matter of political cognizance we know that this court is acting as a tribunal created by the constitution of 1861, that its members have sworn to support it as the constitution of the state: and as a matter of political information we must take notice that all of the departments of the state government have been and are acting solely under the authority of this constitution: and no question can be made but that it is the ratified constitution of the state. . . ."[17] Then, examining the provisions of the 1861 document, the Court concluded that since it provided that the next general election for state officers would be on the first Monday in October of 1862, the governor would be elected at that time and that the sheriff should be ordered to advertise such election.

The authority of the existing Supreme Court rested upon Article VI, Section 7 of the 1861 Constitution which provided that the first appointment by the Governor of Supreme Court justices would "take place at the session of the General Assembly next before the expiration of the term for which the judges of the Supreme Court now in office expire, respectively." Thus, the existing justices were able to continue to act.

Other cases involving interpretations of the 1861 Constitution included *State v. Clendenin, Judge*, 24 Ark. 78 (1862) (involving election of state senators) and *Burt v. Williams*, 24 Ark. 91 (1863) (declaring unconstitutional an act continuing pending cases).

There are not many cases reported in the Supreme Court for 1862 and 1863, and none for 1864. The Reports begin again with the December term, 1865, and *Rison v. Farr*, 24 Ark. 161 (1865), involving a constitutional question—now dealing with the 1864 Constitution, which declared the 1861 Constitution to be "null and void" and not binding upon the people. The question raised in *Rison* involved the right to vote of the former Confederates. The Court held that "whatever might otherwise have been the effect of his having borne arms against the United States, or of his having aided the so-called confederate authorities, he has now been fully pardoned and forgiven, and is no longer amenable to any authority for his acts in that behalf. . . ." 24 Ark. at 173. The Court invalidated a "test oath" act against former rebels under which they had to swear that they had not borne arms against the United States since April 18, 1864, as being violative of the voting eligibility provisions of the 1864 Constitution. Another act barring former rebels from collecting their debts in Arkansas was struck down in *Vernon v. Henson*, 24 Ark. 242 (1865).

Clearly, the most important case during this period, however, was *Hawkins v. Filkins*, 24 Ark. 286 (1866), which raised the question of the legitimacy of legal proceedings while the 1861 Constitution was in force. Hawkins had obtained a judgment against Filkins on a promissory note in the September, 1861 term of Pulaski Circuit Court. On July 25, 1865, execution was issued by the clerk and levied on Filkins' property. Filkins filed a motion to quash based on the argument that at the time the judgment was rendered there was "no legal court" in Pulaski County and the judgment was void. The Circuit Court granted the motion to quash. In a long opinion, Chief Justice David Walker held that the 1861 convention was properly called and that no acts of that convention were void except those that were contrary to the allegiance to the federal government. He stated that Arkansas had no power to withdraw from the compact that had been entered into with the United States, but that this void act could not affect the validity of the constitution and government of Arkansas in other respects. "[N]o one will contend," said the Court, "that there can exist a government, without the adoption of some fundamental rules, by which the sovereignty is transferred from the individual members of society to a corporation of their own creation." "If the convention of 1864 had power to do this, then, a state convention may destroy its state government. This we have already said the state cannot do, whether attempted by ordinance or otherwise." 24 Ark. at 319. This is required by "the covenant of duty" with the federal government. The Court added:

> Upon principle, if the convention of 1864 had power to declare the constitution of 1861 void "*ab initio*," most clearly that of 1861 had a like power to declare the consti-

tution and government of 1836 void. The people, from whom all power is derived, never delegated to any convention the power to destroy all government; nor, as we have seen, can any such power be exercised by the people of any state, without violating its compact with the federal government. 24 Ark. at 319.

Therefore, the 1864 Constitution was construed to mean that the actions of the 1861 constitutional convention were "null and void" only with respect to the effort to sever ties with the United States. The September, 1861, judgment was therefore held valid, and the writ of execution was appropriate to enforce it.

This opinion would seem to fall under the category of decisions of substantial significance which receive less attention than they deserve because people are inclined to say, "well, of course, that is the law." However, what was written in *Hawkins v. Filkins* was an appropriate interpretation of what should have been the law and was a result that any sensible court would have reached. It is probably what the drafters of the 1864 Constitution intended since any contrary result would have been chaotic. However, it was not what that document had declared when it said that "all the action [sic] of the State of Arkansas under the authority of said convention [of 1861], of its ordinances, or of its Constitution, whether legislative, executive, judicial . . . was and is, hereby declared null and void. . . ." except as it might affect the rights of individuals. Nonenforcement of the debt in this case would have adversely affected the rights of the plaintiff, but the sweeping language that invalidated all judicial acts would seem if taken literally, as the defendant argued, that the court action granting the judgment was void. This case assured that law and society, despite the upheaval of secession, were not plunged into chaos.

It may seem that the year 1864 was devoid of legal process, unlike the preceding and succeeding years. But it appears that these cases were simply deferred until later. Certainly, the case law appears to be more sparse during the war years, which would be expected considering the upheaval and societal disarray of the time. But the basic fabric of the law, whether it existed under the federals or the confederates, although damaged and strained, did not break.

The situation in Arkansas, however, as throughout the South, was one of disruption. As D. Y. Thomas wrote in I *Arkansas and its People* 138 (1930):

> The situation in Arkansas during 1864 was not favorable to normal State government loyal to the United States. The loyalties of the people, as well as the territory of the State, were divided between the Confederate State government headed by Governor Harris Flanagin with his capital at Washington, Hempstead County, and the Murphy government with its capital at Little Rock. Roughly, the northern half of the State was dominated by Unionists and the southern held by Confederates. Moreover, the loyalism of 1864 was often an intangible thing, and Governor Murphy expressed doubt about the loyalty of many professed Unionists. Irregular warfare . . . prevailed. . . . Raids and counter raids kept the people in an unsettled state. ... Organized business had collapsed, means of transportation were lacking, farm stock had become scarce, and negroes were demoralized as laborers. . . . ... For the most part the direction of civil affairs was in the hands of untried, if not unknown, men.

The societal chaos that encompassed the law during the war is illustrated by the fact that George C. Watkins, a leading attorney, "privately informed the governor of 'an inability to enforce the criminal code.' "[18] Prisoners were required to be sent to the penitentiary under certain laws and that was impossible when it was under federal control.[19] In an address to those who were able to attend a legislative session in 1864, Governor Harris Flanagin cited, among other things, for the failure of the war effort in Arkansas that "the liquor laws had failed because of the irregularity of the courts and the willingness of the defendants to pay the fines and continue operation."[20] By that time, the burden had passed in some measure to military courts, at least as far as the confederate soldiers were concerned.[21]

After word came of Lee's surrender, there seems to have ensued a period of occasional anarchy and civil unrest. Governor Flanagin, the wartime Confederate governor, was permitted to deliver the state archives to Little Rock, but other proposals aimed at restoration of civil government did not meet with approval of the federal authorities in Little Rock.[22] The problem of civil unrest continued for years. Guerrilla bands roamed the Ozarks for years and some people who had gone away feared to return. One scholar has written that although Arkansas seemed somewhat remote from the major areas of conflict, "the destruction, the ruin, and the hatreds were, if anything, greater than in Virginia or Tennessee."[23]

Perhaps the most significant aspect from a legal standpoint is that law, in one form or another, though its institutions suffered the same difficulties as society in general, managed to survive the upheaval and gradually reclaim its proper place during reconstruction and the years that followed. Another important aspect of all this was that a number of men who had begun to come to prominence before the war and continued in that respect during it became the mainstays of the late 19th century.

Reconstituting a State

The period after the defeat of the South in the bloodiest war in American history is commonly referred to as Reconstruction. Historians, however, usually limit that period to the time before white Southerners were restored to their civil rights and the era was generally considered ended as far as the federal government was concerned.

The effects of the Civil War lingered far beyond the limited period designated as reconstruction. Although most of the basic framework of the State had been put back together by the end of the 1870's, a major part of which was the adoption of the 1874 Constitution, the aftermath of the war extended far beyond that time and actually into the 20th century. Most of the repair to governmental institutions and the work of reconstituting Arkansas occurred during the late 19th century, however. The wealth of the South before the war was tied up primarily in land and slaves. In a recent law review article, Professor Scott Stafford points out that in 1860, the Arkansas slave population amounted to 26% of the total population and numbered 111,115.[24] Slaves were extremely valuable, with the average Arkansas slave being worth more than an eighty acre farm or a substantial residence.[25] Slaves were considered personal property,[26] and cases involving slaves were among the leading cases in the development of Arkansas law involving chattels. However, in 1860, less than four percent of Arkansas whites owned slaves.[27] Consequently, the result of freeing the slaves was to take away very valuable property from a limited number of people, most of whom lived in eastern or southern Arkansas. The result was more widespread economically than might appear. When such capital was taken away, it affected borrowing, the banks and commerce in general. The wealthy were made much poorer and the effect was felt by lower middle classes and the poor. However wrong slavery was, both morally and legally, the economic effect of abolition was devastating since, beyond the large landowners and slaveowners, the general economy was agrarian in nature, and commerce, trade and employment depended on it. Because of the absence of available cash after the war, the landowners developed the sharecropper system under which the former slaves would be given land to work and would receive a share of the crop and probably occupy living quarters on the land.

From a legal standpoint, two significant events occurred only about six years apart, and these were the enactment of the state constitutions of 1868 and 1874. Of course, the latter one is still in effect along with its frequent amendments. It resulted in large measure in reaction to the 1868 document which was viewed as a Republican product.

The Constitution of 1868 has both its dark side and its more favorable aspects. In *The History of Arkansas* by Fred Berry and John Novak, it is stated that the election of delegates "has the reputation of being one of the dirtiest in the state's history" and one in which "fraud was commonplace" and in which ballots were cast in the names of women (who did not have the vote at the time), children and the dead.[28] Most of the delegates, they say, were newcomers to Arkansas, and the document was condemned as an alien document forced upon the people.[29]

However, it is pointed out that the document contained some worthwhile and progressive provisions, among them: (1) Blacks were given full citizenship with all the rights of white people; (2) it established a system of public schools, allowing people to obtain a free education; and (3) it provided for a state university and other higher education institutions.[30]

But it also was skewed toward maintaining the Republicans in office. It gave the governor extensive powers of appointment. Election districts were apportioned in such a way as to help Republicans.[31] The white conservatives who comprised the Democratic Party were certain to change it as soon as they got the chance.

The ensuing six years were rather turbulent. The Republicans were divided over the iron-handed rule of Governor Powell Clayton and the corruption within his administration. Eventually, they split into two factions headed by Joseph Brooks on the one hand and Elisha Baxter on the other. When Baxter defeated Brooks for the governorship, in 1872, it led to the "Brooks-Baxter War" in 1874, in which Brooks with the aid of his militia physically forced Governor Baxter out of office. Baxter then recruited his own militia. Prior to that time, in 1873, Governor Baxter had successfully supported a constitutional amendment restoring voting rights to all legally qualified white men. The predictable result of the approval of this was to allow the Democrats to regain control of the legislature. They supported Baxter. Eventually, after both sides had appealed to Congress and President U. S. Grant, it was decided by Grant on the advice of the Attorney General that the state legislature had jurisdiction to decide the matter. Baxter was restored to the governorship and the "war" ended. This also marked the end of the era of Reconstruction in Arkansas and opened the way to the 1874 Constitution.[32]

In reaction against the concentration of power in the state government, particularly in the governor, the 1874 document severely limited the powers of state government. It was a document produced largely by conservative Democrats. Practically all state offices were made elective rather than appointive. Most state and county officials had to be elected every two years. Severe limits were placed on the borrowing and taxing powers. Some of these provisions have greatly handicapped the state ever since in attempting to meet obvious needs.[33] Although there have been several attempts to adopt a new Arkansas Constitution, most recently in 1980 and 1970, the people have failed to pass these more modern and progressive documents. Each time, the proposals have been nitpicked to death by some interest group seizing upon a limited provision. The result has been that this antiquated document now has over seventy amendments.

One of the most important figures of the latter part of the 19th Century was Augustus H. Garland who was elected to succeed Baxter as governor in 1874. A former Congressman, he had previously been elected to the U. S. Senate in 1867, but he was not allowed to take his seat because Arkansas was not recognized as being in the Union.[34] He had practiced law in Little Rock after that and before being elected governor. He established himself as a superior lawyer. In 1877, he was elected again to the U. S. Senate to succeed Senator Powell Clayton, and he served in the Senate until 1884 when he was appointed by President Grover Cleveland as Attorney-General of the United States—the first Southerner to serve in the cabinet after the Civil War. In early 1899, he suffered a stroke while concluding an argument before the Supreme Court and died shortly thereafter in the clerk's office.[35]

Garland was one of the attorneys and was the petitioner in *Ex Parte Garland*, 71 U.S. 333 (1867), one of the test oath cases decided by the Supreme Court after the war.[36] Under a federal statute, attorneys who practiced law in federal courts had to swear that they had not supported the Confederacy. Garland and most Southern lawyers could not take the oath because they had supported the Confederacy. (Garland had served in the Confederate Congress and Senate.) In a 5 to 4 opinion written by Justice Stephen J. Field, it was held that the law violated the Constitution's ban on bills of attainder and ex post facto laws. The law was a bill of attainder in that it subjected a specified class of individuals to punishment without giving them a trial, and it was ex post facto in that it subjected people to punishment for acts that were not criminal when committed or inflicted additional punishment if the acts were criminal. Garland had been fully pardoned by the President in 1865.

In *Ex Parte Garland*, Justice Field wrote:

> Attorneys and counsellors are not officers of the United
> States. . . . They are officers of the court, admitted as such
> by its order, upon evidence of their possessing sufficient le-
> gal learning and fair private character. It has been the gen-
> eral practice in this country to obtain this evidence by an
> examination of the parties. In this court the fact of the
> admission of such officers in the highest court of States to
> which they respectively belong, for three years preceding
> their application, is regarded as sufficient evidence of the
> possession of the requisite legal learning. . . . ... They hold
> their office during good behavior, and can only be deprived
> of it for misconduct ascertained and declared by the judg-
> ment of the court after opportunity to be heard has been
> afforded.[37]

In other words, although the majority opinion did not expressly say
so, the legislative branch should keep its hands off of the regulation
of attorneys in the practice of law because that is a function of the
judicial branch. It may "prescribe qualifications for the office" of
attorney, but the question is not that, "but whether that power has
been exercised as a means for the infliction of punishment against
the prohibition of the Constitution."[38]

Augustus H. Garland is a fit subject to end this discussion of
Reconstruction because he typified, along with U. M. Rose and
some others who have been discussed, the high qualities of lawyering possessed by leading Arkansas lawyers in the Reconstruction
period and the years that immediately followed. The focus in the
next chapter will be upon the organized bar which began on a
permanent and sustaining basis with the formation of the Arkansas
Bar Association about the time of Garland's death.

One other leader of this period was Grandison Royston of Hempstead County who in the pre-war days had served as a prosecuting attorney, had been a delegate to the constitutional convention of 1836, had served in the first state legislature and was Speaker of the House. He was named U. S. Attorney in 1841 by President John Tyler. He was later elected to the state Senate, and when the Civil War came, he was a member of the Confederate Congress. In 1874, he served as President of the constitutional convention.[39]

There are a number of interesting stories from this period following the Civil War, and some are contained in *The Old Town Speaks*, a book by Charlean Moss Williams containing recollections of the old town of Washington in Hempstead County. For example, I will repeat in full a story that she got from Judge Will Steele of Texarkana:

> Judge J. D. Conway of Washington, an able attorney, a unique character, shortly after the War instituted suit against the railroad, whose line ran through Washington, for the killing of a cow belonging to a widow. He asked for $10 damages. The cause proceeded to trial. The engineer and fireman testified the killing of the cow [was] accidental and unavoidable. His case looked desperate. In looking about over the jury, he observed that there were eight Confederate veterans on the jury. When he arose to conclude his argument, he said: "Gentlemen of the Jury, I realize the fact that I am trying this case under a serious handicap—that I represent a poor widow woman; that she is helpless; that the defendant I am suing is a rich, opulent, ruthless railroad corporation; that it is represented by one of the ablest attorneys in the state. But Gentlemen of the jury, it wasn't always this way.

Only a few years ago, this poor widow woman had a husband and three stalwart sons. When the tocsin of war was sounded in the struggle between the North and South, they enlisted in the Southern army and fought under the banner of the Stars and Bars. I can see them now as they marched away to enter the bloody conflict, as she stood on the steps of that humble cabin in the gathering twilight and waved them goodbye.

The father was killed in the Battle of Bull Run; the oldest son fell amid the earthquake of Shiloh, where Albert Sydney Johnson died. The second son died amid the floods of living fire at Chancellorsville, where Stonewall Jackson fell. The last, the baby boy, died yonder in the gloom of the Wilderness, where angry divisions and corps rushed upon each other, mixed and mingled and rolled together in the bloody mire.

An old Confederate veteran, member of the jury, leaped to his feet and shouted: "God Almighty, Joe, why didn't you sue for a thousand dollars?"[40]

That case and similar cases involving the basic law of contracts, torts and property were typical of that period as far as Arkansas state law was concerned.

One of the unusual situations in the latter part of the 19th century in Arkansas, of which much has been written, occurred in Fort Smith. U. S. District Judge Isaac C. Parker has been called "the hanging judge" because of all the men he tried and hanged after they were apprehended in the Indian Territory by U. S. marshals. You have to remember that the Indian Territory at that time comprised most of what would become the State of Oklahoma in the early 20th century, but at that time it was a haven for a large number of bandits, killers and assorted desperadoes.

Judge Parker was not like Roy Bean, "the law west of the Pecos," or Wyatt Earp. He was a lawyer who was born in Ohio in 1838 and after studying law was admitted to the Ohio bar in 1859. Chief Justice William H. Rehnquist is the source for that, having spoken about Judge Parker at the UALR Law School in 1983 as a part of the Altheimer Lecture Series.[41] After being admitted to the Ohio bar, Isaac Parker moved to St. Joseph, Missouri, opened a law office and served successively as city attorney, circuit prosecutor, and state circuit judge. In 1870, he was elected to Congress and served two terms in that office, and then in 1875, was named U. S. District Judge for the Western District of Arkansas by President Grant.[42] He had jurisdiction over all offenses not subject to trial by the Indian courts, and the Indian courts generally had jurisdiction only over Indians. Few crimes in those days were triable in federal court, and the statutes of that time did not contemplate a federal judge with such sweeping jurisdiction. Consequently, until 1890, no appeal was authorized from his criminal rulings, not even to the Supreme Court. The only remedy for a convicted criminal was to seek executive clemency from the President.[43] While that is rarely granted today, Judge Parker's notoriety is that of the 172 men he sentenced to be hanged about half of them either died in jail or escaped the noose by presidential reprieve or by commutation.[44]

There was no question that Judge Parker was a "hanging judge," although the number he hanged varies in different accounts. Two of the books cited previously refer to his hanging eighty-eight men, but a Fort Smith attorney wrote in *The Arkansas Lawyer* that he only hanged seventy-nine, some having received executive clemency.[45] These men who were hanged were convicted of first-degree murder, and the congressionally ordained penalty for that was hanging.[46] These were callous, brutal men, and the idea that Parker was not much better was as false as the idea that he was ignorant or not learned in the law. One of these hangings in his very first year as a judge gained a great deal of notoriety when he hanged six men on the courthouse lawn on the same day. These multiple hangings attracted newspaper reporters from Little Rock, St. Louis and Kansas City, along with a large crowd, estimated at 5,000 by one newspaper, who came early and in many cases brought their lunches.[47] It is easy to see why he came to the attention of U. S. Presidents. But as Chief Justice Rehnquist wrote:

> But the statistics tell only part of the story. ... After the Civil War, with all the dislocation and lawlessness which inevitably follows such a conflict, fugitives, desperadoes and ne'er-do-wells drifted into the Indian Territory. Because it was difficult, if not impossible, to extradite them from this jurisdiction, it became known as "Robber's Roost." These criminals preyed on Indians and whites alike, throughout the territory, and they did so with impunity until, as the statistics indicate, they became grist for Judge Parker's mill.[48]

Consequently, instead of being viewed as an extremist, Parker was much liked in Fort Smith and praised editorially by the newspapers. After the Supreme Court gained the right of appellate review of his cases, Parker was reversed a number of times on legal technicalities. But the Supreme Court some years later criticized itself for one of these reversals and reversed the earlier holding.[49] Moreover, Judge Parker was praised and the Supreme Court criticized by Dean Wigmore in his monumental work on evidence to this effect: "These [Supreme Court] cases, on the point of presumption, were ill advised to assume the position of monitor over a great and experienced trial judge."[50]

These criminals were apprehended by U. S. Deputy Marshals who were paid six cents per mile and fifty cents for service, and two dollars for execution of warrant and ten cents per mile if they brought the prisoner in alive. They had to pay their expenses and the sustenance of the prisoner out of this compensation. More than 200 men served as deputy marshals during Judge Parker's tenure, and about 65 of them were killed as a result.[51] In the fictional novel, *True Grit*, by Charles Portis, the hero, Rooster Cogburn, is a deputy marshal; he was played in the movie version by John Wayne who won an Academy Award for best actor as a result. In one dramatic scene, Rooster explains to an outlaw, Lucky Ned Pepper, how the law worked in the Indian Territory and in Fort Smith:

> Rooster said, "I mean to kill you in one minute, Ned, or see you hanged in Fort Smith at Judge Parker's convenience! Which will you have?"
> Lucky Ned Pepper laughed. He said, "I call that bold talk for a one-eyed fat man!"
> Rooster said, "Fill your hand, you son of a bitch!"[52]

We move now to the next chapter which deals with the history of the organized bar. That began at the end of the 19th century and will carry us through the 20th century. Changes in the way law was practiced were not extensive as the 19th century merged into the 20th. It was still a basic, meat and potatoes, sort of thing. Federal law, however, became much more complicated with the rise of regulatory agencies during World War I and particularly during the Great Depression and World War II. These resulted from the efforts of President Franklin D. Roosevelt to alleviate unemployment and boost the economy in the 1930's and to deal with the war effort in the early 1940's. That was the most noticeable change in the law in the first half of the 20th century. Another striking aspect of the post-World War II period was the beginning of specialization. For a time after the war, Charles Eichenbaum and Gaston Williamson were the only tax lawyers in Little Rock and probably in Arkansas. With specialization, law firms began to grow much larger, and where seven or eight lawyers at one time would have been considered a large firm for Arkansas, that is no longer true with several numbering over fifty lawyers. Moreover, in the last quarter-century, we have seen women become lawyers and judges, an event that constitutes the most striking change in that period of time. So, in the last half-century, we have seen monumental change that dwarfs what came before.

Notes

1. D. Thomas, 1 *Arkansas and its People*, 115-116 (1930).
2. F. Hempstead, I *Historical Review of Arkansas* at 208-209 (1911).
3. Thomas, *supra* n. 1 at 121.
4. *Id.* at 123.
5. Hempstead, *supra* n. 2 at 213.
6. B. Ruby, "General Patrick Cleburne's Proposal to Arm Southern Slaves," 30 *Ark. Hist. Q.* 193 (1971).
7. *Ibid.*
8. Hempstead, *supra* n. 2 at 221.
9. Thomas, *supra* n. 1 at 130.
10. J. Woods, *Rebellion and Realignment* 137 (1987).
11. See generally, *id.* at 133-152.
12. *Ibid.* And see, *id.,* 166-169.
13. Section six on trial by jury and sections ten, eleven and fourteen, relating to due process in various forms, used this terminology, for example.
14. Sections one, four and six of Article IV so provided, for example.
15. Art. IV, Section 22.
16. 23 Ark. 1, 347, 429 (1861).
17. 24 Ark. at 4-5.

18. M. Dougan, *Confederate Arkansas* 123 (1976).

19. *Ibid.*

20. *Id.* at 124, citing the Governor's message of September 28, 1864.

21. *Id.* at 125.

22. *Id.* at 126.

23. *Ibid.*

24. Stafford, "Slavery and the Supreme Court," 19 *U.A.L.R. L.J.* 413, 414 (1997).

25. *Id.* at 418.

26. *Ewell v. Tidwell*, 20 Ark. 136.

27. *Stafford, supra* at 419.

28. F. Berry and J. Novak, *The History of Arkansas* 113 (1987).

29. *Ibid.*

30. *Id.* at 114.

31. *Ibid.*

32. *Id.* at 118-121.

33. *Id.* at 121.

34. See F. Hempstead, 1 *Historical Review of Arkansas* 284 (1911).

35. *Id.* at 284-285.

36. The other was *Cummings v. Missouri*, 71 U.S. 277 (1867).

37. 71 U.S. at 378.

38. 71 U.S. at 379-380.

39. C. Williams, *The Old Town Speaks*, introductory material, and at 225-227 (1951). This same book has an extensive chapter on Augustus H. Garland at 176-190 and about Albert Pike at 169-175.

40. *Id.* at 223-224.

41. W. Rehnquist, "Isaac Parker, Bill Sikes and the Rule of Law," 6 *U.A.L.R. L.J.* 485 (1983). On Judge Parker, see also W. Gard, *Frontier Justice* (1949); S. Harman, *Hell on the Border: He Hanged Eighty-eight Men* (1953); H. Croy, *He Hanged Them High: An*

Authentic Account of the Fanatical Judge Who Hanged Eighty-eight Men (1952); F. Harrington, *Hanging Judge* (1951).

42. Rehnquist, *supra* at 487.

43. *Id.* at 487-488.

44. W. Gard, *supra* at 285.

45. B. Dobbs, "A Lawyer's Appraisal of the Parker Court," *The Arkansas Lawyer* 4 (Oct. 1968).

46. *Ibid.*

47. W. Gard, *supra* at 283-284.

48. Rehnquist, *supra* at 489.

49. *Garland v. Washington*, 232 U.S. 642, 646-647 (1914) reversing and criticizing the result in *Crain v. United States*, 162 U.S. 625 (1896).

50. J. Wigmore, *Wigmore on Evidence* Sec. 276, at 116, n. 3 (2d ed. 1940).

51. Dobbs, *supra* at 4.

52. C. Portis, *True Grit* 200 (1968).

Chapter IV

THE ORGANIZED BAR BEFORE 1946

The Arkansas Bar Association of today traces its roots back to 1898 as its stated year of formation as the "Bar Association of Arkansas." The oldest books available about its proceedings are in the Arkansas Bar Center in Little Rock and the UALR Law School, and the very oldest available is a bound volume, "Proceedings, 1900-1905, Bar Association of Arkansas." In this bound volume, both the 1900 and 1901 title pages refer only to the "Report of the Proceedings of the Annual Meeting" for that year. However, the 1902 title page states that it is a "Report of the Proceedings of the *Fifth* Annual Meeting of the Bar Association of Arkansas." If 1902 was the fifth annual meeting, then the first annual meeting would seem to have been in 1898.

However, this is complicated by the fact that all references to the first bar association president, U. M. Rose, state that he served in 1899. He was definitely the president in 1899 and until early 1900 because the proceedings for the 1900 annual meeting on January 2-3 begin with the introduction of "the President, U.M. Rose, who delivered" the address reprinted there. One possibility as to what may have occurred, if the 1898 date is correct, is that the association was formed during late 1898 and possibly elected officers for the bar year, 1899, to serve until early January 1900. It appears also that a bar year initially was a calendar year because by the time of the next meeting in January 1900, less than five months later on May 29-30, 1900, in Fort Smith, a new bar president had been chosen to replace Henry C. Caldwell who had taken office at the end of the January meeting. A letter from St. Paul, Minnesota, dated May 21, 1900, was read to the meeting in which Judge Caldwell, Chief Judge of the U.S. Circuit Court of Appeals, writes as follows:

" . . . If, when I was elected President of the Bar Association, I had known that its next meeting would come on in May of this year, I would of course have declined the place [presumably, the position]. I never knew until after my election and until after the Bar Association had adjourned, that the 29th of the present month had been fixed on for the next meeting. I deeply regret my inability to be present. . . ." (The federal appeals court was in session in St. Paul at that time.) The Committee on Officers for the following year had at the annual meeting on January 2-3, 1900, in Little Rock, selected Judge Caldwell as president. However, this becomes somewhat more confusing when in the proceedings of the Fort Smith meeting in May, the president is listed as Sterling R. Cockrill of Little Rock several pages before the letter from President Caldwell was read to those assembled. Apparently, Judge Caldwell served only a short term.

We know that U. M. Rose was still recognized as president in the early January meeting of 1900. The meeting time was changed to May, which seems to have been the source of Judge Caldwell's confusion. Judge Caldwell served from January until the May meeting when his successor was chosen. At that point, the association began to meet annually in late May or in early June just as it does now in June.

Sterling R. Cockrill had earlier served as Chief Justice of the Arkansas Supreme Court for eight years and was Judge Caldwell's successor as bar president. He died on January 12, 1901, before his term ended, and was described by the Committee on Memorials at the 1901 meeting as perhaps rendering "a greater service to our jurisprudence than any other one man who has sat upon our bench."[1]

It would seem reasonable to conclude, as the association historically has, that the organization was formed in 1898 based on the characterization of the May 1902 meeting as the "Fifth Annual Meeting" as well as the subsequent characterization of the May 1903 meeting as the "Sixth Annual Meeting." But the fact that U.

M. Rose, the first president, is listed as holding the position for 1899 and the fact that documents are apparently non-existent for 1898 and 1899, suggests that the association began its operations no earlier than 1899. The reason the 1902 meeting was the fifth annual meeting was because there were two "annual" meetings in 1900. However, the Fort Smith meeting in May is not referred to as the "annual" meeting in the report of those proceedings although the structure of the proceedings is identical to an annual meeting format. It would seem, however, that by 1902 it was considered that there were two annual meetings in 1900. That would explain how the association apparently commenced formal operations in 1899 rather than 1898 unless it organized in 1898. The confusion about all of this has continued to more recent times. In a speech to the bar association in 1958, Edward L. Wright, then the Bar Association President, cited a speech the year before by Bar President Eugene A. Matthews about the earlier state bar organizations and added "but it was in 1898 that our forebears at the Bar reorganized the Association in its present form."[2] However, what President Matthews actually said was: "If we measure the age of this Association from the time of its reorganization in 1899, then this year [1957] we celebrate its 58th anniversary."[3]

According to microfilm in the Arkansas History Commission records, under a headline, "The Arkansas State Bar Association," it is written: "The Arkansas State Bar Association was first organized in 1882. It had a period of successful experience—of about ten years. But from 1890 to the beginning of the present year but little good was effected through it. *A reorganization was effected on the 9th day of January, 1899*, at which time Judge U. M. Rose was elected president, George E. Dodge was elected treasurer, and De E. Bradshaw secretary."[4] It may be assumed that the meeting was planned in 1898, but it would appear that the effectuation of the plan took place nine days into 1899.

Here again, it should be recognized that we are talking about an association that maintained continuity from that time to the present. Arguably, the bar association began earlier because reference is made in subsequent bar publications to several other efforts.[5]

In the *Bench and Bar of Arkansas* (1935), on page 18, it is stated that on November 24, 1837, nineteen lawyers from Little Rock, Fayetteville, Batesville and Helena organized the first "Bar Association of the State of Arkansas." A meeting took place on January 15, 1838, "when action was taken looking to the establishment of a Supreme Court library. No further record is available, and there is no evidence that the organization was maintained." If we ignore continuity, we may assert that the organized bar in Arkansas has a lineage of over 160 years. The initial membership of the 1837 organization is listed in the paper by George B. Rose entitled "Previous Bar Associations in Arkansas" which is found in the Proceedings of the Bar Association of Arkansas, May 26-27, 1932, at page 122.[6]

A more serious effort was made in 1882 in the office of U. M. Rose, according to this same publication. Judge Rose, "then and for many years the Nestor of the bar," offered a resolution that was adopted creating a state association "to advance the science of jurisprudence, to promote the administration of justice, to uphold the honesty of the profession and to encourage cordial intercourse among the members of the bar." The initial meeting was held in the House of Representatives on May 24, 1882, and the formal organization was completed with a membership of eighty-nine and a vice-president for each of the twelve judicial districts. The first officers were M. L. Bell of Pine Bluff, president; Sterling R. Cockrill of Little Rock, secretary; and George B. Dodge of Little Rock, treasurer. This organization is said to have met regularly during the 1880's but lapsed during the 1890's.

Then, it is asserted in this 1935 publication that the "Bar Association of Arkansas" reorganized the lawyers in "the year of 1899" and "by January, 1900, the first formal meeting, the membership had grown to 212." It states that the second meeting was held in May, 1900, and after that regular meetings were held annually in May or June, usually at Little Rock or Hot Springs but sometimes at Fort Smith, Texarkana, Pine Bluff, and Memphis (the latter being in conjunction with the Tennessee Bar Association).

Whether 1898 or 1899 was the beginning of the present association is something that may remain a matter of historical dispute. Maurice Mitchell has stated, for example, that his conclusion several years ago that 1898 was the correct date was disputed at the time.[7] From all of the above, it seems more likely that 1899 is the correct date, particularly considering the statement in microfilm material on file with the Arkansas History Commission which is quite specific about the date being January 9, 1899.

These early annual meetings of the Bar Association of Arkansas all had a similar format. There were reports from officers and from committees. There were speeches or papers delivered usually by the association president and often by other attorneys or judges of substantial repute in the bar. These papers or speeches amounted to an early form of continuing legal education. U. M. Rose and George B. Rose often dwelled on great philosophical issues and the thoughts or sayings of great philosophers of the Western world. Other presentations were on specific legal topics, such as the presentation by Judge Jacob Trieber on June 2, 1905, on the jurisdiction of the federal courts in actions in which corporations are parties, or by a guest, Henry D. Ashley of Kansas City, on the effect of precedent or *stare decisis* on American law. The committees came forth with reports which often resulted in resolutions. Some of the committee reports could be eloquent or offer strong condemnation even in the same report. A report of the Committee on Law Reform, after endorsing adoption of the

ABA-proposed Negotiable Instruments Law as "an admirable codification of the law on the subject," then stated in its second paragraph that the Arkansas "laws of curtesy is [sic] barbaric and unsuited to a civilized age" because if "a man has by a woman a child born alive he becomes entitled to all her lands for life, and may turn her offspring out to starve," which it stated was often done in regard to the children of a former husband. It advocated abolition of common law curtesy and the award of one-third of the wife's property to the husband if she has children and that her dower rights be equal in that circumstance.[8]

Apparently, no meetings of the statewide bar association were held except the annual meeting—and excepting, of course, what happened in 1900—in the early years. That is explainable easily enough by the conditions of transportation in the early part of the 20th century. Presumably, local bar meetings and local bar associations had to suffice in the meantime. Continuing legal education, as we know it, did not exist.[9]

Early Leaders in the Arkansas Bar Association

It is difficult to talk about a few leaders in the bar without inappropriately neglecting others. There have been many over the years who contributed greatly to the bar association in so many ways that it is impossible to cover them all here. The object here is to talk about a few people who particularly distinguished themselves in various ways through their contributions to the work of the organized bar.

Obviously, a great deal of attention must be paid to U. M. Rose, who was the primary organizer of the Bar Association of Arkansas and who also was one of the founders of the American Bar Association. Judge Uriah M. Rose was born in Kentucky in 1834, read law in a law office, and later attended the Transylvania Law School, from which he graduated in 1853. He married and moved to Batesville, Arkansas, where he practiced law until his appointment in 1860 by Governor Elias Conway as Chancellor of the Pulaski Chancery Court. That court had a general jurisdiction of a special nature in the sense that it had been created to act on matters connected with the Real Estate Bank anywhere in Arkansas. The war disrupted the Arkansas court system to a certain degree, as mentioned earlier, and after the war, Judge Rose was succeeded in 1865 by Judge Lafayette Gregg, a prominent Fayetteville lawyer. He then formed a firm with Judge George C. Watkins, known as Watkins & Rose. Later, after Watkins' death in 1872, he practiced alone and then in partnership with his son, George B. Rose, being subsequently joined by Judge W. L. Hemingway and later by James F. Loughborough and Deaderick H. Cantrell in the firm of Rose, Hemingway, Loughborough & Cantrell. He was described as not a politician, but as dedicated to law practice, and as an accomplished scholar who spoke several languages, a literary person who was an incessant reader, a lecturer, a gifted orator who made many important addresses, an extensive traveler, and a poet who translated into English Schiller and portions of Goethe's "Faust."

In the autumn of 1905, President Theodore Roosevelt visited Arkansas and was so impressed with Rose that he appointed him not long after that to the American Commission to the Peace Tribunal at The Hague in 1907.[10]

Judge Rose compiled the first 23 volumes of the Arkansas Reports into "Rose's Digest" and was an examiner or reviewer of Mansfield's Digest published in 1885.[11]

What the organized bar remembers him the most for, however, is his work in organizing the Arkansas Bar Association—an effort of both the 1880's and the 1890's, as has been discussed. He was also one of the founders of the American Bar Association in 1878.

The American Bar Association was organized at Saratoga Springs, New York, in the summer of 1878 by a group of lawyers, most of whom were from the South, who traveled to this spa in the

Adirondacks to escape the rigors of the Southern summer.[12] The annual meeting of the association after that time took place only at Saratoga Springs until 1889, and a "convivial group of Southern lawyers" accustomed to vacationing there each August "formed the largest single element in the original membership."[13] "For many years election was a highly selective, personalized matter; for at least twenty years the atmosphere of the Association was mainly social."[14] However, this was soon to change, as it did in the late 19th century when the ABA took on the project of the improvement of legal education and in the period from 1892-1912 when it sought to promote uniformity of common law and statutory law in the states.[15] In 1906, in an influential address to the ABA on causes of popular discontent with the administration of justice, Roscoe Pound placed defects in the various court systems high on the list of such causes.

U. M. Rose served as President of the ABA in 1901. Subsequently, his bust was selected to be one of two from Arkansas in Statuary Hall in the nation's Capitol. The Rose Law Firm bears his name, although the firm traces its origins back before him to George Watkins and before him to Chester Ashley and Robert Crittenden. Writing only two years before Judge Rose's death in 1913, Fay Hempstead stated that "Judge Rose stands preeminently as Arkansas' foremost citizen."[16] In 1958, Justice Felix Frankfurter wrote: "In my early years at the bar, U. M. Rose was one of the luminaries of our profession—not merely a very distinguished practitioner but a highly cultivated, philosophic student of civilization and of the role of law and the lawyers in the progress of civilization. Mr. Rose inspired me in my formative years as a lawyer."[17]

Other early leaders of the state Bar, other than the ones already mentioned, included the following as Bar Presidents through 1909-10 (in addition to Rose, Caldwell and Cockrill, the first three): Thomas B. Martin, Little Rock (1901-02); George B. Rose, Little Rock (1902-03); James F. Read, Fort Smith (1903-

04); Allen Hughes, Jonesboro (1904-05); Joseph M. Stayton, Newport (1905-06); Joseph W. House, Little Rock (1906-07); William H. Arnold, Texarkana (1907-08); John M. Moore, Little Rock (1908-09); N. W. Norton, Forrest City (1909-10); and W. V. Tompkins, Prescott (1910-11). The meetings were always held either during the last week in May or the first week in June.

By this time the Bar Association was well-established and had much the same format—committee reports, resolutions, speeches (many of which had obviously taken a great deal of time and thought to prepare), and social events.

Two of these are of particular note. In July 10-12, 1906, there was a joint meeting of the Arkansas and Texas Bar Associations held in Texarkana. The two met jointly in an initial session and then broke into separate sessions for their regular meetings. The joint meeting was held at the Miller County Courthouse (which would suggest, at least, that Arkansas had made the overture). The Arkansas President was Joseph M. Stayton, who introduced the Vice-President, W. H. Arnold of Texarkana, for opening remarks. He stated that the "invitation to meet in Texarkana was not only extended by the united bar of our two cities, but by its business men, who fully realize the honor as well as the great advantage that will be gained by reason of this great meeting. . . ."[18] Both Mr. Arnold and Joe T. Robinson of Lonoke, who followed him, praised Texas in the grand style of the day and to an extreme seldom lavished on the Lone Star State by people from Arkansas. After a flowery response by Edward F. Harris of Galveston on behalf of the Texas Bar, President H. M. Garwood of Texas introduced President Stayton of Arkansas who delivered his annual address which was followed by Stayton's introduction of Garwood who in turn delivered his annual address. After that, Judge U. M. Rose delivered a paper on "The Code of Napoleon" and several others from both States read papers. The first session concluded by Stayton's announcement of a reception the following night at the

Elks Hall and a banquet on another night. As it was growing late, Stayton stated that he was "speaking for Mr. Garwood and myself, and will say it is getting very dry at this end of the house."[19] They adjourned, after which it presumably got wetter.

On June 4-6, 1907, there was a joint annual meeting of the Bars of Arkansas and Tennessee. This is the first time that the caption sheet of the proceedings refers to the "Arkansas Bar Association" rather than "the Bar Association of Arkansas." However, in the text, reference is still made to the Bar Association of Arkansas. This meeting was held at Memphis in the Goodwyn Institute Building and involved both the joint meeting and separate meetings. The format was very similar to the joint Arkansas-Texas meeting. F. H. Heiskell, the Tennessee Bar President, introduced James H. Malone of Memphis who delivered an address of welcome. Then, Arkansas President Joseph W. House introduced O. N. Killough of Wynne, who responded to the welcome. There were other speakers including both Bar Presidents. Papers were also delivered during the next two days. Entertainment included a "Dutch Lunch" in the *evening*, a smoker, automobile parade and luncheon at the Country Club, a separate luncheon for the ladies at the Country Club, and a boat ride on the river followed by a banquet. The speeches were just as flattering as those of the preceding year in praising the wonderful achievements of each of the states and the attorneys and statesmen found among the citizenry and the beauty of the women.

By the time of the 1908 annual meeting, held on May 22-23 in Little Rock, the joint meetings were over for then, although there would be another in 1926. Without knowing, one might suspect that the time consumed in interaction of the two bar associations reduced or detracted from the available time for conducting the business of each one. For many years, state bar associations have limited the interaction to inviting presidents or presidents-elect of the bars of surrounding states to be guests at the annual meeting.

The annual meetings that followed in the early part of the 20th Century all had the same essential format previously described. Aside from committee reports, resolutions, the election of officers and appointment of committee chairs and members, and the memorials to deceased members, the proceedings were consumed in large measure with an early form of continuing education in which papers were read. An examination of this material showed that it varied from presentations of the law on certain subject matter to memorial presentations about respected and well-known lawyers who had died to learned or esoteric presentations of a philosophic nature. In the 1908 proceedings, in addition to finding the presentations made at that meeting, there is a list of presentations made in the nine preceding meetings from 1900 to 1907 (including both of the meetings held in 1900). These included "bread and butter" presentations on matters of law. There were two different addresses dealing with the life of the late former Chief Justice Sterling Cockrill which were basically memorials.

Many of the speeches dealt with more philosophical, historical or esoteric subjects. U. M. Rose's presidential address in January 1900—the first one of record—was on Beccaria, "the author of that remarkable book on 'Crimes and Punishment,'" a book which he thought had a profound influence in shaping present laws. He compared his work with that of other writers from early times, the middle ages, and the authors of the enlightenment. In 1901, George B. Rose gave a talk on "Literature and the Bar," in which his thesis was that lawyers by the nature of the profession ought to know everything, but since they cannot, they should read as much literature as possible in order to have their thought, outlook and ability shaped by the great writers, speakers and philosophers of the past. Jesse Turner of Van Buren, at the 1902 meeting, wrote about "The Case of Macauley v. Poe" suggesting that Edgar Allan Poe had plagiarized some of his material from Thomas Babington Macauley. Judge U. M. Rose in 1906 presented a paper on "The

Code Napoleon," and at the same meeting, Justice David M. Brewer of Washington lectured on two periods in the history of the U.S. Supreme Court. In 1907, N. W. Norton of Forrest City addressed the joint Arkansas-Tennessee bar meeting on "Progress in the Law as Compared with Other Professions." Although critical at times of the legal profession, he concluded:

> Other professions are unselfish, loyal, noble, and filled with a great manhood; but in their trust and confidence in each other, and their profound respect for and appreciation of each other, and the resultant good-fellowship, the sun in its rounds finds nothing like the legal profession.[20]

May we say that with credibility today—or has incivility in the practice of law eroded it to a point not recognizable ninety years ago?

It seems that by this time, just preceding World War I, the Arkansas Bar Association had established a permanent, structured organization that had overcome the lack of continuity of previous efforts. It could not be faulted for meeting only annually in late May or early June. Transportation and ease of travel were a major problem with chief reliance being on the railroads. The motor car was in its infancy and roads outside of the major towns were only muddy or dusty trails used largely by horse-drawn wagons or buggies or by men on horseback.

As noted earlier, the agenda for the annual meetings was now set by custom and there was little difference except for the speakers and the content of the papers delivered, committee reports and resolutions. For that reason, concentration during this intermediate period will focus only on some of the personages involved and some of the noteworthy events.

One noteworthy paper presented in 1909 was U. M. Rose's account of the "Life and Character of Chester Ashley."[21] It provides not only great insight with respect to the influence and state and national prominence of Ashley, but also as to various persons of historic prominence during that period and events such as the ill-advised and ill-fated Real Estate Bank.

By the 1910 meeting, held in Pine Bluff on June 1-2, there were standing committees on Law and Law Reform, Uniform State Laws, Public Service Corporations, Public Improvements and Local Assessments, Practice in the Supreme Court, Practice in Chancery Court, Practice in Circuit Court, Memorials and Legislation.[22] The most interesting thing about that meeting, however, is something the members never heard. It was a paper "read by Judge U. M. Rose on the Magna Carta, before the old Arkansas Bar."[23] The caption to it states that the address was made before "the Arkansas State Bar Association at its Annual Meeting about 1882."[24] One of the interesting events he discusses is the opening of the tomb of King John in the Cathedral of Worcester in 1797 to determine if in fact John was actually buried in the tomb that bore his effigy. He points out that John by then had been dead for almost 600 years having been "laid to rest . . . with an unparalleled dearth of tears."[25] The skeleton in the tomb conformed to contemporary descriptions of John and the body had been clothed exactly as represented by the effigy "except that the hands were not encased in gloves, and that in lieu of a kingly crown it wore a monk's cowl, put on at the king's dying request, in the hope that it might scare the devil away, or deceive the keen vision of the Angel of Resurrection."[26] The tomb was close to those of two holy saints who "as he trusted, would charitably intercede for him at the last day. By means of these prudent precautions he hoped to slip along with the elect into the Kingdom of Heaven."[27] If there is any doubt that his description of John differs from the universal judgment of historians, he later refers to him as "the greatest enemy of free government that was ever seen in England" and "one of the vilest of the champions of wickedness."[28] The paper goes on to tell of the events that led to the Magna Carta which, most people do not know although Judge Rose knew, was largely and in its lasting parts the work product of Stephen Langton, Archbishop of Canterbury. It was based in part on an old charter of King Henry I, circa 1100, granting certain privileges to the people, and perhaps to some degree on the more liberal laws of the revered Edward the Confessor, the next-to-last of the Saxon kings, whose death and succession by Harold led to the Norman Conquest.

This is an outstanding document and one that should be reprinted for use in courses in legal history.

By 1910, the Bar Association seemed sufficiently well-established that the years that followed will be considered in a less-intensive way. The essential pattern of these annual meetings was settled and is illustrated by the preceding discussion. Consequently, what follows will attempt to emphasize some of the highlights of the years that followed.

1911 to 1920

The 1911 proceedings featured an extensive report on circuit court practice by its chair, Judge Gus Fulk. A substantial part of the report was devoted to a comparison of English criminal practice with Arkansas criminal practice that had been taken from a study by a national committee. The comparisons favored the English system. In one case a comparison was made of an English case with a similar Missouri case in each of which the murder victim was poisoned. Over a period of about six weeks, the accused Englishman was indicted, tried, found guilty and sentenced to die, the case was affirmed and he was hanged. However, in Missouri over a period of about thirteen months, the accused was indicted, tried, convicted, sentenced to die, the conviction was reversed by the state supreme court (after seven days of argument), and the case was reversed. It was obvious that the English system was superior.

There was a learned speech by W. V. Tompkins of Prescott, the president, on the relationship between church and state, and an interesting talk by U. M. Rose on practice in Arkansas in the early days.

The featured speaker in 1912 was the President of the American Bar Association, Stephen S. Gregory of Chicago (whose presence almost certainly was secured by Past President U. M. Rose). Part of the introduction by Arkansas President Ashley Cockrill has relevance even today. The end of the introduction was this:

> "Stephen S. Gregory is endeavoring to preserve the American Bar Association so as to make it possible for the Southern lawyers, and those who hold their views on social questions, to remain members of that great Association."[29]

Some things never change. But some do in that a modern-day ABA President such as Phil Anderson would talk about the Association or some current theme, but Gregory gave a long, learned speech on Lord Mansfield.

Nothing of particular significance seems to have happened at the 1913 meeting, and the 1914, 1915 and 1917 proceedings are missing from the bound volume that purports to contain them.

In 1916, Judge T. H. Humphreys of Fayetteville read a paper on international peace, the year before the country entered World War I ("the Great War"), and W. H. Rector of Little Rock delivered a paper on the need for a new state Constitution. Although the Rector address printed out at just under forty pages, he cautions at the beginning, ". . . nor will your attention be called to every instance wherein the present constitutional system fails adequately to provide for the efficient expressions of the various functions of governmental power."[30] We have the same document today, except for many additional amendments, more than eighty years later.

The 1918 meeting opened with a resolution presented by federal Judge Jacob Trieber which put the Bar Association squarely on the side of the U.S. and against the Germans. It passed unanimously.[31] President Thomas C. McRae of Prescott spoke about "the War and Lawyers," and W. H. Arnold of Texarkana spoke about the American Bar Association and its history and development. The 1918 proceedings listed local bar associations in Arkansas.[32] There were eighteen at that time—Little Rock, Mississippi County, El Dorado, Eighth Chancery Circuit (in extreme northeast Arkansas), Pike County, Ninth Judicial Circuit (in southwest Arkansas), Little River County, Phillips County, Fayetteville, Bentonville, Eureka Springs, Fort Smith, Pope County, Booneville, Jefferson County, Malvern, and the Eastern District of Clay County (Piggott).

A highlight of the 1920 convention was a speech by Roscoe Pound, Dean of the Harvard Law School, entitled "The Revival of Personal Government." Pound was made an honorary member of the Bar Association immediately following the address.[33]

1921 to 1930

(Proceedings of the Bar Association for 1919, 1921, 1922, 1924, and 1925 are missing. The 1923 meeting was not particularly eventful, although it had the usual round of speeches and a resolution urging an increase in judicial salaries.) In 1926, the meeting in Texarkana was held jointly with the Texas and Louisiana Bar Associations. The three associations held separate meetings and then met jointly. The Arkansas Bar meeting was presided over by President George B. Pugh whose address was entitled "Our [Arkansas] Supreme Court." It was a brief history of the Court up to the time of moving into the new State Capitol in 1914. The speech recalls some stories about judges that are particularly entertaining, including some about Archibald Yell that appear in this book. He also discusses the events of the Brooks-Baxter War, and that also appears in this material.[34] By this time, the Bar Association seems to have been quite well-established and the list of its members and their communities consumes fourteen pages printed in small print.[35]

The joint meeting consisted of a series of addresses by prominent lawyers and judges, including one on "The Progress and Development of the Law" by Chief Justice E. A. McCulloch of Arkansas, another by Senator Thomas J. Walsh of Montana on "The Reform of Federal Procedure," and one by former Senator (and prominent historian) Albert J. Beveridge of Indiana on "The Development of the American Constitution under John Marshall." Henry P. Dart, Sr., of New Orleans made a presentation on the colonial legal systems of Arkansas, Louisiana and Texas. Professor William R. Vance of Yale, former Dean at Washington and Lee, George Washington and Minnesota, spoke on what universities should do for the legal profession. He viewed their potential assistance as being in the area of law reform through legal research, viewing law as a social science. American Bar President Chester I. Long, former U.S. Senator from Kansas, spoke on "Liberty with Government." Former U.S. Attorney General T. W. Gregory of Texas spoke on "Woodrow Wilson and the League of Nations." It was an impressive occasion, presided over by W. H. Arnold of Texarkana, who apparently was instrumental in developing the program, serving as its General Chairman, and who made an introductory address.

A joint banquet was held after this and much of it, although not all, was humorous. It seems dubious that members of the present bar associations of any of those states would be enthusiastic about introductory remarks followed by seven speeches that occupy twenty-nine printed pages. The most welcome remark must have come from ABA President Chester Long when he said in the closing remarks: "I will not attempt to make a speech tonight. The only thing you expect of me is to say, 'Good-bye.' "[36]

Nonetheless, it was an impressive gathering.

In 1927, 1928 and 1929, the Bar Association met alone in Hot Springs. In each of those years, only three addresses were given, and this may lead one to believe the largesse of 1926 might have been more than was desired. Although there was some dispute over revising and redigesting the statutes in the 1929 session—a proposal that was approved—not much happened in those meetings. Among new members, Edward L. Wright was admitted in 1928 and Robert A. Leflar in 1929.

The 1930 meeting was somewhat more interesting, not because it had four addresses rather than three, but because one of them was by Senator Joe T. Robinson on "Naval Arms Limitation Treaty of the London Conference." He explained the treaty and what it accomplished in reducing the tonnage of the United States, Great Britain and Japan. Senator Robinson had been instrumental in its approval by the Conference.[37] Association President T. D. Wynne of Fordyce gave a speech on "The Courts in Relation to Social Progress" in which he lamented the "recent and acrimonious debate in the United States Senate, in which opposition to the nomination and confirmation of the present Chief Justice of the Supreme Court was expressed, [emphasizing] the growing tendency to assess judicial qualifications not alone according to superior legal attainments and judicial temperament, but also in accord with political and economic predilections."[38]

American Bar President Henry Upson Sims of Alabama gave a talk on "The Relation of Bar Organization to Law" and Judge J. R. Keaton of Oklahoma, its Bar President, spoke on "Incorporation of the Bar in Oklahoma" as the result of a legislative act of 1929 which created a unified or integrated bar.

1931 to 1940

In 1931, a featured speech was delivered by U.S. Senator T. H. Caraway, who died a short time after the Convention. The type-written copy of the speech that was given by him was never found. Bar President T. C. Trimble, Jr., of Lonoke made a presentation on the profession discussing legal development in England, the bifurcation between barristers and solicitors and the Inns of Court. He discussed requirements for admission to the bar in England, France and the United States. He noted that thirteen of the states did not require any general education as a prerequisite, including Arkansas, and that seven states, including Arkansas, did not re-quire any definite period of law study. He deplored this situation, stating that the "outstanding contribution that we in America have made in the field of the law has been the modern law school."[39]

In 1931, a symposium on state government was led by J. H. Carmichael, Chairman of the Executive Committee. One of the subjects covered was a new Constitution or amendments to the old one. Judge S. H. Mann of Forrest City advocated an amendment process, and that view was concurred in by Charles A. Walls of Lonoke. W. H. Arnold of Texarkana disagreed and viewed the amendment process as haphazard in nature. W. H. Rector of El Dorado agreed with Arnold, stating that he did not "believe in patching up an old constitution which has outlived its day."[40] That was in 1931; in the 21st Century, we still have the much amended, patched up Constitution of 1874.

The symposium of 1931 was resumed at the 1932 annual meeting with Judge J. H. Carmichael again serving as the mod-erator. He referred to the pressing "need for reorganization" of state government. The difference between the partisans seemed not to relate to the need for change and institutional improvement but how to do it. Some favored "reorganization" of state govern-ment, presumably by statutes or constitutional amendments, while some favored a new constitution. The 1932 speakers, including Carmichael, Judge J. M. Futrell, Charles A. Walls, and others were reorganization advocates.

Two excellent papers delivered in 1932 were "Isaac C. Parker" by Arkansas Bar President Harry P. Daily of Fort Smith, and "Previous Bar Associations in Arkansas" by George B. Rose (which dealt more with the leaders of the Bar in those years than with associations). A paper about U. M. Rose, delivered previously in 1914, was reprinted.

The 1933 meeting featured an address by American Bar President Clarence E. Martin of West Virginia on "Shall We Abolish Our Republican System of Government." The obvious answer was "no," but what he was actually concerned about was the nationalization of child labor laws. He viewed that as socialistic and an "ingenuous attempt to nationalize children."[41] Also in 1933, a paper on "Racial Exclusion in Jury Trials" was delivered by Henry M. Armistead of Little Rock. He argued that the "states should cease to give grounds for the objection of exclusion of negroes from juries."[42] These papers were indicative of the concerns for the times and a harbinger of national issues yet to come. On a more objective note, David D. Terry made a presentation on the work of the 1933 legislature and President-elect Paul Jones of Texarkana discussed the law of oil and gas.

In 1934, the usual small handful of new members increased to five pages. The membership chairman was W. H. Arnold of Texarkana. The Proceedings list "Special Ambassadors to the Bar"—one or more for every county—who, presumably, were responsible for recruiting members at the local level. The result dwarfed any previous year.

By 1934, some familiar names—some still living and some deceased within easy memory—began to show up in leadership positions. They included, among many others, George K. Cracraft (father of the retired Court of Appeals judge of the same name),

Harry C. Ponder, Beloit Taylor, N. J. Gantt, Jr., James Seaborn Holt (later of the Supreme Court), Ed F. McFaddin (also to become a Justice), Archer Wheatley, E. Charles Eichenbaum, Richard B. McCulloch, Ben Shaver, Archie House, Thomas B. Pryor, Jr., Harry J. Lemley (later of the federal bench), Pat Mehaffy (also to become a federal judge), Charles Frierson, Jr., Adrian Williamson, John L. McClellan (later U.S. Senator), Oscar Fendler, Robert A. Leflar, C. E. Daggett, J. Mitchell Cockrill, Heartsill Ragon (federal judge) and many others. By the 1930's, the emerging bar leaders included many who would continue to lead in the post-war period and the decades of the 1950's and 1960's.

The 1934 meeting featured a speech by Earle W. Evans of Wichita, Kansas, the American Bar President. What spurred the most interest was a presentation on the integrated bar by an Oklahoma lawyer, L. A. Rowland, a former Texarkana resident. A resolution was proposed by Judge J. H. Carmichael, Chairman of the Committee on Incorporation of the Bar, endorsing the concept and proposing that a bill be drafted for the legislature creating such a Bar. Despite opposition, the resolution was adopted.[43] Nonetheless, President Paul Jones appointed Joseph M. Hill, Chairman, and J. H. Carmichael, W. H. Arnold, J. F. Loughborough, W. F. Coleman, W. R. Donham, and John McClellan to prepare and draft the bill.[44]

The 1935 meeting featured an unusual format that had not been used before. After the welcoming speeches, there were four separate presentations in different meeting rooms. In one, Governor J. Marion Futrell presented a paper on "Cooperative Acts of the Legislature of 1935 and Federal Agencies." This was followed by a presentation of three other papers dealing with the federal housing administration by Walter L. Pope, the Reconstruction Finance Corporation by Harry E. Meek, federal banking and savings and loan organizations by Clyde E. Pettit, and the home owners loan act by J. S. Utley. A second meeting room, presided over by

Ed F. McFaddin, featured four papers on different aspects of bankruptcy. A third meeting room provided a discussion of taxation and improvement districts and featured two papers by George Vaughan and Charles W. Frierson with Archer Wheatley presiding. W. R. Donham presided over the fourth meeting room with the topic being personal injury practice and with papers presented by J. F. Loughborough and T. W. Campbell. This was something of a forerunner of what is done today—in which more than one presentation is available to attendees.

On the second day, the controversial bill over the incorporation of the Bar was discussed. It had passed the Senate but died on the calendar in the House. The leadership persevered in its support of incorporation, and a new resolution was passed supporting the "movement" for integration of the Bar. By now, the list of Bar members covered twenty-three pages.

The integration of the Bar issue was still alive in 1936, and it was again endorsed by an almost unanimous vote. The "Junior Bar Section" was created by an amendment to the Bar constitution. Miss Aurelle Burnside of El Dorado gave a talk entitled, "The Woman Lawyer—Why?" Among other things, she said:

> But, as a practical matter, it would be idle and unreal to assume that women have equal opportunities with men in the practice of law, largely by reason of woman's natural timidity in availing herself of her opportunities. But, even for the more aggressive, the profession of law is too old and too firmly encrusted in tradition to be affected so soon by reason of woman's devotion. He is a sophisticated old gentleman, impervious to flattery, and confident that his affection may not be won easily by woman. The way to his heart is difficult, requiring the highest attributes of heart and mind. . . .[45]

A hurried examination of the roster of the Arkansas Bar in 1936 suggests that it had only nineteen women members at that time counting Miss Burnside.

The 1937 meeting dealt with some peripheral matters such as the creation in 1936 of the American Bar House of Delegates. Judge W. H. Arnold of Texarkana who had attended that meeting in Boston and two other meetings in Columbus and Kansas City was elected delegate. Another matter concerned the Arkansas annotations to the American Law Institute's Restatements. J. R. Wilson of El Dorado reported on his committee's work on this project. The Bar President, Judge J. F. Gautney, was blindsided by a motion by former Governor Tom Terral to endorse President Franklin D. Roosevelt and Senator Joe T. Robinson in their efforts to increase the membership of the Supreme Court [the court-packing bill]. Chancellor Gautney ultimately ruled the motion out of order "in view of the fact that neither Senator Robinson nor President Roosevelt is running for office at this time."[46] Whatever his ruling had to do with anything, the Bar Association never endorsed the court-packing bill (about which Senator Robinson actually had grave misgivings).

The most annotated speech ever given to that time was delivered by Joe C. Barrett of Jonesboro on the rule making power of the courts. The text more resembles a law review article.

The 1938 convention featured a paper delivered by Bar President Walter G. Riddick on "The Supreme Court of Arkansas as an Active Power in the Administration of Justice." It was critical of the Court on that ground, particularly with regard to evidentiary rulings. The paper was discussed at some length. George B. Rose stated that he had practiced law for almost sixty years and "the greatest curse in the administration of justice in Arkansas is weak and timid judges, who think that by being weak and timid they will secure continuance in office."[47]

The Report of the Executive Committee for 1938 revealed that in 1934 the dues were reduced from $5.00 to $2.00 and that, despite the dues reduction, a great many members had been lost. The Association was in poor shape financially and the proceedings of 1937 could not be printed in time for the 1938 meeting. They recommended considering a joint dues program with the American Bar.

Also, in 1938, the Special Committee on Regulation of the Bar recommended that the Arkansas Constitution be amended to provide that the Supreme Court "shall make rules regulating the practice of law and the professional conduct of attorneys-at-law."[48] Pursuant to it the Canons for Judicial Ethics and Canons for Professional Conduct of Lawyers of the American Bar Association were approved and appear in the 1940 Proceedings of the Association. Also, the Bar Rules Committee was established in 1939.[49]

1941 to 1946

By 1941, there were 23 local bar organizations that are listed in the Proceedings.[50] The Executive Committee's Report revealed that in 1940, President N. J. Gantt, Jr., of Pine Bluff had appointed a committee to inaugurate a series of legal institutes in Arkansas. These were pronounced a success. This was the beginning of continuing legal education in Arkansas with the exception of the addresses at the annual meeting.[51] Membership and dues remained as problems. There was an extensive report recommending changes in the practice and procedure in the courts.[52]

World War II was being waged in 1942, and the program seemed shorter than most. Possibly it was partly because Henry Moore, Jr., of Texarkana, the Bar Association President, had died a month before the meeting. He had written the President's Address on "Freedom of Speech," which was read by C. E. Daggett of Marianna.[53] Another talk, "Improving the Administration of Justice," was delivered by Senior Circuit Judge John J. Parker of the U.S. Court of Appeals for the Fourth Circuit. The Arkansas Annotations to the Restatements were discussed, and it was announced that George Rose Smith's annotations to the Restatement of Trusts were the only ones that had been completed. The Legal Institutes Committee had been very active, and a substantial number of programs had been conducted in the regional Chancery Circuits.

A telegram was read from Lt. Oscar Fendler of the U.S. Navy saying that he was sorry he could not attend.

E. H. Wooten of Hot Springs, Joe C. Barrett of Jonesboro, and Terrell Marshall of Little Rock were elected President, Vice-President and Secretary-Treasurer, respectively.

The Junior Bar met before the Bar convened in 1943. The Bar was very concerned with the war effort. There were only four addresses and two of them concerned the Soldiers and Sailors Relief Act and the role of the lawyer in war work. Prior to the 1942 meeting, a Committee on War Work had been created. Wartime restrictions on gasoline were responsible for nearly terminating the legal institutes program—only two were held in the preceding year. The Committee proposed the creation of a journal published by the "Law Department" of the University of Arkansas to keep the bar informed. The Executive Committee had debated the question of whether to even have the annual meeting but unanimously voted to do so.

In the summer of 1942, after the annual meeting, one of the long-time leaders of the Arkansas Bar died on his 82nd birthday. He was George B. Rose, the son of the founder, U. M. Rose. Aside from other services, he presented many scholarly, well-written papers to the Association, whom he had served as President in 1902. Aside from his legal scholarship, he had written books on the art of the great painters of the Renaissance as well as numerous articles on literature. He had truly lived the life of a Renaissance man in the late 19th and the 20th centuries.

Despite the war effort and gasoline rationing, there were 28 local bar associations in 1944.[54] However, the Association Secretary, Terrell Marshall, wrote a letter published in the Proceedings urging more lawyers to join. He said that Martindale's listed 1,489 lawyers in Arkansas (even though the Supreme Court Clerk listed over 2,000). An American Bar analysis, however, showed only 956 full-time lawyers in the State—the others being part-timers, military lawyers, public officials and the like. He noted that the last annual meeting had endorsed a resolution urging the appointment of a committee to confer with the Supreme Court about integrating the Bar.[55] The Association had 570 members, of whom 387 were active, dues-paying members, 119 were exempt because of military service, 18 were exempt as special members, and 46 were exempt as judges. Thus, almost one-third paid no dues.[56]

The war was taking its toll aside from military service and gasoline rationing. The Executive Committee had met only once, and both the Committee on Arkansas Annotations to the Restatements and the Committee on Legal Institutes had suspended their work. The effort to create a law journal in cooperation with the University had been halted due to the war. The most active committee was the one on war work. As a result, the year could not help but be a low point in the life of the Bar. The highlights were thoughtful speeches by President Joe C. Barrett and Dean E. M. Morgan of the Harvard Law School. A third talk was about legal assistance to the armed forces. There were two distinguished guests present at the annual meeting, both of whom made some comments—Senator Harry S. Truman of Missouri and Governor J. M. Broughton of North Carolina. E. A. Henry was elected President for 1945.

These war-related problems constituted the reason that there was no annual meeting held in 1945. Thus, the Proceedings of

1944 state that it is the 47th annual meeting, and the Proceedings of 1946 state that it is the 48th annual meeting. Although the war was nearing its end by the spring of 1945, Germany did not surrender until May 7 and Japan held out until August 15. The annual meeting was customarily held in early May in those days. This did get things back on track somewhat since there had been two meetings in 1900. The work of the Association went on, however, and the Executive Committee Report of 1946 stated that the membership had grown from 600 in 1945 to 777.[57] There were six full pages of new members from August 1, 1944, to September 1, 1946.[58] Consequently, by 1946, with the end of the war and under old President Henry, it had survived and under new President Lamar Williamson, it had revived. Mr. Henry gave an account of his stewardship during 1944-45. He recalled the absence of many of the younger members in the war effort, the problems caused by the rationing of gasoline and tires, and the scarcity of cars. He then said that despite the determination to discontinue legal institutes, many were held. He said that within the next two years there would be an Annotated Digest, and as a result of Association efforts, the Supreme Court had appointed a Digest Committee consisting of Robert A. Leflar, Chairman, Cecil Warner, Charles W. Norton, Paul Jones and Guy E. Williams, the Attorney General. He explained that the 1945 Annual Meeting, aside from other war-related problems, could not be held in Hot Springs because the federal government had taken over practically all of the hotel space. Plans to replace it with a meeting in Little Rock failed because they were advised by the government that no more conventions could take place during the war.

Notes

1. Report of the Proceedings of the Annual Meeting, Hot Springs, 1901, p. 16.

2. Wright, *Sixty Years: We have Come of Age*, 12 ARK. L. REV. 260 (1958).

3. Mathews, *Looking Backward—To See Forward*, 11 ARK. L. REV. 273 (1957). Emphasis supplied.

4. Emphasis supplied. This is found in SMC Box LII, No. 3, entitled "Proceedings of the Arkansas Bar Association—1882-89, 1900-68," and Constitution of 1838.

5. In the speech by Eugene Matthews, he discusses briefly these earlier bar associations.

6. This article is largely a discussion of early leading lawyers in Arkansas, such as Chester Ashley, Albert Pike, George C. Watkins and others. It is quite interesting and well-written.

7. Telephone interview with Maurice Mitchell, October 14, 1997.

8. Proceedings, Eighth Annual Meeting of the Bar Association of Arkansas, Hot Springs, June 1-2, 1905, pp. 10-11.

9. Robert R. Wright was appointed to the law faculty and Director of Continuing Legal Education by Dean Ralph C. Barnhart in 1963. Before that, after World War II, the annual meeting and later the mid-year meeting and Fall Legal Institute, and some local meetings, formed the basis for CLE.

10. F. Hempstead, I *Historical Review of Arkansas*, at 335-341, 1100 (1911).

11. *Id.* at 347.

12. J. Hurst, *The Growth of American Law: The Lawmakers*, 287 (1950).

13. *Ibid.*

14. *Ibid.*

15. *Id.* at 71-72.

16. I Hempstead, *supra* n. 10 at 348.

17. "History of Rose Law Firm," by Rose Law Firm at pp. 2-3.

18. Proceedings of the Arkansas Bar Association, 1906-08, p. 6.

19. *Id.* at p. 22.

20. Proceedings, Joint Meetings of the Bar Association of Tennessee and Bar Association of Arkansas, June 6, 1907, p. 199.

21. Proceedings, Annual Meeting, June 1-2, 1909, pp. 137-163.

22. Proceedings, Annual Meeting, Bar Constitution, pp. 28-29.

23. *Id.* at 27.

24. *Id.* at 135.

25. *Id.* at 136.

26. *Id.* at 137.

27. *Ibid.*

28. *Id.* at 138.

29. Proceedings, Fifteenth Annual Meeting, Bar Association of Arkansas, June 3, 1912, p. 11.

30. Proceedings, Nineteenth Annual Meeting, Bar Association of Arkansas, p. 91.

31. Proceedings, Twenty-First Annual Meeting, Bar Association of Arkansas, p. 13.

32. *Id.* at 43.

33. Proceedings, Bar Association of Arkansas, June 3, 1920, p. 16.

34. Proceedings, Bar Association of Arkansas, April 22-24, 1926, p. 18, *et seq.*

35. *Id.* at 79-93.

36. *Id.* at 175.

37. Proceedings, Bar Association of Arkansas, June 4-5, 1930, p. 13; address by Senator Robinson at p. 109 *et seq.*

38. *Id.* at 85.

39. Proceedings, Bar Association of Arkansas, 1931, p. 102.

40. *Id.* at 155.

41. Proceedings, Bar Association of Arkansas, 1933, p. 97.

42. *Id.* at 112.

43. The Proceedings for 1934 state that it was adopted unanimously—a dubious conclusion, in light of the opposition and the fact that years later, the same idea was rejected on at least two occasions.

44. Proceedings, Bar Association of Arkansas, 1934, p. 23.

45. Proceedings, Bar Association of Arkansas, 1936, p. 142.

46. Proceedings, Bar Association of Arkansas, 1937, p. 90.

47. Proceedings, Bar Association of Arkansas, 1938, p. 155.

48. This became Amendment 28 to the Arkansas Constitution as approved in November 1938.

49. Proceedings, Bar Association of Arkansas, 1940, pp. 18-44.

50. *Id.* at 46.

51. Proceedings, Bar Association of Arkansas, 1941, p. 131, and pp. 138-141.

52. *Id.* at 132-137.

53. Two other officers, Cecil Shane, the Vice-President, and Roscoe R. Lynn, the Secretary, had also died during the preceding Bar year.

54. Proceedings, Bar Association of Arkansas, 1944, pp. 43-44.

55. *Id.* at 45.

56. *Id.* at 160.

57. Proceedings, Bar Association of Arkansas, 1946, p. 294.

58. *Id.* at 70-75.

Chapter V

THE ORGANIZED BAR AFTER WORLD WAR II

1946 to 1950

The organized Bar had obviously been adversely affected by the war and, before that, the great depression. But by 1946, the Association was ready to achieve more than it ever had. It was ready to take off.

The 1946 Executive Committee report stated that the Association had accomplished the following: (a) put on a Bar refresher course for returning lawyer-veterans; (b) created a Committee on Taxation; (c) appointed a committee to work with the Arkansas Public Expenditures Council; (d) appointed a Public Relations Committee to improve the image of the Bar; (e) appointed a Committee on Constitutional Changes to work with a Governor's committee to remove archaic sections from the Constitution; (f) joined with other state bar associations and the American Bar to urge Congress to pass the Federal Administrative Procedure Act; and (g) successfully worked to increase membership.

The Committee on Jurisprudence and Law Reform had numerous recommendations for improvements, including curbing the abuse of the nonsuit statute, passing the Uniform Declaratory Judgments Act, making findings of fact by Circuit Judges in non-jury cases have the same effect on appeal as the findings of a Chancellor, adoption of a state administrative procedure act, making certain pre-trial procedure mandatory, creating a Judicial Council, creating a committee on re-codifying probate law, and reforming the judicial system. Obviously, many of these things came to pass (such as the adoption of the Probate Code of 1949) and some did not (reforming the judicial system, which the Bar is still involved

120

with today). Twelve to fifteen legal institutes had been conducted since the end of the war, that committee reported.

There were several addresses in 1946. President Lamar Williamson attacked the elective system for judges (something that appears periodically in this material). He called it "an anomaly scarcely known outside of the United States, illogical and indefensible." "Judges," he added, "are skilled, career technologists, and only persons competent to judge their skill should be responsible for selecting them."[1] He advocated a modified version of the Missouri Plan, but with the Chief Justice substituted for the Governor. The Judicial Council, composed of selected judges, lawyers and laymen, would be the nominating body. The Chief Justice himself would be appointed by the Governor subject to confirmation by the Senate.[2] A proposal involving some type of selection and appointment process has long been recommended by the American Bar Association and the American Judicature Society, but it is still being discussed without any proposed change. The elective system remains the main reason for diversity of citizenship cases in the federal courts.

Another address was delivered by Glenn R. Winters, then the Secretary-Treasurer and editor of the journal of the American Judicature Society. After some discussion of other subjects, he presented a discussion of judicial selection. He pointed out that in the colonial period and for about half-a-century after formation of the United States, judges were appointed by the Governor or selected by the legislature. The change to election was due to Jacksonian populism. He endorsed the Missouri Plan, which combines the appointment and election process, with the original selection being through an appointment process and with the determination as to continuance in office being decided at the ballot box.[3] He presented a proposed plan for the organization of the Arkansas judiciary.[4]

The Executive Council report for the 1947 annual meeting indicated that President Max B. Reid had devoted a great deal of time and effort, along with a special committee appointed by him, to the Court Reorganization Plan mentioned previously. Another item of some note was that the Association, based on a discussion with Dean Robert A. Leflar, would in a one-year experiment publish a law review quarterly that would involve joint financing by the Association and the University. The two entities would create a joint board of control. This, of course, was the genesis of the *Arkansas Law Review and Bar Association Journal*, as it was originally called.

George Rose Smith, as chairman, reported that Arkansas annotations to the Restatements would resume, the committee having been dormant during the war. The Committee on Constitutional Changes reported that the state urgently needed a new Constitution and recommended that work begin on that immediately. The Committee on Court Reorganization filed a lengthy report stating that they had rejected some suggestions of former President Williamson as being too "idealistic rather than practical, and others because they were not adaptable to the needs, traditions or background of our state."[5] However, the plan submitted in 1947 was "designed to improve the method of the selection of judges. . . ."[6] It still provided for an appointive system and is set out in full in pages 19-27 of the 1947 Proceedings. A report of the Committee on the Integration of the Bar indicated that that committee was active and moving forward with its plans, which ultimately came to naught. A long report from the Probate Law Committee would ultimately be more productive. The Model Probate Code of 1946, a product of the American Bar Association, was now available and would ultimately form the core of the work product of the committee. As amended, it would become the Arkansas Probate Code of 1949. There was a particularly long report in 1947 of the Committee on Publication of a Journal, headed by William Nash of the

Rose firm. This, of course, would result in the law review as mentioned previously.

Invigorated by the return of the veterans and a burgeoning membership, the Bar Association in 1947 was a hotbed of activity, all of which was worthwhile, and some of which would come to fruition.

For the first time, in 1947, part of the Association proceedings appeared in the new law review and bar journal. There were two principal addresses, those being by President Max Reid and former Congressman Hatton W. Sumners of Texas. President Reid's speech, "We Are Life Tenants," dealt with professional obligations, law reform and particularly judicial reform.

Wilson W. Sharp of Brinkley presided over the 50th annual session of the founding of the Association in 1948. Ever since the war, the Committee on Taxation—now a Section—had been increasingly active. Presided over by its chairman, E. Charles Eichenbaum, the committee or section had a very active session in 1948 with eight papers being presented. Prior to World War II, there had only been a limited tax practice in Arkansas.[7] But after the war, it had apparently blossomed.

Probably the high point of the 1948 meeting was that the Arkansas Probate Code had been completed by a committee under the chairmanship of Adrian Williamson of Monticello, with the very active and able involvement of Maurice Cathey of Paragould, and it had been received favorably in presentations to local bar associations. It was now ready to go to the legislature.

President Sharp gave an address, "The Court Supreme," which was highly critical of the U.S. Supreme Court's recent decisions. There was a nostalgic, very interesting speech by Tappan Gregory, the President of the American Bar Association, about the history of Arkansas lawyers and the bar. Justice Frank Smith of the Arkansas Supreme Court made a speech about the Court and some of its history.

By 1948, the Law Review Committee was able to report that the Bar Association, by means of a dues increase and an annual contribution of $2,000, was planning for the continuance of the publication on a permanent basis.

In the introduction to the 1949 annual meeting, President A. F. House was able to announce that the Probate Code had become law and that the Association had been given an Award of Merit by the American Bar Association for its efforts over that year and the previous years following the war.[8]

There was once again a substantial tax seminar with five papers being presented by Henry Gregory, Jr., J. E. Gaughan, Walter E. Paul, J. S. Daily, and Leonard L. Scott. It was again presided over by E. Charles Eichenbaum. An address on tax problems of farmers was also given by Professor Jack R. Miller of Notre Dame and there was an address by the IRS Chief Trial Attorney on trial techniques.

Although the Probate Code had passed, the Court Reorganization Plan had run into trouble. The Bar was divided. Dean Robert A. Leflar addressed the Junior Bar on its behalf. Archie House's President's speech was an interesting piece of history involving Justice Stephen J. Field, David Dudley Field and Augustus H. Garland.

There was once again a major tax seminar in 1950 with seven papers delivered and with a luncheon speech by a judge of the U.S. Tax Court. The Junior Bar, now led by Fred M. Pickens, Jr., of Newport, heard an address from Robert A. Leflar who was still the Dean of the Law School but also an Associate Justice of the state Supreme Court. The court reorganization plan was still being amended and studied. President Cecil R. Warner criticized federal taxation and spending designed to promote social goals and the inordinate expansion of what is meant by "general welfare." Senator John L. McClellan made a speech in which he decried the phenomenal growth of the federal government and the impact on budgetary obligations and the appropriations process. Robert P. Patterson, Secretary of War during World War II and a former federal circuit judge, also addressed the convention, as did Dr. Lillian E. Schlagenhauf of Quincy, Illinois, whom the women lawyers had invited as a speaker.

Volume Five of the *Arkansas Law Review and Bar Association Journal*, in addition to the annual meeting proceedings, contained a bar association section with local bar notes and committee reports. One committee, headed by J. L. Shaver of Wynne, had been active in proposing court reorganization. The legal institute committee had been particularly active, and thirty-one lawyers had volunteered to speak on various subjects at the circuit institutes. Also active was a committee on revision of civil procedure, its goal being essentially to adopt the Federal Rules. They were too late for submission to the legislature in 1951 but would continue their work.

1951 to 1960

In a foreword to the proceedings of the Fifty-Third Annual Meeting in 1951, President John H. Lookadoo could point to the recent enactment of the Probate Code, the civil procedure revision, the legislative approval of preserving oral testimony in the Chancery Courts, the legal institutes, and the effort to obtain a law clerk for each member of the Supreme Court. The Tax Section again had its seminar with four papers being presented. Louis Ramsay of Pine Bluff was elected Chairman of the Junior Bar.

There were addresses by Justice Tom C. Clark of the U.S. Supreme Court, Justice Sam Robinson, Judge Burnita Shelton Matthews of the District of Columbia federal district court, Dr. Kenneth McFarland, and President Lookadoo. Among the obituaries was that of Justice Frank G. Smith, who served on the Arkansas Supreme Court for thirty-seven years, the longest tenure to that time, exceeding by one year the service of Justice Carroll D. Wood. He wrote more than 3,000 opinions during his time on the Court.

Another fairly extensive tax program was put on in 1952. Among the items approved that year was a bill to be presented to the legislature creating a procedure for asserting claims against the state. The Junior Bar Section presented addresses from various people in support of presidential candidates, Eisenhower, Kefauver, Harriman, Kerr, and Russell. Paul Young succeeded Louis L. Ramsay, Jr., as Chairman of the Junior Bar. Speeches were made by Bar President Terrell Marshall, New Orleans Editor William H. Fitzpatrick, John D. Randall of the ABA, and Harry E. Meek. Meek's after-dinner speech entitled "Things" was likely the best received because it was very clever. He even delivered a poem he had written about *Horsley v. Hilburn* (a fee tail case).[9]

The Tax Section again presented several papers on various aspects of taxation at the 1953 meeting. J. Gaston Williamson, Chairman of the committee, was introduced by Paul Sullins, the Chairman of the Executive Committee. Mr. Sullins announced that the Secretary-Treasurer, Gerland Patten, had resigned and had been replaced in that capacity by Maurice Mitchell. Mr. Mitchell announced that on the date of his appointment the Association had 1,058 active members. It was announced that Bar President A. F. Triplett had appointed a committee to draft a new corporation code for Arkansas, the committee consisting of Harry E. Meek, Chairman, Ralph Barnhart, Paul Sullins, J. E. Gaughan, E. J. Butler, G. Thomas Eisele, and Edgar Bethell.[10]

On Friday, May 15, 1953, the Bar Constitution was amended to change the name of the Association from "the Bar Association of Arkansas" to the "Arkansas Bar Association." Also, the annual dues for members admitted to the Bar more than three years was raised to $10.00 and for those admitted less than that time to $5.00.[11]

Speeches in 1953 were made by President Triplett criticizing the jury system, by American Bar President and SMU Dean Robert G. Storey of Dallas on the future of the legal profession, and by Dorothea Blender, President of the National Association of Women Lawyers (and an invitee of Neva Talley).[12]

At the 1953 meeting, there appears the first reference to "a mid-year meeting workshop," which the Executive Committee had decided to hold in carrying out a suggestion made by Oscar Fendler. The first such meeting was held on January 16, 1953, was chaired by Edward L. Wright and proved a success.[13] By the 1954 annual meeting, President J. L. Shaver could report that the meeting held on December 4, 1953, had been attended by a large number of lawyers and that the mid-winter meetings would continue.[14] Also in 1954, it was announced that the Association would join with the Law School in holding an annual legal institute in Fayetteville each fall.[15]

Credit for the idea of a mid-year meeting should go in part to the Junior Bar for conducting a successful "Fall Seminar" in Little Rock on December 14, 1951.[16]

At the 1954 meeting, the Taxation Committee, chaired by E. Charles Eichenbaum, put on a seminar consisting of four presentations. At the Association's lunch, there was an address by Dean Ray Forrester of the Tulane Law School (a Little Rock native). There was an afternoon address by the General Counsel of the NLRB, George Bott. The next day, there were addresses by the Chairman of Public Relations of the Oklahoma State Bar, by U.S. Senator Estes Kefauver of Tennessee and by Bar President J. L. (Bex) Shaver. The banquet address was by Hicks Epton, Immediate Past President of the Oklahoma Bar. Dr. Lillian E. Schlagenhauf, an Illinois state senator, spoke at the women's luncheon.[17]

By this time, the Bar Association had hired a staff person, Mrs. Clyde D. Calliotte, to staff its office in the Pyramid Life Building. The Bar Association passed a resolution urging the construction of a building (the Justice Building) to house the Supreme Court and the Attorney General.

The 1955 meeting featured addresses by Arkansas Chief Justice Lee Seamster; Texas Attorney General John Ben Shepperd; Robert G. Storey, Jr., the American Bar Junior Bar Vice-Chairman; D. C. Court of Appeals Judge Thurman Arnold; Diana J. Augur, President of the National Association of Women Lawyers; Bar President Jack M. Smallwood; and two tax specialists presented by Taxation Committee Chairman William H. Bowen. There was a panel discussion on ethics presided over by U.S. Circuit Judge Shackelford Miller, Jr., of the Sixth Circuit and with panelists Fred M. Pickens, Jr., Paul Sullins, and Edward L. Wright. Nathan Gordon presided over most of the meeting as Chairman of the Executive Committee, and Chairman John C. Deacon presided over the Junior Bar Section proceedings.[18]

Among the obituaries of prominent lawyers were those of Chief Justice Griffin Smith, W. W. Sharp, Joseph W. House, Judge Gus Fulk, and C. E. Daggett.

The 58th meeting on June 7, 1956, was presided over by John A. Fogleman, Chairman of the Executive Committee. As usual, it featured an extensive program from the Taxation Committee, which was chaired by Ed Bethell. Tax consequences of certain problems were discussed by Dan B. Dobbs, William H. Bowen, William B. Riley, Jr., and W. P. Hamilton, Jr., and this was followed by an address by Lewis R. Donelson, III, of Memphis on tax problems in the preparation of wills. The luncheon featured an address by Vanderbilt Law Professor Paul H. Sanders on recent developments in race relations law. Committee reports were presented in the afternoon, and the Junior Bar Section, chaired by Edward Lester, heard an address on law office management by Ralph R. Neuhoff of St. Louis. On the following Friday, there were more committee reports and a memorial to deceased Bar President Shields M. Goodwin presented by Richard B. McCulloch, Sr. Fred M. Pickens, Jr., made a talk entitled "Justice—For a Price," calling for higher judicial salaries.

At the luncheon, Neva B. Talley introduced Victoria V. Gilbert of Shelbyville, Tennessee, President of the National Association of Women Lawyers, who was the speaker. Following the luncheon, U.S. District Judge John E. Miller introduced the main speaker for the meeting, U.S. Circuit Judge Alfred P. Murrah of Oklahoma City, who spoke on "Justice Now or Never," which dealt with different aspects of the judicial process and the administration of justice.

There were yet more committee reports after that. The banquet speaker in the evening was Dean Robert Farley of the University of Mississippi Law School, whose speech was entitled "The Deuteronomy of the Dilemma."[19]

In 1957, Eugene A. Matthews was Bar President, Oscar Fendler was Chairman of the Executive Committee, and Neva B. Talley, who had always been a major force in organizing the women lawyers in Arkansas, had become President of the National Association of Women Lawyers.

Once again, the Taxation Section, now under the chairmanship of Leonard L. Scott, had an extensive program with talks on the preparation and trial of a federal income tax case, the tax uses of trusts for the general practitioner, and social security benefits to the lawyer. One of the speakers, Randolph W. Thrower, would later become Commissioner of Internal Revenue. The Thursday luncheon speaker was Congressman Brooks Hays discussing "The Due Process of Law Making." Robert M. Lowe presided over the Junior Bar Section program which featured a speech by ABA President David F. Maxwell. The banquet speaker was U.S. Court of Appeals Judge John R. Brown of the Fifth Circuit. The following morning there were more committee reports, followed by a speech by Association President Matthews entitled "Looking Backward—To See Forward," a thoughtful presentation.

In the afternoon, NAWL President Talley introduced the
luncheon speaker, U.S. Circuit Judge Florence E. Allen of the
Sixth Circuit, who spoke on "The Living Power of Law." When
the convention reconvened, Bill Smith introduced Senator John F.
Kennedy of Massachusetts whose address was "The World Around
Us."

Senator Kennedy had been narrowly defeated for the Democratic Nomination for Vice President in the preceding year by
Senator Estes Kefauver. One of the approaches of the Bar Association during that period of time, continuing into the 1960's, was
to obtain speakers of some prominence (including political prominence) whose speeches would be transcribed by a court reporter
and printed in the *Law Review*. It would seem to be appropriate to
reinstate that effort with there being an appropriate mix of speakers in the political realm.

Senator Kennedy's speech was entertaining and instructive in
dealing with the labor union mismanagement and racketeering of
the day.[20] The most important speech, however, was that of Bar
President Matthews. It "looked backward" to the beginning of the
organized Bar, particularly the current bar association, which he
believed to have begun in January 1899. He considered some of the
important matters advocated over the years by the Bar Association—adequate compensation for judges (advocated as early as
1902 and reasserted several times, including 1955), the expansion
of the Supreme Court from five to seven members in 1924, sufficient personnel for the courts, procedural reform, reform of the
criminal procedure beginning in 1934 with Abe Collins (later Bar
President) as chairman and Robert A. Leflar as secretary, the annotated statutes, the Probate Code, the creation in 1936 of a Junior
Bar (the first officers being Eugene Warren, Gordon Young, and
E. L. McHaney), the establishment of legal institutes throughout
the state and then the Fall Legal Institute in Fayetteville, the mid-
winter meeting of the Bar with its workshops, the work of the Bar

on setting standards for the admission to the practice of law, the creation of the *Arkansas Law Review and Bar Association Journal*, the opposition to the unauthorized practice of the law, the funding and construction of the Justice Building, and several other efforts. He described in detail the effort to establish a unified or integrated bar, including the successful adoption of a constitutional amendment to provide the Supreme Court with rule-making authority relative to the practice of law.[21]

Aside from the Justice Building, then under construction, the Bar had turned its attention to the need for a permanent Bar Association building. By 1957, a committee headed by W. S. Mitchell had begun the planning process, and a resolution was approved authorizing the Executive Committee to proceed with the project, including any necessary borrowing of money and making of contracts.

In 1957, Edward L. Wright was elected President of the Arkansas Bar for the coming year; John A. Fogleman was elected Vice-President; and Maurice Mitchell was again elected Secretary-Treasurer.[22]

The sixtieth annual meeting took place in 1958 with W. S. Mitchell presiding as Executive Council Chairman. At the luncheon on Thursday, Dean Joe E. Covington made a talk on the Law School. This followed another extensive Taxation Committee program, the highlight of which was the interview of Judge Bolon B. Turner of the U.S. Tax Court by William H. Bowen. In the afternoon, American Bar President Charles S. Rhyne made a speech about preserving peace under law and weapons control. At the evening banquet, Harry E. Meek gave another entertaining talk called "Idem Sonans." The presidential address by Edward L. Wright began at 11:15 a.m. and was entitled, "Sixty Years: We Have Come of Age." Among other things, he said:

Sixty years ago and for a considerable period thereafter the Arkansas Bar Association was a loosely knit, comparatively small band of lawyers who constituted little more than a congenial social group which met once a year, listened to several speeches verging on the profound, and convivialized a bit on the side. There is nothing original on my part to observe that the tempo of the turn of the twentieth century was a leisurely one in contrast with our own. Public travel was exclusively by steam train . . . [and] there were at least sixteen Arkansas counties whose borders were not touched by a single passenger train.[23]

He discussed how the law had changed in the interim period and how the organized Bar had grown and developed. He spoke at some length on the need for a permanent Bar headquarters building. He reviewed the extensive work of the Association committees, which he tied to the building need.

On Friday, the women's luncheon speaker was Jean J. McVeety of Minneapolis, who discussed the family court. That afternoon, Judge Harold L. Medina, a prominent jurist from the U.S. Court of Appeals for the Second Circuit, took "A Look at America."

During the period of the late 1950's and 1960's, the Bar Association had the services of the very capable Dorothy M. Orsini as a full-time staff director.

E. L. McHaney, Jr., Chairman of the Executive Committee, presided over the 1959 meeting. (By this time, the custom was firmly established of having the annual meeting at the Arlington Hotel in Hot Springs in early June.) After the traditional program on taxation, Oscar Fendler, Chairman of the Conference of Local Bar Associations, introduced C. Sidney Carlton of Sumner, Mississippi, who spoke on "Help for the Lawyer." This luncheon address related in large measure to Bar organization and lawyer income. He revealed that according to the 1950 Census, the median annual income of lawyers in Arkansas at that time was $4,536—the lowest in the nation. Mississippi lawyers had a median income in 1950 of $5,286, which by 1956 had risen to $12,418 gross income. Presumably the Arkansas figure had risen also. After the meeting reconvened, Herschel H. Friday, Jr., the Bar Association Delegate to the ABA, introduced ABA President Ross L. Malone who spoke on professional responsibility. After this, the Junior Bar Section took over, and R. Ben Allen, the Chairman, introduced ABA Junior Bar Chairman Kirk M. McAlpin who addressed the convention. The dinner was presided over by Phillip Carroll, as toastmaster, and he presented Carl F. Conway, Vice-President of the Iowa Bar, the speaker.

At the following morning's session, Bar President John A. Fogleman addressed the convention on "Where Do We Go From Here?" Recalling the speeches of his two predecessors as relating to the past and the present, he chose to address the challenges of the future. The four he selected were the unauthorized practice of law, the economics of law practice, the rule of law and the courts, and public relations. He quoted statistics and data compiled by the American Bar's Special Committee on the Economics of the Law Practice that demonstrated how lawyer income had failed to keep up with other wage-earners and professionals despite an increased need for legal services, national wealth and prosperity, and a diminution in the number of lawyers and law students. Much of the talk, however, was devoted to the rule of law and recent criticism of the courts, particularly the U.S. Supreme Court. "Much of the criticism that has been directed toward our courts, and the judges of them, has been emotional, irresponsible, irrational, intemperate and unjustified" and "the Bar . . . has been too slow to respond."[24] But respect for the courts cannot be manufactured, and so it is the duty of the Bar to try to determine what is justified and what is not. "We owe as great a duty to the courts and to the public to preserve the balance [of checks and balances among the three branches of government] as we do to protect the courts from criticism."[25] He drew a measured course in a time of criticism, not only from irresponsible sources, but also from such agencies as the National Conference of [State] Chief Justices.

After a luncheon talk by Judge Annie Lola Price of the Alabama Court of Appeals, there was a presentation by Charles J. Bloch on the "Role of the American Lawyer in the Protection of the American Constitution," a talk Mr. Bloch said had originally been named "The Role of Southern Lawyers in the Restoration of Constitutional Government." The speech was quite critical of the Supreme Court for not following *stare decisis* and for deciding cases more on whim or the individual philosophy of the justices.[26] It was a difficult time of societal upheaval that had only begun.

By 1959, it could be announced that the Arkansas Bar Foundation had been organized, and its inception was connected directly to the acquisition of a permanent headquarters. Moreover, for the first time, a membership directory was compiled and published, as was a brochure containing pictures and information about Law School seniors who wished to practice in Arkansas.[27] Prior to adjournment, Willis B. Smith, W. S. Mitchell and Phillip Carroll were elected President, Vice-President and Secretary-Treasurer respectively.

The annual meeting format that had been followed rather strictly was once again in place in 1960. With Edward L. Westbrooke, the Chairman of the Executive Committee, presiding, the morning program again led off with presentations on what had become the Committee on Taxation, Trusts and Estate Planning, chaired once again by Leonard L. Scott. This was followed by the luncheon with the speaker being Russell L. Dearmont, President of the Missouri-Pacific Railroad. At 3:00 p.m. the Junior Bar under the chairmanship of William I. Prewett took over, and Robert V. Light introduced Gibson Gayle of Houston, Chairman of the Junior Bar of the American Bar, who addressed the assembly. Dale

Price, the Junior Bar convention chairman, made announcements which were followed by reports. The toastmaster for the banquet was William B. Putman, who introduced Justice George Rose Smith to discuss "Television As I View It."

On Friday morning President Willis B. Smith addressed the subject of "The Responsibility of Lawyers to Clients, To Fellow Lawyers, To the Bench, To the Bar, and To the Public." Maurine H. Abernathy, President of the National Association of Women Lawyers, was the speaker at the women's luncheon. In the afternoon, John C. Satterfield of Jackson, Mississippi, the President-Elect nominee of the ABA, spoke on "Is American Democracy Fading Away?" It was not reproduced but was probably in keeping with the critical tone of that period in relation to social change that had disturbed the relatively placid fifties.

Progress in 1960 could be reported on several fronts. The Arkansas Bar Foundation, in particular, had been quite active even though it was less than two years since its formation. The organization of the Bar Foundation for 1959-60 listed W. S. Mitchell, President; Ned Stewart, Vice-President; and Gaston Williamson, Secretary-Treasurer. The Directors were those three and John A. Fogleman, Heartsill Ragon, Fred Pickens, and Louis Ramsay.[28] By 1960, the Bar Foundation had entered into negotiations for the purchase of the old Rose Law Firm building at 314 West Markham in Little Rock as a permanent bar headquarters. (This was later accomplished, and it remained the Bar Association offices until the construction of the present Bar Center.) By the time of its report by Chairman Louis L. Ramsay in 1960, the Foundation had received $3,662 in donations. It had put this money to use in the form of law student scholarships, a grant to the compilation of the Arkansas Annotations to the Restatements, awards to law review students for outstanding publications, guidance books for high schools, the graduating senior publication, and a study of construction and renovation of court buildings. It had also begun the

Outstanding Lawyer, Lawyer-Citizen, and Bar Association Awards.[29]

For its work in 1959-60, the Arkansas Bar Association received the Award of Merit from the American Bar Association, ranking first among all bar associations with fewer than 2,000 members.

1961 to 1970

By the 1961 Annual Meeting, the Bar Foundation had completed acquisition of the old Rose Firm building at 314 West Markham in Little Rock and in January, 1961 had moved the headquarters there from the rented space in the Pyramid Life Building. By this time both the Mid-Winter Meeting and the Fall Legal Institute had proved successful and were firmly ensconced as the major state-wide CLE events of the Bar year. The Foundation had obtained tax-exempt status and had a fund-raising goal of $300,000.00—an objective, it later confessed, that was thought overly ambitious by some leaders at the time. The Foundation under new Chairman Louis L. Ramsay, Jr. was by then discussing the eventual construction of what is now the Arkansas Bar Center. Bar President Will Mitchell was heavily involved in all of this as Chairman of the Headquarters Building Committee which negotiated the purchase of the Rose Law Firm building for $57,500.00. The formation of the Foundation and the acquisition of a building to house the Bar headquarters were integrally related.[30] (There is a fallacy currently entertained by some younger members of the Bar that the plan for construction of the current Bar Center was originally undertaken in connection with the need to house the Little Rock Division of the University of Arkansas Law School. That is incorrect. The University did not acquire (what in 1961 was) the Arkansas Law School until 1965 and discussion of its inclusion in the Bar Center, and the plans for same, did not come until later.)

After the acquisition of the Rose property, Executive Committee Chairman Howard Cockrill reported that some $4,000.00 was spent in cleaning and refurbishing the premises.[31] The plan to acquire adjoining property in the rear and to the west of the building was also in effect and was subsequently carried out.[32]

Proposals from committees included revision of the election laws and a constitutional amendment creating a Family Court.

Speechmakers included the former Chief Counsel of the IRS, the Presiding Judge of the Oklahoma Court of Criminal Appeals, James R. Browning, the Clerk of the U.S. Supreme Court on the history of the Court, Joe Barrett on private international law, Justice Lorna Lockwood of the Arizona Supreme Court, Thomas F. Lambert, Jr., the Editor of the NACCA Law Journal, and President Mitchell. Mr. Barrett's speech on the Hague Conference on Private International Law is especially interesting.[33]

The committee reports for 1962 reveal that the ALI Arkansas Annotations to the Restatement were still being compiled—this time by law clerks of the Supreme Court employed for that purpose. The Public Education Committee, headed by W. H. Dillahunty, had made Clint Huey State Chairman for Law Day—USA, and Hubert Mayes, Jr., was editing "It's the Law," a column for weekly newspapers.

President Heartsill Ragon reported that Edward L. Wright had been elected Chairman of the House of Delegates of the American Bar Association and that Dorothy Orsini had taken office as President of the National Association of Women Lawyers. Gaston Williamson, the 1961-62 Bar Foundation Chairman, reported that the Foundation had received pledges totaling $250,750.00 from 626 attorneys. The earlier goal of $300,000.00 was now pronounced "too modest." William J. Smith would head up an effort to secure pledges from selected businesses and Edward L. Wright would seek to obtain pledges from memorials. The Bar Center Committee would go out of business and the Foundation would replace it. There was now annual income of $5,000 from the Bar Center which would pay the Foundation's annual office expense and for all projects except for the Model Jury Instructions. The Foundation Report gave special credit to Oscar Fendler, Will Mitchell, Ed Wright, Courtney Crouch, Bruce Bullion and Abner McGehee for their efforts in fund-raising.

The Fall Legal Institute for 1961 had been a very extensive program on the UCC, and the first Oil and Gas Institute had been held.

The Outstanding Lawyer and Lawyer-Citizen Awards went to Harry E. Meek and James C. Hale, respectively, and the local bar association awards went to Sebastian County (large bar) and the Tri-County Bar (small bar).

Speeches were given, in addition to the president, by Lyndon B. Johnson, Vice-President of the United States, Senator John L. McClellan, Federal Judge Sarah F. Hughes of Dallas, and American Bar President Sylvester C. Smith.

Comer C. Boyett presided over the Junior Bar. New officers were Jack Lessenberry, Chairman; Ted G. Boswell, Vice-Chairman; and Jerry T. Light, Secretary. The Conference of Local Bars elected J. C. Deacon as President; W. H. Dillahunty, Clint Huey, C. R. Warner, Jr., Robert C. Compton, and Edward Gordon as regional Vice-Presidents, and Philip S. Anderson, Jr., as Secretary-Treasurer.[34]

President Oscar Fendler's address in 1963 was a call to reform the state judicial system that was presented in substantial detail and was forward-looking in nature. As usual, few changes resulted. The Executive Committee had met with the University of Arkansas President about the Law School taking over the Arkansas Law School in Little Rock, the state accredited but nationally unaccredited operation whose history is discussed in greater detail in the chapter on legal education. The University, in 1962, agreed to insert a provision for this in its budget request but stated in 1963 that sufficient funds had not been provided by the legislature to undertake the project.[35]

On the subject of legal education in Little Rock, the Board of Law Examiners had expressed concern over the inability of Arkansas Law School (Little Rock) graduates to pass the Bar. The Committee stated bluntly: "If the University does not undertake to carry on an accredited program in Little Rock, it is almost certain that one of two other institutions will."[36] The plan then described is essentially the one that eventually was followed. The report discussed the advantage of the Law School having an operation in Little Rock, particularly for research and CLE purposes. Budget cuts in the legislature had failed to provide the funding for this to take place in 1963. The Committee expressed its desire to persevere in the proposal.[37]

There was a long report from Judge Paul Wolfe about the plans of the Arkansas Supreme Court Committee on Jury Instructions which the Court created on February 12, 1962, by per curiam order. Chairman Wolfe discussed in some detail the problems, how other states had dealt with the situation, and how he proposed to proceed. The original committee members appointed were W. H. Arnold, III, Judge Lyle Brown, Kaneaster Hodges, Robert L. Jones, Jr., Dale N. Price, W. B. Putman, Professor Frederic K. Spies, Justice George Rose Smith, Judge Audrey Strait, James I. Teague, Henry Woods, and Paul B. Young. Associate members were Philip S. Anderson, Jr., Winslow Drummond, and Jacob Sharp, Jr. The Executive Secretary was Phillip Carroll. Ex-officio members were the Chief Justice, the President of the Judicial Council, the President of the Arkansas Bar Association, the President of the Arkansas Bar Foundation, and the Dean of the U of A Law School.[38]

Continuing Legal Education was given increased emphasis by the appointment of a faculty member at the Law School as of July 1, 1963, to serve half-time as Director of Continuing Legal Education.[39] CLE was moving forward. The first Federal Tax Institute had been held in September 1962, and it began to replace in part the extensive tax programs that had been presented at the Annual Meeting ever since World War II.

There was a long Judiciary Committee Report by Chairman Edward Gordon on the committee's extensive efforts and recommendations for court reform.

There were speeches, among others, by retired Justice Charles E. Whittaker of the U.S. Supreme Court and Walter E. Craig, the President-Elect of the American Bar Association. These were reprinted in the Arkansas Law Review, but unfortunately an address on "Raccoon Valley Recollections" by the Honorable Erby L. Jenkins of Tennessee is lost to posterity.

The 1964 Annual Meeting speakers included Solicitor General Archibald Cox and former Secretary of State Dean Acheson.

The Bar Foundation reported that $264,000.00 in pledges had been made, of which over half had been paid. A building committee consisting of Paul B. Young, Robert L. Jones, Jr., John T. Williams, Gaston Williamson and Bruce Bullion had been appointed. Only $18,000.00 and accrued interest remained to be paid on the joint Rose and Revilo properties on which the new Bar Center would be built. Plans of other bar buildings were being studied and Ed Cromwell had been selected as Consulting Architect.

In other Bar matters, the Arkansas Bar Title Company, Inc., was in business under President Phillip Carroll with the aid of a Foundation grant. The "preceptorship" program of placing law students with law firms during the summer between the second and third years of law school had begun. The model jury instructions program under Judge Wolfe was nearing completion. A special study committee of the Association structure and activities headed by W. S. Mitchell made extensive recommendations including the creation of a Legal Education Council to coordinate CLE activities. The CLE Committee had outlined six major events for 1963-64 and had formed a speakers' bureau. The unauthorized practice litigation with the realtors that had been going on for a year or two had been lost although negotiations continued.

President Louis Ramsay's address, "A Look in the Mirror," was a reflection of his desire that lawyers be more active in civic affairs—community, state and nation. He decried the diminution of lawyers in the legislature (which is reduced even more today). He examined the historic duty of lawyers to be the leaders in society and to shape law and government.

The President of the Conference of Local Bar Associations was Clint Huey. James E. West was elected to replace him with Marion Gill, Sidney Davis, Gene Schieffler, Joe Woodward and Phil Dixon as regional vice-presidents and with Boyce Love as secretary. Ted Boswell was Chairman of the Junior Bar and was replaced by James D. Cypert with John A. Davis III as vice-chairman and John Echols as secretary. The name of the Junior Bar was changed to the Young Lawyers Section.

Speakers in 1965 included American Bar President Louis F. Powell, later to be a Supreme Court Justice, and U.N. Ambassador and former two-time Democratic Presidential Nominee Adlai Stevenson (who died forty days later, but whose remarks are preserved in 19 ARK. L. REV. 257 (1965)).

President Bruce Bullion's address was a discussion of the Judiciary Commission Report of 1965—a three-volume comprehensive study of the Judicial Department—chaired by John A. Fogleman and with members Audrey Strait, James Pilkington, Clayton Little, Walter Hussman, M. T. Hickingbotham and Russell Benton, and with Walter Niblock as Secretary. Some of the proposals did become law although most of it did not. The general tenor of the report likely served to point up problems that were dealt with at least partially to the extent that they were dealt with at all. Certain aspects considered by the Commission and recommended were ultimately addressed—judicial salaries, the need for judicial redistricting to correct case load imbalances, retirement, discipline and some others. Consequently, when the intransigence of the legislature and the judiciary itself is considered, the Commission's efforts were definitely worthwhile and were partially successful in the long run.

However, these periodic expenditures of great energy and time by leaders in the Bar in attempting to improve the judicial system have to be undertaken by pragmatists who are willing to accept a part of the loaf now and hope for more later. These efforts sometimes fail completely as in 1990 and sometimes they succeed a little bit. One must suppose that they are at least some better than the search for the Holy Grail, the lost Ark and the elusive quark in that the failure is not always total and occasionally a small morsel of victory can be snatched from the jaws of defeat.

President Bullion closed with the observation that the Bar in cooperation with the American Judicature Society was going to conduct a citizens and lawyers conference on the courts in September. The Commission's recommendations would be the centerpiece of the conference. (The conference did take place. It was hoped then and had been hoped since that involvement of prominent citizens in the work of court reform would lend impetus to the Bar's efforts in connection with the legislature and the public in general. It has never worked out that way to any appreciable degree. The House of Representatives has historically been impervious to any proposal for widespread change and, in 1991, after the effort of 1990, did not even trust the people enough to submit the proposed judicial article to them for a vote.)

On a more successful note in 1965, Judge Paul Wolfe presented a final report on the model jury instructions book and its contents.[40]

In 1966, President Courtney Crouch appointed a committee to study the need for changes in the Probate Code and also for the laws on homestead, dower, descent and distribution. He praised the CLE program headed by Chairman Robert Shults and the Director. He also discussed involvement in legal aid, the Keogh Act, financial support for the Law School, the model jury instruction book, the establishment in Little Rock of the evening division of the Law School, and the Bar's dues structure. He praised the committee that had worked diligently for the passage of the new Corporation Code. He urged continued support for passage of the recommendations on judicial reform.

F. William McCalpin, a member of a substantial law firm who had a rich background in legal aid work in St. Louis and in the ABA, spoke on legal services to the poor. One of the programs he advocated was Judicare, a program adopted by the Wisconsin State Bar based on the English system and involving volunteer work by private attorneys (similar to what would become VOCALS in Central Arkansas).

Senator Joseph P. Tydings of Maryland and Congresswoman Martha Griffiths of Michigan were other speakers.

The Young Lawyers passed a resolution favoring an integrated Bar. Boyce Love was elected Chairman; Richard Mays, Vice Chairman; and Joe Buffalo, Secretary, for the coming year.

Thomas B. Pryor was elected President of the Conference of Local Bar Associations; Joe L. Boone, James Neill Smith, Fines F. Batchelor, Jr., Dennis L. Shackleford and Claibourne W. Patty were elected Vice-Presidents, and Charles R. Ledbetter was chosen Secretary-Treasurer.

Outstanding lawyer and lawyer-citizen awards went to O. A. Graves and Donald H. Smith, and the Southwest Arkansas Bar and Benton County Bar won the large and small bar association awards.[41]

The 1967 presidential speech by Maurice Cathey was largely a defense of the Fifth Amendment. Much attention that year was devoted to legal education and talks on that subject were presented by Dean Ralph C. Barnhart of the Law School and by Dean Page

Keeton of the University of Texas. Dean Barnhart focused on the change in award of the degree in American law schools from the LL.B. to the J.D. He also stated the University would now require an undergraduate degree as a prerequisite to Law School admission. He pointed out the need for better trained lawyers along with his belief that the Law School was falling behind financially. He was especially appreciative of the efforts of Representative Ray Smith in obtaining an additional appropriation of $100,000 for the Law School. Dean Keeton went into great detail about the need for additional funding for legal education. He pointed out the necessary involvement of law faculty in the work of the Bar and in law improvement efforts. As for lawyers, "we . . . know that the lawyer is a free society's best trained trouble shooter; he is society's generalist; he is society's only remaining Jack-of-all-trades; that we must have lawyers to resist all efforts of those who would defy law and order while at the same time altering, reforming, and changing the law in such a way as to command the respect of the people."[42]

The Continuing Study of Probate Law Committee was active. In its first phase, it had proposed amendments to the Probate Code of 1949, and these had been adopted. Now it was undertaking a study of inheritance law. The Committee stated that it was anticipated that this would be "a codification of existing law" "not intended to revise present law, unless there is something which the Committee clearly feels should be changed."[43] Actually, what eventuated was the Inheritance Act of 1969, many of the ideas of which came from the third working draft of the Uniform Probate Code. It substantially changed the pattern of descent and distribution in Arkansas, almost (but not entirely) wiped out ancestral estates, abolished the doctrine of worthier title (to the extent that it existed) along with some other ancient anachronisms, and clarified some aspects of the existing law. It was primarily the product of Harry E. Meek with help from the Co-Chairs Judge Thomas F. Butt and Owen C. Pearce, Richard Williams, G. D. Walker, Albert Graves, Charles Roscopf, Adrian Williamson, Edward L. Wright, E. B. Meriwether, J. H. Bowen, Maurice Cathey, Judge Murray Reed, Judge Richard Mobley, Judge Claude E. Love, Judge Paul X. Williams, Judge Ford Smith, Walter H. Laney, Jr., DuVal L. Purkins, Robert R. Wright, Oliver Clegg and James B. Sharp.

The Legal Aid Committee was also very active because of the new legal services program of the Office of Economic Opportunity.

The new officers of the Conference of Local Bar Associations were Fines F. Batchelor, Jr., President; Charles M. Mooney, Charles B. Roscopf, James B. Blair, Richard H. Mays, and Isaac A. Scott, regional Vice-Presidents; and Thomas G. Graves, Secretary-Treasurer. The new Young Lawyers Section leaders were Richard H. Mays, Chairman; William Henslee, Vice-Chairman; and Joe K. Mahony, II, Secretary.[44]

In 1967, the first issue of *The Arkansas Lawyer* appeared. It was a magazine type of publication with a format similar to *The American Bar Association Journal* or one of the ABA Section publications. It would ultimately replace the "Bar Association Journal" aspect of the *Arkansas Law Review*. In the first issue there was a long interim report by Maurice Cathey on bar association activities that was quite similar to the annual reports submitted to the Bar.[45] There were also reports of projected activities for the following year by President-Elect William S. Arnold and a report on the status of the Bar Center project by Bruce Bullion.[46] In the second issue in September, 1967, there was a report from Bar President Arnold and articles on tort liability and revision of the state constitution, and two articles on legal aid. In the December, 1967, issue, there was the President's report and additional articles. The March, 1968, and June, 1968, issues also contained interim reports from the President and articles directed to law practice. Regular features were Juris Dictum by C. R. Huie, dealing with the courts, and reports on continuing legal education and law school news by CLE Director Robert R. Wright.

The Citizens' Conference on the Courts was held in the 1967-68 Bar year and was duly reported to the 1968 Annual Meeting by Chairman Edward Gordon of the Judiciary Committee. The Probate Code Advisory Committee was fully involved with the second phase of its work (*i.e.*, the Inheritance Act of 1969), and this was reported by Judge Butt and Cul Pearce, the Co-Chairs. The Legal Aid Committee, which had been quite active for several years under the chairmanship of W. S. Miller, filed a long report on its work and its projected program. Because of the relatively new Arkansas Tax Institute, the Taxation Committee under Chairman Leonard Scott was now putting its major emphasis there rather than in its previous extensive presentations at the Annual Meeting (although those would continue for some time yet). The Uniform Commercial Code Committee under the head of Joe C. Barrett announced that the 1967 legislature had adopted its proposed changes.

President William S. Arnold's address dealt with the professional obligations of the Bar in a rapidly changing society. In other presentations there was a debate between two law professors, Jeffrey O'Connell of Illinois and David J. Sargent of Suffolk, on the Keeton-O'Connell "basic insurance plan" of no-fault insurance.[47] Dean Robert Figg, Jr., of the University of South Carolina spoke on "Free Press Versus Fair Trial," the topic having come from a special advisory committee appointed by ABA President Lewis F. Powell, Jr., to consider that subject in connection with criminal justice standards. This committee, on which Dean Figg served, produced the "Reardon Report," which was named for its Chairman, Massachusetts Supreme Court Justice Paul C. Reardon. The Report was "assailed by a wide segment of the press" "with little restraint," according to Dean Figg.[48] He called for cooperation between the two and mutual respect for the interests of both values, with resulting synergistic benefit to the public. This was before "Watergate," of course, and before the press had in more recent years descended to its current depths.[49]

By the time of the first report of new President Gaston Williamson in the August, 1968 issue of the *Lawyer*, he could report on the effort to improve jury selection, the considerations entering into a constitutional convention to revise the 1874 document, a proposal to establish a public defender system, the appointment of a committee on bar unification, and the activities of various other committees. His October, 1968 report was devoted to the constitutional revision study commission and the proposal to call a constitutional convention. The February, 1969 report was devoted to the death of LeRoy Gaston, who had served as Executive Director for about two years and the appointment of Col. Clarence E. Ransick as the new Executive Director. The President's report of May, 1969 details the passage of several bar-sponsored bills by the legislature—Inheritance Act, Jury Selection Act, increases in judges' salaries, and Uniform Arbitration Act—but deals largely with the proposal for a unified bar.

At the 1969 Annual Meeting, President Williamson devoted his address to discussing the "revolutionary period of profound social change" that we had entered and the duty of lawyers to restore respect for the law. "The spirit of rebellion is loose in the land,"[50] he said, and it was typified in the passage in earlier years of "patently unconstitutional laws" to evade school integration, disorder and "mob actions" on college campuses, as well as more pedestrian violations of the law.[51]

Fittingly enough, there was a debate at the Annual Meeting on the resolution of whether deliberate violation of the law as a means of social protest was morally justified. The proposition that it was not justified was argued by Thomas A. Glaze and David B. Bogard, both to become long-term judges, while the contrary position was taken by Philip E. Kaplan and Jim Guy Tucker. Mr.

Kaplan stated that "Mr. Tucker and I are taking a very conservative position."[52] He said that they were echoing the philosophy of the framers of the Declaration of Independence and the Constitution. (Actually, the Declaration of Independence was a document that justified the right of revolution, something that was thought by 1861 to have no legal justification as far as the Union was concerned.) In any event it is nice to note that later on, Mr. Kaplan became a prosperous lawyer and pillar of society and Mr. Tucker after also prospering in law and business became Governor of Arkansas. Moreover, their arguments were couched in legal and constitutional tradition. This illustrates, combined with the presidential address, the problems and concerns of the country and the legal profession in 1969, however.[53]

There was also a speech in 1969 by Glenn R. Winters, Executive Director of the American Judicature Society, favoring the unified bar.[54] (The unified or integrated Bar, mentioned previously, consists of all people admitted to practice in the state. Most of the state bar associations are unified. The unified Bar, as opposed to a voluntary Bar such as ours, takes on an added role with the Supreme Court because it assumes the responsibility for disciplinary and other administrative duties.) In form at least, there are two Bars in Arkansas now—the voluntary Arkansas Bar Association and the Supreme Court Bar consisting of all attorneys licensed to practice in Arkansas. The question of whether to have a unified Bar structure has been a subject of considerable discussion and occasional heated debate in Arkansas on several occasions.

Beginning in 1969, the *Law Review* ceased to publish committee reports, and in 1970, it only published the address of the bar president. A few years later, it ceased that practice and thus was no longer the "Bar Association Journal" even to a limited extent. The new *Arkansas Lawyer* was viewed as having replaced the necessity for the old journal. However, the eventual effect in later years and in more recent years is that much of the information contained in the full committee reports, the speeches, the proceedings and the like is no longer available in printed form because as the *Lawyer* matured, it eliminated or cut back extensively on such material.

Robert L. Jones, Jr., in his September, 1969 report in the *Lawyer* emphasized the need for Bar involvement and assistance in the constitutional convention then under way. A successful convention was one of his goals. His second goal was the unified bar proposal. The Bar Association planned to petition the Supreme Court to create a unified Bar. Other concerns were legal aid and the new ABA Model Code of Professional Responsibility drafted by a committee chaired by Edward L. Wright, the President-Elect of the American Bar. He appointed a committee chaired by Joe D. Woodward to study the new Code and report with recommendations. The long and detailed petition for the reorganization of the Arkansas Bar into a unified Bar is reproduced in that issue of the *Lawyer*. Also, it reported that the American Bar Association Award of Merit for excellence had been received by the Arkansas Bar Association at the preceding annual meeting and a similar award had gone to the Craighead County Bar Association.

Speeches by Edward L. Wright on the Model Code and by Justice Arthur Goldberg of the U.S. Supreme Court, delivered at the preceding annual meeting, were reproduced in the December issue of the *Lawyer*. In the president's report, it was stated that the Executive Committee had approved the Model Code, filed for its adoption by the Supreme Court, and that the Supreme Court had adopted it by per curiam order.

By March, President Jones could report in the *Lawyer* that the Supreme Court had denied the bar unification proposal. He wanted to make the Association more democratic and he thought unification would have achieved that. He also wanted to provide for law student involvement in the Association. Establishment of a client's security fund and providing adequate funding for the Committee on Professional Conduct were new goals. The 17th annual mid-year meeting had drawn 175 despite wintry weather, the *Lawyer* reported. The Ninth Annual Oil and Gas Institute, which began in 1962, was scheduled for April 19-20, 1970 in Hot Springs.

By the June issue of the *Lawyer* in 1970, the plans for the annual meeting could be announced. Both Bernard G. Segal and Edward L. Wright, the President and President-Elect of the American Bar Association, would be in the receiving line for the President's Reception. Senator John L. McClellan would be presented a special award by Senator J. William Fulbright on behalf of the Association. There would be speeches by ABA President Segal, former Justice and Director of the Federal Judicial Center Tom C. Clark, and Astronaut William Anders. A Law Student Division of the Association would be created.[55] At the meeting, Bar Foundation President Clint Huey presented a special award to Neva B. Talley for becoming the first woman to chair an American Bar Association Section—the Family Law Section. A. F. House received the Outstanding Lawyer Award and W. H. Arnold received the Outstanding Lawyer-Citizen Award posthumously.[56]

President Jones in his address at the annual meeting announced the appointment of committees headed by Gaston Williamson and Winslow Drummond to consider some of the situations addressed by the unified bar proposal (which had been defeated). Winslow Drummond's committee was to study ways to make the Association more democratic, and Gaston Williamson's committee was to consider ways to improve disciplinary enforcement. The virtues of the new ABA Code of Professional Responsibility were extolled. The work of Bar members in the constitutional convention was applauded. The new Model Student Practice Rule adopted by the Supreme Court permitting third-year law students to gain some courtroom experience representing indigents under the supervision of a licensed attorney was praised.[57]

John C. Deacon became President of the Bar at the end of the 1970 meeting. By the November, 1970, issue of the *Lawyer*, he could announce that an Association Committee had redrafted the Bar Constitution and By-Laws to provide for a House of Delegates divided into four districts based (in large part) on equal representation in the districts, an Executive Council chosen by the Delegates, and the rotation of the President-Elect among the four districts. This was Winslow Drummond's committee consisting also of Judge Thomas F. Butt, Philip E. Dixon, Julian B. Fogleman, Richard H. Mays, James B. Sharp, and Henry Woods. In addition, the Association was studying the ABA Minimum Standards for Criminal Justice with the intention of making some changes.

1971 to 1980

In August 1970, Edward L. Wright became the second Arkansan to be President of the American Bar Association. The January, 1971 issue of the *Lawyer* and most of Jack Deacon's report was devoted to that. The report also stated that a seminar was being scheduled on the Criminal Justice Standards and that the Association was seeking to establish a day division and construct a new law school building in Little Rock and to build an addition to Waterman Hall.

The 1971 annual meeting featured American Bar President Edward L. Wright and Chesterfield Smith, Past President of the National Association of Bar Presidents (and later to become American Bar President himself), along with Richard Markus, President of the American Trial Lawyers Association. Governor Dale Bumpers was the banquet speaker.

President Deacon paid tribute to the creation of the Law Student Division—the first in the nation and one that would be emulated in other bar associations. Don Schnipper "who knew how to communicate with the law students" was the first Chairman. Mr. Deacon discussed efforts to improve the criminal justice system and the bar-sponsored law to authorize the Supreme Court to make rules of criminal procedure, practice and pleading. The Association Constitution and By-Laws revision was approved to provide essentially for the present form (although there have been some changes since then). A revised Desk Book had been prepared. A full-time disciplinary office for lawyers had been established by the Supreme Court.

By May, 1972, Bar President Paul B. Young could report on three Association activities—the proposal to hire a lobbyist to represent the Bar in the legislature, the creation of a special committee on corrections to implement the work of the ABA Special Commission on Correctional Facilities, and a special committee to develop a plan for prepaid legal services.[58]

In his address to the Bar Association, Mr. Young dealt largely with changes in the practice of law. He discussed law schools and law students, criminal justice, correctional systems and penal reform, and prepaid legal services. (At that time, much more was expected of prepaid legal services in terms of importance and magnitude than what eventuated. His high expectations were not at all unusual for that period of time.)[59]

Plans for the new Bar Center were being finalized and were given a great deal of attention. Incoming American Bar President Robert Meserve addressed the Convention. The '72 Gridiron under the superb direction, production and composition of Griffin Smith, Jr. was becoming a fixture at the meetings.

One situation in 1971-72 that was unique to that Bar year was that the President of the Bar Association and Chairman of the Bar Foundation were law partners, Paul B. Young and Stephen A. Matthews.

Henry Woods succeeded Paul Young as Association President for 1972-73. Few men of our time have had a greater impact on various aspects of the law in Arkansas than Henry Woods, whether as a prominent trial lawyer, author of articles and books (such as his work on comparative fault), as supporter and mover and shaker in connection with legal education, as a federal judge, as a friend and confidant of political figures such as the great Sid McMath in his early career and Bill and Hillary Clinton later on (particularly Hillary), and as a leader in the legal profession.

In his July, 1972 report in *The Arkansas Lawyer*, he pointed out the challenge facing the Bar in implementing the changes made by the new Bar Constitution. He discussed the need for a membership drive, since only slightly more than half of the lawyers admitted to practice belonged to the Association. He called for support for the new Bar Center, discussed the work of the building committee headed by Ed Lester, and urged increased financial support from the Bar members. He pointed out the need for a "legislative liaison" (lobbyist), established deadlines for the submission of proposed legislation, and set a new timetable for the process. (The Bar-sponsored legislation had taken a beating in the 1971 session.) No-fault insurance legislation was sure to come up in the 1973 session, and he urged the members to educate themselves on these proposals. A Client Security Fund should be adopted and implemented by the Bar. He praised efforts being made in corrections. He spoke of the search for a new Dean to replace retiring Dean Ralph Barnhart and lamented "bitter factionalism among the faculty" in Fayetteville.[60]

By September, President Woods could report that substantial contributions had been made to the Client Security Fund and that after the fund drive, the Supreme Court would be asked to establish the mechanics of the fund. Moreover, the House of Delegates had taken a position against a federal no-fault insurance proposal.[61]

The Bar Center was nearing completion, according to the January, 1973 report, and President Woods stated that he had been working almost full-time on the project. This work primarily involved fund-raising, and it had been successful. Briefing sessions with legislators and Governor Dale Bumpers had been held in support of the Bar's legislative package.

The mid-year meeting had been an exceptional program on trial practice put on in conjunction with Hastings College of the Law, which is part of the University of California. In addition to two top law professors from Hastings, it featured some of the top lawyers and judges in the country. There were 443 lawyers in attendance. Similarly, the annual meeting focused on environmental law, commercial law class actions, tort law and criminal law, again with some of the top lawyers in the country being involved—Tom Foran, who prosecuted the "Chicago Seven"; Henry Rothblatt, a prominent criminal defense attorney; Moe Levine; Jake Fuchsberg; Steve Sussman; Jim Jeans; Francis Hare; Judge Robert Van Pelt; and Tom Lambert as the banquet speaker. It was the 75th annual meeting.

In his President's Report, Judge Woods could state that he had accomplished all ten of his objectives set out by him the year before: increase Association membership by 20%; raise the money and let the contract for the new Bar Center; devise a better method of handling the legislative program; propose and have enacted a broad, progressive legislative program; secure enactment of reasonable no fault legislation; provide leadership in connection with prison and correctional reform; secure additional financial support for legal education; make possible a meaningful scholarship program for law students; establish a client security fund [approved by the Supreme Court in April 1973]; and expand the Bar's public relations efforts. One piece of legislation providing support for legal education was Act 207 levying a fee on the filing of cases with the money to be used for the law schools.

At this meeting, James E. West of Fort Smith became the new Bar President. His report in the September issue of the *Lawyer*[62] highlighted a series of trial practice seminars scheduled for various regional locations, the success of a Disaster Legal Services Program for tornado victims, the construction of the Bar Center and the need to collect outstanding pledges, and the planned dedication of the Bar Center at the mid-year meeting with Justice Roger Traynor of California as the featured speaker.

The Fall Legal Institute was held in Little Rock that year, and Judge Pat Mehaffy was honored for his having become Chief Judge of the Eighth Circuit.

The January, 1974 issue of *The Arkansas Lawyer* was devoted to the Bar Center dedication and the organization, formation and hard work of the Arkansas Bar Foundation. At the formative meeting of the Foundation on January 22, 1959, the first directors elected were W. S. Mitchell, John A. Fogleman, Fred Pickens, Heartsill Ragon, Gaston Williamson, Louis L. Ramsay, Jr., and Ned Stewart. Others pictured as organizers include H. Maurice Mitchell, Edward L. Wright, and Willis B. Smith. Participants in the ground-breaking ceremony for the Law Center were Chief Justice Carleton Harris, Bar President Henry Woods, Bar Foundation Chairman Edward Lester, Executive Council Chairman James B. Sharp, Building Committee Chairman John P. Gill and County Judge B. Frank Mackey. The dedication of the building took place during the mid-year meeting on January 10-12, 1974. Co-Chairmen were President West and Chairman Philip S. Anderson of the Bar Foundation. Co-Hosts were past Presidents Henry Woods and Edward L. Wright. Speakers included Justice Roger Traynor, Governor Dale Bumpers, past Foundation Chairman Edward Lester, and American Bar President Chesterfield Smith. There was a Dean's panel consisting of the former living Deans of the University of Arkansas Law School—Robert A. Leflar, Ralph C. Barnhart and Joe E. Covington—and the then current Dean, Wylie Davis.

The annual meeting was on "the Good Old Days." Robert A. Leflar reminisced about the "Good Old Days at the Law School" and J. L. "Bex" Shaver about the "Good Old Days" of lawyering. Richard A. Williams presented J. Harris Morgan and Robert P. Bigelow to discuss law practice management for the solo and small firm. A new edition of an Arkansas Model Jury Instructions book was discussed by Justice George Rose Smith, Henry Woods and Winslow Drummond. President James E. West wrote a poem commemorating the Arkansas Bar Center and spoke extensively about the relationship between the Law School and the Bar.[63] He also provided an impressive list of his activities in his bar year and stated that membership had gone to 1,930, a new record.

Incoming President James B. Sharp gave an inaugural address that appears in 27 ARK. L. REV. 766-777 (1973), and it was criticized in an "Editor's Forum" [Editorial] following the "Legislative Notes" earlier in volume 27, written by N. M. (Mac) Norton, Jr., who at that time was presumably one of the editors. In essence, the address by President Sharp criticized then current legal education methodology such as over-reliance on the case study method, advocated more clinical education, and urged establishment of a day division in Little Rock. The response in the "Editor's Forum" was largely critical of creating a second full-time law school in the State and of over-reliance or over-emphasis on clinical legal education.

Because of construction on Waterman Hall, the Fall Legal Institute was again held in Little Rock. An addition to Waterman Hall was projected for completion in the early summer of 1975. A session of the House of Delegates featured a debate between Dean Wylie Davis and past Bar President Henry Woods over whether to establish a day division in Little Rock. The controversial resolution would ask the Board of Trustees to do so. After some continued debate in the House, the resolution passed by a narrow margin. The House also, after some debate, approved a proposal to establish a statewide public defender system, and it endorsed passage of the Equal Rights Amendment.[64]

By January 1975, the legislative program had been promoted through a series of dinner meetings with legislative leaders, judges and local lawyers throughout the State arranged by Henry Woods, the Legislative Chairman, and James R. Rhodes, the Bar's new Liaison Representative to the legislature.[65] The legislative session in 1975 was particularly significant for legal education in Arkansas. Act 19 of 1975, as President Sharp expressed in his report in the April issue of *The Arkansas Lawyer*,[66] "granted a complete divorce to the Law School in Little Rock from the Law School in Fayetteville." He refers to "a struggle over a period of nearly ten years" as to whether a full-time day program should be established in Little Rock. This event is discussed at greater length in the chapter on legal education. What the legislature did, aside from the day division, was to transfer the Law School in Little Rock to the University of Arkansas at Little Rock instead of maintaining it as the evening division of the University (Fayetteville) Law School for part-time students. It was a major event because it had the effect of creating two separate, full-time law schools in Arkansas in separate locations, although both campuses remained under the control of the same Board of Trustees. The emotions that surrounded this event are discussed in the chapter on legal education. Basically, opposition to a Little Rock day division stemmed from the fear in Fayetteville that this would ultimately lead to the closing of the Law School there, and indeed there has been some periodic legislative pressure over the years that followed to have only one law school. That seems unlikely.

Annual meeting speakers for 1975 included former Watergate Independent Counsel and former ABA President Leon Jaworski, Governor David Pryor, and past President of the Texas Bar, Leon Jeffers. Incoming Bar President Robert C. Compton's remarks were the last to be published in the *Arkansas Law Review*.[67] In 1975, the Spring issue[68] of the *Law Review* dropped "Bar Association Journal" from its title. Bob Compton's relatively short incoming President's address decried the attacks on the legal profession, urged strict ethical conduct by lawyers and competence in our work as well as public service.

The new Justice Building was dedicated on January 9, 1976. George Hartje, Chairman of the Justice Building Commission, presided. J. L. (Bex) Shaver spoke on behalf of the Commission. Bar President Compton spoke on behalf of the Association. Robert A. Leflar delivered the dedicatory address.[69] About two weeks later, at the mid-year meeting, there was an in-depth study of the new Arkansas Criminal Code and the Rules of Criminal Procedure. Almost 400 people attended.[70]

The 1976 Association meeting featured programs on law office economics put on by Richard A. Williams, Chairman of the American Bar Section on Economics of the Law Practice, in conjunction with Alston Jennings, the Annual Meeting Chairman. Governor David Pryor delivered the keynote address. Former Governor Sidney S. McMath also spoke. There were other speakers on prepaid legal services and delivery of legal services.

Herschel H. Friday, who shared a long-term involvement in Bar activities and served for many years as its ABA Delegate, became President at the end of the meeting. Along with Edward L. Wright, Herschel was probably the most loved and most influential member of the Bar, on both a state and national basis, of the latter half of the 20th Century. When you add Jack Deacon to the group, they were our main ABA triumvirate until Phil Anderson came along in the 1990's to add a fourth. Oscar Fendler was also a leader in the ABA in that same time period with occasional service on the Board of Governors and House of Delegates and as one of the founders and Chair of the General Practice Section. The new President's report in the July 1976 *Arkansas Lawyer* pointed out that this was his 30th consecutive Annual Meeting. He outlined a plan of action—a legislative newsletter to inform members of proposed legislation affecting lawyers, support for the law schools and a professional utilization survey, the effective utilization of the new statewide lawyer referral service, a new youth education for citizenship program, a new committee on specialization and advertising, a judicial poll evaluating performance of judges, and consideration of mandatory continuing legal education.[71]

The Fall Legal Institute was again held in Little Rock. It was on "Winning Trial Tactics" and was chaired by Henry Woods, featuring some of the top trial lawyers in the country. In addition, there were presentations on practice skills by the Young Lawyers Section under the leadership of George D. Ellis and Jerry Jackson and a bar leadership conference under the co-chairmanship of John P. Gill and Sidney H. McCollum. The preparation of practice systems had begun, and the first one was to be the *Corporation System* by George Plastiras, Richard Williams, and Tom Overbey. It would be the focus of the mid-year meeting.[72]

The development of the various practice systems of the Association, the *Arkansas Form Book*, and other such practice publications should not be passed over without meritorious comment. The Association was one of the first and one of the most energetic at developing such practice aids. They have been of enormous value to members of the profession and have helped the legal profession in Arkansas practice in those areas efficiently and effectively.

At the May meeting of the Executive Council in 1977, it was reported by new Little Rock Dean Robert K. Walsh that a "line" had been approved by the legislature for a Director of the Continuing Legal Education Institute. Thus, the focus for the statewide CLE program was shifted from Fayetteville to Little Rock apparently without any objection from Fayetteville Dean Wylie Davis. Some Bar entities would continue to do their own programs (such as the Oil and Gas Institute and the Tax Institute).[73]

At the annual meeting, Herschel Friday and Robert S. Lindsey, the Executive Council Chairman, left office, although Cyril Hollingsworth remained as Secretary-Treasurer. Walter Niblock became Association President, and James D. Cypert was the new Executive Council Chair. President Niblock devoted his first report to a no-fault insurance bill then pending in Congress that had been endorsed by President Carter and a judges omnibus bill that would increase the number of federal judges. He advocated adoption of a LAWPAC to allow the hiring of a full-time legislative liaison. He expressed concern about lawyer advertising in the wake of the U.S. Supreme Court's decision in *Bates and O'Steen v. State Bar of Arizona*. Jeff Starling was Chair of the Specialization and Advertising Committee, and his committee had adopted a proposal from the ABA to try to contain the problem, and this was approved by the House at a September meeting.[74] At that meeting, Justice John A. Fogleman urged the creation of "an additional Appellate Court" (that became the Court of Appeals). Also, the House approved a *Probate System* that would be the feature of the mid-year meeting. A *Wills and Trusts System* and a *Workers Compensation System* were being prepared, and work had begun on the *Form Book*.

By April, President Niblock could report that LAWPAC had been created. The House had approved a feasibility study on whether the Bar could have its own prepaid legal insurance plan. In the mill were systems on creditor's rights, domestic relations and worker's compensation. The Annual Meeting would feature a trial practice program chaired by Henry Woods and featuring eight of the "superstars" of the day.[75]

Wayne Boyce became President at the end of the 1978 meeting, and Phil Carroll was named Executive Committee Chairman. His October report was directed in large measure toward the dedication on July 14-15 of the Old Federal Building as part of the Law School in Little Rock.[76]

The history of the renovation of the Old Federal Building for UALR Law School purposes is told in an article in the January, 1979 issue of *The Arkansas Lawyer*, at pages 4-7, by Dean Robert

K. Walsh. The renovation was accomplished through a $20,000 donation from the Association presented by President Herschel Friday at the 1977 Annual Meeting and was coupled with a $10,000 pledge from the University of Arkansas Foundation.[77]

In the summer of 1978, Philip S. Anderson was appointed by President Carter to a nominating committee to recommend a replacement for Judge William Webster. E. Charles Eichenbaum created his scholarship fund that summer also—the occasion of his having practiced law for fifty years. New Secretary-Treasurer James A. Buttry, in his Executive Council report, stated that the Association recommendation to the Supreme Court to form an Unauthorized Practice of the Law Committee was still pending; that the Association was seeking two new federal judgeships for Arkansas; that appointments had been made to Arkansas Legal Services, Inc.; that Articles of Incorporation were being drawn for a prepaid legal insurance entity; that LAWPAC corporate papers had been drafted and would be filed; and that George Campbell would be Chair of the Constitutional Reform Committee whose work would be related to the forthcoming Constitutional Convention.[78]

The Executive Council in the Fall of 1978 voted to seek the recodification of the Arkansas Statutes; Bobby McDaniel announced that no-fault had been defeated; and the American Bar Association once again presented its Award of Merit to the Association for the development of the systems.[79] In December, 1978, the Supreme Court created its committee on the unauthorized practice of law, and in the same month, the Garland County Bar Association honored Senior Judge John E. Miller in a special federal courtroom ceremony.

In his President's Report in January, 1979, President Boyce told about the Florida Bar's authorization for lawyers to place their funds being held for clients in interest-bearing trust accounts with the interest to be used for public interest programs related to the legal profession.[80] Thus did news about IOLTA first come to Arkansas.

The mid-year meeting in January, 1979 involved the new Rules of Civil Procedure and attracted 701 registrants. AICLE was quite active under its new Director, Claibourne W. Patty, Jr. The House of Delegates voted to recommend a new intermediate Court of Appeals.[81]

The Annual Meeting was on "Handling Major Litigation" and "Coping with Stress," and featured some outstanding trial lawyers such as John C. Shepherd, Chairman of the ABA House of Delegates, and ABA President S. Shepherd Tate. John Thomason, Chair of the ABA General Practice Section, and his wife, Sally, presented the "Coping with Stress" program. At the end of the meeting, E. Harley Cox, Jr. became Bar President and John F. Stroud, Jr. became Chairman of the Executive Council with Jim Buttry continuing as Secretary-Treasurer.

President Cox's October report called for efficiency and ethics among lawyers, stated that the Bar and the Supreme Court committee were considering the new American Bar Association Standards for Professional Discipline, and announced that the Fall Legal Institute would feature a presentation of the new *Arkansas Form Book* drafted by Robert R. Wright.[82] Judge Judith Rogers received the Arkansas Democrat Woman of the Year Award for 1979 and was also honored by the Pulaski County Bar Association.[83] Henry Woods was nominated in the Fall of 1979 to be U.S. District Judge for the Eastern District.[84] Jack Deacon became President of the National Conference of Commissioners on Uniform State Laws. General Hugh Overholt became Assistant Judge Advocate General of the U.S. Army (and would subsequently become Judge Advocate General).[85] Judge C. R. Huie retired on December 31, 1979, as Executive Secretary of the Arkansas Judicial Department and was replaced by Jim Petty.[86] Judge Huie had written a column, "Juris Dictum," for *The Arkansas Lawyer* during his tenure which occasionally quoted such sources as *The Miller County Fulminator*, a satirical and seldom "politically correct" publication circulated privately by Philip G. Alston ("Titius Proudfoot"), Senior Law Clerk to Federal Judge J. Smith Henley ("Justinian S. Blackstone").[87] Ruth Lindsey retired as Supreme Court Librarian after many years of service and the Court appointed Jacqueline S. Wright as her replacement, a position she held until 1999.[88]

By January 1980, two issues were attracting considerable attention from the bar leadership. In that issue of *The Arkansas_Lawyer*, in side by side columns, Bar President Harley Cox wrote about his support for mandatory continuing legal education (and that it was being studied by a committee headed by Don Schnipper), and Bar Foundation Chairman Boyce Love wrote favorably about interest on trust accounts. As of October 31, 1979, Bar Association membership stood at 2449.

A leadership conference was held in April 1980 to determine which projects should be given priority. The attendees were divided into three groups with the group reporters being David Epstein, Dean at Fayetteville, Robert K. Walsh, Dean at Little Rock, and Chris Barrier. Epstein's team listed these priorities: Mandatory CLE, a bar exam preparatory course, interest more lawyers in bar activities, and increase professionalism. Walsh's group's priorities were law reform, the cost of legal services (which they wanted to reduce by limiting interrogatories and unnecessary discovery), improvement of the judicial system, law student support (in connection with the bar exam), public information and the high cost of litigation. Barrier's group urged more clinical education, was concerned with access to lawyers and meeting the need for legal services, sought more economic delivery of legal services (particularly through more "systems"), and was concerned with better professional relationships through public relations efforts.[89]

The Annual Meeting in early June at the Arlington in Hot Springs, as usual, was on the subject of Law Office Economics and

Management and featured some national experts from the ABA Economics of Law Practice Section as well as some local experts. Phillip Carroll became President at the end of the meeting and Don Schnipper became Chairman of the Executive Council. W. Christopher Barrier replaced James A. Buttry as Secretary-Treasurer.

In the October, 1980 issue of *The Arkansas Lawyer* appears an article by Dean Robert K. Walsh on the proposed 1980 Constitution, a project that consumed a great deal of time for a number of lawyers. It failed, of course, as its predecessor did also, ten years before. Arkansas would enter the 21st Century with a 19th Century Constitution from the horse and buggy days when the U.S. Cavalry was still protecting Western settlers against Indian attacks and the cowboy was only beginning to evolve into a romanticized legend.[90] Also, in 1980, John Purifoy Gill and Marjem Jackson Gill published their interesting book, *On the Courthouse Square in Arkansas*, containing the pictures and some history of the county courthouses.[91]

Two items were concerning the Bar in 1980 that had actually first appeared earlier. They were the attempt by the Federal Trade Commission to inject itself into the practice of law and the Kutak Report proposal that each lawyer be required to contribute a large number of hours to pro bono work each year. (The latter had not been adopted at that time by the ABA House of Delegates and the document the Executive Council had before it was not adopted.)[92] By the end of September, 1980, Phil Carroll could proudly report that the House of Delegates had overwhelmingly approved the proposed new Constitution which gave voters a choice also between merit selection of judges and non-partisan election of judges.[93] The electorate did not heed the Bar's endorsement.

1981 to 1990

By the Spring of 1981, the FTC inquiry into the practice of bar associations in the United States (presumably aimed at price-fixing) was dead. Although it didn't happen until several years later, plans were made to convert the printed "systems" of the Association for use with word processing equipment in addition to the printed volumes.[94]

A number of Arkansas lawyers were honored in the 1980-81 Bar year. Alston Jennings was named President-Elect of the American College of Trial Lawyers. Jack Deacon was elected to the ABA Board of Governors. Robert L. Jones, Jr., was re-elected to the Board of Directors of the American Judicature Society. E. Charles Eichenbaum was reappointed Chair of the ABA Standing Committee on Retirement of Lawyers. Neva B. Talley received two ABA awards for contributions to family law. Patrick Henry Hays was elected Clerk of the ABA's Young Lawyers Division Assembly.[95]

The new officers following the Annual Meeting in 1981 were James D. Cypert, President, and Robert D. Ross, Chairman of the Executive Council. Chris Barrier remained Secretary-Treasurer. Herman Hamilton replaced Sidney McCollum as Chairman of the Foundation. At the Annual meeting, outgoing President Carroll could report that things were going well for AICLE and the Bar Foundation. Moreover, the Association was in sound shape financially. However, for several years, there had been friction between the Bar and the Bench over the judicial poll and there had been a squabble over the judiciary's so-called "gag order." The Supreme Court had rejected the Association's efforts to tighten up on lawyer behavior with regard to advertising and specialization, and "pursuing mandatory continuing legal education at this time [with the Supreme Court] seems pointless."[96]

In September 1981, the Fall Legal Institute returned to Fayetteville with a program on trial practice planned by Dean David Epstein. A tax seminar for the general practitioner was held in Little Rock in October and the mid-year meeting was scheduled to deal with law office management loss control and tax problems in estate planning. Chairman Harry Truman Moore was praised for his efforts with the Young Lawyers Section (which had won some awards from the ABA at its Annual Meeting, including one for a speakers bureau in support of the proposed 1980 Constitution organized by Louis "Bucky" Jones). By this time, the fledgling Court of Appeals was suffering from a case load that was "almost unmanageable," according to President Jim Cypert's President's Report.[97] In the House of Delegates, there was a debate over expansion for the Court between former Appeals Judge David Newbern and former Chief Justice John Fogleman. The matter was deferred until the mid-year meeting. Chief Judge Pat Mehaffy of the U.S. Court of Appeals for the Eighth Circuit, who had died, was memorialized at a special ceremony in St. Louis.[98]

The Annual Meeting had an unusual format planned by David Epstein, the Chairman, in that Friday afternoon had no scheduled activities. At the end of the meeting, President J. L. (Jim) Shaver, Jr., took office for 1982-83 with Richard Hatfield as Chairman of the Executive Council. Randall W. Ishmael succeeded Herman Hamilton as Bar Foundation Chairman. Annabelle Clinton became the new Secretary-Treasurer. Frank C. Elcan II was the Chair of the Young Lawyers Section. Jim Shaver's inaugural address lamented the decline in the number of lawyer-legislators.

At the House of Delegates meeting in September, President Shaver could point to the publication of the "Legislative Digest" newsletter as one of the services to members. Also, LAWPAC now had 119 contributors, and the money was being used to fund the legislative program. The specialization plan of the Association had been approved by the Supreme Court. The standards for criminal justice were being considered by a committee headed by John Fogleman.[99]

The proposal on interest on lawyers' trust accounts was prepared for submission to the Supreme Court by a committee headed by Herman Hamilton and was subsequently approved. Colonel C. E. Ransick, the Executive Director, wrote an article for the January, 1983 *Arkansas Lawyer* detailing problems in connection with trust accounts.[100] Eighteen bills were submitted by the Bar to the 1983 General Assembly. In the Spring, during the racing season, the YLS hosted a regional outreach of affiliates from six other states in Hot Springs. They also worked with FEMA to coordinate disaster relief caused by tornados and floods.[101] Prior to that time, the Executive Council approved and recommended to the House a YLS project to provide pro bono legal services for the low-income elderly.

Walter Niblock chaired the Annual Meeting in 1983, and the CLE presentation was "Anatomy of the Tort Trial" featuring seven nationally prominent tort specialists and litigators. Judge Henry Woods presided over the presentations and later spoke on judicial attitudes toward the trial. The keynote speaker for the luncheon was Governor Bill Clinton. At the end of the meeting, Dennis L. Shackleford took office as Bar President, James H. McKenzie became Chairman of the Executive Council, and Annabelle Clinton remained Secretary-Treasurer. Cyril Hollingsworth became Bar Foundation President.

In President Shackleford's first report, he discussed long-range planning for the Bar. It had begun with a long-range planning conference called by Wayne Boyce in 1978 and pursued again by Phil Carroll in 1982. Jim Cypert had appointed the first Special Planning Committee which conducted a long-range planning conference in April, 1982. Jim Shaver had appointed Robert K. Walsh head of that committee with instructions to hold a planning session in the Spring of 1983. That culminated with the approval in June, 1983 of the Report of the committee. Although specifics were provided, the general plan called for promoting access by the public to lawyers and allocating legal resources to meet such needs, improving professional competence and accountability and fulfilling the profession's responsibility to the community, continuing and strengthening programs to protect the future of the organized bar, improving and strengthening the Bar's legislative efforts, improving the judicial system, providing alternatives to litigation, and protecting and providing for the future of the judiciary.[102] It was decided to limit the number of Bar legislative proposals to ten. James R. Rhodes, III, the Bar's lobbyist, reported at the Annual Meeting of the House that the Bar did not fare well in the 1983 Session. All four uniform act proposals failed as did four other bar-sponsored bills. Moreover, the Supreme Court denied the proposal to establish a rule governing interest on lawyers' trust accounts.[103]

During the years since its formation, the Arkansas Bar Foundation had continued to expand its scope and improve its activities. In addition to providing scholarships and making awards to outstanding lawyers, the Foundation had provided booklets to aid the elderly and the poor and to support in general the work of the Association. Colonel C. E. Ransick, the Executive Director, had been much involved with the Foundation efforts, and upon his retirement, he was honored with the creation of the Colonel C. E. Ransick Award of Excellence, to be awarded for exceptional service to the legal profession.[104]

At the fall meeting of the House of Delegates, committees were appointed to study the new Model Rules of Professional Conduct and mandatory CLE. Herschel Friday was named to Chair the former and Russ Meeks the latter. A joint committee of the Association and the Judicial Council was created to help promote public and professional understanding of the judiciary. The problem of "too many lawyers" was considered. Tommy Womack presented a brief history of the Bar's long range planning conferences. Dean J. W. Looney of Fayetteville reported that the *Agri-*

Law System would be presented and would be the subject of the next fall institute.[105]

Writing in the April, 1984 issue of *The Arkansas Lawyer*, Dennis Shackleford stated that a "principal characteristic of the . . . current year is an awareness of the legal profession's commitment to the judiciary."[106] The effort was directed primarily at establishing "an open communication between the organized bar and the judiciary." This had been ranked as the number one problem for discussion at the National Conference of Bar Presidents. At the suggestion of the joint Bench-Bar committee chaired by Kelvin Wyrick, a committee headed by Sheffield Nelson was appointed to study and propose legislation creating a Judicial Compensation Commission. Twenty states had such commissions, most of which were of recent vintage. The Executive Council approved another proposal by Mr. Wyrick to lower the dues for judges.

A long range planning conference was held on March 29, 1984, with Tommy Womack as coordinator. Nationally, the ABA Task Force on Professional Competence, chaired by Herschel Friday, had reported, and its recommendations included mandatory CLE and endorsement of specialization. Development of "how to do it" bridging-the-gap courses also were being focused upon by the Association.[107]

The last report as Bar President by Dennis Shackleford is also concerned in large measure with the judiciary. The Judicial Compensation Commission proposal would be submitted, a new "judicial critique" (poll) had been prepared with the results to be confidential to the judge, with the judges being discouraged from releasing the results to the news media, and with the judge being given the results only on him or her.

The 1984 Annual Meeting in Hot Springs was on Appellate Advocacy and was chaired by John Stroud. An update of the *Appellate Advocacy Handbook* by Jacqueline Wright was available for distribution at the meeting. Presentations were made by U.S. District Judge Myron H. Bright, Federal Appellate Judges J. Smith Henley and Richard S. Arnold, and State Appellate Judges George Rose Smith, Richard B. Adkisson, Darrell D. Hickman and Melvin Mayfield. The gridiron presentation, "Hamelot," was presented with Griffin Smith and Bill Blair as Co-Chairs. At the end of the meeting, William R. Wilson, Jr., became Association President; David M. (Mac) Glover was Chair of the Executive Council; Robert L. Jones, III, was the new Chair of the Foundation; Annabelle Davis Clinton remained Secretary-Treasurer; and Martha Miller replaced Carl Crow as Chair of the YLS. Ms. Miller also became the new Association lobbyist at this meeting.

Carrying out the theme created by Dennis Shackleford, the first report from President Wilson was to call for reducing "unnecessary" friction between the bench and bar. He employed that term "since I suppose there will always be some tension between those of us who try lawsuits and those will invariably rule against us from time to time."[108] Judge John T. Jernigan, the Judicial Conference President, appointed Judge Perry Whitmore to work with the Bar in implementing trial practice seminars.

After having turned it down previously, the Arkansas Supreme Court approved the IOLTA proposal on September 17, 1984.[109] (Of course, it was wounded fatally, in terms of the use of the money, by the U.S. Supreme Court's decision that the interest belongs to the clients in June, 1998.) At a meeting of the House of Delegates on September 21, 1984, a controversial resolution was presented that stated "that any effort to screen candidates for judicial office through interrogation utilizing past published decisions be held improper and any such actions are hereby repudiated and condemned."[110] The resolution was enmeshed in politics surrounding allegations relating to Congressman Ed Bethune (who denied having done anything of that type), but despite pleas from some that the Bar should stay out of politics and despite the recommendation of the Resolutions Committee that action be postponed, the resolution passed by a narrow vote of 25 to 23.[111]

The Annual Meeting in 1985 featured two different topics—Trial Practice and the Growing Federalization of Divorce and Family Law. The keynote speaker for the trial practice program was Jerry Spence, the famed cowboy-appearing lawyer from Wyoming. At the end of the meeting, Don M. Schnipper became Bar President; Philip E. Dixon was named Chair of the Executive Council; Annabelle Clinton was selected again as Secretary-Treasurer; Richard L. Ramsay became Chair of YLS; and Martin Gilbert was named Chair of the Foundation. The House of Delegates approved with two amendments a mandatory CLE proposal submitted by Committee Chair Russ Meeks, and the Supreme Court would be petitioned to effectuate the program. Thomas L. Overbey reported that malpractice insurance rates were increasing by 25-30% and that an independent consultant would be hired to make recommendations on group insurance.[112] New President Schnipper commended President Wilson for the effectuation of the IOLTA program and for the development of the mandatory CLE proposal during his administration.[113]

At the Fall Institute meeting of the House of Delegates, Herschel Friday resigned as Association Delegate to the ABA in order to serve on the Board of Governors and Jack Deacon was appointed to fill out the unexpired term. (Herschel Friday would return to the Delegate position later on and, at the time he died, he had served more years in the House of Delegates than any other person in ABA history.) Dennis Shackleford and his legal education study committee were commended for their work. They recommended the continuation of two law schools in Arkansas and suggested that research be done to explore creative ways to provide additional funding for legal education. The *Criminal Law Handbook* was introduced at the Fall Institute; the *Agricultural Law Sys-*

tem was nearing completion; and the *Workers Compensation System* was scheduled to be finished in time for a seminar on it in April.[114]

At the mid-year meeting of the House, Robert D. Ross was appointed to chair the Sesquicentennial Committee, Larry Wallace was appointed chair for the annual meeting, and Mac Glover was named chair of the 1986 long range planning conference. It was announced that IOLTA's implementation was being made possible by a $25,000 grant from the Ford Foundation and smaller grants from the Bar Foundation, the Arkansas Justice Foundation, and the Legal Services Corporation. Thirteen proposed bills had been submitted to the Jurisprudence and Law Reform Committee, according to Chair Vincent W. Foster, Jr. AVLE (Arkansas Volunteer Lawyers for the Elderly) was approved as a permanent Association project. Charles L. Carpenter reported that the Judicial Council had voted to pursue implementation of a Judicial Compensation Commission.[115]

The Bar's Annual Meeting for 1986 presented "The Latest in the Law" with programs on various areas of the law. It also featured "Arkansans Coming Home" (from Washington, D. C.) in keeping with the Sesquicentennial observance. The four who were featured were Jim Burnett, Chair of the National Transportation Safety Board; Delia B. Combs, Assistant Commissioner of the Immigration and Naturalization Service; Major General Hugh R. Overholt, the Judge Advocate General of the Army; and Senator David Pryor. At the House of Delegates meeting, it was announced that Suzanne Roberts had been appointed executive director of IOLTA. The recruitment of lawyers to participate was being headed by Mark Lester. James M. Moody, chair of the Tort Reform Committee, submitted three proposals to address the legislature's concern about the "perceived crisis in the insurance industry," and these were adopted. W. Russell Meeks, III, reported that the state Supreme Court had denied the mandatory CLE proposal and that it would be resubmitted with more data on funding and court administration. Vince Foster presented the legislative package and five were approved and eleven were rejected. Action was postponed on a proposal for the merit selection of state court judges.[116]

Richard F. Hatfield became Bar President at this meeting and named Randall W. Ishmael to Chair the Executive Council. Sandra Wilson Cherry became the new Secretary-Treasurer. James A. McLarty, III, became the Bar Foundation Chair, and J. Thomas Ray became Chair of the YLS. President Hatfield targeted eight areas of Association involvement: the "insurance crisis," IOLTA, support for constitutional amendment 64 to raise the dollar limits on municipal court jurisdiction, mandatory CLE, pro bono work, revision of the Arkansas Tax Code, specialization and advertising, and celebration of the bicentennial of the Constitution. He appointed John P. Gill to head the bicentennial committee.[117]

At the fall legal Institute meeting of the House, it was reported that there had been a net gain of 134 members; that the Supreme Court had included in its budget a request that a court administrator be funded to administer mandatory CLE; that bills on notice to creditors in probate matters, on revision of the garnishment statutes, and on allowing personal representatives to pay small claims of less than $3,000 without petitioning to do so had been approved for the Bar's legislative package; and that there should be no bifurcated trials or change in the Rules of Civil Procedure by legislative action. Claibourne W. Patty, Jr., who had served as CLE Director for many years, had resigned, and the new Director, Dr. Rae Jean McCall was introduced.[118] The legal profession during this period had come under attack from the insurance industry seeking tort reform that they argued would lower the cost of liability insurance and make it more affordable. The main areas under attack included joint and several tort liability, contingent fees, the collateral source rule, punitive damages, and pain and suffering damages. President Hatfield stated that a "select committee" of both plaintiffs and defense lawyers had been appointed to study the matter. Moreover, the House had taken action to support Insurance Commissioner Robert Eubanks' efforts to obtain information from insurance companies to determine the reason for the increase in rates; to support a mandatory seat belt law; to support a policy that punitive damages not be covered by insurance; and to adopt Rule 11 to allow courts to impose sanctions on frivolous lawsuits. Because no information had been forthcoming from the insurance companies, the Bar had opposed other changes that had been proposed.[119]

The mid-year meeting heard that 700 attorneys were now participating in IOLTA, that it would be 1988 before mandatory CLE could be implemented, that the proposed revision of the Arkansas Code was completed and that it would completely replace the current Arkansas Statutes, that the legislative package would consist of eight bills, and that certain committees should be eliminated.[120]

"How to Succeed at Lawyering" was the theme of the Bar Association Annual Meeting, and different aspects of that were explored including the presentation of the case, meeting the media, computerized legal research for the small law firm, the law office of the future, leadership and communication, and avoiding "the bear traps." Speakers included Judge Henry Woods, Chief Justice Jack W. Holt, Jr., ATLA national President Robert L. Habush, TV anchor Steve Barnes, columnist John Brummett, radio host Pat Lynch, Winslow Drummond, Dennis L. Shackleford, George Plastiras, Thomas D. Ledbetter, Head Razorback Football Coach Ken Hatfield, Lawrence J. Smith, Jerry W. Cavaneau, Berl S. Smith, Howard W. Brill, Thomas L. Overbey, James M. Moody, James R. Harper, and Martha M. Miller.

At the House meeting, Philip E. Dixon reported that membership now stood at 3,440. A motion by Russell Meeks to increase Supreme Court dues to pay for administrative expenses of the mandatory CLE program was approved. Martha Miller reported that the legislature had adopted six of the eight Association bills, including the Corporation Code and the new Arkansas Code compilation. John F. Stroud, Jr. became the new President, and he named Vincent W. Foster, Jr., as Chair of the Executive Council. Sandra W. Cherry was re-elected as Secretary-Treasurer, and Philip E. Dixon became President-Elect. Michael W. Crawford became YLS Chair.[121]

In his first report, President Stroud stated what was being done to amend the state Constitution to create a Judicial Compensation Commission.[122]

By the autumn of 1987, President Stroud could report that the *Arkansas Corporation System* would be ready by the mid-year meeting and the *Debtor/Creditor System* was expected to be completed by April. A long-range planning meeting was scheduled for April. Petitions were being circulated to obtain sufficient signatures to place the Judicial Compensation Commission amendment on the ballot in November, 1988. The House approved a resolution authorizing consideration of LEXIS group membership for Association members.[123]

In his second report, John Stroud could advise that mandatory CLE had become a reality through approval of the program by the Supreme Court. IOLTA also had matured and approximately $120,000 would be available during 1988 for law school scholarships and legal services for the indigent or other worthy projects.[124]

The mid-year meeting of the House involved discussion of a proposed Code of Ethics. Executive Council Chair Vincent W. Foster, Jr., reviewed what had been done, and Webb Hubbell, a member of the Governor's Code of Ethics Commission, discussed the objectives of the Commission in drafting the proposed Code. On a motion by Lamar Pettus, the Code was approved. Dennis Shackleford sought a financial commitment from the members and responsibility for obtaining petition signatures for the Judicial Compensation Amendment.[125]

In his report in the April, 1988 issue of *The Arkansas Lawyer*, John Stroud previewed the annual meeting. The featured speaker would be Judge William Webster, formerly a judge on the Eighth Circuit Court of Appeals and former FBI and CIA Director. There would be panels on a variety of subjects. The new *Arkansas Form Book* would be presented by Robert R. Wright. Justice David Newbern would speak on judicial ethics, and Chief Justice Jack W. Holt would discuss the mandatory CLE requirements. The Stroud report also expressed some concerns about the proposed Code of Ethics approved by the House as it applied to lawyers.[126]

By the time of the annual meeting, it had become apparent that the effort to create a Judicial Compensation Commission had fallen short of obtaining enough signatures to be placed on the ballot. However, discussion had begun about a broader effort that would ultimately lead to the drafting of a proposed new Judicial Article to the Arkansas Constitution. The annual meeting also provided a first in the form of a joint meeting between the Arkansas Judicial Council and the Arkansas Bar.[127]

Mandatory continuing legal education was not yet in operation by June, 1988, but R. Christopher Thomas had been appointed director. It would become operational during the coming bar year. It was announced during the House meeting that E. Charles Eichenbaum had been given the prestigious Fellows Award by the American Bar Foundation. Philip E. Dixon took office as President at the end of the meeting and appointed Jack McNulty as Chair of the Executive Council. David M. (Mac) Glover was certified as President-Elect, and Sandra Wilson Cherry continued as Secretary-Treasurer. Edward Boyce became chair of the YLS.[128] New President Dixon said that one of his main goals would be to build and promote a closer association between local bars and the Arkansas Bar. Mandatory CLE would be developing and would need the active support and assistance of the Bar, and that would be another of his goals.[129] In furtherance of the goal of promoting the relationship between local bars and the Association, a Bar Leaders Conference was held in October, 1988, chaired by Phillip Carroll, a past president.[130] Eighty bar leaders representing 31 state and local bars, specialty bars, and committee and Section chairs from the Association attended.[131] Also, by the fall meeting of the House of Delegates, Chris Thomas had developed a plan for implementing mandatory continuing legal education (MCLE) which was approved. The new Office of Professional Programs of the Supreme Court, headed by Thomas, would be responsible for the administration and enforcement of MCLE. The Mandatory CLE Committee of the Bar, chaired by Russell Meeks, had worked with Thomas to develop the plans for the program. There was appointed an Arkansas Continuing Legal Education Board to assist and advise Thomas in promulgating the rules, guidelines and requirements for MCLE. There would be twelve hours of CLE credit required each year, and the reporting period was moved to June 30, 1990, for the first period.[132]

Carrying over to the fall meeting from the summer, the need for a new Judicial Article was emphasized by E. Charles Eichenbaum and Judge Eugene Harris. A committee was appointed to report back on how best to go about the drafting process. Subsequently, by the summer of 1989, a Task Force for a New Judicial Article had been formed, co-chaired by Harris and Eichenbaum. The other participants and leaders in this undertaking were to co-chair four divisions dealing with various aspects of the judiciary. They were Justice Donald L. Corbin and Judge Warren O. Kimbrough on financing the judiciary; Judge Ellen B. Brantley and Herman Hamilton on qualifications and election/selection; Judge James Hannah and Don Schnipper on administration; and Judge Sidney McCollum and John F. Stroud, Jr., on court structure and personnel. Robert R. Wright was to chair "the Control Center" on collection and dissemination of research and information.[133]

The mid-year meeting of 1989 was one largely composed of resolutions. Those that were passed included the recommendation that all state and federal courts provide that counsel appointed to represent persons having a constitutional or statutory right to counsel receive reasonable fees and compensation for expenses; another that would present legislation directed at achieving the goal of the preceding one including the increase in maximum fees allowed for state criminal appointments; and a third that would support the legal challenge to the constitutionality of the statutory maximum fee schedules. These were all presented by Ralph Brodie. Another resolution supported a salary increase for judges and that the compensation of federal judges not be tied to compensation for congressmen.[134]

At the annual meeting in Hot Springs, a number of trial lawyers who were members of the American Board of Trial Advocates (ABOTA) presented a trial to a jury composed of persons drawn from an actual jury panel in Hot Springs. The new President David M. (Mac) Glover appointed Fred S. Ursery as Chair of the Executive Council. Charles B. Roscopf became President-Elect, and Rodney E. Slater was elected the new Secretary-Treasurer.[135] Rosalind M. Mouser became Chair of the Young Lawyers Section. President Glover stated four objectives for 1989-90: Implementation and promotion of MCLE; strengthening relations between the Bar and the judiciary; encouraging women and minorities to take leadership roles in the Bar; and the revision of the Judicial Article to the Arkansas Constitution.[136]

Not incidentally, with mandatory CLE in force, all previous records were broken at the annual meeting in June, 1989, as 834 lawyers attended, who could obtain all or almost all of their hours at that one meeting.

By the end of the year association members were voting on amendments to the Association Constitution resulting from a re-districting study headed by Winslow Drummond. The Northwestern District had grown larger than the Southern and Northeastern Districts combined, and the Central District (Pulaski County) was three times the size of each of the two smallest districts. As redistricted, the Central District would elect a President every three years and four smaller districts of about 450 members each would each elect a President every six years. The four smaller districts would each have fifteen delegates, and the Central District would have twenty-one.[137] This was approved.[138]

The annual meeting in June, 1990 was again a joint meeting with the Arkansas Judicial Council. Its President was Judge John R. Lineberger. Vince Foster chaired the annual meeting, and there was an extensive exhibit hall which has been the case ever since.[139] Benjamin R. Civiletti, former U.S. Attorney General, was one of the featured speakers. There was a huge CLE program offering 24.5 credit hours, of which fourteen were possible to attain.[140] At the end of the meeting, Charles B. Roscopf became President, James H. McKenzie was President-Elect, Rodney E. Slater remained as Secretary-Treasurer, Gregory T. Jones became Chair of the Young Lawyers, and Richard A. Williams became Chair of the Executive Committee. David Solomon was elected President of the Bar Foundation. At its meeting, the House of Delegates voted to oppose civil justice "reform" in the form of an act pending in Congress relating to changes in tort litigation.[141]

In the fall, an open forum and House of Delegates meeting took place on November 3, 1990, to consider the proposed new Judicial Article to the Arkansas Constitution. This culminated a two-year effort by many lawyers and judges, as previously mentioned, and the group was headed by E. Charles Eichenbaum and Judge Eugene S. (Kayo) Harris.[142] The House of Delegates approved the Judicial Article.[143] The plan was to then have the General Assembly submit it to the people for a vote. It was subsequently approved for submission by the Senate, but it failed in the House by two votes. David R. Matthews, Chair of the Legislative Action Committee, held a "Lawyers' Day" in both January and February to support the legislative package, including the Judicial Article, but it failed despite that effort.[144]

1991 to Present

Members voted in the spring on a proposal to amend the Bar Constitution to require an affirmative vote by a majority of the members of the Bar before the Bar could sponsor any proposed Amendment to the federal or state Constitutions. This was proposed by former President James B. Sharp and opposed by the current bar leadership including President Roscopf.[145] Despite the opposition, it passed. The effect was to take that power away from the House of Delegates.

At the annual meeting in June, 1991, L. Stanley Chauvin, the Immediate Past President of the American Bar, was one of the featured speakers. John G. Lile was the Chair for the convention.[146] James H. McKenzie became President at the end of that meeting with John C. Everett as the new Chair of the Executive Council. John P. Gill was the President-Elect, and Rodney E. Slater continued as Secretary-Treasurer. Lynn Williams took office as the Chair of the Young Lawyers. The Association membership had reached 4,000 by the summer of 1991. Work was progressing on updated versions of the *Domestic Relations*, *Probate Law* and the *Debtor/Creditor* handbooks as well as the *Arkansas Form Book*.[147]

The Association had previously taken a position against the statutory caps on fees awarded to lawyers appointed by a court to defend indigents, and it filed an *amicus* brief in a case on the subject. The Supreme Court ruled the caps unconstitutional in accordance with the Bar's arguments.[148]

The hot topic at the fall meeting of the House of Delegates was the creation of a statewide public defender system. After a long debate the House authorized Bar sponsorship of a bill that would create such a system. This was an outgrowth of the Supreme Court decision declaring unconstitutional the statutory caps on attorney's fees in criminal cases involving indigent defendants. Also, prior to that meeting, and pursuant to House of Delegates action taken at the annual meeting, the Model Code of Judicial Conduct Committee filed a petition with the Supreme Court for adoption of the Code.[149]

In an "extra" issue of the Bar *Newsbulletin* for October/November, 1991, it was reported that federal Judge Henry Woods had approved a consent decree in a suit brought by Eugene Hunt on behalf of African-American residents of judicial districts in which certain state judicial districts were divided into African-American majority subdistricts and white majority subdistricts. The judges elected would exercise district-wide jurisdiction. This suit was filed under the federal Voting Rights Act which had been applied by the U.S. Supreme Court to states having an elected judiciary. The result of this case was to increase the number of minority judges in Arkansas and to make special judges of about nine white judges who would continue to serve until the end of their terms, retirement or resignation, or until December 31, 1994.

About this time, in late 1991, Barbara Tarkington celebrated twenty years of staff service to the Bar.[150] She received a plaque commemorating her long service. Then, shortly thereafter, Assistant Executive Director Judith Gray was honored at a reception and dinner at the Capitol Hotel for her twenty-five years of service to the Bar. She received a gold pendant inscribed "Arkansas Bar Association First Lady." She had worked by then with three executive directors and twenty-five presidents.[151]

The 1992 Annual Meeting featured United States Solicitor General and former federal Circuit Judge Kenneth Starr, past

ABA President John C. Shepherd and ethicist Matthew Josephson. No one had reason to anticipate the future interaction between Kenneth Starr and various prominent persons in the State of Arkansas. Starr was the keynote speaker at the Convention.[152] Hillary Rodham Clinton received the Outstanding Lawyer Citizen Award on behalf of herself and her husband, Governor Bill Clinton.[153] John P. Gill took office as the new Bar President, Rosalind M. Mouser as Chair of the Executive Council, E. Lamar Pettus as President-Elect, and Rodney Slater remained as Secretary-Treasurer. Lucinda McDaniel was chosen to Chair the Young Lawyers.[154]

In August of 1992, it was decided that AICLE would merge with the Arkansas Bar Association effective September 1. AICLE staffers became Association employees. Now all CLE activities including those at the annual meeting would be under the CLE department of the Association.[155] Sarah Jane Polk, the Director of AICLE, became the Association Director of CLE although she resigned not long thereafter to accept another job.

At the August meeting of the American Bar Association, Philip S. Anderson became Chair of the House of Delegates.[156] He would later become President-Elect in August 1997, and President of the American Bar in August 1998, following in the footsteps of U. M. Rose and Edward L. Wright.

At the midyear meeting in January, 1993, the House of Delegates raised dues for the first time since 1979 to $150.00 for those admitted more than ten years. Lesser amounts applied to those admitted from four to ten years, three years or less, judges, nonresidents, military personnel, and retired members. The By-Laws were also updated to reflect current practices and to make them internally consistent.[157]

Bar President John Gill wrote a column on "Notes for the Future of the Bar" in the *Newsbulletin* that set out his perspective on the future. He discussed hiring a "year-round" lobbyist; expanding bar services; developing a consulting service on law office management; a mechanism (a Board) for keeping current the Bar's systems and handbooks; a growing public relations activity; support of new lawyers; bar-related malpractice insurance; improvement of the lawyer referral service; CLE; more staff help to committees and sections; improvement of Bar office facilities; further development of the publications program; improved procedures for timely rule-making by the Supreme Court; fee dispute arbitration; and computer availability and access to court and other public records.[158]

Deb Garrison, formerly Assistant Director of AICLE, was named Director of CLE to replace Sarah Jane Polk around the first of the year.[159]

In the legislative session of 1993, seven of the ten bar bills passed. A public defender bill passed that was a hybrid of the bar bill and legislatively provided provisions. Another added six judges to the Court of Appeals. Yet another provided three legal assistants to twenty-one judges who had no employees at all.[160]

Featured speakers at the annual meeting were Governor Jim Guy Tucker, Jay Foonberg (the leading authority on how to start and build a law practice), and Morris Dees (head of the Southern Poverty Law Center and the winner of some huge awards against hate groups).[161]

The new officers were President E. Lamar Pettus, President-Elect Robert L. Jones, III, Executive Council Chair Russ Meeks, YLS Chair Brian Ratliff, and Secretary-Treasurer Jeanette Hamilton.[162] During the summer of 1993, there were several notable actions taken. The client security fund rules were revised in several ways, and the amount a client could collect was raised to $40,000.00.[163] A "BarNet" personal computer access to informational data bases was expected to soon be in use.[164] An *Arkansas Law Office Manual* was now available.[165] The Arkansas Supreme Court had undertaken administrative restructuring and had placed some scattered administrative and budgeting activities under the

Administrative Office of the Courts, which was directed by James D. Gingerich.[166] Five thousand *Consumer Law Handbooks* or *Veterans Handbooks* were mailed. An *Arkansas Trial Notebook* was available.[167] The fourth annual "Best of CLE" seminar drew 529 attendees from five states.[168]

At the fall, 1993 meeting of the House of Delegates, a referendum was called by the House on support of a "comprehensive IOLTA." This would require lawyers who maintain pooled trust accounts to place them in interest bearing accounts with the Bar Foundation receiving the interest. The IOLTA Board was contemplating petitioning the Supreme Court to require that pooled trust accounts become IOLTA accounts. ("Pooled accounts" were those containing client funds that were too small in amount or held for too short a time for it to be practical to put the money in a separate interest-earning account for the benefit of the client.)[169]

At the mid-year meeting of the House of Delegates, Dee Davenport Ball, M. D. Buffalo and Chief Justice Jack W. Holt, Jr., were honored for their work with the Committee on Opportunities for Women and Minorities in the Legal Profession. Wendell Griffen reported that the committee had drafted an ethical rule dealing with the use of hate speech and gender and racial bias by attorneys. YLS Chair Brian Ratliff reported that the *Elder Law Handbook* would come out in May, 1994. It was announced that Carolyn Witherspoon was the President-Elect Designee. The Arkansas Young Lawyers were selected by the American Bar to make a presentation on *their Consumer Law Handbook* at a spring affiliate outreach national conference.

After a spring long range planning conference, the Annual Meeting met. Featured speakers included Governor Jim Guy Tucker, former American Bar President Chesterfield Smith, Doreen Weisenhaus, the Legal Affairs Editor of the *New York Times Magazine* and former editor-in-chief of the *National Law Journal,* and humorist Mark Russell.[170] At the end of the meeting

Robert L. Jones, III, took office as President, Carolyn B. Wither-spoon became President-Elect, Frank B. Sewell was elected Sec-retary-Treasurer, Robert M. Cearley, Jr., was the new Executive Council Chair, and Steve Quattlebaum became Chair of the Young Lawyers.

There was a long discussion about the Lawyer Referral Service in the House of Delegates meeting. The House eventually voted to allocate $30,000 out of the 1993-94 budget if there were profits to offset the expenditure. In effect, they adopted the recommendation of Chair Ann West who recommended hiring a full-time staff person, giving the service its own phone line, doing more yellow-page advertising for the service, revamping the way attorneys are listed, and raising the annual referral membership fee substantially.

Other events involved national organizations. John C. Deacon, one of the Arkansas Bar's leaders for decades, was named President of the American Bar Foundation. Todd Greer, a second-year law student at UALR, became Chair of the Law Student Division of the American Bar and thereby also became a member of the ABA House of Delegates. In a tragic airplane accident, while attempting to land his aircraft at his own private landing strip during a thun-derstorm, Herschel H. Friday, Jr., was killed. Herschel served the Bar in many capacities, both here and nationally, and served in the House of Delegates of the American Bar longer than any other person in its history. His contributions are reviewed in greater depth elsewhere.

At the American Bar Convention, the Arkansas Bar for the first time in its history presented a resolution supporting voluntary alternative dispute resolution (ADR) but opposing mandatory ADR as a prerequisite to jury trials in federal courts. The resolu-tion was submitted by Robert R. Wright, who succeeded Herschel Friday as Bar Delegate, and by H. William Allen, State Delegate. Judge G. Thomas Eisele was the principal speaker for the resolu-tion. Judge William R. Wilson, Jr. had previously spoken to the

Southern Conference of Bar Presidents on its behalf. The Arkansas resolution was joined in sponsorship by South Dakota, Georgia, Mississippi and the ABA General Practice Section. It was adopted as American Bar policy.[171]

In October of 1994, the state Supreme Court approved IOLTA as a requirement for all lawyers practicing law in Arkansas as the Bar Association had urged. The IOLTA Executive Director by then was Lisa DeLoache Melton. The IOLTA Foundation awarded $130,000 in grants to fifteen organizations for 1995. Also, in the fall of 1994, Stacey Allison DeWitt was named Director of Communications/ Lobbyist. Lucinda McDaniel was selected as the Arkansas and Oklahoma American Bar Young Lawyers Division district representative. Robert M. Cearley, Jr., was re-elected to the Board of Directors of the American Judicature Society. Judge Thomas F. Butt, who had been a Chancellor and Probate Judge since January 1951, received the Certificate of Merit for his service as the first chair of the Judicial Discipline and Disability Commission.

In the winter issue of the *Arkansas Lawyer* in 1995, Robert L. Jones' column dealt with professionalism, a theme that several presidents before him had also pursued.[172] Steve Quattlebaum, Chair of the YLS, promoted a charitable fund-raiser called "the three-point attack" to raise money for the American Cancer Society. He was soliciting lawyer donations to a campaign that originated from a proposal that people pledge $3.00 for every three-point shot made by the Arkansas Razorback basketball team.[173]

By spring, President Jones could report that a "blue ribbon committee" was preparing to make recommendations to the state Supreme Court following the U.S. Supreme ruling in a Florida case on lawyer advertising. Also, he reported that Ann West had made substantial progress in reorganizing the lawyer referral service and that Theresa Dixon was the new full-time director of the program.[174] A court funding bill had passed the legislature providing for a state-funded administrative assistant/case coordinator for every trial judge, and he regarded it as one of the highlights of his term as bar president.[175]

The featured speaker at the annual meeting in 1995 was Justice Antonin Scalia of the United States Supreme Court, who discussed his view of constitutional interpretation. Other speakers included George Bushnell, President of the American Bar Association; Joe Jamail, the famed trial lawyer from Houston; Governor Jim Guy Tucker; and I. S. Leevy Johnson, Past President of the South Carolina Bar.

Carolyn Witherspoon took office as President of the Bar Association, the first woman to hold that position. Harry Truman Moore became President-Elect; Sandra Wilson Cherry was named Chair of the Executive Council; Frank B. Sewall was elected Secretary-Treasurer; and Stuart P. Miller was named Chair of the Young Lawyers Section.[176]

Around the same time, Chief Justice Jack Holt, Jr., announced his retirement from the Supreme Court and Bradley Jesson was appointed to fill out his unexpired term. Ann Dixon Pyle became Executive Director of the Arkansas Bar Foundation. Ann Orsi Smith became President of the Arkansas Association of Women Lawyers.[177] The Association entered into an agreement with Law Office Information Systems (LOIS) to make Association books available on CD-ROM with the disks also to contain the Arkansas appellate cases and the Arkansas Code.[178]

In the fall of 1995, lawyer advertising was the most intensely discussed topic at the House of Delegates meeting. (The Association had had a petition pending before the state Supreme Court for more restrictive lawyer advertising rules since 1993.) The U.S. Supreme Court's ruling upholding the Florida Bar's ban on direct mail solicitation of accident victims within thirty days of the accident was of much interest to Bar leaders. The Court had relied heavily on studies conducted by the Florida Bar which showed harm to the public as justifying the restriction. Consequently, studies in Arkansas were being contemplated.[179]

It was also announced in the fall that IOLTA would fund a statewide conference on domestic violence to take place in the spring.[180] In terms of outside activities by Bar members, Phil Anderson was a candidate for President-Elect of the American Bar Association; Robert R. Wright was elected Chair-Elect of the ABA General Practice Section; Judge Ellen B. Brantley was named Judge of the Year by the National Child Support Enforcement Association; and Sam H. Boyce was elected President of the National Organization of Social Security Claimant's Representatives.[181]

On January 10, 1996, Wendell L. Griffen, John F. Stroud, Jr., and Olly Neal were sworn in as new Court of Appeals judges. Judge Stroud had previously served by appointment on the Arkansas Supreme Court.[182]

At the mid-year meeting, the House approved Chair Donis Hamilton's recommendation to conduct a survey on how the public was affected by lawyer advertising. Randy W. Ishmael, Chair of the Uniform Probate Code Committee, reported that his committee would favor passage of the UPC as modified and that this should be bar-sponsored legislation in 1997.[183]

William Aubert Martin, who had followed C. E. Ransick as Executive Director of the Association, had announced his retirement as of the end of 1996, and a search committee had been appointed under the chairmanship of Past President David M. (Mac) Glover.[184] Bill Martin served the Association faithfully for many years, looked after its finances very carefully, and worked with Judith Gray, the Associate Executive Director, to carry out the goals and policies of the Association and to further its development. He has remained active in both the Arkansas Bar and the American Bar.

In April 1996, the Gayle Pettus Pontz Award of the Women's Law Student Association at the U of A Law School in Fayetteville presented the award to Judge Andree Roaf. Previous award winners had been Carolyn Witherspoon, Paula Casey, Judge Annabelle Clinton Imber, Kathlyn Graves, Sandra Wilson Cherry, Hillary Rodham Clinton, Judge Mary Davies Scott, Judge Judith Rogers, Judge Elsijane Trimble Roy, and Gayle Pettus Pontz (who was the first female graduate of the University of Arkansas Law School in 1937). The award recognizes the achievements of a female lawyer who best represents the accomplishments of women in the legal profession.[185]

At the 1996 Annual Meeting, there was again a joint proceeding with the Arkansas Judicial Council, whose President was Judge Jim Hannah. David Matthews was Chair of the meeting.[186] Speakers included Senator Dale Bumpers; Michael Josephson, a well-known ethicist; Clay Jenkinson, who portrayed Thomas Jefferson; and many other prominent speakers. The program offered a potpourri of various presentations on different topics from which to choose, all accorded some degree of CLE credit.[187]

At the House of Delegates meeting, the House approved a legal services funding bill to be a part of the legislative package. H. Maurice Mitchell, chair of the Legal Services Task Force, asked for inclusion of the bill due to severe federal funding cuts. Also, the House endorsed authorization of the Association lobbyist to work with the AARP to develop a "Uniform Probate Code based bill" adapted to Arkansas needs.

The new officers who took office at the end of the 1996 Annual Meeting were Harry Truman Moore, President; Jack A. McNulty, President-Elect; Daniel R. Carter, Secretary-Treasurer; J. Thomas Ray, Executive Council Chair; and Denzil P. Marshall, Jr., Chair of the YLS.

During the summer of 1996, *The Arkansas Lawyer* was awarded the first annual "AWAE excellence in communications award" by the Arkansas Society of Association Executives. Later, at the American Bar Convention, Judge Thomas F. Butt of Fayetteville received the national Award of Judicial Excellence presented by the National Conference of State Trial Judges, an affiliate of the ABA Judicial Administration Division.

The House of Delegates in October, 1996 approved the appointment of Don Hollingsworth, Executive Director of Legal Services of Arkansas, to be the new Executive Director of the Association to succeed William A. Martin at the end of the year.[188]

Despite all the work that had been done on the Uniform Probate Code proposal and despite its sponsorship by the AARP, it failed to get very far in the legislature. Former Dean Lawrence H. Averill, Jr., of the UALR Law School, in particular, had put in a large amount of time in assembling the revised text.

In 1997, Judith Gray, the pillar of the Arkansas Bar Association, celebrated thirty years of service to the Association. Pictures and quotes from prominent lawyers were featured in *The Arkansas Lawyer* in the Winter issue of 1997, pp. 24-25. The respect and love bestowed by Judith Gray upon the Arkansas legal profession is clearly shared by the same respect and love that the profession feels for her. Her hard work and dedication has been an integral part of the success of the Association.

There were some substantial additions to the Supreme Court and Court of Appeals to begin 1997. W. H. (Dub) Arnold became Supreme Court Chief Justice, and the new Associate Justices were Ray Thornton and Annabelle Clinton Imber. They joined Associate Justices Tom Glaze, David Newbern, Robert L. Brown and Don Corbin. Judges Margaret Meads, Andree L. Roaf, Terry L. Crabtree and Sam Bird joined Court of Appeals Judges John M. Pittman, John F. Stroud, Jr., James R. Cooper, Judith Rogers, John E. Jennings, Olly Neal, Wendell L. Griffen, and Chief Judge John B. Robbins.[189] (When Justice Newbern retired from the Supreme Court, Lavenski Smith, an African American Public Service

Commissioner, was appointed by the Governor to complete his term, beginning in 1999.)

Lawyer advertising was the prime topic at the mid-year meeting of the Association, now being held annually at the Peabody Hotel in Memphis. The Florida Bar's Supreme Court-approved rule prohibiting direct mail solicitation of personal injury victims for thirty days after the accident was proposed and received a tie vote in the House of Delegates. President Moore voted in the negative to break the tie. A proposed requirement of lawyers claiming special expertise to provide potential clients with a written description of experience and training also failed by one vote. Another issue was the use of actors or non-members of law firms in broadcast or print advertisements, and the House voted by a substantial margin to stop this practice, recommending that the Supreme Court amend its Rules of Professional Conduct accordingly.[190]

The 1997 Annual Meeting listed seventy-nine speakers and numerous CLE offerings most of which had to do with some aspect of trial practice. At the end of the meeting, Jack A. McNulty became President of the Association; Robert M. Cearley, Jr. became President-Elect; Daniel R. Carter remained Secretary-Treasurer; Jack Davis became Executive Council Chair; and Scott Morgan was named to head the Young Lawyers.[191] The first article by new President McNulty referred to a century of professionalism and service, as the Association moved toward 1998 and the celebration of its centennial.[192]

President McNulty was able to report to the Association that as a result of the steady increase in the size of the Association, it now had two Delegate positions in the American Bar House of Delegates. Because Robert Wright had been named a Delegate from the ABA General Practice, Solo and Small Firm Section and vacated his Delegate position, two new Delegates were added—Past Presidents Carolyn Witherspoon and Harry Truman

Moore. Joined with State Delegate H. William Allen and ABA President-Elect Philip S. Anderson, the Association now had five delegates in the ABA House of Delegates.[193]

Since 1990, under the leadership of E. Charles Eichenbaum and Judge Eugene (Kayo) Harris, the Bar Association and the Judicial Council had been engaged in an effort to reform the Judicial Article to Arkansas' ancient Constitution through the amendment process. This 1990 effort had failed, following approval for submission to the voters of the Judicial Article by the Arkansas Senate, when the House of Representatives refused to allow the voters to pass on it by a very narrow margin. In the *Newsbulletin* for Fall, 1996, it was reported that the Judicial Council was proposing to refer an amendment to the Judicial Article to permit retired judges, with their consent, to be recalled for service when a sitting judge was in need of assistance. This was supported by the Bar Association and was submitted to the voters.

A subsequent major effort for an entirely new Judicial Article, however, began in the Spring of 1997 when a joint committee of the Bar Association and the Judicial Council was named to again propose a new Judicial Article. On March 14, 1998, the House of Delegates approved the draft submitted. (Subsequently, it was overwhelmingly approved by a vote of the entire Association membership.) The plan was to submit the proposal to the 1999 General Assembly for submission to the voters as a constitutional amendment in the November, 2000 general election.[194] The document in its final form would merge the separate courts of law, equity and probate into one court of general jurisdiction to be called the Circuit Court; merge the municipal and other local courts into one court of limited jurisdiction to be called the District Court; provide for non-partisan election of judges; vest rule-making authority in the Supreme Court; and continue popular election of judges rather than a system of merit selection.[195] Merit selection, although favored by the American Judicature Society, the American Bar Association and practically all legal scholars, was overwhelmingly rejected by the Arkansas judiciary.

In the spring of 1998, the National Board of Trial Advocacy honored Judge Henry Woods as a founding Board member and Judge William R. Wilson, Jr., as the first dual-certified attorney in Arkansas at a joint reception with the Association. Thomas M. Carpenter of Little Rock became national President of NBTA.[196]

Much of the activity of President McNulty's year was devoted toward planning for the 1998 Annual Meeting celebration of the Centennial of the Bar. An enormous program was planned with enough CLE credit to last for several years if the credits could have been carried over that far.[197] Featured speakers included Justice Clarence Thomas of the U.S. Supreme Court; Judge Richard S. Arnold, until April, 1998 the Chief Judge of the U.S. Court of Appeals for the Eighth Circuit; Governor Mike Huckabee; incoming President Philip S. Anderson of the American Bar Association; and James W. McElhaney, a trial practice expert. Former Governors Sidney S. McMath, Dale L. Bumpers and David H. Pryor spoke on "when lawyers head the state."[198] It was a magnificent occasion and one in which old U. M. Rose would have been proud to be a participant.

The attendance of 1,108 lawyers and judges, constituting 26% of the members, set a record. One other Southern state bar association had recently set a record when 3% of its membership attended.[199]

At the conclusion of the Centennial celebration in June 1998, Robert M. Cearley, Jr., took office as President for 1998-99; Louis B. Jones, Jr., became the President-Elect; H. Murray Claycomb was named Secretary-Treasurer; and Philip E. Kaplan was appointed Chair of the Executive Council. Gwendolyn D. Hodge was elected Chair of the Young Lawyers Section.[200]

Louis B. (Bucky) Jones of Fayetteville became President of the Bar in June, 1999. Ron D. Harrison of Fort Smith became Presi-

dent in June, 2000. Sandra Wilson Cherry of Little Rock becomes
President in June, 2001.

Conclusion

When you take all the trees that comprise the forest and look
at the Arkansas Bar Association and its history as a whole, you are
struck by the fact that the Association's instinct and desire from
the very beginning to the present has always been to improve the
legal profession and the courts. At times, this has gone beyond improvement and taken the approach of outright legal reform as it
has in the rather moderate proposed Judicial Article. None of it has
ever been radical; none of it has departed from what was viewed at
the time as best for the profession, the judiciary and the court
structure and its rules at a particular time and in a particular day.

The people, however, particularly as manifested in the controlling elements within the House of Representatives of the legislature, have too often lagged behind, resisting change, resisting improvement and reform, even though the ultimate beneficiaries
would be the people. The accomplishments of the Bar have been
won at the price of struggle and persuasion, and when it has ven-
tured outside the confines of the profession, the Bar has lost as
much as it has won. It has never, however, halted its perseverance.

The Bar itself has historically fixed its sights on moderate,
rather modest, goals with which few within the profession can
quarrel. Beset by occasional wrongdoing or by breach of ethics by a
few lawyers, however, the profession has developed a poor reputation with the people. This is aided and abetted by "lawyer jokes"
and by misunderstanding of Shakespeare's quotation about killing
all the lawyers. This is a large part of why it is so difficult to promote moderate improvements in the law and legal structure. If a
multi-million dollar campaign had been launched to discredit the

profession, it could not have done any better than the volunteers who enjoy bashing lawyers.

Those who engage in this activity are basically ill-informed people. Before law, there was no civilization. Civilization began with law. Even in "law of the tribe" or "law of the cave" of prehistoric times there was a kind of law. To paraphrase Thomas Hobbes, man in a state of nature lived a life that was nasty, brutish and short. We have today as a part of our arsenal the heritage of centuries of experience and concepts that draw upon the finest thoughts and aspirations of those who have gone before. We absorbed into English law the heritage of Rome and Greece and Judeo-Christianity. England added the Magna Carta, the Petition of Right, the English Bill of Rights, and the Writ of Habeas Corpus, along with a grand body of jurisprudence constituting the great and common law. To that, we added the Declaration of Independence, our great Constitution and Bill of Rights. We are now in an age of honing and perfecting all of that as best we can, while at the same time adapting our heritage to new problems, conditions and challenges. And we are the keepers of the keys. As Alexis de Toqueville wrote in *Democracy in America* over 150 years ago: "It is at the bar or the bench that the American aristocracy is found."[201]

How well we do in keeping our trust with the past, in nurturing and developing our institutions and laws, and in adapting that heritage to modern conditions and the never-ending change and newness of the law, will determine how well we have fulfilled our duty and met the challenge as individual professionals and as an organized Bar.

If we do our job well, then we will not have to proclaim our virtue for it will be there for all to see.

Notes

1. Proceedings, Bar Association of Arkansas, 1946, p. 145.
2. *Id.* at 146.
3. *Id.* at 155.
4. *Id.* at 168-224.
5. Proceedings, Bar Association of Arkansas, 1947, p. 17.
6. *Id.* at 18.
7. Interview with E. Charles Eichenbaum, p. 13; Interview with J. Gaston Wiliamson, Dec. 2, 1993, pp. 5-6.
8. 3 Ark. L. Rev. 247 (1949)
9. 6 Ark. L. Rev. 337 (1952).
10. Proceedings, Fifth-fifth Annual Meeting, 7 Ark. L. Rev. 179-181 (1953).
11. *Id.* at 184.
12. *Id.* at 213-236.
13. 7 Ark. L. Rev. 97 (1953)
14. 8 Ark. L. Rev. 244 (1954)
15. *Ibid.*
16. 6 Ark. L. Rev. 22 (1951-52).
17. 8 Ark. L. Rev. 266-268 (1954).
18. 9 Ark. L. Rev. 216-218 (1955).
19. Bar Association Section, 10 Ark. L. Rev. 301-438 (1956).
20. He was a member of the McClellan Committee which was involved in investigating union racketeering.
21. Of course, the integrated bar never came to pass, and in fact, by secret ballot, the Bar Association repudiated its support for an integrated Bar in 1953. (Matthews, 10 Ark. L. Rev. 284-85.)
22. Proceedings, 11 Ark. L. Rev. 220-350 (1957).
23. 12 Ark. L. Rev. 260 (1958).
24. 13 Ark. L. Rev. 221-222 (1959).
25. *Id.* at 222.
26. *Id.* at 238-256 (1959).

27. Executive Committee Report, 13 ARK. L. REV. at 272 (1959).
28. *Id.* at 186
29. 14 ARK. L. REV. 251-52 (1960).
30. *Id.* at 262-263.
31. Executive Committee Report, 15 ARK. L. REV. at 232.
32. Arkansas Bar Foundation Report and the Bar Center Report, 15 ARK. L. REV. at 322-23 and 324-26 (1961), by Louis L. Ramsay, Jr., and J. E. Lightle, Jr., respectively. The other property was referred to as "the Revilo property" by the Foundation. The Foundation report states that the eventual plan is for a new Bar Center building. It is stated that this ties in with the plans of the city for a mall in that area. The Bar Center report itemizes the uses of the $300,000.00 that the Foundation sought to raise: $57,500 for the Rose property; $75,000 for the Revilo (or "Revelo") property; $10,000 for interest and carrying charges on loans; $7,500 for fund-raising expenses; and $150,000 for part of the cost of building construction.
33. 15 ARK. L. REV. 232-93 (1961).
34. 16 ARK. L. REV. 324-98, 318-22 (1962).
35. 17 ARK. L. REV. 321 (1963).
36. *Id.* at 332.
37. Report of Committee on Law School Expansion, *id.* at 331-334 (1963). The Chairman was Paul B. Young, and members were Thomas C. Trimble, Jr., James B. Sharp, Bruce Bullion and Heartsill Ragon. Advisory members were William J. Smith, Herschel Friday, Will Mitchell and Leon Catlett. The committee answered one opponent to the effect that its aim was not to move the Law School from Fayetteville to Little Rock.
38. *Id.* at 232-38.
39. This was Robert R. Wright. Continuing Legal Education Report, *id.* at 240 and Executive Committee Report, *id.* at 322.
40. 19 ARK. L. REV. 205-269 (1965).
41. 20 ARK. L. REV. 211-276 (1966).

42. 21 ARK. L. REV. 379 (1967).

43. *Id.* at 391.

44. *Id.* at 110-121, 360-392.

45. *Arkansas Lawyer*, v. I, no. 1, 3, 22-25, 27-29.

46. *Id.* at 5, 16.

47. 22 ARK. L. REV. 574-606 (1968).

48. *Id.* at 607.

49. Bar Ass'n Section, *id.* at 565-625.

50. 23 ARK. L. REV. 518 (1969).

51. *Id.* at 517-525.

52. *Id.* at 539.

53. *Id.* at 517-565— Bar Ass'n Section; debate, 536-555.

54. *Id.* at 526-535.

55. *Arkansas Lawyer*, June, 1970, p. 47.

56. *Arkansas Lawyer*, Sept. 1970, p. 98.

57. 24 ARK. L. REV. 391-398 (1970).

58. *Arkansas Lawyer*, May, 1972, p. 75.

59. 26 ARK. L. REV. 254 (1972).

60. *Arkansas Lawyer*, May, 1972, p. 119.

61. *Arkansas Lawyer*, Sept. 1972, p. 179.

62. *Ibid.*

63. 28 ARK. L. REV. 169 (1974).

64. *Arkansas Lawyer*, Oct. 1974, p. 159.

65. *Arkansas Lawyer*, Jan. 1975, p. 2.

66. *Id.* at 42.

67. 28 ARK. L. REV. 420 (1974).

68. 29 ARK. L. REV., number one (1975).

69. *Arkansas Lawyer*, July, 1976, pp. 90-93.

70. President's Report, *Arkansas Lawyer*, April 1976, p. 51.

71. *Id.* at 94-95.

72. President's Report, *Arkansas Lawyer*, Jan. 1977, p. 2.

73. *Arkansas Lawyer*, July, 1977, p. 122.

74. *Arkansas Lawyer*, Jan. 1978, p. 36.

75. *Arkansas Lawyer*, April, 1978, pp. 58-59.

76. *Arkansas Lawyer*, Oct. 1978, p. 54.

77. The legislature had previously appropriated $250,000 for the project in a bill sponsored by Senator Max Howell and Representative Bill Foster, and that figure was matched by the federal government. An additional $70,000 was pledged by the Arkansas Commemorative Commission and the Ben J. Altheimer Foundation.

78. *Arkansas Lawyer*, Oct. 1978, p. 192.

79. *Arkansas Lawyer*, Jan. 1979, p. 22-23.

80. *Id.* at 2.

81. *Arkansas Lawyer*, April, 1979, pp. 86-87.

82. *Arkansas Lawyer*, Oct. 1979, p. 138.

83. *Id.* at 188.

84. *Arkansas Lawyer*, Jan. 1980, p. 32.

85. *Id.* at 51.

86. *Id.* at 116.

87. See *Arkansas Lawyer*, Oct. 1975, p. 182.

88. *Arkansas Lawyer*, Oct. 1980, p. 213, contains a biographical sketch.

89. *Arkansas Lawyer*, July, 1980, pp. 126-127.

90. *Arkansas Lawyer*, Oct. 1980, p. 206.

91. *Id.* at 280.

92. *Arkansas Lawyer*, Jan. 1981, p. 41.

93. *Id.* at 2.

94. *Arkansas Lawyer*, April, 1981, p. 52.

95. *Arkansas Lawyer*, Jan. 1981, p. 43.

96. Executive Council Notes by Chris Barrier, *Arkansas Lawyer*, Oct. 1981, p. 146.

97. *Arkansas Lawyer*, Jan. 1982, pp. 2-3.

98. *Id.* at 14.

99. *Arkansas Lawyer*, Jan., 1983, p. 2.

100. *Id.* at 50.

101. *Arkansas Lawyer*, April, 1983, p. 65.

102. *Arkansas Lawyer*, Oct. 1983, pp. 2, 173.

103. *Id.* at 177.

104. *Id.* at 143.

105. *Arkansas Lawyer*, Jan. 1984, pp. 2-3, 37.

106. *Id.* at 47.

107. *Arkansas Lawyer*, April 1984, pp. 47, 61.

108. *Arkansas Lawyer*, Oct. 1984, p. 159.

109. *Arkansas Lawyer*, Jan. 1985, p. 3.

110. *Id.* at 51-52.

111. *Id.* at 52.

112. *Arkansas Lawyer*, Oct. 1985, p. 186.

113. *Id.* at 143.

114. *Arkansas Lawyer*, Jan. 1986, pp. 43-44.

115. *Arkansas Lawyer*, April, 1986, pp. 127-128.

116. *Arkansas Lawyer*, Oct. 1986, pp. 213-214.

117. *Id.* at 175.

118. *Arkansas Lawyer*, Jan. 1987, pp. 35-36.

119. *Id.* at 2.

120. *Arkansas Lawyer*, April, 1987, pp. 79-80.

121. *Arkansas Lawyer*, Oct. 1987, p. 163.

122. *Id.* at 122.

123. *Arkansas Lawyer*, Jan. 1988, pp. 43-44.

124. *Id.* at 2.

125. *Arkansas Lawyer*, April 1988, pp. 135-136.

126. *Id.* at 46.

127. President's Report, *Arkansas Lawyer*, July, 1988, p. 138.

128. *Arkansas Lawyer*, Oct. 1988, pp. 233-34.

129. *Arkansas Lawyer*, July, 1988, pp. 141-143.

130. President's Report, *Arkansas Lawyer*, Oct., 1988, p. 190.

131. President's Report, *Arkansas Lawyer*, April, 1989, p. 46.

132. *Id.* at 87-88.

133. President's Report, *Arkansas Lawyer*, July, 1989, p. 94.

134. *Arkansas Lawyer*, April, 1989, pp. 87-88.

135. Rodney E. Slater's career subsequently took a turn when President Clinton appointed him U.S. Secretary of Transportation.

136. *Arkansas Lawyer*, July, 1989, p.112

137. "Newsbulletin," p. 1, Nov./Dec., 1989.

138. "Newsbulletin," p. 1, Feb./March, 1990.

139. "Newsbulletin," p. 2-3, April/May, 1990.

140. *Id.* at 5, 6.

141. "Newsbulletin," p. 1, 2, July/Aug. 1990.

142. "Newsbulletin," p. 1, Sept./Oct. 1990.

143. "Newsbulletin," p. 1, Nov./Dec. 1990.

144. "Summary from the Hill," p. 4, supplement to "NewsBulletin."

145. "Newsbulletin," p. 1, March/April, 1991.

146. 1991 Annual Meeting News.

147. "Newsbulletin," pp. 1, 2, 5, July/Aug. 1991.

148. *Id.* at 1.

149. "Newsbulletin," p. 1, Oct./Nov. 1991.

150. *Id.* at 3.

151. "Newsbulletin," p. 2, Jan./Feb. 1992.

152. Annual Meeting News, pp. 1, 3.

153. "Newsbulletin," p. 4, Summer, 1992.

154. *Id.* at 1.

155. "Newsbulletin," p. 1, Fall, 1992.

156. *Id.* at 3.

157. "Newsbulletin," pp. 1, 6, Winter, 1993.

158. *Id.* at 4.

159. *Ibid.*

160. "Newsbulletin," p. 1, Spring, 1993

161. *Ibid*, Annual Meeting Supplement, p. 1.

162. "Newsbulletin," p. 1, Summer, 1993.

163. *Id.* at 6.

164. *Id.* at 2.

165. *Id.* at 3.
166. *Id.* at 7.
167. *Id.* at 8.
168. *Ibid.*
169. "Newsbulletin," p. 1, Fall, 1993.
170. "Newsbulletin," Joint Annual Meeting issue.
171. "Newsbulletin," Summer, 1994.
172. *Id.* at 6.
173. *Arkansas Lawyer*, Winter, 1995, pp. 20-21.
174. *Arkansas Lawyer*, Spring, 1995, p. 6.
175. *Ibid.*
176. "Newsbulletin," Summer, 1995, p. 1.
177. *Id.* at 6.
178. *Id.* at 7.
179. "Newsbulletin," Fall, 1995, p. 1.
180. *Id.* at 5.
181. *Id.* at 1, 2, 4.
182. "Newsbulletin," Spring, 1996, p. 1.
183. *Id.* at p. 2.
184. *Ibid.*
185. "Newsbulletin," Annual meeting edition as a part of the Spring bulletin, 1996. Most of the discussion of the accomplishments of women lawyers are contained in the separate chapter on that subject.
186. *Id.* at 1.
187. *Id.* at 2-3.
188. "Newsbulletin," Fall, 1996, p. 2.
189. *Arkansas Lawyer*, Spring, 1997, pp. 10-15.
190. "Newsletter," Winter 1997, p. 2. See, *Arkansas Lawyer*, Lawyer, Spring, 1997, p. 22-23, the article by William A. Martin, "Truth in Lawyer Advertising," for a more detailed discussion, complete with citations.
191. *Arkansas Lawyer*, Summer, 1997, p. 1.

192. *Id.* at 3.

193. *Arkansas Lawyer*, Fall, 1997, p. 3.

194. "Newsbulletin," Winter 1998, p. 1.

195. *Ibid.*

196. "Newsbulletin," Spring 1998, p. 1.

197. You cannot. You can only carry over a maximum of 12 hours of credit from one year to the next.

198. "Newsletter," 100th Annual Meeting, Spring 1998. The individual speakers and topics were so extensive that, like the Indians at the Custer massacre, we will not attempt to name them all.

199. *Arkansas Lawyer*, Summer 1998, p. 4.

200. *Id.* at 1.

201. A. de Toqueville, *Democracy in America* 139 (44 *Great Books* (1993)).

Chapter VI

LEGAL EDUCATION IN ARKANSAS

Early Legal Education in America

In the early days of the Republic, there was no system of legal education as we know it today. A system of apprenticeship combined with a formal examination, which might vary considerably as to its scope or depth, was the sought-after standard by leading lawyers at the time of our independence.[1] Although not compulsory outside of urban areas, apprenticeship was the common method of legal training in the late 18th Century. Outgrowths of law offices of successful practitioners occasionally resulted in private schools, the most famous of which was Litchfield in Connecticut, established in 1784. Litchfield grew out of the teaching activities of Tapping Reeve and under Reeve and James Gould, studies were offered based upon Blackstone as adapted to the new Republic.[2] One of its famous attendees was John C. Calhoun, for example, but although its students came from all of the former colonies, the apprenticeship method remained predominant.

Blackstone's *Commentaries*, particularly as annotated with American authority by St. George Tucker, and published in the United States in 1803, was a basis for study along with such treatises as *Coke on Littleton*. Such treatises formed the basis also for decisions by the judges who rode circuit and could carry few books with them in their saddlebags. Roscoe Pound has commented on the great effect that doctrinal writing had upon case decisions in the early years of our country.[3]

In terms of formal education in colleges, the first step was the inclusion in the faculty of a professor of law, who served in a manner similar to that of Blackstone's Vinerian professorship at Oxford. The most influential of the two chairs that were established was the one created at William and Mary due to the influence of Thomas Jefferson. It was held by his old teacher, Chancellor George Wythe. The other was the professorship of law at Columbia held by James Kent. Wythe, who was eventually succeeded by his former student, Henry St. George Tucker, was particularly influential. Some of his students included John Marshall, Spencer Roane, John J. Crittenden, and John Breckenridge, as well as Tucker.[4] Chancellor Kent's influence at Columbia was manifested more through his writings, the most important of which was his *Commentaries on American Law*, first published in 1826.[5]

A third short-lived professorship that should have had great promise was that established at the College of Philadelphia for James Wilson, who was then a Justice of the U. S. Supreme Court. After two years it died, apparently due to lack of students.[6]

In these early days, however, Litchfield was the closest thing to anything resembling a modern law school. Instruction was by lecture, but its course of study purported to cover the whole of the law as contained in 48 titles (many of which received cursory treatment). Nonetheless, it exercised great influence for its day with its students coming from all over the country. Two of its graduates became vice-president; three sat on the U. S. Supreme Court; thirty-four sat on the highest courts of their states; six served in the cabinet; two were foreign ministers; one hundred one were elected to the House of Representatives, and twenty-eight to the Senate; fourteen became governors and twenty became lieutenant governors of their states.[7]

Although other educational institutions such as Harvard and Yale followed the practice of creating professorships, these professors as well as Litchfield followed the practice of meeting the basic needs of the soon-to-be lawyer. Both were an expansion of the apprenticeship route, although without some of the onerous and "by rote" clerical duties of the law office apprentice.[8]

The beginning of the modern law school came in 1870 when new President Charles W. Eliot of Harvard appointed Christopher Columbus Langdell as Dean of the Harvard Law School. Langdell's practice in New York City had involved little trial work and had largely been an office and library practice involving preparation of opinions, briefs and pleadings. He was viewed as what we would refer to today as a scholarly genius. He believed that law was a science and that all of the available materials of that science were found in books.[9]

The law school that Langdell created at Harvard embodied components that remain today in every law school in the country. He installed the written examination system, and it not only became the central examination device in law schools but also became the way to determine admission to the Bar.[10] He believed in the in-depth study of the law, so that over a period of two decades the hours of instruction offered at Harvard roughly doubled, although the number of courses was reduced.[11] Langdell installed the case study method as opposed to reliance on the summary of treatises. This methodology had been used to some extent before, but Langdell relied not just on lectures, but also on a class discussion of successive court opinions designed to reveal the basics of the subject and also to involve the student in the process. Thus began the Socratic method of law study.[12] This new form of legal education obviously called for something else—a permanent, full-time faculty engaged primarily in teaching different areas of the law with relatively little or no involvement in active law practice.[13]

By the early 20th century, all leading American law schools had adapted to this model, and the basics of the modern law school had been established.

Early Legal Education Efforts in Arkansas

Early legal education in Arkansas was of the apprenticeship method in its entirety except for certain lawyers who had the benefit of some time at Litchfield or under a law lecturer at an Eastern college. Those were few in number.

The University of Arkansas Board of Trustees in 1886 received a special committee report that a law school would be desirable but would probably be impracticable at that time.[14] Prior to that time, however, there had been a Little Rock Law Class in existence since 1868 in which students received instruction from prominent local attorneys in a smaller, less prestigious context than what had been done at Litchfield.[15] This involved the lecture method.

Although it was proposed that this organization be affiliated with the University as its law school, an attempt was first made to establish a school in Fayetteville which was called the "Department of Law." This was created in 1890 with Frank M. Goar named as Dean. Goar and four others were designated as professors in specified areas of the law. The four professors were practicing attorneys in Fayetteville.[16] This was to be a two-year law course which would only last one year if the students could pass their examinations. Apparently, Dean Goar made a genuine effort to create a law school, but the practicing lawyers did not devote much energy to their lectures and met class irregularly. By 1891, the University catalog omitted all reference to the Law Department. There had only been seven students enrolled, and the two recommended by the law faculty to receive degrees were denied them by the University.[17]

Dean Goar then moved to Little Rock, reorganized the twenty students of the Little Rock Law Class, and it became the Law Department of the "Arkansas Industrial University" (as it was then called) in 1893. It was "to be operated and conducted on the same basis as the Medical Dept. of the University [with] no financial obligation to be incurred by the University Board in the conduct of said Law Dept."[18] The lack of financial commitment to legal education in Arkansas was thus manifested at an early date and has continued to the present although it has departed from the "no financial obligation" concept. As had been done in Fayetteville, Dean Goar recruited four leading Little Rock practitioners to join him as professors in different areas of law.[19] There were thirty-six students enrolled in 1893, and eleven graduated in 1894, nine of whom practiced successfully in Little Rock and two of whom achieved considerable financial success outside of Arkansas.[20]

Three new faculty members replaced three of the original faculty in 1897, one of whom was one of the first graduates, John H. Carmichael, who was later to become dean of the school.[21] The smooth operation of the school was affected by the sudden death in 1898 of Dean Goar, who had become a candidate for Attorney General against Jeff Davis (later three-time Governor). The stress of the campaign was apparently too much for Goar who died of apoplexy while campaigning at Huntsville.[22]

Carmichael had been serving as Acting Dean by appointment of Dean Goar, but the Board of Trustees decided to name Judge Mark Valentine of Little Rock as the permanent Dean. There was a complete turnover in faculty, and the Board declared the Department to be under its "supreme control" and "in immediate charge of the Dean, who is responsible to the Board."[23]

What had happened was that the Board had refused to follow the desires of alumni, students and faculty that Acting Dean Carmichael be appointed the permanent dean. As a result of the schism, Dean Carmichael and his faculty conducted classes elsewhere, and the Board appointees were left without any students. When that year ended, the Board threw in the towel and appointed John Fletcher, a prominent Little Rock attorney and member of the Carmichael faculty, as Dean and Carmichael as Assistant Dean. In less than a year, Fletcher resigned, and Carmichael was named Dean with the privilege of selecting his own faculty.[24] This situation continued for the rest of Carmichael's life, and the school became known to some as "Dean Carmichael's Law School."

This law school continued as a part of the University but operated essentially as an independent, autonomous unit without much contact with the central administration in Fayetteville and with no control exercised over it by the President or the Board. In 1910, the Board of Trustees appointed a committee to negotiate as to "taking over" the law school and moving it to Fayetteville under "the exclusive control of this Board."[25] Nothing was accomplished, and so in 1913, the Board ordered that all reference to the law school be deleted from the University catalog, and Dean Carmichael was to be directed to cease using the name "University of Arkansas" in that regard after the 1913-14 academic year. Students who would graduate in 1915 would, however, be able to receive their degrees from the University. An effort was made in 1915 to reconcile the conflict, but the conditions drawn up by President John C. Futrall in a meeting in the office of Governor George W. Hays, which included Board control over the law school, were rejected outright by Dean Carmichael in a rather petulant letter which cut off further negotiations.[26]

Neither side distinguished itself in the history of these events from 1893 to 1915. The seeds of ill feeling were sowed early on when the Board took charge of the Little Rock operation and sought to run it in an autocratic way with little or no regard for the people who were faculty, students or lawyers involved in the operation. On the other hand, few come across as dictatorial as Dean Carmichael, who wished to operate the Little Rock school without brooking any interference or accepting any advice from the University President in Fayetteville or the Board of Trustees. Having set sail on a separate course, Dean Carmichael's school was renamed the Arkansas Law School, and he presided over it until he died in 1950. At that time, William Nash of the Rose Law Firm became the dean.

It is of historical note that the struggle over legal education between Fayetteville and Little Rock did not have its genesis in the last thirty or so years—but over a century ago. We shall see, instead, how in at least the last few years the matter seems to have stabilized although some sources of discontent remain.

The University of Arkansas Law School in Fayetteville

The Board of Trustees had by no means given up on establishing a law school in Fayetteville. However, for nine years there was no University of Arkansas Law School. Julian Seesel Waterman was a young economics professor at the University who had studied law periodically at the University of Chicago and from which he had received the Juris Doctor degree in 1923. (It might be noted that unlike most other law schools which followed the English practice of awarding the LL.B. as the first degree in law, Chicago has always followed the civil law practice of awarding the J.D. All American law schools had changed to that practice by the 1970's.)

Waterman had been born in Pine Bluff in 1891, his father being a German emigrant who was the first permanent settler in the town of Dumas. He had received a B.A. from Tulane in 1912 and an M.A. from Michigan in economics in 1913. While he was still in law school in 1923, President Futrall asked him to study what would be required to create a sound law school in Fayetteville. He conferred with Dean James Parker Hall of Chicago on the subject and reported to Futrall the basic facts that are commonly known among legal educators today (but which also are sometimes to this day ignored or resisted by central administrators or faculty in undergraduate disciplines). His recommendations as to smaller teaching loads, higher salaries, a substantial law library, and higher administrative and academic standards gave Futrall pause, and he decided not to recommend establishment of a law school to begin in 1923-24.[27]

However, the plan was not abandoned, and Waterman, who was now head of the University economics department, was assigned the task of preparing for the establishment of a law school that was to be named the "law department." It was to be of sufficient quality to meet the requirements of the American Bar Association and the Association of American Law Schools. At least two years of undergraduate education would be required by 1925; there would be three years of law study required; at least 2500 books would be provided for the first year; and course offerings would be staggered with only first year courses being offered during the first year and with that expanding until three full years were offered. Waterman would be the head of the department and one other instructor would be hired.[28]

Futrall made a trip to Harvard and personally hired the second faculty member, a recent graduate of the Harvard Law School named Claude D. Pepper,[29] later to be United States Senator and United States Congressman from Florida and, in his later years, a national champion for the elderly.

Thirty-four students enrolled in the first class, of whom twenty were part-time. The entire operation, including the small library, was housed in the basement of Old Main. Ten students comprised the first graduating class in 1927, all of whom engaged in law practice in Arkansas, largely in the north or west.[30] The law school was approved by the American Bar Association in 1926 and became a member of the Association of American Law Schools in 1927. It increased in enrollment even during the early years of the Depression and maintained a steady enrollment until World War II when it diminished to very few.[31]

Its most distinguished professor, for whom the school is now named, Robert A. Leflar, joined the faculty in 1927 and taught there continuously until he reached the age of 70, with the exception of one year each at Harvard, as an S.J.D. candidate and recipient, and at Kansas and Missouri as a visiting professor.[32] After teaching at Vanderbilt and Oklahoma for a salary, he was permitted to return and teach for free. Because of his impact on the law school, this material will take up other aspects of his career in some detail subsequently in this chapter.

In Leflar's book on the history of the University of Arkansas, and in his article on *Legal Education in Arkansas* in 16 ARK. L. REV. 191 (1962), there is contained more extensive information about the early law faculty members in Fayetteville. Only certain of the faculty members will be mentioned here, including some of the early ones.

One of these was Edward Baylor Meriwether, otherwise known as Judge Meriwether (although no one was ever certain of what court he had ever presided over, unless perhaps a stint as a municipal judge in his native Alton, Illinois). Judge Meriwether came to the law school in 1930 and was a law graduate of both Washington University in St. Louis and the University of Chicago. A property teacher, he loved to say that the "law of property is historical in its origins, not logical," and then proceeded to conduct about the first three weeks of the course on the peculiarities of the feudal law in medieval England—a practice that mystified the students who had not contemplated a course in English medieval history. Nonetheless, the judge was a jovial, short, very rotund man who wore black suits and black ties in the winter and seersucker suits and black ties in the summer. While student views as to his professorial quality differed, he was remembered fondly by many who accepted his educational tendencies with equanimity.[33]

Judge Meriwether lived in a small house with his mother not far from the campus. However, he earned some substantial outside money in investments, particularly in the local Dr. Pepper company. Whenever a student was poised before the cold drink machines about to buy a coke and the judge approached, he usually came into a sudden urge for a Dr. Pepper. The judge had many expressions that he used to abundance. If a student attempted to distinguish the situation in a case to the judge's dissatisfaction, he might say, "Ah, but that is a horse of a different collar." Generous with the law students, the judge's gifts, loans and scholarships helped many a worthy, struggling student. He was an active member of the Arkansas Bar committee which drafted the 1949 Arkansas Probate Code. He retired in 1963.

J. William Fulbright taught in the law school as a part-time lecturer in constitutional law and equity, beginning in 1936. He was scheduled to begin full-time faculty work in 1939, but the death of President John C. Futrall in an automobile accident led to his being named President of the University instead.[34] He was subsequently fired as President by a Board of Trustees controlled by a Governor who was engaged in a political fight with Fulbright's mother, a Fayetteville newspaper publisher. This led him into politics and, somewhat later, to his candidacy and election to the United States Senate, defeating the same man who had him fired.

In the post-war years of the late 1940's, there was an influx of veterans who were older and more serious students. These years of the late 1940's and early 1950's were generally regarded as the golden years of law teaching by faculty of that vintage.[35] Those years, of necessity, brought with them the need to increase the holdings of the law library and the size of the faculty. New faculty who came in during the late 1940's or early 1950's included Edwin Eagle Dunaway of Little Rock, a graduate of the Columbia Law School who had been Prosecuting Attorney of Pulaski County and had served an appointed stint on the state Supreme Court; and Wylie Herman Davis, a graduate of Mercer Law School who had an LL.M. from Harvard, and who would later become Dean of the Law School. Another was Ralph Clayton Barnhart, a graduate of

Cincinnati, who would become Dean of the Law School prior to Wylie Davis and who would serve many years in that capacity. Dean Barnhart was instrumental in the formation of the Little Rock Division of the Law School, which will subsequently be discussed.

Dean Joe Covington succeeded Robert A. Leflar as Dean. He was a quiet, thoughtful man, originally from Delight, Arkansas, and the major course he taught was contracts. During his time at the University, he also became Provost and Acting President of the University. He later left to become Dean of the University of Missouri Law School at Columbia. After his service as Dean and while still on the Missouri faculty, he married his second wife, Ann Covington, who is at present Chief Justice of the Missouri Supreme Court.

Some of the better teachers at Fayetteville after the War were Arkansas natives. In addition to Leflar and Covington, Ray Trammell specialized in tax law and was University Counsel. David Newbern taught for several years and then became a Justice of the Arkansas Supreme Court. Jake Looney came in 1980 to head the new Agricultural Law program.

In the late 1950's, faculty expansion brought several people to the Fayetteville faculty who devoted most of their careers to teaching there, notably Albert M. Witte, Frederic K. Spies, Charles N. Carnes and, in 1965, Morton Gitelman. Charlie Carnes was rather quiet and introspective, with the result that there are few stories about him. On the other hand, there are so many stories about Spies and Witte that they could form the subject of an entire book.

Fred Spies was a short fellow who graduated from Dickinson Law School in Pennsylvania, held an LL.M. from N.Y.U., and was on the Dickinson faculty for several years before coming to Fayetteville. He was a ham radio operator and enjoyed spending an hour or so in the evening with his equipment. During the geophysical year in the 1960's he spoke to people all over the world, including such remote spots as Madagascar. Fred's scholarly interests were primarily in Law and Medicine and the Uniform Commercial Code. He particularly liked "L and M" and enjoyed taking his students to the Medical School in Little Rock to witness the dissection of a corpse. In 1976, Fred joined the law faculty in Little Rock where he remained until his untimely death from cancer a few years later.

Albert M. Witte grew up in Erie, Pennsylvania, the recipient of a Jesuit upbringing. After receiving a master's degree in English from the University of Chicago, he taught that subject for a time at Ripon College in Wisconsin. Eventually, he turned to law and received his degree from the University of Wisconsin Law School. He came to the University in 1957, and left only once for any period of time to teach at Emory. He returned after several years at Emory in the late 1960's. A superb classroom teacher, he taught also in visiting stints at Oklahoma, Baylor and for several years at UALR.

One of Witte's high points was becoming President of the Southwest Conference, a position which Leflar also held at one time. His highest point in that area, however, was his service as President of the National Collegiate Athletic Association. As an adviser on athletic rules and regulations to Athletic Director Frank Broyles, the University remained out of trouble with the NCAA on a consistent basis. Witte retired in 1995, and although he continues to teach occasionally, he relinquished his position as faculty adviser to the Athletic Department to Professor Howard Brill of the Law School.[36]

By 1970, the law faculty in Fayetteville consisted in part of the following persons (along with their student-given nicknames): Al Witte (the Big Al), Fred Spies (Freddy K.), Robert Wright (Rapid Robert), Morton Gitelman (Mort), Rafael Guzman (Ray Baby), Ray Trammell (Baby Ray), T. J. McDonough (Tee Jay or Uncle

Heavy), James Gallman (Booger Jim), Charles Carnes (Deputy Dawg), Robert A. Leflar (the Doc or Bobby Jack), Dean Ralph Barnhart and a few others. The student nicknames made it sound like either the Mafia or a collection of clowns. Students are that way.

Before bringing the Law School down to the present, I think it is appropriate to mention some of its graduates who distinguished themselves in academia. To start naming leading lawyers or politicians who graduated from the Law School would be an endless matter, since that has been true of the great majority of Arkansas lawyers or politicians, and if you combine the list with those from Little Rock, only a few law graduates from other law schools would remain.

In *The First 100 Years*, Leflar's centennial history of the University of Arkansas, he mentions two of these academic alumni on page 270: Joe E. Covington and Robert R. Wright.[37] As mentioned previously, Joe Covington had been on the law faculty and had served as Provost and as Acting President of the University. He served as Dean of the Law School from 1954 until 1958 when he accepted the deanship at the University of Missouri in Columbia. Robert R. Wright served on the Fayetteville faculty from 1963 to 1970 when he became Dean of the University of Oklahoma College of Law and Director of its Law Center. Leflar mentions Wright's book, *The Law of Airspace*. Before Wright left the faculty, he published the first edition of his casebook on land use. It is now co-edited by him and Distinguished Professor Morton Gitelman of the Fayetteville law faculty, and West Publishing Company has recently printed its fifth edition. Wright has also published the nutshell on land use for West, a book on eminent domain, two on probate, and edited the first and second editions of *The Arkansas Form Book*. He has been, since 1977, Donaghey Distinguished Professor of Law at the Law School in Little Rock.

Morris S. Arnold was serving as Dean and Professor at Indiana University School of Law in Bloomington at the time of his appointment as U. S. District Judge and has since become a judge of the U. S. Court of Appeals for the Eighth Circuit. He also served as Professor of Law and Vice-President of the University of Pennsylvania and held the Altheimer Distinguished Professorship at UALR. Judge Arnold is a prolific writer and scholar in the field of Arkansas legal history. Despite his judicial duties, his scholarly writing continues as time will permit. He is clearly one of the law school's most distinguished graduates.

Other graduates have achieved prominent status in academia, one of the most prominent being Dan Byron Dobbs of the University of Arizona College of Law. Professor Dobbs is a nationally recognized expert on the law of remedies and the law of torts and has produced major books in both areas of the law. He taught at North Carolina before going to Arizona. Professor William S. McAninch holds a chair or distinguished professorship at the University of South Carolina and has also written extensively. Professor Don Smith of Emory died several years ago, but not until after having achieved distinction in his field which prompted his appointment as head of the Federal Power Commission. Susan Webber, now Susan Webber Wright, was Professor of Law at UALR before becoming a U. S. District Judge and wrote extensively on oil and gas and land use law.

Another of the Law School's prolific scholars is Steve H. Nickles, formerly holder of the Roger Noreen chair in law at the University of Minnesota and currently the Bess and Walter Williams Distinguished Professor at Wake Forest University. Professor Nickles has written extensively on the Uniform Commercial Code, debtor-creditor law, and bankruptcy. He has a three-volume set with two co-authors on bankruptcy, a casebook on debtor-creditor with two others, and a book on common law and equity under the UCC with two others.[38]

Several graduates of UAF are faculty members at UALR. W. Dent Gitchel has written a book on the Arkansas law of evidence and is in charge of the trial advocacy curriculum. James W. Spears is another, as was U. S. District Attorney Paula Casey prior to assuming her present position. Former Dean William H. Bowen of UALR graduated from Fayetteville in the post-World War II years having become the Dean at UALR following a long and outstanding career in the practice of law and as the CEO and Chairman of the Board of the largest bank in Arkansas, First Commercial, and following a short stint as President of Health-Source.[39]

Law Deans in Fayetteville since Wylie Davis have been David Epstein, a distinguished professor and scholar at the University of Texas, who left to become Dean at Emory and then went with a large Atlanta law firm and recently accepted a chair at Alabama; J. W. (Jake) Looney, the founder of the agricultural law program which offers an LL.M. degree in that subject; Leonard Strickman, who formerly served in the same capacity at Northern Illinois; and Robert B. Moberly, the current Dean, who is a graduate of Wisconsin and came to Fayetteville in 1999 after serving as Professor and Director of the Institute for Dispute Resolution at the University of Florida. Under their leadership, the school has continued to prosper and at present it extends beyond Waterman Hall (which has been built onto several times) across the street to what was once a small woman's residence hall and later, a sorority house. The clinical program, once a salient feature in Little Rock, has been expanded greatly in Fayetteville as has the legal writing program under the leadership of former Dean Strickman.[40]

Morton Gitelman, a prolific scholar in the area of land use law and evidence, is co-editor of a casebook on land use with Robert R. Wright and served under Dean Strickman as Associate Dean. He holds the rank of Distinguished Professor. Robert T. Laurence, a prolific writer on the law of future interests, holds the Leflar Professorship, and John J. Watkins holds the Arkansas Bar Foundation Professorship. Phillip Norvell has served on the Arkansas Oil and Gas Commission and has published in that field of law. Robert B Leflar (—and that is "B" and not "A"—) has performed substantial work in law and medicine, and others also add quality to the current faculty.[41]

Robert A. Leflar

One cannot depart from a discussion of the University of Arkansas law School or a consideration of legal education in the state without a discussion of the enormous impact of Leflar on both. When he was forcibly retired in 1971 because of the University's mandatory retirement policy at age 70, numbers 1 and 2 of 25 Arkansas Law Review, pages 1-200, were devoted to him. Articles and short texts were written about him and different aspects of his life and contributions to the law by Chief Justice Warren Burger, Chief Justice Roger T. Traynor of California (retired), Professor Elliott E. Cheatham of Columbia and Vanderbilt, Professor Ralph Bischoff of N.Y.U., Dean and Professor Robert B. McKay of N.Y.U., President David W. Mullins of the University, Senator J. William Fulbright, American Bar President Edward L. Wright, Arkansas Bar President John C. Deacon, Justice George Rose Smith, New Hampshire Chief Justice Frank R. Kenison, Louisiana Supreme Court Justice Albert Tate, Jr., Associate Director Fannie J. Klein of the N.Y.U. Institute of Judicial Administration, Dean and Professor Robert R. Wright of Oklahoma, Joe C. Barrett, former Arkansas Bar President, Edgar E. Bethell, George E. Campbell, James R. Campbell and Richard B. McCulloch.

This outpouring was phenomenal and the articles illustrate his great achievements. Moreover, the authors could not anticipate that he would live for over a quarter-century after that and continue to contribute as a teacher, scholar, writer—and as the all-time Dean of the Arkansas Bar.

The law school in Fayetteville was begun by its first Dean Julian S. Waterman as noted earlier, and its building is quite properly named for him. But the school itself bears Leflar's name as it should. The law school was very much the product that he created, particularly from the 1940's following the death of Dean Waterman until his retirement. He became a national figure in legal education and in legal scholarship, particularly involving the law of conflict of laws and tort law. As the pre-eminent scholar in the law of conflict of laws, he was honored by a rare symposium conducted at the annual meeting of the Association of American Law Schools. It had only to do with his writings and his ideas.[42]

As long ago as 1968, in reviewing Leflar's newest edition of his book, *American Conflicts Law*, published the same year, Professor Albert A. Ehrenzweig of the University of California at Berkeley, himself one of the greatest of conflicts scholars, stated:

> Here a great judge and scholar, to my knowledge uniquely, has at the same time achieved both a first edition with a totally fresh approach and a new title, and a third edition building on the experience and growing perfection of two predecessors. In 1938, Leflar published his first text on the conflicts law of Arkansas. Not only did he thus decisively and definitively shape the law of his state. But everybody knew that the modest title concealed a national treatise which avoided the pretense and diffusiveness of other texts by concentrating on the complete analysis of the case law of one state. When in 1959 this book was followed by a Student Edition on THE CONFLICT OF LAWS, Leflar raised the curtain, quickly to occupy the stage with the leading scholars in the field.[43]

Indeed, Leflar's writings in the field of conflict of laws shaped not only the thinking of scholars but also the law of this nation. This is discussed in some depth in Wright, *Robert A. Leflar: A Tribute to a Professional*, 25 ARK. L. REV. 120, 132-138 (1971). (His views continued to influence the development of the law long after that was written.) As an Annotation in 29 A.L.R.3d 603, 631 (1970) stated: "Professor Robert A. Leflar has made a major contribution to American conflicts law in identifying 'five choice-influencing considerations which seem to incorporate all the basic considerations. . . .' "[44]

Leflar, the scholar, continued to be a prodigious writer until a few years before he died. However, by 1971, Richard B. McCulloch, the first Editor-in-Chief of the Arkansas Law Review (of which Leflar was founder), could identify 64 law review articles, 16 symposiums, 31 book reviews, five bar association addresses, and five books published by him.[45] That was before several of his books and a great many other articles were published.

As a public servant, in addition to his law school work, he served as President of the Constitutional Conventions that produced the proposed new Constitutions in 1980 and 1970, as Chairman of the Arkansas Constitutional Revision Commission in the late 1960's, as a Commissioner on Uniform State Laws, as Chairman of the Arkansas Statute Revision Commission, as a member of the regional War Labor Board during World War II, as Assistant Solicitor for the War Relocation Authority also during the war, and as a member of the Arkansas Commission on Criminal Law Reform during the 1930's.[46] He also was a pioneer as a teacher not only of law students, but of appellate judges. He was Director of the Appellate Judges Seminar at New York University from its inception in 1956, which operated under the Institute of Judicial Administration of that same institution. His students were state and federal appellate judges. His students included judges of the highest courts of 49 states, judges from all of the circuits of the U. S. Courts of Appeal, several justices of the U. S. Supreme Court, judges from England and Ireland, and appellate judges from the Supreme Court of Canada and the highest courts of Alberta, Nova Scotia, Ontario, Quebec, Saskatchewan and Puerto Rico. By 1971, more than three-quarters of the highest appellate court judges in the nation had attended these seminars.[47]

As a law teacher he excelled. At the 1965 Fall Legal Institute, he set out some salient points as to what a law school should be. About teaching, he said, "the first test of a law school's quality is the teaching that is done in it," but good law teachers are made, not born. They have to work at it, and they are also expected to demonstrate their scholarly abilities through periodic articles and research. But a law teacher's main job is teaching, and if he does not take it seriously, he ought not to be in teaching.[48]

Probably, during his lifetime, Robert A. Leflar taught at least one course to at least two-thirds, if not more, of the current Bar of Arkansas. No one ever exerted that kind of influence over the Bar of a single state, before or since, and no one will again.

The University of Arkansas at Little Rock Law School

After the University abandoned legal education in Little Rock and left it essentially in the hands of Dean Carmichael, the school continued to exist independently as an unaccredited institution. Its graduates were permitted to take the Arkansas bar examination but were ostracized in other states unless admitted on reciprocity. Nonetheless, the school produced a fairly substantial number of lawyers, most of whom practiced in Pulaski County or not very far away. After the death of Dean Carmichael in 1950, the Arkansas Law School as it was known continued to be operated by members of the Little Rock bar, particularly by several who were members of the Rose Firm. Like Dean Carmichael, who had carried on an extensive and successful law practice and was a leader in the Arkansas Bar Association, they were full-time practitioners. Thus, the Arkansas Law School had existed prior to 1965 much in the pattern of Litchfield, as opposed to the modern law school model originated at Harvard in the late 19th century. Because its teachers were practitioners, the classes were held in the evening.

For a number of years after Judge Carmichael's death, there had been expressions of interest by the Little Rock lawyers who taught there of having the University take over the Arkansas Law School. There was relatively little interest at first on the part of the University in doing this. However, outside forces affected the situation to some extent and perhaps to a greater extent than has ever been noted. This can be traced in the rise of Arkansas State from a two-year institution to a four-year institution, from a state teachers college to, at first, Arkansas State College and then Arkansas State University at Jonesboro. The energetic leader in its expansive role in these later years had been its president, Carl Reng. All of a sudden, Arkansas State was looked upon as a potential rival for leadership in higher education to the University of Arkansas.[49]

Whether there was ever anything to it of consequence is of little importance, but the idea began to develop that Arkansas State would like to gain a foothold in Little Rock and would relish the idea of having its own law school, particularly since the U of A Law School had long been a major force in producing the political, professional, social and economic leaders in the State. The Little Rock lawyers associated with the Arkansas Law School were growing restless, and the Arkansas State possibility was communicated to Dean Ralph C. Barnhart by one or more of them.[50]

For the University to take over the Arkansas Law School would be a major step, and it was not taken lightly. After considerable study by Dean Barnhart[51] and consultation by him with the Bar and also with many of the faculty, the faculty had a rare special meeting one evening at Fred Spies' house which was located up above Razorback Stadium. After some discussion, the motion to take over the Arkansas Law School was made by Robert Wright, seconded by Fred Spies, and the faculty voted without dissent to proceed accordingly when authorized to do so by the General Assembly. In March, 1965, the legislators passed the necessary legislation and provided that the operation had to be in place by August, 1965 for fall classes.[52]

There were many things to be done in an extremely short period of time. Not the least of these was to iron out the accreditation problems with the ABA Section of Legal Education and Admissions to the Bar, which was the federally recognized accrediting agency for law schools. They were quite helpful and acted in an advisory capacity with guidelines that they set down being carefully followed. Students at the Arkansas Law School were given some credit for coursework that they had previously taken. However, they did not receive credit for all of the hours accumulated at the unaccredited school. The entering class, some of whom had already taken some hours at the Arkansas Law School, started essentially anew. Sheffield Nelson, Robert Leslie, Buddy Raines, Art Givens and other well-known Arkansawyers were members of that first class.

Another major problem was obtaining a satisfactory facility. It had to be done in a short period of time, and it had to be a structure with a large enough space and sufficient support structure to house a modest library. The Pulaski County Law Library, which had been the library source for the Arkansas Law School, was to be transferred to this space in addition to books purchased by the University or sent down from Fayetteville.[53] The building eventually leased was named the Gay Building and was located at the corner of Third and Broadway in Little Rock. The space leased was over an automobile glass repair shop called Everett's Glass Shop. It had a flashing sign attached to the building on the Third

Street side and was visible to the law school's second floor offices and classrooms. Everett's motto was "Give us a break," and that could have been and should have been the motto of the Little Rock Division of the University of Arkansas Law School.[54]

The operation in Little Rock was intended merely to replace the unaccredited night law school that then existed with an accredited part-time program at night. In other words, the object was to achieve accreditation of the evening operation as a part of the University of Arkansas Law School. Initially, Robert R. Wright was sent from Fayetteville to serve locally as Assistant Dean, subject to Dean Barnhart, who would come weekly from Fayetteville to Little Rock to oversee the new operation. D. Fenton Adams, a member of the Dickinson Law School faculty, an established law school in Carlisle, Pennsylvania, was hired as Professor of Law, and Ruth H. Brunson, a clerk at the Arkansas Supreme Court, was hired as law librarian.[55] Along with some adjuncts, these were the initial law faculty in Little Rock.

This was in accord with what was "directed and authorized" by the 1965 General Assembly. This was intended to be an evening operation, and a small budget was approved for it for the 1965-67 biennium.[56] Accreditation was never a problem because the Little Rock Division was a part-time extension of Fayetteville and, theoretically at least, the faculty of both was the same. Students at both places received the same degree and wrote for the *Arkansas Law Review*.[57]

This did not play out as well in practice as it might seem, however. Robert R. Wright left after one year as Assistant Dean to pursue an S.J.D. degree, which he received in 1967, and then returned to Fayetteville according to his agreement with Dean Barnhart. That left Dean Barnhart as the only permanent link between Fayetteville and Little Rock. The Little Rock faculty grew gradually, but out of necessity, as its student body grew and its burdens increased. Most of the Little Rock faculty had never taught at Fayetteville and only mingled with the larger faculty when joint faculty meetings were held. There was some jealousy on the part of the Little Rock faculty of the Fayetteville faculty which was viewed as somewhat of an elitist and uncaring group with bet- ter facilities and probably better salaries (although the latter, at that time, was uncertain). The friction led to strained relations and some personality clashes. Moreover, the ABA was showing increased concern over part-time legal education, particularly that which existed outside of a university structure—and Little Rock was inside of a university structure more in form than in an interactive reality.[58]

Consideration of the possibility of establishing a full-time operation at the Little Rock Division, fueled by interest in the Bar and among civic leaders in Pulaski County, was aided by the fact that the University of Arkansas had acquired Little Rock University. It had become the University of Arkansas at Little Rock. This acquisition had seemingly slammed the door on any Arkansas State aggrandizement in Central Arkansas, a matter mentioned earlier. These two facts, however,—the Little Rock Division and UALR—were independent of each other when the question of a full-time as well as a part-time operation at Little Rock was under consideration beginning in the early 1970's. The University of Arkansas had other operations in Little Rock that were not affiliated with UALR, such as the Medical Sciences campus and the Graduate Institute of Technology, and so, it would not have been unusual for the Little Rock Division to continue as a full-time operation connected to Fayetteville.

In both the 1971 and 1973 sessions of the General Assembly, the question of a full-time law school in Little Rock arose. Opposition from the University and from Northwest Arkansas legislators deflected the proposal.[59] In October 1974, however, President Charles E. Bishop appointed a special committee to consider the feasibility of this move. The committee consisted of Dean Wylie

H. Davis of Fayetteville, U. S. District Judge G. Thomas Eisele of Little Rock, Herschel H. Friday, Jr., of Little Rock, Assistant Dean Glenn E. Pasvogel, Jr., of Little Rock, Dean Joshua M. Morse, III of Florida State University and formerly of Ole Miss, and Dean James P. White of Indiana University-Indianapolis, the ABA Consultant on Legal Education. The committee recommended that a separate, accredited law school be created to be part of the University of Arkansas at Little Rock with full-time and part-time divisions to be housed ultimately in a building to be built on the UALR campus.[60]

Four years earlier, Dean Page Keeton of the University of Texas Law School, a legend in legal education, who ultimately served for almost thirty years as Dean at Texas and Oklahoma, had written in a consultation report for the combined law schools that it "is . . . clear to me that the University of Arkansas should maintain and operate a law school with a day division at Little Rock, and that this should and would become in the long run the major legal education program."[61] He did not recommend discontinuance of the law school in Fayetteville. However, the report was alarming to the Fayetteville faculty, who perceived or speculated that this would lead to a unification of the two divisions in Little Rock. The report of the special committee appointed by President Bishop led to the same fear. This fear that the two law schools would be unified in Little Rock has persisted to this day in Fayetteville and exists even as you read this.

These recommendations as to the UALR Law School came to fruition in the General Assembly of 1975 with the endorsement of the President and Board of Trustees of the University. However, the bill initially prepared was met with skepticism and criticism by supporters of the Little Rock operation who believed the initial proposal to be no more than a ploy. Emotions were running high. Several Arkansas Bar leaders, including Henry Woods, Edward Lester, and Herschel Friday of Little Rock, James B. Sharp of

Brinkley, Louis L. Ramsay of Pine Bluff, John C. Deacon of Jonesboro, and Oscar Fendler of Blytheville had conceived a plan to provide financing for a building to house the Little Rock Division, including the Pulaski County Law Library and the law school's collection, and to provide classroom and office space.[62] All of this was to be in the Arkansas Bar Center, which would also house the Arkansas Bar Association and Bar Foundation.

In accord with this plan, Senator Max Howell of Pulaski County and Representative William F. Foster, Sr., of Lonoke County introduced identical bills in the 1975 legislative session which would create both full and part-time operations in Little Rock and transfer control over the Little Rock division to UALR.[63] These bills encountered strong opposition from the University of Arkansas and the Northwest Arkansas legislators. But under the direction of their sponsors the common bill passed both houses within eight days of introduction and was signed into law by Governor David H. Pryor as Act 19, 1975 *Ark. Acts* 43-A to 46-A on February 3, 1975. Former Dean Lawrence H. Averill, Jr., describes the final decision of the Governor as follows:

> The story that concerns the day of reckoning for this legislation is infamous. With University of Arkansas President Charles E. Bishop, and five or more trustees and others on one side, and Senator Max Howell on the other, the Governor asked for their opinions. The legislative branch prevailed. . . .[64]

Of course, there was more at stake than an issue involving the law schools as far as the University President and Trustees were concerned. UALR, at that time, was a fledgling institution with a small graduate program offering degrees at the master's level. The desire in Northwest Arkansas, and among the Trustees, was to keep it that way. In that way, it served as a buffer against other institutions in Central Arkansas while not interfering with the development of the main campus in Fayetteville. The addition of a law school to UALR was an expansive move of much significance to UALR and a step in the wrong direction in the viewpoint of the University administration and the Trustees. As might be expected, UALR officials, such as Chancellor Robert Ross, had to remain largely noncommittal and out of sight during the encounter. The situation also stirred narrower emotions among those concerned only with legal education. Dean Wylie H. Davis, Distinguished Professor Robert A. Leflar, and the Fayetteville faculty in general were very much opposed to what transpired, and the prevalent fear was that this was the first step toward combining the two law schools in Little Rock.

With this as background, the Little Rock Division became the University of Arkansas at Little Rock School of Law and occupied its new facilities in the Arkansas Bar Center on West Markham Street in the Fall of 1975. David R. Hendrick, Jr., a professor on the law faculty, was appointed as Acting Dean and a Dean's Search was begun for a permanent Dean. During his administrative year, Dean Hendrick recruited Susan Webber, who was serving as law clerk to Judge J. Smith Henley of the U. S. Court of Appeals for the Eighth Circuit, to serve the following year as Assistant Dean and Assistant Professor, and he agreed with Dean Robert R. Wright of the University of Oklahoma to come as Visiting Distinguished Professor in 1976-77. Robert K. Walsh, an administrator and faculty member at Villanova University Law School, was ultimately selected as the new Dean.

Although under separate units of the University System and under separate Deans, the two law schools were still subject to the same governing board—the U of A Board of Trustees. However, the accreditation that was enjoyed by the Little Rock Division was no longer in effect because the ABA viewed the Little Rock operation as a new law school. After some ambivalence over the situation, the ABA decided to continue the part-time program as accredited as it had previously been, but to consider accreditation of the full-time day operation separately. The full-time day program began in the fall of 1976 and received provisional accreditation in June 1977, subject to the Law School renovating and occupying as additional space the Old Federal Building at Center and Second Streets, which was accomplished. In 1978, full ABA accreditation was accorded.[65]

The Association of American Law Schools (AALS) is not a federally recognized accrediting agency, but it is a venerable organization of which every law school of any quality aspires to be a member. The AALS took the position that Little Rock was no longer a member and would have to reapply. At the AALS annual meeting on January 3, 1979, the UALR Law School became the 135th member of the AALS.[66]

The building situation is one of several that plagued the law school in Little Rock and was not solved on anything approaching a permanent basis until its move into its present facilities during the summer of 1992. The Gay Building (consistently referred to as "Third and Broadway" by the early law school administration) was never anything more than a temporary stop-gap. The Arkansas Bar Center, although much better and having an attractive library with a two story atrium, was not well thought-out in terms of its usefulness as a law school. The library, for example, was designed to hold only the number of volumes required at the time by the ABA and AALS and expansion was not taken into account. Office space was inadequate for a faculty of adequate size serving both a full-time and part-time operation. Its major attributes were that it put the law school in direct contact with the state and local bar associations, and the building had a lovely view of the Arkansas River looking north from the back offices and classrooms on the sixth and seventh floors. A major handicap to students and faculty alike was the parking problem, and it was not alleviated by the Old Federal Building addition and continued until the new building was occupied.

The Old Federal Building acquisition was essential for accreditation purposes and AALS membership. There was so much enthusiastic energy expended over it that its occupancy was somewhat misleading. It was renovated for a little over $500,000 by a local architecture firm headed by Charles Witsell that specializes in restoring old buildings. It was a fascinating old building that, because of the furor that gunboats had caused on the Arkansas River during the Brooks-Baxter War, had very thick walls on the side that faced north toward the river. (At least that is legend—whether true or not.) It had been the federal courts and post office building in Little Rock until the mid-1930's. Dean Robert K. Walsh presided over a major ceremony befitting the dedication of a brand-new building with the principal speaker being Justice Byron White of the U. S. Supreme Court.[67] The fact that this was only a temporary answer to the facilities problem was lost on all but a few professionals, including Millard Ruud, the Executive Director of the AALS, who attended the event.[68]

During the administration of Dean Lawrence H. Averill, Jr., who succeeded Dean Walsh after the latter had returned to private practice with the Friday law firm, plans were begun for a permanent structure, designed as a law school, to replace these facilities in the heart of downtown. There were three basic locations under consideration—the UALR main campus, the property in Cammack Village donated to the University by the late Kate B. Cammack and which had to be used within a period of years or lost under a Chancery Court decree, and a building originally constructed in the 1930's by the WPA that was occupied by the U of A Graduate Institute of Technology and other offices and was originally constructed for the Medical School. The University Board of Trustees, guided by President Ray Thornton, chose to renovate the latter location and to build a President's home on the Cammack property (a location which had been favored by many of the faculty).[69] The financing for the multi-million dollar renovation of the building at 1201 McAlmont came from some funds provided by the State with the support of Governor Bill Clinton plus a bond issue.

The old building on McAlmont, adjoining MacArthur Park, was completely gutted except for the walls and supporting structures. A large library addition and a large courtroom, later dedicated in honor of Herschel H. Friday, Jr., and called the Friday Courtroom, were additions to the existing structure. The architects, Wittenberg, Delony and Davidson of Little Rock, did an excellent job in combining the old with the new, so that even the new brick was indistinguishable from the old. Having been designed originally as a classroom building for the medical school, it was not difficult to redesign it for a law school. The result was a very fine building with extensive parking and fully adequate for the indefinite future.

Between the time of the planning process, the building construction and the move into the building, Dean Averill resigned as the dean and accepted a position as chief of staff to Chief Justice William Rehnquist of the United States Supreme Court. He was replaced by Dean Howard B. Eisenberg, who had been a professor and director of the legal clinic at Southern Illinois. Dean Eisenberg and Library Director Lynn Foster supervised the move into the new building, although he resigned after serving for only three years to become Dean of the Marquette University Law School in Milwaukee.

During the latter part of Dean Eisenberg's service, he became increasingly disenchanted with the breach of promises made to him by the UALR administration when he originally decided to accept the position. These promises were almost entirely unfulfilled because UALR's flawed accounting system eventually was shown to have suffered a loss of some seven million dollars (and perhaps more) under the chancellorship of James E. Young, who had hired Dean Eisenberg. The necessary result under new Chancellor Charles Hathaway was a period of austerity and retrenchment in which the law school suffered equally with other units, even though it was eventually reported in the *Arkansas Democrat-Gazette* that the law school had been the lender of some $700,000 to UALR during that period—a loan unknown to the law school, but which had apparently helped keep UALR afloat. Salaries were frozen during that period and law school salaries, already low, plummeted in comparison to those of other law schools, including Fayetteville. That remains essentially the same today with the result that UALR law school faculty salaries are among the worst in the United States, although better than the law schools in Puerto Rico, something which is hardly a fact for celebration.

The overreaching by UALR into law school funds and its treatment of the law school as a "cash cow" partly because of the special legislative appropriation intended for enrichment of legal education in Arkansas, a fund which is shared by the two law schools equally, caused enormous friction in recent years between the law school and the campus administration. The result was that Dean Eisenberg, before leaving, entered into an agreement with the campus administration under which the law school would receive all of its funds from all sources and would pay UALR for overhead. Unfortunately, the overhead figure was fixed at about 24% of its total funding, whereas about 15% is the usual figure in American universities, with the result that the law school remained in the hole, continuing to lose ground in faculty salaries and staff support. A 1996 report of an ABA inspection team strongly criticized this situation. Adjustments have recently been made.

Dean Eisenberg was replaced for a fixed two-year term by Dean William H. Bowen, whose background was not in academics but in banking and the practice of law. He was a former President, CEO and Chairman of the Board of First Commercial Bank and had engineered the merger of First National Bank and Commercial National Bank in Little Rock some years before. Prior to that, he had been a partner in Smith, Williams, Friday & Bowen, the predecessor law firm to Friday, Eldredge & Clark. Moreover, he had served in many public service capacities with the state and local chambers of commerce and various civic and eleemosynary organizations. He was clearly one of the top business and professional leaders in Arkansas. It was thought that he could add to the fund-raising start initiated by Dean Eisenberg, who had raised around a million dollars in private funds in connection with the new building. It was also hoped that he could straighten out the law school's financial mess. He was ably assisted by Associate Dean Charles W. Goldner, Jr., who managed matters internally, and succeeded Dean Rodney Smith on July 1, 2000.

A highlight for the law school in the spring of 2000 was the renaming of it the UALR William H. Bowen School of Law, in honor of its former Dean and kind benefactor. President Clinton was the featured speaker for his former Chief of Staff as Governor when Clinton was running for President.

The history of the law school in Little Rock from its genesis in 1965 through the 1990's, except for the construction of the present physical facilities and the addition of faculty to provide for the full-time program during the late 1970's and early 1980's, was one of consistent undersupport. The operation had been a bare bones program in which, because of the necessity for duplication in the full-time and part-time programs, the curriculum largely consisted of either required courses or very basic courses common to all law schools. Electives were mostly core courses, many of which were subjects covered on the bar examination and were taken by most law students. Some degree of enrichment came through the Altheimer lectures in which prominent judges, lawyers and academicians of national notoriety were brought in to deliver a paper, visit with the students and faculty, and perhaps teach a course or two.

Moreover, the law school in Little Rock became aggressive in its intercollegiate participation in appellate advocacy and other such programs, particularly under Professor Dent Gitchel, and enjoyed a substantial degree of success and hosted some of these events. The fact that despite its budgetary inadequacies, the law school had a substantial degree of success educationally was illustrated by the fact that its graduates, with few exceptions, have consistently performed better on the Arkansas bar examination than either Fayetteville or out-of-state law school graduates ever since it became a separate institution.

Much of this success was due to the quality of the faculty. Arthur G. Murphey, Jr., the Arkansas Bar Foundation Professor, and James W. Spears were with the faculty for thirty years or more. Kenneth Gould and Glenn Pasvogel served on the faculty from the early 1970's. Fenton Adams, who recently retired, served on the faculty for between twenty and twenty-five years (with a six year sojourn at Ole Miss in between stints) and twice served as Acting Dean. Robert R. Wright accumulated over twenty years on the faculty, after serving on the Fayetteville faculty during the 1960's and as Dean and Professor at Oklahoma during 1970-76 as well as visiting on occasion at Iowa and Cincinnati. Robert K. Walsh, mentioned earlier and currently the Dean at Wake Forest, was a long-time faculty member and was instrumental in the development of the law school. Lawrence H. Averill, Jr., his successor, aside from planning the new law school, is a nationally recognized scholar in probate law, and he and Wright are Academic Fellows of the American College of Trusts and Estates Counsel, in addition to being fellows of the American Law Institute. Judge Morris S. (Buzz) Arnold of the U. S. Court of Appeals for the Eighth Circuit was Altheimer Distinguished Professor for several years and also served, before his first judicial appointment, as Dean and Professor at Indiana and, before coming to UALR, as Vice-President and Professor of Law at the University of Pennsylvania.

Professor Fred Peel, who was Altheimer Distinguished Professor subsequent to Professor Arnold, was an outstanding tax expert who was nationally recognized for his work on consolidated tax returns. John R. Pagan left the faculty in 1994 for a position as Director of an international graduate study program at New York University Law School and then became Dean of the University of Richmond Law School. M. Eugene Mullins has published books on drafting legislation and for administrative law judges. Lynn Foster is nationally recognized for her work in law librarianship, having succeeded to her position after the retirement of Ruth H. Brunson, the founder and original developer of the law library. In the 1997-98 academic year, Lynn Foster left her library position to become Associate Dean and was replaced by Michael Beaird, Acting Law Library Director at St. John's and former Law Library Director at the University of Mississippi. There are many other promising younger faculty who are already making their mark through law review publications and in other ways, such as Scott Stafford, Philip Oliver, Andrew McClurg, John DiPippa, Sarah Jenkins, Tom Sullivan and Terri Beiner, to name only a few.

Although it is difficult for an understaffed, underfinanced law faculty to be productive from a scholarly standpoint, many of the faculty have distinguished themselves through law review writing. Additionally, Wright's casebook on land use with Morton Gitelman of the Fayetteville faculty is now in its fifth edition, and his nutshell publication is in its third edition, both of which are published by West. Averill's nutshell on the uniform probate code also has undergone three editions with West. Peel's book on consolidated tax returns has been mentioned, and he and Professor Philip Oliver have completed another recently published book on tax policy. Glenn Pasvogel and Robert Wright have written a number of books for the Arkansas Bar, including Pasvogel's system on debtor-creditor law and two editions of the two-volume *Arkansas Form Book* by Wright. Former faculty member Buzz Arnold has been a prodigious scholar in connection with early Arkansas history and has published two books on that subject with another under way.

Student publications receive note through the University of Arkansas at Little Rock Law Journal,[70] and many faculty publish in it also, although many faculty publish in outside law reviews, including some considered to be national law journals.

In public service, both Professors Scott Stafford and Dent Gitchel served terms as special assistants to the Governor and Professor Stafford has previously served on the Public Service Commission. He too is a steady scholar who has published extensively. Professor Averill has served the Bar as an advisor on its Uniform Probate Code Special Committee and has served in capacities nationally with ACTEC and ALI. Professor Wright has served as a member and Chair of the Little Rock Planning Commission and as an officer and Chair of the American Bar Association General Practice, Solo and Small Firm Section, as well as on the Arkansas Bar Executive Council, its House of Delegates, and as its Delegate to the ABA. Others have served in various public service capacities.

A recent Dean of the University of Arkansas at Little Rock School of Law was Rodney K. Smith, a veteran dean who previously served in that capacity at both Capital University in Columbus, Ohio, and at the University of Montana. He had also taught at three other law schools. He was a graduate of the Brigham Young University Law School and held an LL.M. and S.J.D. from the University of Pennsylvania. He had written numerous law review articles, and although his first book was *Sports Law* in 1986, his preoccupying interest was probably manifested by his second one in 1987, *Public Prayer and the Constitution: A Case Study in Constitutional Interpretation*. He was a first amendment scholar, and one of his first actions as Donaghey Dean was to bring some outstanding constitutional scholars to the campus to present a symposium dealing with freedom of religion primarily as it was affected by the recent Supreme Court decision in *Flores v. City of Boerne*. Unfortunately, Dean Smith resigned effective June 1, 2000 to accept an endowed "chair in excellence" at the University of Memphis. He was succeeded by Associate Dean Charles W. Goldner, Jr., a law graduate of the University of Oklahoma and with an LL.M. from Georgetown.

Dean Smith was very active since coming to Arkansas in the summer of 1997 in getting acquainted with the members of the Bar, the alumni and business leaders. He also elevated the fundraising efforts. In his first year, he instituted plans for a second publication in addition to the Law Journal that will deal with appellate practice and procedure. He had plans for an Arkansas Law Institute that would provide research and law reform assistance to the legislature and to state government in general. He placed great emphasis on faculty scholarly activities, writing and research, as well as public service. The relationship of the law school with the Altheimer Foundation, which began restoration under Dean Bowen, has been restored. The Altheimer distinguished professorship and the Altheimer lectures by distinguished scholars and judges have returned. The financial relationship with the central administration has been corrected in large measure. *Hearsay*, the alumni publication, has taken on a new look and new quality. During 1997-98, Dean Smith's first term in office, the law school hired a new Director of the Law Library; three new staff to work in arbitration or mediation have been added to Gerry Glynn's increasingly high quality Legal Clinic; a new full-time writing and research Instructor has been added; and the school is looking for another half-time writing Instructor who will also edit the new appellate publication. Other new positions are being filled.

As a new Dean, Smith came to UALR with high recommendations from his former colleagues. Aside from his energy, vigor, ideas and intellectual qualities, they were speaking of collegiality.

"You will like him" is the simplest way to put it. They were correct and the law school wishes him well in his new position.

Ralph C. Barnhart

I close this history of the UALR School of Law much as it began with the Evening Division of the University of Arkansas. (Of course, if the long history of the Arkansas Law School is included, it would go back much beyond 1965.)

It is safe to say that there would be no University of Arkansas Law School in Little Rock, connected with UALR, were it not for Ralph C. Barnhart. Although the Dean at Fayetteville, Ralph recognized the essential connection that the University of Arkansas must have with the rest of the state. The largest collection of the legal profession by far was located outside of Northwest Arkansas. He knew that the University must serve the entire state and the entire profession. His first outreach to the statewide Bar was in 1963 with the appointment of a Director of Continuing Legal Education (half-time) and an Assistant Professor of Law (half-time) to the faculty. It was essential that the CLE Director conduct programs in other parts of Arkansas, outside of Fayetteville, in order that the Law School would be of service to all of the lawyers. Every program could not be at Fayetteville or Little Rock. There had to be outreach to the other sections of Arkansas. That was how the CLE program developed; in addition to the Fall Legal Institute, there would be regional programs. Sometimes, the same "traveling road show" would be conducted in as many as five or six regional locations.

With the Arkansas Law School eager to close, it was only logical to Dean Barnhart that its evening operation should be taken over by the University of Arkansas. There had been a part-time night program in Little Rock for decades, and without the University's intervention, it was certain that it would be replaced in some way, perhaps by some other institution. Leaders in the Arkansas Bar thought it only appropriate that the University (which was the alma mater of most of them) take over the operation. Ralph Barnhart had developed a close relationship with bar leaders during his deanship, and he agreed. There was some faculty opposition, but in the end the faculty realized that this had to be done. Probably to some, it was a purely defensive measure. But to Ralph Barnhart, it was an assertion of the University's role as the sole accredited provider of legal education in Arkansas and was an obligation that the University had to perform as a service to the people and to the legal profession.

Ralph Barnhart did many other worthy things during his career. He was a progressive educator who tried to keep abreast of developments in legal education and implement them, as best he could, within a limited budget. In his writings, he was an advocate of constitutional reform among other things. He sought to improve and to build.

Most of all, however, he will be remembered for his leading role in the establishment of the Law School. His painting hanging in the Deans' Gallery is the first and foremost.

The Future of Legal Education in Arkansas

The question of whether Arkansas should support two law schools continues to provide an unsettling climate for stable legal education in the State. Oddly enough, when people argue about duplication in legal education, no one ever mentions the eight or nine state-supported colleges of education in the State, even though that form of education is generally acknowledged as the least academically challenging of all forms of educational endeavor. Law, on the other hand, was described by Martin Mayer in *The Lawyers* as the best of all forms of education (and Mayer was not a lawyer).

If Arkansas would support a law school the way that it should be supported to achieve national or regional prominence, then a case could be made for having only one law school no matter where it was located. That argument, suggesting the possibility of combining the faculties, libraries and facilities, for the purpose of achieving something of high quality other than one of the Razorback teams or the Razorback program, has been made. However, it is an unrealistic assumption that anyone would want to achieve that objective. The General Assembly would not view it that way—it would view the elimination of one of the two law schools as simply a way of saving money. By that same line of thought, if all state institutions were closed except for about five which were strategically and regionally located, a great deal of money could be saved from the expenditure on higher education. Would the survivors be benefited from such savings by an infusion of most of the funds that had been recaptured? It is at least somewhat questionable.

The fact of the matter is that, as this chapter has shown, for over a hundred years the battle between having legal education exclusively in Fayetteville or in Little Rock has continued, only broken by periods of relative calm in between times of siege. It is time to put an end to a foolish battle which has no basis in achieving excellence at either law school or in any precise location. Such quality as either achieves has been and will continue to be the product of individual effort and initiative operating within a minimal financial framework.

It is a matter of history, perhaps unfortunate although not unfair in the process that was followed, that the University of Arkansas was located in such a remote, although scenically beautiful, part of the State. This is probably the major reason why there has been such a proliferation of educational institutions throughout the balance of the State. The location of the University was not unfair in that Washington County, in a bidding process provided for by the legislature, offered one of the two highest and best bids.[71] The result, however, was that many people in Eastern, Southern and Central Arkansas sought other alternatives. The pursuit of a legal education did not differ in that respect.

It seems clear now that legal education must exist both in the rapidly growing Northwest Arkansas area and in the State's only metropolitan area in Central Arkansas. The demand exists in both places. The main campus of the University should have a law school as should the people in that most rapidly growing part of Arkansas. The law school in Fayetteville is available to anyone in Arkansas who wishes to go there and is particularly important to those in its immediate area, including portions of Missouri, Oklahoma and Kansas. About forty-five percent of the Arkansas Bar Association practices law in Pulaski County alone, and Little Rock is readily accessible to Eastern and Southern Arkansas as well as to Central Arkansas. The need for a law school there to serve the people of those areas is readily apparent and finds its support not only in demographics but in history. Moreover, every State bordering Arkansas has two or more law schools, whether public or private. Arkansas has the advantage of having both of its schools under the control of a single governing board and thus subject to a common policy and controlled goals and objectives.

Some benefit can come from two law schools if there is more interaction between the two than there has been in the past. Perhaps even greater coordination of effort could be achieved by appointment of a Chancellor for Law, who would be the overall coordinator and director for both, and by putting both on a separate, independent budget, subject to the President and Board of Trustees, as in the case of Medical Sciences. This has been done on other campuses and is a possible arrangement of some benefit for Arkansas.[72]

Whether that structure takes shape or the current structure remains, the time has come to end the cloud that looms over both law schools every time the legislature meets. The time has come to recognize that both schools serve a purpose and have a place to fill. History has demonstrated that fact.

Notes

1. R. Stevens, *Law School* 3 (1983).
2. *Ibid.*
3. 3 R. Pound, *Jurisprudence* 387-388, 428-429 (1959). Pound wrote: "Doctrinal writing has been a much more active and important formulating agency in Anglo-American law than our theory leads us to admit. Coke formulated the medieval law authoritatively for the classical era, the seventeenth to the nineteenth century. Nor did doctrinal writing stop. On the contrary, it gained in importance in the nineteenth century. While in form our law is chiefly the work of judges, in great part judges simply put the guinea stamp of state's authority upon propositions which they found worked out for them in advance." *Id.* at 387.
4. J. Hurst, *The Growth of American Law* 257 (1950).
5. *Ibid.* In 1830, Chancellor Kent published the fourth and final volume of his *Commentaries*. These were based on his lectures at Columbia. According to Hurst, this "immediately became the standard general treatise on law in the United States . . . ."
6. *Id.* at 258.
7. *Id.* at 259.
8. *Id.* at 260.
9. *Id.* at 261-262. Hurst quotes Langdell from his preface to his *Selection of Cases on the Law of Contracts* (1871): "Law, considered as a science, consists of certain principles or doctrines. To have such a mastery of these as to be able to apply them with constant facility and certainty to the evertangled skein of human affairs, is what constitutes a true lawyer; and hence to acquire that mastery should be the business of every earnest student of law."

10. *Id.* at 263.

11. *Ibid.*

12. *Id.* at 261-266, particularly at 264. "Langdell's contribution was to translate the idea into the prevailing method of a whole law curriculum." See also, B. Schwartz, *The Law in America* 146-147. "The Langdell innovations transformed legal education. . . . Langdell had established the first modern law school, which set the pattern for legal education for the better part of a century. By 1910, the case method had become dominant throughout the country."

13. Schwartz, *supra* n. 12, at 147: In 1873, Langdell hired another full-time faculty member, James Barr Ames, who succeeded him some years later as Dean. "His appointment inaugurated the career of the scholar-teacher who devoted his professional life to law teaching."

14. R. Leflar, *The First One Hundred Years* 257 (1972). See also, Leflar, *Legal Education in Arkansas: A Brief History of the Law School*, 16 ARK. L. REV. 191, 195 (1962).

15. *Ibid.* Leflar, *supra*, 16 ARK. L. REV. at 195. A newspaper article in 1886 from the *Arkansas Gazette* stated that the Little Rock Law Class had organized with W. A. Webber as President, E. C. Johnson as Vice-President, Joe Loeb as Secretary-Treasurer, and Johnson, A. C. Carden and F. M. Hyatt as the Executive Committee. It said: "Prof. Noon, who has recently taken charge of the Arkansas University, was present and with hearty encouragement pledged the efforts to that institution to further and perpetuate the success of the class. This class has a faculty composed of some of the most eminent and accomplished members of the Arkansas bar. . . ." University records, however, do not disclose who "Prof. Noon" was. *Ibid.*

16. *Ibid.* The four Fayetteville lawyers, all of whom were given professorial rank, were Judge L. Gregg, B. R. Davidson, R. J.

Wilson and J. V. Walker. See also, R. Leflar, *The First One Hundred Years, supra* n. 14, at 258.

17. R. Leflar, *supra* n. 14, at 258. The two students recommended for graduation were William Theophilus Stanford and Michael K. Duty. Although denied graduation, they were listed as alumni in later lists of the Little Rock School's annual catalog. Leflar, *supra*, 16 ARK. L. REV. at 196, fn. 20.

18. R. Leflar, *supra* n. 14, at 258-259.

19. These were George B. Rose (often mentioned in the chapter on the organized bar), Thomas B. Martin, Wilbur F. Hill, and Morris M. Cohn. Leflar, *supra*, 16 ARK. L. REV. at 196-197, and R. Leflar, *supra* n. 14, at 259.

20. R. Leflar, *supra* n. 14, at 259. The graduates of 1894 were John H. Carmichael (later to be Dean, a power in the Arkansas Bar, a judge, and a successful practitioner), DeEmmet Bradshaw, J. Fairfax Loughborough, Sam W. Reyburn, Lawrence C. Maloney, W. H. Andereck, Lewis Rhoton, W. Sprigg Brown, John D. Shackleford and John W. Black. (Bradshaw and Reyburn were the two who achieved financial success in other states.)

21. *Ibid.* The other two were John Fletcher and J. C. Marshall.

22. *Ibid.*

23. *Id.* at 256-60. This lay the groundwork for the ultimate schism between Carmichael and the Board and between legal education in Little Rock and Fayetteville.

24. *Id.* at 260.

25. *Id.* at 260-61.

26. *Id.* at 261. Futrall's statement of conditions were not unusual either then or now for a law school that forms part of a university: The faculty was to be appointed by the Board subject to the recommendations of the President and Dean with salaries fixed by the University. The entrance requirements were prescribed by the University, and graduation had to include two full years in law school [now three]. At least part of the teaching would be in the day. Law

246 A HISTORY AND REMINISCENCES OF THE BAR OF ARKANSAS

funds would be handled by the University Treasurer, and tuition and fees would be set by the Board. Carmichael's reaction was to write a strong letter suggesting that deserving young men would be deprived of a legal education as a result of the proposal and stated that there was "no further use nor necessity of an attempt on the part of either of us to consolidate the law school as it now exists with the University of Arkansas." One can only conclude that he wanted it to be the Carmichael Law School, under his total command, whether it was part of the University of Arkansas or not. The conclusion also appears inescapable that, although he apparently was a very capable man and able lawyer, he did not know much about how legal education had developed in the United States over the previous forty years. He still related to the Litchfield model. President Futrall, an educator although not a lawyer, apparently had kept up with the developments. Futrall was perhaps the University's greatest president and was certainly one of its finest.

However, as indicated in the text, the Board had helped to fuel the fire through its own heavy-handed tactics also. There was enough fault to go around.

27. All of this is discussed in greater depth in R. Leflar, *supra* n. 14 at 263. Futrall did not abandon the idea of establishing a law school in Fayetteville but simply decided "to hold the thing over until next year, thus giving time to study [it] thoroughly." *Id.* at 264.

28. *Id.* at 264.

29. Pepper only taught one year at Fayetteville. Two new teachers were added: W. Ney Evans, a recent Harvard law graduate who had practiced briefly in Missouri and Judge William Armistead Falconer, a University of Virginia law graduate who had been serving as a chancellor in Fort Smith. Evans left after two years to join the law faculty at the University of North Carolina. Falconer was also a scholar of the classics who had published nationally and

who died at age 58 in his third year of teaching. Before he died, a fourth faculty member, John S. Strahorn, Jr., was added. He taught at Arkansas for four years before leaving for a distinguished career at the University of Maryland Law School where he taught until his death. R. Leflar, *supra* n. 14 at 265, fn. 7-9.

30. The first graduating class of 1927 were W. E. Beloate, Jr., O. R. Bridgeforth, Ben Henley, Jack Holt, I. W. Howard, Joe McCoy, W. B. Owens, John T. Parker, Tom Pearson, and Donald Poe. *Id.* at 265.

31. *Id.* at 265-66. It had highs of 124 students in 1934 and 1935 and was over 100 from 1933 to 1940.

32. *Id.* at 266.

33. *Id.* at 266-67. Only a part of this comes from Leflar. The balance comes from my own recollection, as did part of what Leflar wrote.

34. *Id.* at 267.

35. The post-war years were years of growth in many ways. From 1929 to 1933, the *Law School Bulletin* was published. It was a forerunner of the *Arkansas Law Review* and consisted of three issues per year of about twenty pages each. Discontinued briefly during the Depression, it resumed in 1936 and was again discontinued during the war in 1942. It resumed in 1946 but was permanently replaced in 1947 by the *Arkansas Law Review and Bar Association Journal* (later to be known only as the *Arkansas Law Review*). Its first student editorial board consisted of young men who would become excellent lawyers and leaders in the Bar. The first editor-in-chief was Richard B. McCulloch, Jr., of Forrest City, and his Board included Richard K. Burke, Jr., Sam Laser, Claude B. Brown, Herschel Friday, Paul B. Young, William S. Arnold, William A. Eckert, Robert L. Jones, Ed Lester, John Mann, Omer C. Burnside, William H. Enfield and Ed Penick. Its financing was underwritten by the Arkansas Bar Association, and it was disseminated without charge to the Bar members. A more complete dis-

cussion is contained in R. Leflar, *supra* n. 14 at 268-269 and in Leflar, *supra*, 16 ARK. L. REV. at 204-206.

36. These brief descriptions of faculty members in the 1950's, 1960's or beyond are taken from recollections of them. Interesting stories about them will not appear in this chapter but in a later chapter of reminiscences about them and others and also of other lawyers about other members of the Bar.

37. *Id.* at 270.

38. All of the foregoing material is from personal knowledge.

39. *Ibid.*

40. *Ibid.*

41. *Ibid.*

42. *Ibid.*

43. A. Ehrenzweig, *Comparative Conflicts Law*, 16 AM. J. COM. LAW 615, 616 (1968).

44. Annot., *Torts—Lex Loci Delicti*, 29 A.L.R.3d 603, 631 (1970). See also, Coyne, *Contracts, Conflicts, and Choice-Influencing Considerations*, 1969 U. ILL. L. F. 323 (1969), and Juenger, *Choice of Law in Interstate Torts*, 118 U. PA. L. REV. 202 (1969). Leflar's contributions in conflict of laws situations most influenced the tort aspects of conflicts but were useful also in contract situations. The tort aspects have presented the most difficult problems in conflicts.

45. McCulloch, *The Founder of the Arkansas Law Review*, 25 ARK. L. REV. 154, 155-159 (1971).

46. Barrett, *Vignette of Robert A. Leflar*, 25 ARK. L. REV. 143, 145-46 (1971). The author was Joe C. Barrett of Jonesboro, one of the great men of the Arkansas Bar, who among other things, served as Arkansas Bar President and as President of the National Conference of Commissioners on Uniform State Laws.

47. Kenison, *The Continuing Contribution of Robert A. Leflar to the Judicial Education of Appellate Judges*, 25 ARK. L. REV. 95, 96-97 (1971). Frank R. Kenison was Chief Justice of the Supreme Court

of New Hampshire and was one of many good friends of Bob Le-flar among the state and federal appellate judiciary.

48. Leflar, *Legal Education: The Making of a Good Law School*, 29 ARK. L. REV. 50-60 (1966). His views are summarized in fifteen basic points in Wright, *Robert A. Leflar: A Tribute to a Professional*, 25 ARK. L. REV. 120, 131-32 (1971).

49. Once again, this is based on the recollection of the author. There are no documents to support the attitudes of the faculty and administration of the University of Arkansas. The rise of Arkansas State into a four year institution with graduate offerings and degrees is well-known.

50. This view was communicated to the faculty by Dean Barnhart, and it was predicated in large measure on his discussion of the situation with prominent lawyers and Bar leaders in Little Rock. He became convinced that something was going to happen to the Arkansas Law School whether the University took it over or not; and that if by default, the University passed up the opportunity, then Arkansas State was a likely suitor. There were other possibilities, of course. He believed that the University of Arkansas should be in charge of legal education in Arkansas. It was that simple.

51. Dean Barnhart went about the matter carefully and cautiously. He had numerous conversations with the Consultant to the American Bar Association Section of Legal Education and Admissions to the Bar (which is the federally designated accreditation agency for law schools).

52. Act 525, Sec. 10, 1965 *Ark. Acts* 1889, 1905.

53. The Pulaski County Law Library had a volume count of less than 30,000 volumes. Averill, *A Short History of the School of Law at UALR*, 8 UALR L. J. 619, 620 (1986). This was to form the library core for the school. However, some unneeded duplications of the Fayetteville library were shipped down, and, in addition, some important new purchases were made, particularly law reviews. These were purchased during the year at a cut-rate price from

Hein and Company, a purveyor largely of reprints and used books. The law reviews were bound in the orient, possibly Taiwan, and came in bright colors—green, yellow, orange, red, blue, purple—looking much like a child's Easter eggs.

54. Obviously, much of this is from memory.

55. See Averill, *supra* n. 53 at 620.

56. *Ibid.*

57. *Id.* at 621. This was not as simple as it may sound. The *Law Review* people in Little Rock sometimes felt that they were treated like second-class citizens, and the same grew in subsequent years to be true of the faculty.

58. *Ibid.* This is discussed here in a slightly different way, however, than in the Averill article.

59. *Id.* at 621. Dean Averill points out that efforts were made in the 1971 and 1973 sessions of the General Assembly to establish a full-time law school in Little Rock. These efforts were not supported by the University and were ardently opposed by Northwest Arkansas legislators. The old Fayetteville-Little Rock battle over legal education had once again surfaced.

60. *Id.* at 633.

61. *Id.* at 622, fn. 5. Prior to that time, Dean Page Keeton had stated the following in an address on legal education at the Law School in Fayetteville (Fall Legal Institute): ". . . I believe the correct policy was followed in the State of Arkansas when the Bar and the University of Arkansas worked together in bringing about the establishment of an evening division of this law school at Little Rock, because under existing circumstances and as long as evening schools are approved there will be a school of some kind in existence in a city the size and importance of Little Rock. *But an evening division cannot be operated as effectively as day divisions for a number of reasons.*" [Emphasis added.] He then went on to explain the reasons for this statement. He clearly intimated then, several years before his advisory report, that a full-time day division should

be in operation in Little Rock. See Keeton, *Legal Education: Developments, Objectives and Needs*, 20 ARK. L. REV. 31, 35 (1966).

62. *Id.* at 623.

63. *Ibid.* S.B. 187 by Senator Howell and H.B. 325 by Representative Foster.

64. *Id.* at 623-24.

65. *Id.* at 625.

66. *Ibid.*

67. *Id.* at 626-27.

68. *Ibid.* The late Millard Ruud, a commercial law professor who served at one time as the Consultant to the ABA Section of Legal Education and for many years as Executive Director of the Association of American Law Schools, said to the author as we were crossing West Markham Street for the dedication of the Old Federal Building: "I hope that they don't think that this is the final solution."

69. *Id.* at 630-32. This is discussed at greater length by Dean Averill in his article. Of course, he was intimately involved in the planning process and was instrumental in bringing the project to fruition.

70. In 1978, shortly after the UALR Law School became a full-time operation, the *Law Journal* was established. Although only two issues per year were published initially, there were three issues in 1981 and by 1982, it began publishing four issues per year. In 1983, the Arkansas Bar Association began subsidizing the *Journal*, as it did the *Arkansas Law Review* by paying for subscriptions for each of its members. The *Journal*, in its twenty year history, has published many outstanding articles from distinguished academicians, judges and lawyers. The first editors of the *Law Journal* were Stephen Jones and Diane Mackey. See Averill, *supra* n. 53 at 629. Jones was Editor-in-Chief and Mackey was Executive Editor. Andree Roaf was Articles Editor; Cynthia Dodge, Notes Editor; Victra Fewell, Research Editor; and William Feland, Sur-

vey/Comments Editor. Associate Editors were Catherine Anderson, Don Dodson, Dub Elrod, Kathy Woodward Goss, Keith N. Johnson, Edward O. Moody, Anne E. Owings, James W. Richardson, Anne Tucker Raney, Margaret Osborn Keet, and Susan A. Newberry. There were nine other staff members and thirteen apprentices. The Faculty Publications Committee consisted of David R. Hendrick, Jr., Chairman; Glenn E. Pasvogel, Jr.; James W. Spears; Frederic K. Spies; Susan Webber; and Claibourne W. Patty, Jr.

71. Governor Powell Clayton, a Republican governor during Reconstruction, who had come to Arkansas as an officer of a Union regiment from Kansas during the war, persuaded the legislature to pass an act establishing a state university in the spring of 1871. This was based on the Morrill Act passed by Congress in 1862 that provided for establishment of land grant universities in the United States. J. Fletcher, *Arkansas* 265 (1947). The Arkansas statute allowed counties and towns interested in acquiring the university to hold elections on local proposals on the first Monday in August. Bids would be presented to the new Board of Trustees when it met in Little Rock in September. The only serious efforts to obtain the university came from Little Rock, Batesville, and Fayetteville-Prairie Grove. A spirited effort was launched for both Pulaski County, which proposed a $150,000 bond issue, and Little Rock, which proposed a $50,000 bond issue. Public debate was vigorous, with opponents pointing out the poor financial condition of both the county and the state. They favored common schools being provided for ahead of a university; they also feared bond sharks; and they mistrusted the Board of Trustees, all of whom were Republicans. The distrust by ex-Confederate Democrats of the ruling Reconstruction Republicans was rampant. The county bond issue failed 756 to 78 and the city bond issue failed 222 to 46. R. Leflar, *The First One Hundred Years* 6-7 (1972).

Batesville, however, was a genuine contender. A county bond issue of $100,000 failed by 590 to 428, but a $40,000 bond issue plus gifts of land by the City of Batesville passed by a vote of 90 to 0.

In Washington County, the county proposed a $100,000 bond issue; Fayetteville proposed a $30,000 bond issue which included some land donations; and Prairie Grove and Viney Grove $23,265 consisting of land and $7,350 of promissory notes. Unlike in Little Rock, the Unionist-Republicans and the Confederate-Democrats had made peace, and the effort was headed by ex-Union Colonel Lafayette Gregg, a State Supreme Court Justice, and David Walker, a former and subsequent State Supreme Court Justice, who had supported and worked for the Confederacy. Despite, this, the county bond issue passed by only eighty votes—400 to 320. The Fayetteville proposal had only two negative votes. *Id.* at 7-8.

The Board's committee visited Batesville in late September and was impressed. The citizens wanted the university and understood what a good university should be. To go to Fayetteville, the committee returned to Little Rock, went by rail to Morrilton (which was then the end of the line), continued by steamboat to Van Buren on the Arkansas River, then took a stagecoach to Fayetteville. On the return trip, they went by stagecoach to either Springfield or Neosho, Missouri, then by rail to St. Louis, and then back to Little Rock by rail. *Id.* at 8-9. The experience of the trip alone should have done in the Washington County/Fayetteville proposal, and in fact, inaccessibility was the main argument against the location. However, they were impressed with the sites and the enthusiasm of the citizens and apparently were wined and dined extensively. When the trustees voted, Trustees Cohn and P. H. Young, both of Little Rock, proposed and supported Batesville, but they were in the minority, and on a subsequent motion by Trustee Bennett of Helena, Washington County was selected unanimously. *Id.* at 9. Travel conditions have improved tremendously since that time, but

254 A HISTORY AND REMINISCENCES OF THE BAR OF ARKANSAS

the location problem remains the same. It still takes over five hours to go to Fayetteville from Texarkana or Helena by car and longer than that from other locations.

72. Louisiana State University's Law Center is on a separate budget and has its own Chancellor—an idea that they adopted from a plan developed for the University of Oklahoma Law Center, which in the 1970's was placed on a separate budget headed by a Dean of the College of Law and Director of the Law Center. Oklahoma has since retreated substantially from the Law Center concept (which it developed with the help of Dean Erwin Griswold of the Harvard Law School). The LSU adaptation remains intact. Under Dean Howard Eisenberg, the UALR School of Law was placed on a separate budget under which it receives all of its income and is responsible for all of its expenses. This plan continued to develop under Dean Rodney K. Smith and Dean Charles W. Goldner. However, the basis of the Law Center concept is that at the core is a Law School or College of Law and that law-related activities ancillary to the basic mission of educating law students are under the umbrella of the Law Center—so that the whole of the profession is administered to through that instrumentality. It is much the same concept that has long been applied to university medical centers which may include colleges of nursing, dentistry, pharmacy, and other health related activities.

Chapter VII

AFRICAN-AMERICAN LAWYERS

According to a scholar who bases his opinion on a letter from prominent Arkansas historian John L. Ferguson, the first black lawyer admitted to practice in Arkansas was probably Thomas P. Johnson in about 1866.[1] Another much older source from 1898 states that T. P. Johnson "is the oldest colored lawyer in the city [of Little Rock] having been in the practice since about 1870."[2] The latter reference refers to Johnson as having "served as a soldier in the 'late unpleasantness'"[and having "marched up from the battle field through blood to the bar of justice. . . ."[3] This refers to his service in the Union army. Johnson was born a slave in either North Carolina or Kentucky, depending upon whether you apply the records of the state constitutional convention of 1868 or the 1870 census. In addition to serving in the 1868 convention, he held office as a justice of the peace and practiced law.[4]

About the same time, William H. Gray, a legislator from Phillips County, was elected to the 1868 Arkansas Constitutional Convention and in that same year seconded the nomination of Ulysses S. Grant for President at the Republican Convention.[5] Supreme Court records reveal that Gray was admitted to the Bar of Arkansas on April 6, 1869.[6] Gray was an ardent defender of the voting rights of black citizens and made an eloquent plea on that subject at the 1868 state Constitutional Convention.[7] At a convention of freedmen in Charleston, South Carolina, in 1871, Gray met Mifflin W. Gibbs. Gray was serving at the time as state commissioner of immigration and lands, and he encouraged Gibbs to settle in Arkansas, stating that the state had "golden prospects and fraternal amenities."[8]

It is clear that the best known and most accomplished black lawyer and most powerful black political leader during and after

Reconstruction was Mifflin Wistar Gibbs, who was born in Philadelphia in 1823, the son of Jonathan C. Gibbs, "a Methodist minister and member of the city's elite black society."[9] Gibbs began working at twelve in the home of Sidney George Fisher, a prominent attorney. He later worked in the construction business as a carpenter and a building contractor. He became active in the abolitionist movement in the 1840's and met Frederick Douglass.[10] He went to California in 1850 as a part of the Gold Rush and worked as a carpenter until the white workers went on strike to protest his presence. He joined a protest by California blacks in 1851 over their denial of voting rights under the new state Constitution and in 1855 founded the first black newspaper in the state, published in San Francisco. Gibbs left for British Columbia in 1858 to prospect for gold and remained there for almost ten years involving himself in mining and railroad ventures. He was twice elected to the Victoria City Council.[11]

Gibbs returned to the United States, attended the Law Department of Oberlin College in Ohio, and graduated in 1870. About the same time, his younger brother, Jonathan, was elected Lt. Governor of Florida, according to one source.[12] (However, another source only mentions that Jonathan was appointed Florida Secretary of State in 1868, unsuccessfully sought a congressional seat in the same year, and was appointed Florida Superintendent of Education in 1873.)[13] In any event, Mifflin Gibbs settled in Little Rock and studied for admission to the Bar in the offices of a white law firm, Benjamin and Barnes. After he passed the Bar, he was appointed County Attorney of Pulaski County.[14] In 1872, he formed a partnership with a prominent black attorney and Republican leader, Lloyd G. Wheeler.[15] Drawn into Republican politics, in 1873, he was elected municipal judge and is said to have been the first black man in the United States to have been elected to such a position.[16] It was not an easy victory. Gibbs had to defeat four other candidates, including a former mayor, to receive the party nomination. The general election was bitterly fought, and his opponent was the incumbent, John S. Triplett, who was strongly backed by the *Arkansas Gazette*. Nonetheless, Gibbs won by 1,001 to 948.[17] Gibbs was defeated for re-election two years later and never again sought political office.[18] One or two years later, he was appointed by President Rutherford B. Hayes registrar of the U. S. Land Office at Little Rock, and he held that position until 1885.[19]

Gibbs' rapid rise was due to his active involvement in Republican politics shortly after coming to Arkansas. He was "the chief black political lieutenant of Governor Powell Clayton."[20] (Clayton was first Governor, and then Senator, and was the leader of the "regular" Republicans.) Gibbs' activity in Republican politics continued even after Reconstruction and the restoration of the power structure to the Democrats. From 1876 to 1904 he was a delegate to every Republican national convention except the one in 1888. He served as secretary of the Arkansas Republican Central Committee from 1887 to 1897. It is said: "For four decades, he was involved in virtually every black political, social, and economic endeavor in Little Rock, and he took a prominent part in the resistance to the state's streetcar segregation act of 1891."[21] Yet he is said to have maintained good relations with the white business community and owned shares in local enterprises including the electric company.[22] His reputation nationally and his political involvement led President William McKinley to appoint him the U.S. Consul at Madagascar in 1897, and he served until 1901.[23] He founded the second black-owned bank in Arkansas in 1903, the Capital City Savings Bank of which he was the president. However, in 1908, the bank went bankrupt due to poor management and numerous lawsuits followed including one in which his personal estate of over $100,000 was seized by the court. He eventually settled the case for $28,000 and remained a wealthy man the rest of his life.[24]

Although Gibbs remained a nominal Republican all of his life, he became disenchanted with the party in the late 19th and early 20th century and even supported Democrat William Jennings Bryan in the 1908 presidential election. Long prior to that, originating perhaps with President Rutherford B. Hayes, the party became convinced that it would not be safe politically until it broke the Democratic control on the South. The key to that, it was thought, was to build a predominantly white party in the South that was entirely white in leadership.[25] Gibbs continued to be favored with appointments even after that, and apparently performed well, but in 1908, the nomination of William Howard Taft set him off. Taft had been Secretary of War in 1906 when blacks were harshly dealt with in the Brownsville, Texas, riot.[26] His endorsement of Bryan led to his being severely attacked by the *Washington Bee*, a nationally prominent black newspaper.[27] However, he remained politically independent for the rest of his life although nominally still a Republican.

His political career tends to obscure his professional and other public interests. He embraced human rights causes even as a young man, starting with the abolitionist movement while he lived in Philadelphia. His interest continued in guarding against forces of racial oppression in California and in Canada.[28] In Little Rock, in 1873, Wheeler and Gibbs successfully represented four influential blacks in filing charges against a barkeeper who refused to serve them. The barkeeper was fined $46.80. In 1883, he called for labor laws that would protect the rights of black tenant farmers. That same year, there was a riot in Howard County in which both blacks and whites were killed. A large number of blacks were arrested and charged, and eventually three were sentenced to hang. Gibbs and other black leaders sought to save them, and he contended that they had only been defending themselves. After raising defense funds, some prominent white lawyers were employed. Eventually the sentences of two of the men were reduced although one of them was hanged.[29] None of this did anything to change his view of the legal system, however, and he believed on into the 20th century that it was unjust to blacks, particularly in criminal matters involving whites and in its racially discriminatory statutes.

In this, he did not confine his views or his efforts to Arkansas. He attended a substantial number of national conventions and protest meetings outside of Arkansas. He also supported the exodus of blacks from the South to Kansas in 1879 partly because they might obtain land on the frontier. He believed that as long as blacks did not own land, they would remain economically enslaved in the manner of medieval serfs. When appointed head of the Little Rock branch of the federal land office in 1877, he advertised in black newspapers seeking blacks to settle in certain counties where there was available federal land. He urged blacks from other former slave states to come to Arkansas and buy land. He had a great deal of confidence in the idea that if a black achieved financial security through landholding or success in business, then he also achieved political and physical independence and security. This was natural because it was in keeping with his own experience. He was already rather wealthy when he came to Little Rock. Wheeler and Gibbs was the pre-eminent black law firm in Little Rock and had a successful practice. The firm also advertised as a real estate agency. Gibbs, in fact, purchased considerable residential real estate and acquired some farm land through payment of past due taxes.[30] His major business failure, as mentioned earlier, was in the failure of his bank in 1908. Even that venture appeared successful until the day the bank collapsed.[31]

In the community, he was much involved in his support of black education. He frequently donated to the library of the M. W. Gibbs School, a public high school. He also donated land and money to create the M. W. Gibbs Old Ladies Home, a rest home for poor elderly women.[32]

After being in declining health for some months, Mifflin Gibbs died on July 11, 1915, at the age of 92, and was buried in the Fraternal Cemetery on Barber Street in Little Rock. A well-educated man, who spoke in flowery English, a product of his extensive reading of the classics and possibly of his long association with the Canadians, he may be said to have been the black equivalent of U. M. Rose. Certainly, like U. M. Rose, he was a greater leader of his time.[33]

Not as much is known about Gibbs' black contemporaries in the Bar until the arrival on the scene of Scipio A. Jones. However, the following will be some brief comments on at least some of them.

In the book by Gaines, cited at the beginning of this chapter, he names several and has nothing but praise for all of them. Apparently, all of them practiced law in Little Rock. He refers to C. T. Lindsay as "among the shining legal lights in this state" with no one enjoying "a fuller confidence of all the people." It is common to hear his name used "in connection with that of such eminent [white] lawyers as Murphy, Rose and Vaughan." As for L. J. Brown, his "scholarship coupled with his legal attainments places him in the front rank of the state's most proficient men." J. A. Robinson, a "young and able lawyer" admitted to the Bar on June 15, 1893, in argument "has all the persuasive powers of a genius which frequently wins for him the victory in a hard legal contest." N. H. Nichols "is honest, cool courageous and deliberate" and such "personal attributes combined with his great store of knowledge make him one of the best prepared young men the writer has had the pleasure to meet." He also extols the virtues of S. A. Jones, about whom more will be written later.[34]

One of the early black lawyers in Arkansas was Wathal G. Wynn who settled in Lake Village in 1871. He had graduated from law school at Howard University and was admitted in the District of Columbia. Also, on March 9, 1871, he was admitted to the Circuit Court in Richmond, Virginia, becoming Virginia's first black lawyer. Why he shortly thereafter left Virginia and that area to move so far west is unclear, but on September 25, 1871, he was admitted to practice in Arkansas and thereby became the first black lawyer in the nation to be licensed to practice law in three jurisdictions.[35]

Wynn had not been in Chicot County very long before a referendum was proposed to "subscribe" $100,000 to each of two railroads that served the area. This was a divisive issue because what it involved was to tax the people to provide support for these railroads. In December 1871, Wynn was visiting a store belonging to a white man named Curtis Garrett and got into a heated argument with John M. Sanders over the issue. A fight followed, and with a third white man named Jasper Duggan blocking the door to keep Wynn from escaping, Sanders killed Wynn with a knife. As the details became known, anger erupted among the black citizens of the county. The county judge, James W. Mason, was a black person who had been educated in Paris, France. After a hearing, Judge Mason had the three white men placed in the county jail. Despite this prompt action, the black citizens rioted, demanded to see Lawyer Wynn's body, and the judge permitted the body to be viewed. That probably was like gasoline on a fire because many white people left the county, fearing for their lives. A mob gathered at the jail to demand that the prisoners be released to them. The sheriff placed a guard of about fifty men around the jail, but in an ensuing struggle, the mob obtained the keys, took the prisoners out and "shot them dead."[36]

Soon after that event, Abram W. Shadd, a former classmate of Wynn's at Howard, came to Chicot County to practice law and was admitted to the Bar on March 25, 1872. Shadd also had a law practice across the river in Greenville, Mississippi, and presumably was admitted in both states.[37]

Two other notable black attorneys of that period were C. A. Otley who was elected city attorney at Helena, and George Napier Perkins who was both elected to the city council in Little Rock and to a delegate's position for the Constitutional Convention of 1874.[38] Lloyd G. Wheeler has been mentioned as being the law partner of Mifflin Gibbs. Wheeler had originally been admitted to the Bar in Illinois in 1869. Richard A. Dawson was admitted also in Illinois in 1870, and practiced law in Pine Bluff.

Although less is known about Wheeler than about Gibbs, Wheeler was also quite successful. In 1871, he was elected by the Quorum Court in Pulaski County to serve as county attorney at a salary of $1,000 a year, which obviously was good pay for a part-time job at that time. He also had matters before the U.S. Circuit Court in 1871. He served as an elector for Ulysses S. Grant in 1872. It is thought that his income probably equalled those of most of the white lawyers at the time.[39]

Despite their apparent success, these black lawyers were considered something of a threat to their customs and way of life by the white people. Both Wheeler and Dawson were constantly criticized in the white press. Eventually, in the late 1870's, Wheeler left the state and returned to Chicago. Another black lawyer who came in 1887 but left for Chicago in 1893 after what appeared to be a successful career was J. Gray Lucas. He was an honor graduate of Boston University School of Law and did exceptionally well on his bar examination. He did mostly criminal defense work, and in 1890 was appointed assistant prosecuting attorney in Pine Bluff. He was elected to the legislature a year later. He then became the first black United States Commissioner for the Eastern District of Arkansas. (A Commissioner in those days was similar to a Magistrate today.) It is thought that he left Arkansas because of the deterioration of race relations.[40]

Daniel Webster Lewis studied law in the office of white lawyers, Judge Robert F. Crittenden and S. P. Swepton of Marion, and was admitted around 1880. He served in the legislature from 1880 to 1882. He was then elected probate judge of Crittenden County and served until 1888. Lewis Jenks Brown graduated from Howard University Law School in 1886 and was the first black lawyer to be admitted upon examination by the Arkansas Supreme Court in 1887. He was admitted to federal District Court two years later. John E. Patterson was a black lawyer admitted in 1873, but there is no other available information on him.[41]

Scipio Africanus Jones' career overlapped with that of Mifflin Gibbs in the late 19th and early 20th century. Second only to Gibbs, he would be considered the dominant black lawyer of his time. He was born a slave around 1863 somewhere in South Arkansas as the owner and his family left their home in Dallas County and fled to Texas to avoid the advancing federal troops. Rumor had it that his father was a white man since he was listed as a "mulatto" and neither of his legal parents was a mulatto.[42] After his childhood in Tulip (Dallas County), he came to Little Rock, worked as a farm hand, and eventually attended what is now Philander Smith and ultimately graduated from Shorter College around 1885.

At this point, he became a school teacher, but began to study law also in the offices of Judge Robert J. Lea, Judge John Martin, and Judge Henry C. Caldwell, a federal District Judge. On June 15, 1889, he passed the bar examination given by a committee of lawyers and was authorized to practice in the circuit court and inferior courts. He was admitted to the Arkansas Supreme Court years later, on November 26, 1900, and in 1905 to the United States Supreme Court.[43]

He formed a partnership with J. A. Robinson, who had been admitted on the same day, but it was not long lasting. Over the years, he also practiced with Archie V. Jones, John W. Gaines, and Thomas Price.[44] His chief clients were black fraternal organizations, the Shriners and the Knights of Pythias. He successfully defended the Shriners in federal lawsuits brought by white Shriners in both Little Rock and Houston over the question of whether the black Shriners could use the name and wear the organizational uniforms. The Knights were in the insurance business, and when they ran into difficulty with the Insurance Commission, he won their case in the state Supreme Court. His largest client was the Mosaic Templars of America, an international fraternity. This organization began in Little Rock in 1882 and by 1924 had over 2,000 lodges in 23 states, South and Central America, the Canal Zone and the West Indies with a total membership of 80,000.[45]

Jones represented several other fraternal groups including the International Order of Twelve, Knights and Daughters of Tabor, Royal Circle of Friends of the World, Order of Eastern Star, Household of Ruth and the Grand Court of Calanthe.[46]

His legal ability won him respect from white attorneys. He was elected once a special municipal judge when the regular judge, Fred A. Isgrig, recused, and he was later elected a special chancellor.[47]

The high point in his career came as a result of the Elaine race riots in Phillips County in 1919. There had been an attempt to organize the black sharecroppers and in the riots that followed, several whites and a larger number of blacks were killed.   Over   a hundred blacks were arrested, and twelve blacks were sentenced to die by white juries. Six days later, on November 24, 1919, a prominent white attorney and former Attorney General, George W. Murphy, was hired by the NAACP to represent the condemned twelve. He chose Scipio Jones to help him with the case. Eleven months later, Murphy suddenly died and Jones became the lead counsel.[48]

Although prominent white lawyer, Archie House of the Rose Firm, has been said not to regard his friend, Jones, as a "sharp technical lawyer," he prepared the briefs when the case reached the U.S. Supreme Court. (The oral argument was made by a prominent white lawyer, Moorfield Storey, a past president of the NAACP.) His brief described the racial situation in Phillips County, where the blacks greatly outnumbered the whites, in great detail. He viewed the case as "the greatest case against peonage and mob law ever fought . . . ."[49]

This case is usually referred to as *Moore v. Dempsey*,[50] which was its name in the U.S. Supreme Court. But the state court appeals had various other names. The legal situation is discussed by Dean Julian S. Waterman and Professor E. E. Overton in "The Aftermath of Moore v. Dempsey," in 6 *Ark. L. Rev.* 1 (1951), a reprint of an article that appeared much earlier in the *St. Louis Law Review*. The original trials lasted only five days and involved the conviction and sentencing of eleven blacks to death, and fifty-four were given penitentiary sentences of one to twenty years. A twelfth black was tried, convicted and sentenced to death about two weeks later.[51] In the appeals, those sentenced to die were considered in two groups. Group one was granted a new trial by the Arkansas Supreme Court because the verdicts were defective.[52] This same group was retried in Phillips County and convicted again, and that was set aside by the Arkansas Supreme Court because blacks were systematically excluded from the jury panel.[53] The group was given a change of venue to Lee County where two terms of court passed without them having been tried which gave them the right to be released under an Arkansas statute, and the state Supreme Court ordered the sheriff of Lee County to release them.[54] Later on the same day, the Circuit Judge ordered the sheriff to take them to the state penitentiary for safe keeping. The warden refused to accept them, so the sheriff left them at the penitentiary gates from where they wandered off. The Circuit Judge held the warden in contempt and fined him $500.00. This was overturned by the state Supreme Court which said that the warden could not be fined for disregarding a void order.[55]

The conviction of the six in Group Two was affirmed by the Arkansas Supreme Court despite the fact that five of them were tried jointly.[56] The United States Supreme Court denied certiorari.[57] Two days before the execution, Chancellor John E. Martineau granted a writ of habeas corpus and enjoined the execution. The Arkansas Supreme Court issued a writ of prohibition against the chancellor and quashed the habeas corpus and the injunction on the basis that equity had no jurisdiction in criminal matters and could not issue a habeas corpus.[58] The U.S. Supreme Court again denied certiorari.[59] After the date of execution had again been set, a petition for a writ of habeas corpus was filed in the U.S. District Court and was granted by Judge Jacob Trieber, who then disqualified himself because of his long years of residence in Phillips County. A federal judge from Oklahoma City, assigned to sit for Judge Trieber, some days later granted a demurrer by the state and discharged the writ, but he certified that there was probable cause for appeal to the U.S. Supreme Court.

On a direct appeal, Justice Oliver Wendell Holmes, speaking for the Court, reversed and remanded with directions to the District Court to find out whether the facts alleged in the petition for the writ were true as to "mob domination and the systematic exclusion of Negroes from the jury panel."[60] Governor Thomas C. McRae, on November 2, 1923, commuted the death sentences to twelve years because of an agreement between counsel. This made the prisoners eligible for parole at once under Arkansas law because they had already served one-third of the sentence. This was prompted in part by a petition favoring commutation from eighteen residents of Phillips County, including some members of the Committee of Seven appointed by Governor Charles H. Brough to investigate the race riots.[61] *Moore v. Dempsey* was then dismissed in U.S. District Court.

Scipio Jones was not necessarily alone in handling these cases. For example, in the *Martineau* case, white lawyers E. L. McHaney and J. H. Carmichael (the Dean of Arkansas Law School) were also of record on his side of the case. Nonetheless, he was involved from start to finish in what clearly was one of Arkansas' most famous cases, and none of these men sentenced to die ever met that fate.

Many of Jones' clients were poor or indigent blacks who could not afford a fee. Despite that, he seems to have accumulated a good bit of property. It is said that he owned a nice home on Ringo Street in 1907, along with "eight or ten other valuable houses or lots."[62] In 1908, he organized the Arkansas Realty and Investment Company through which members of his race might acquire homes and improve them.[63] He had several other incorporators and shareholders including his law partner, Thomas J. Price. However, this company never did succeed, and in 1911 it was dissolved.[64] Another business venture was the People's Ice and Fuel Company, which was successful until it failed in the depression. Jones lived well and even had a chauffeur-driven Cadillac, but when he died his estate was valued at only $1,497.50, not including his house.[65]

During his life, Jones was also active in civic affairs, serving on the Board of Shorter College, assisting an old folks' home, and serving as a director of a forerunner to the United Fund.[66] He also helped the mayor of Little Rock obtain a bank loan for the city by some not-so-subtle arm-twisting. During World War I, he had the Mosaic Templars purchase some $125,000 in Liberty Bonds.[67]

Although he had many white friends, including Governor George Donaghey and Dean J. H. Carmichael, and although he had an excellent rapport with white friends, jurors, judges and lawyers, he fought for the rights of his fellow blacks. He devoted time to fighting discriminatory legislation such as that used to prevent black voter participation. He deplored discrimination in the penal system and with the help of Attorney General Jeff Davis, got the system changed to enable county prisoners to work out their fines faster.[68]

Like Mifflin Gibbs and most black men of his day, he was a Republican and was active in the party. Around the turn of the century, he became increasingly embroiled in internal squabbles with white Republicans. In 1920, a struggle ensued when Augustus C. Remmel, the white leader of the Pulaski County Republicans, moved the county convention from the Marion Hotel to the Capital Hotel without giving advance notice to the black members. Since the convention's principal business that day was to select delegates to the state convention, it was momentous. The blacks organized their own delegation headed by Scipio Jones, but the credentials committee refused to certify them. They held a new and separate convention and selected a slate for the national convention, but the regular white delegation was seated.[69] This exemplified the rising racial split in the Republican Party in the South during that period of time that was earlier mentioned in the discussion of Mifflin Gibbs.

The black Republicans, however, reached an accommodation with the white Republicans in 1928. Scipio Jones was elected a delegate to the Republican National Convention and his alternate was also a black man. Moreover, blacks continued to be elected to Republican positions on into the early 1940's, and Jones served as a delegate to the 1940 Republican Convention that nominated Wendell L. Willkie. Scipio Jones died on March 28, 1943.[70]

The most prominent black lawyer following the death of Scipio Jones was probably W. Harold Flowers. In fact, an article about him by Judge Andree Roaf in 1985 referred to him as "the Dean of the black bar in Arkansas."[71] At that time, he had practiced longer than any black lawyer in the state, having been admitted for fifty years. He was born in Stamps in Lafayette County on October 16, 1911, his father being manager of a life insurance company and his mother a school teacher. His mother was referred to as "the aristocrat of black Stamps" by another Stamps native, Maya Angelou, in her autobiography, *I Know Why the Caged Bird Sings*.[72] In his youth, his father would take him to the county courthouse in Lewisville to listen to the court proceedings.[73]

Flowers attended Philander Smith College in Little Rock before going to Washington, D.C., to the Robert H. Terrell Law School, which was all black, graduating from it in 1937.[74] He had already passed the Arkansas bar exam in 1935. When he returned from Washington, he opened his law office in Pine Bluff in 1938. Quoting from Geraldine R. Segal, *Blacks in the Law* 276 (1983), Judge Andree Roaf wrote that at that time there were only twelve black lawyers in Arkansas and only ten in 1970.[75]

Although he was involved in a number of high profile criminal trials, Flowers regarded the high points of his life as building up the NAACP (which he served as president in Arkansas); involvement in the enrollment of Silas Hunt as the first black law student at the law school in Fayetteville; being co-founder and eventually president of the National Bar Association; and being the founder of the black lawyers' association in Arkansas that bears his name. He also was appointed judge of the Arkansas Court of Appeals to serve out the unexpired term of Judge George Howard, Jr., when Judge Howard was appointed to the federal bench. He also served various churches as a minister and religious leader.[76]

In the latter half of the 20th Century, Harold Flowers was probably the most influential black lawyer in Arkansas. He was also politically involved and was a big supporter of Governor Sid McMath in the late 1940's and early 1950's. He was a noted orator whom Judge Lawrence Dawson of Pine Bluff regarded as having "no equal."[77]

Ruth C. Flowers, the wife of Harold Flowers, was also a 1946 graduate of the Terrell Law School, but she apparently failed to pass the bar examination by a narrow margin. She was admitted to the bar of the District of Columbia in 1946, but she never practiced in Arkansas.[78]

Legal Education of Blacks in Arkansas

At this point, we reach the time of the more contemporary black lawyers, most of whom are still living and active and most of whom were educated at the two law schools in Arkansas or at other law schools that were traditionally or predominantly white. Consequently, it is important at this point to focus on the acceptance of blacks by the University of Arkansas in Fayetteville, an event of significant importance.

To understand the background of what happened in Fayetteville, you have to consider the lack of available legal education to blacks in America. When Mifflin Gibbs went to Oberlin College, it was one of only a handful of white colleges with law departments admitting blacks—only one of four in the nation when John Mercer Langston, who became the first Dean of the Howard Law School, graduated there in 1849.[79] (Women did not fare much better. Harvard did not accept women until 1950, although a large percentage of the students at Columbia and Yale during World War II were women.)[80] Consequently, black law schools came into being. Howard began in 1868 and continues to this day.[81] Freylinghuysen University was found in Washington, D.C., in 1906 to provide education "for colored working men and women," and it had a law school as a component part until 1927 when the D.C. Board of Education refused to permit it to grant LL.B.'s.[82] Two others, Virginia Union and Simmons in Kentucky disappeared about 1931 and 1932.[83] Much of this was due to rising standards in legal education that moved it out of the reach of many minorities.[84] There were some law schools that admitted a handful of minorities. John Marshall Law School in Chicago had two blacks in the class of 1928.[85]

This situation began to change as early as the 1930's as the result of litigation beginning in the border states of Maryland and Missouri. Even in the era of "separate but equal," there was nothing to be compared with as being "equal" although "separate" in most states. Consequently, the state courts ordered a black applicant admitted to the University of Maryland in *University of Maryland v. Murray,* 169 Md. 478, 182 A. 590 (1936).[86] The next case was of more national note because it was decided by the U.S. Supreme Court and was a test case sponsored by the NAACP to challenge the "separate but equal" doctrine as it applied to equal access to educational facilities. Lloyd L. Gaines, a black applicant, had been denied admission to the all-white University of Missouri Law School, and the state courts had upheld the denial. In a 6-2 opinion written by Chief Justice Charles Evans Hughes, the Court ordered the admission of Gaines despite the offer from Missouri to pay his tuition to an out-of-state law school and the state's professed intention to establish a law school for blacks at Lincoln University. *Missouri ex rel. Gaines v. Canada*, 305 U.S. 337 (1938).[87]

These cases, and others that followed, led to the creation of law schools for blacks in the South. In addition to Lincoln in Missouri, South Carolina created a law school at State College of South Carolina rather than admit John Wrighten to the University.[88] A landmark case on the subject was *Sweatt v. Painter*, 339 U.S. 629 (1950), involving the application of Herman M. Sweatt, a Houston mail carrier, to the University of Texas Law School in 1946. His application was denied, and fierce litigation ensued while the State of Texas scrambled to create a law school for blacks (which it did at Texas Southern). Chief Justice Fred M. Vinson declared for a unanimous Court that the newly created law school was in no way equal to the University of Texas and that "separate but equal" was not realistically attainable in higher education.[89] A companion case reaching the same result was *McLaurin v. Oklahoma State Regents for Higher Education*, 339 U.S. 637 (1950), involving the application of George W. McLaurin to the University of Oklahoma. It differed in that McLaurin was ordered admitted by the Federal District Court, but in class he had to sit on a row "reserved for Negroes," study at a separate table in the library, and eat at a separate table in the cafeteria. In a short, terse opinion by Chief Justice Vinson for a unanimous Court, these practices were declared to violate the equal protection of the laws.[90]

This was not the complete picture, however, when Edward W. Jacko, Jr., applied for admission to the University of Arkansas Law School in June, 1938. In *The First 100 Years: Centennial History of the University of Arkansas* (1972), former Arts and Sciences Dean Guerdon D. Nichols wrote the segment dealing with admission to blacks to the law school, although former Law Dean Robert A. Leflar was the author of the book. (This was because of Leflar's involvement with the admission of blacks, according to a prefatory note.) Dean Nichols writes that Jacko's "application was deftly turned aside."[91] He adds, however, that Dean Julian S. Waterman of the Law School "was becoming increasingly concerned about the problem."[92] In fact, according to Leflar in a long article on legal education in Arkansas, Dean Waterman had been keeping a file on the subject of "Negro applications commencing in 1937, and was active in arranging for tuition payments to out-of-state law schools attended by Arkansas Negro students."[93] He explains in a footnote that early tuition grants were paid from University funds, but Act 345 of 1943 was enacted by the legislature to provide separate "tuition grants" for black students "studying in fields not available to them in Arkansas state colleges."[94] Prior to that time, for example, the University had provided funds, at the request of Scipio A. Jones, to fund the attendance of Prentice A. Hilburn at Howard University.[95] According to Dean Nichols, by the end of World War II, the State Department of Education had up to 100 requests for tuition funding.[96] One persistent complainant was Clifford Davis of Wilton, a graduate of Philander Smith, who "from his first application for out-of-state tuition in December, 1944 until his final refusal in the fall of 1948 to enter the law school under the segregated teaching conditions in force at that time" "kept up a running battle by correspondence with authorities over the payment of tuition to Howard and Atlanta Universities and for admission to the University of Arkansas law school."[97] Moreover, on March 9, 1946, Clifford Davis filed an application for admission to the University of Arkansas Law School for the fall semester.[98]

Dean Leflar wrote a memorandum to himself describing five possible courses of action, but the one that he favored was the last one—"set up facilities for teaching Negro students in connection with the regular law school."[99] He thought there would be powerful opposition to this action and that in the beginning, at least, there would have to be separate study rooms and classes; that duplicate books would be provided but bodily access to the law library would be denied; and that other books could be delivered to them upon request. Dean Nichols thought Leflar viewed this as "a sugarcoated integration pill that Dean Leflar was about to persuade the state to take, based largely on its inevitability and the dim outlook for any of the alternatives."[100]

Leflar was most disturbed about the possibility of litigation because of the bad publicity and unfavorable race relations that would result.[101] He approached the law faculty, and it agreed. He then approached Herbert L. Thomas, Chairman of the Board of Trustees, and in June 1946, the Board authorized the law faculty "to exercise its own judgment but to move no faster than was necessary."[102] Unlike many Southern states, Arkansas had no law barring racially integrated higher education, and in 1872, the University Board of Trustees had adopted a resolution that had never been rescinded "throwing the institution open to all without regard to race, sex or sect."[103]

Governor Ben Laney was from South Arkansas and had been involved with other Southern governors in the Dixie opposition to liberal forces within the Democratic Party and in the Southern support for racial segregation.[104] It was necessary for Dean Leflar to smooth the way by obtaining the Governor's consent. By this time, Leflar had become Acting President of the University, pending the arrival of Lewis Webster Jones, President of Bennington College in Vermont, and President-designate of the University. When he consulted President Jones, he was advised that Jones' position should be that of the Board and that Dean Leflar and the law faculty should solve the problem as best they could.[105]

William J. Smith was Executive Secretary to Governor Laney, a position that he had served in through several previous gubernatorial administrations and would ultimately serve in again. Bill Smith arranged for an appointment with the Governor. Leflar presented his position in some detail, pointing out the substantial cost of starting a separate law school, and the relatively modest cost of his plan. He stressed the importance of preserving favorable racial relations and avoiding adverse publicity. Governor Laney listened carefully and without interruption and finally said that if that were the way it was, the University could proceed and he would not interfere. He kept his word.[106]

The result was that blacks would be admitted to the Law School but on the segregated basis previously mentioned. Leflar writes that one applicant "from Little Rock, already studying at Howard in Washington, D.C., withdrew his application because he was unwilling to accept the latter condition," i.e., the segregated aspects.[107] That apparently was Clifford Davis. The first black student to enroll was Silas Hunt of Texarkana, a war veteran and honor graduate of Arkansas A. M. & N. (now UAPB), on February 2, 1948.[108] He had come to the Law School on that day accompanied by Harold Flowers, Wiley Branton (not yet a lawyer or law student) and a reporter for a black newspaper. The registration was brief and routine.[109] Hunt's qualifications were exceptional. He had already been admitted to the Indiana University Law School.[110]

However, war wounds suffered in the Battle of the Bulge continued to plague him, and he eventually developed tuberculosis and died before completing his legal education.[111]

He was followed in the fall of 1948 by Jackie L. Shropshire, a graduate of Wilberforce College in Ohio, and he became the first black to graduate from the University of Arkansas in June 1951.[112]

During Silas Hunt's time at the Law School, he studied in a separate basement room and met classes there with regular faculty members. One or more white students, though not required to do so, attended his classes also. Shropshire also began with a similar situation, but there were so many entering law students that no single room could hold all of them. The entering class was divided into two sections, and Shropshire was placed in the small section which soon filled. He had to sit behind a railing separated from the others, but Leflar recounts, "one day the railing was torn down and never replaced."[113]

What happened to the railing has for years been a mystery: Did students tear it down in the dark of night, or did God himself in his vengeance do away with it? The mystery was solved in an interview with Robert A. Leflar on October 2, 1992, as follows:

Wright: You temporarily had a rail in the Law School. It separated the black law students from the whites, and the rail disappeared, and I've always suspected that you tore it down.

Leflar: Well, yes, I did. I remember getting up in the middle of the night. I lived out at my wife's old home and knew what I was going to do that night, so that I didn't really take my clothes off. I went to bed with my clothes on and waited till after midnight.

Then, he slipped into the Law School unnoticed, tore down the railing and hid it temporarily in a closet in the Dean's office. So ended segregated classes at the Law School.

Leflar regarded this episode in his life in admitting black students to the Law School as one of the high points. "I take genuine pride," he said, "in the fact that the University of Arkansas was the *first* to admit blacks, south of the Mason-Dixon line."[114] In addition to being the first law school of the states of the Confederacy to admit blacks, it appears that no black was ever denied admission once the issue was squarely presented. Clifford Davis received tuition funds to go elsewhere, which he accepted, but apparently was admitted subject to his compliance with the segregation rules that were later accepted by Silas Hunt. Davis was unwilling to comply. Dean Nichols refers to his "final refusal in the fall of 1948 to enter the law school under the segregated conditions in force at that time."[115] Prentice A. Hilburn received tuition funds from the University itself to go to Howard, as mentioned previously. This seemed to be satisfactory to him and Scipio Jones, and presumably his application was dropped. If any black applicant were turned down, it would have to be Edward W. Jacko, Jr. in the late 1930's. According to Dean Nichols, his application "was deftly turned aside."[116] Does that mean it was rejected, withdrawn or not completed? We do not know, and it is unlikely that University records would reveal anything since Jacko was never a student. Be that as it may, the Law School avoided the legal and social problems of other Southern and Southwestern law schools in handling legal education for blacks, and that was due almost entirely to the careful and thoughtful manner of handling the matter by Dean Leflar. The actions of the Board of Trustees and its Chairman, Herbert Thomas; President Lewis Webster Jones; William J. Smith; and Governor Ben Laney all illustrate a reasonable, non-confrontational approach to a very sensitive matter. It also illustrates why, before the Central High School milieu in 1957, Arkansas was viewed as one of the more progressive of the Southern states.

Three other black law students entered the Law School in the fall of 1949, Wiley A. Branton, George W. Haley, and Christopher C. Mercer, Jr. Chris Mercer entered private practice after graduation and has engaged in a general practice ever since. His office is in Little Rock. Wiley Branton and George Haley, on the other hand, developed national recognition out-of-state (although initially Branton practiced law in Pine Bluff and was engaged in some high profile civil rights cases).

Wiley Branton graduated from the Law School in 1953 with a reputation of being very intelligent and a hard worker. After ten years of practice in Pine Bluff, he became director of the Voter Education Project of the Southern Regional Council in Atlanta and served in that capacity from 1962-65. He then was appointed by President Lyndon Johnson as Special Assistant to the Attorney General, a position he held from 1962-65. He also served at various times in the 1960's as Executive Director, Council of United Civil Rights Leadership, and as Director of the community and social action Alliance for Labor Action. During the 1970's, he was a partner for six years in a law firm that he helped form and was of counsel to the racially mixed Little Rock firm of Walker, Kaplan and Mays. In 1978, he became Dean of the Howard University Law School. He also served on the Board of Directors of the NAACP Legal Defense and Education Fund and was active in its cases. He received numerous awards for participation in civil rights litigation including the Henry W. Edgerton Award presented to him by the ACLU in 1977, and the Charles Hamilton Houston Medallion from the National Bar Association in 1978.[117] He died at age 65 on December 15, 1988. His son, Wiley A. Branton, Jr., is a Judge of the Chancery Court, Juvenile Division, in Little Rock.

George Williford Boyce Haley, now 73, was born in Henning, Tennessee, and is the brother of the late Alex Haley, the author who wrote *Roots* and other books. After graduation from the Law School in 1952, he moved to Kansas City, Kansas, where he worked as a Deputy City Attorney and was elected in 1954 to the Kansas State Senate. He moved to Washington, D.C., in 1964 to become Chief Counsel of the Urban Mass Transportation Administration. After that, he served in several positions in Washington including Associate Director and then General Counsel of the E.E.O., U.S. Information Agency and Counsel for E.E.O., N.A.S.A. He was Chairman and later a Commissioner for the Postal Rate Commission. He held positions during part of this time in UNESCO. He received two outstanding alumni awards from the University of Arkansas and was honored by Morehouse College.[118]

Contemporary Black Lawyers and Judges

In contrast to the time when Harold Flowers entered law practice, there are a substantial number of black lawyers today—too many to mention all of them. One prominent black lawyer who entered the University of Arkansas Law School shortly after those mentioned previously was George Howard, Jr., who was appointed U.S. District Judge by President Jimmy Carter in 1980. He was the first, and so far the only, black Article Three federal judge in Arkansas. At the time he was appointed, he was serving on the Arkansas Court of Appeals by appointment of Governor Bill Clinton.

After service in the Navy Seabees during World War II, graduation from high school, and undergraduate work at Lincoln University in Jefferson City, Missouri, he applied to and was accepted by the University of Arkansas Law School in 1950. He lived initially with a prominent black family in Fayetteville but moved into the Lloyd Hall complex in the spring of 1952. Lloyd Hall consisted of temporary housing primarily for war veterans and was a collection of converted army barracks. Judge Howard won election as President of Lloyd Hall, defeating two white opponents, and became the first black to win a student elective office at the University. He graduated from the Law School in 1954 and was its fourth black graduate. His graduation and entry into practice was thus in the same year that the U.S. Supreme Court decided *Brown v. Board of Education* requiring desegregation of the public schools.

Returning to his home town of Pine Bluff, Judge Howard practiced law for twenty-five years and, along with Wiley Branton and John Walker, became active in school desegregation cases in Arkansas in the 1950's and 1960's. His most famous case was the Dollarway desegregation matter involving a lawsuit that he filed in federal district court. One of the students admitted as a result to the formerly all-white school was his daughter, Sarah, who was in the tenth grade. Today, Sarah Howard Jenkins is a professor of law at the U.A.L.R. Law School.

Judge Howard was active in cases in the 1960's involving state legislation or city ordinances aimed at limiting the activities of the NAACP and the denial of blacks to equal access in restaurants and hotels and motels. He served as president of the Pine Bluff chapter of the NAACP in 1962 and president of the Arkansas NAACP in 1967. He was honored in 1980 by a special award from the Little Rock NAACP for his work in civil rights. He was appointed in 1965 to the Arkansas Advisory Committee to the U.S. Civil Rights Commission.

In 1969, he was appointed by Governor Winthrop Rockefeller to a six-year term on the State Claims Commission and was subsequently appointed for another term by Governor David Pryor. He served during most of 1977 on the Supreme Court Committee on Professional Conduct. On December 5, 1977, he was appointed to fill the remainder of the unexpired term of Justice Elsijane Trimble Roy who had been appointed by President Carter to the federal district court. Shortly after that term ended, he was appointed on July 15, 1979, by Governor Bill Clinton to the newly created Arkansas Court of Appeals. In addition to being the first black appointed to the federal bench, he was the first one to serve on the Supreme Court and Court of Appeals.

Judge Howard has won other honors. In 1974, he was elected President of the Jefferson County Bar Association. He was chosen by the Arkansas Trial Lawyers Association to receive its Outstanding Judge Award in 1984-85. He expressed his judicial philosophy in an article written by Phyllis Harden Carter for *The Arkansas Lawyer* in the July 1987 issue:

> I try diligently to show compassion, to be understanding. I try to be patient and most of all to see that the voiceless, the underprivileged, the have nots, the forsaken and the alleged outcasts are afforded the same opportunities as those who have—shall we say—unlimited resources or have prestigious beginnings. I think this is part and parcel of every individual's duty. More is expected of one who has achieved more and this is what I strive to do in those cases over which I preside.[119]

The most recent appointment of a black Supreme Court justice is that of Lavenski R. Smith, who had been serving on a state commission. He is a graduate of the U of A School of Law.

As this chapter is being written, there are three black judges on the Arkansas Court of Appeals: Olly Neal, Wendell L. Griffen, and Andree Layton Roaf. Judge Andree Roaf had a bachelor's degree in zoology from Michigan State University and worked twelve years as a research scientist before she enrolled in the University of Arkansas at Little Rock School of Law. She graduated in 1978, and in 1979 joined the firm of Woodson Walker and Associates in Little Rock with the intent to specialize in commercial matters along with some probate and domestic relations practice. Eventually, she built up the commercial practice to the point it constituted about one-half of her work. In the mid-1990's she was appointed to the Arkansas Supreme Court to fill out the unexpired term of Justice Robert H. Dudley, who retired. After that term was up, she was appointed to a judgeship on the expanded Arkansas Court of Appeals.[120]

Judge Olly Neal was also an appointee to the expanded Court of Appeals. After graduation from the University of Arkansas at Little Rock School of Law in 1979, he practiced law in Marianna and Eastern Arkansas and was involved in a variety of legal matters including civil rights and criminal practice. He served later as a Deputy Prosecuting Attorney for a number of years and then as Prosecuting Attorney of the First Judicial District for about fifteen months before he became Circuit Judge. He served as Circuit Judge for two years, from January 1, 1993, to December 31, 1995. He became Judge of the Arkansas Court of Appeals on January 1, 1996, and has served ever since. He has served in many capacities including as a member and Chair of the Winthrop Rockefeller Foundation (1990-96) and on the Board of Directors of the Arkansas Judicial Council.

Judge Wendell Griffen graduated from the University of Arkansas Law School in Fayetteville where he was a member of the Editorial Board of the *Arkansas Law Review*. He joined the Wright, Lindsey & Jennings law firm in Little Rock, one of the top law firms in the state, and in due course became a partner. He also was and remains an ordained minister. Active in civic and bar work, he was selected in the late 1990's as President of the Pulaski County Bar Association. He was appointed Chair of the Workers Compensation Commission in April 1985 by Governor Bill Clinton, and was appointed to the expanded Arkansas Court of Appeals by Governor Jim Guy Tucker effective January 1, 1996. A deeply religious man, he combines his efforts in two professions, law and religion, and his numerous civic and professional activities, in an energetic, productive way.[121]

It is no longer unusual to find lawyers of African-American descent occupying judicial offices in Arkansas. Probably this is due in part, and perhaps in large measure, to the extension of the federal Voting Rights Act to judicial offices in states that elect their state court judges by popular vote. Nonetheless, the result has been that in Pulaski County alone you find Circuit Judge Marion A. Humphrey and former Judge Morris Thompson, recently removed from office in 2000 by the Supreme Court. Chancery Judges are Wiley A. Branton, Jr., Alice S. Gray and Joyce Williams Warren. Not all occupy state court judgeships. Judge Henry Jones is a U.S. Magistrate for the Eastern District of Arkansas.

The foregoing material has focused to a large extent on black judges and those who might be considered pioneers. We should not ignore by any means those black lawyers who have largely just practiced law. One who comes immediately to mind is John W. Walker whose efforts on behalf of black clients in school desegregation matters is legendary. His principal case has been the long-running case involving the Little Rock, North Little Rock and Pulaski County School Districts, but he has been involved in numerous other school desegregation cases in other parts of the state. Further, he has represented numerous clients with complaints relative to racial discrimination, employment discrimination, and other civil rights matters.

Other black lawyers who have largely just practiced law include Woodson Walker and Darrell Brown of Little Rock and Eddie Walker of Fort Smith. Some prominent black lawyers have combined regular law practice with governmental or judicial positions. Richard L. Mays and P. A. (Les) Hollingsworth have served by appointment as Associate Justices of the Arkansas Supreme Court. Jerry Malone practiced law for some years in the Friday law firm and more recently has served in a top administrative position in the U.S. Department of Transportation.

Rodney Slater occupies one of the highest positions of any black lawyer in the country, serving as U.S. Secretary of Transportation under President Clinton. He served as Federal Highway Administrator prior to that. In Arkansas, he was Vice President for

Governmental Relations at Arkansas State University, was a Commissioner on the Arkansas Highway Commission and was president of the Harold Flowers Law Society. He also has served as Secretary-Treasurer of the Arkansas Bar Association.[122]

There are other prominent black lawyers who have contributed of their time and energy to the practice of law and to involvement in the community. The situation at the time of Harold Flowers' admission to practice in the late 1930's when there were only a few black lawyers in the state has changed. It began to change with the voluntary admission of black students to the University of Arkansas Law School. As black lawyers continue to serve capably and honorably in positions of trust, they should solidify this evolution in the early part of the 21st century.

Notes

1. J. Smith, *Emancipation: The Making of the Black Lawyer 1844-1944* 321 (1993).
2. D. Gaines, *Racial Possibilities As Indicated by the Negroes of Arkansas* 85 (1898).
3. *Ibid.*
4. E. Foner, *Freedom's Lawmakers: A Directory of Black Officeholders During Reconstruction* 119 (1993).
5. Smith, *supra* n. 1 at 321, citing the letter from Dr. Ferguson. In Dillard, "Golden Prospects and Fraternal Amenities: Mifflin W. Gibbs's Arkansas Years," 35 *Ark. Historical Q.* 307, 309 (1976), Gray's name is spelled "Grey."
6. *Ibid.*, based on a letter from the Clerk of the Arkansas Supreme Court.
7. *Ibid.*
8. Dillard, *supra* n. 5 at 309, quoting from Gibbs, *Shadow and Light* 126 (1902). Gibbs wrote that he came to Arkansas as "a stranger to every inhabitant."

9. Foner, *supra* n. 4 at 84.

10. *Id.* at 85.

11. *Ibid.*

12. Smith, *supra* n. 1 at 321.

13. Foner, *supra* n. 4 at 84.

14. Smith, *supra* n. 1 at 322. Although Smith states that Gibbs passed the Bar in 1870, he apparently did not come to Arkansas until 1871, according to Dillard, *supra* n. 5 at 309.

15. Dillard, *supra* n. 5 at 309

16. Smith, *supra* n. 1 at 322.

17. Dillard, *supra* n. 5 at 310-311. Dillard writes that the *Arkansas Gazette* branded Gibbs as "a carpetbag negro." The entire "regular Republican" ticket won in the election, and Gibbs was a firm ally of Senator (and former Governor) Powell Clayton and the regulars. Governor Elisha Baxter, who had seemingly prevailed in his struggle with his rival, Joseph M. Brooks, (although the "Brooks-Baxter War" was yet to come) had offended many Republicans when he became Governor by dealing with the Democrats, even to the point of transferring state printing contracts from the *Little Rock Republican* to the "rabidly" pro-Democrat *Arkansas Gazette.* *Id.* at 310.

18. Foner, *supra* n. 4 at 85.

19. Smith, *supra* n. 1 at 322, states that he was appointed in 1876 and held the office for thirteen years. Foner, *supra* at 85, says that Gibbs was appointed in 1877 and held office until 1885. It would seem that the 1885 date would be correct because the Democrats regained the White House that year with the election of Grover Cleveland.

20. Foner, *supra* at 85.

21. *Ibid.*

22. *Ibid.*

23. *Ibid.* Also, Smith, *supra* n. 1 at 322.

24. *Ibid.*

25. Dillard, *supra* n. 5 at 317.

26. *Id.* at 321.

27. *Id.* at 322.

28. *Id.* at 323.

29. *Id.* at 323-324.

30. *Id.* at 325-326.

31. Dillard, *supra* n. 5 at 327-330 discusses the establishment, growth and ultimate failure of the bank in some detail.

32. *Id.* at 331.

33. Reference works on Mifflin Gibbs, in addition to those cited, include Tom Dillard's Master's thesis, "The Black Moses of the West: A Biography of Mifflin Wistar Gibbs, 1823-1915," at the University of Arkansas, Fayetteville, which would be available through the Mullins Library; Gibbs' own autobiography, *Shadow and Light*; and W. Gatewood, *Aristocrats of Color: The Black Elite, 1880-1920* 268-269 (1990).

34. Gaines, *supra* n. 2 at 87-89.

35. Smith, *supra* n. 1 at 322.

36. *Id.* at 322-323.

37. *Id.* at 323.

38. *Ibid.*

39. *Ibid.*

40. *Id.* at 324.

41. *Id.* at 324-325.

42. Dillard, "Scipio A. Jones," 31 *Ark. Historical Q.* 201-202 (1972).

43. *Id.* at 204.

44. *Ibid.*

45. *Id.* at 205.

46. *Id.* at 205-206, citing E. Woods, *The Blue Book of Little Rock and Argenta* 59 (1907).

47. *Id.* at 206.

48. *Id.* at 206-207.

49. *Id.* at 208.

50. 261 U.S. 86 (1923)

51. Waterman and Overton, "The Aftermath of Moore v. Dempsey," Ark. L. Rev. 2 (1951).

52. *Banks v. State*, 143 Ark. 154, 219 S.W. 1015 (1920).

53. *Ware v. State*, 146 Ark. 321, 225 S.W. 626 (1920).

54. *Ware v. State*, 159 Ark. 540, 252 S.W. 934 (1923).

55. *Martin v. State*, 162 Ark. 282, 257 S.W. 752 (1924). This situation is discussed in Waterman and Overton, *supra* n. 51 at 2-3.

56. *Hicks v. State*, 143 Ark. 158, 220 S.W. 308 (1920).

57. 254 U.S. 630 (1920).

58. *State v. Martineau*, 149 Ark. 237, 232 S.W. 609 (1921).

59. *Martineau v. Arkansas*, 257 U.S. 665 (1921).

60. Waterman and Overton, *supra* n. 51 at 4-5, fn. 28.

61. *Id.* at 5-6.

62. Dillard, *supra* n. 5 at 209.

63. *Id.* at 209-210.

64. *Id.* at 210.

65. *Ibid.*

66. *Id.* at 211.

67. *Id.* at 212.

68. *Id.* at 212-213.

69. *Id.* at 215-217.

70. *Id.* at 218.

71. Roaf, "Generations in the Law: W. Harold Flowers," *The Arkansas Lawyer*, p. 112 (July, 1985).

72. *Ibid.*

73. *Id.* at 112-113.

74. *Id.* at 113.

75. *Id.* at 113.

76. *Id.* at 114.

77. *Id.* at 115.

78. Smith, *supra* n. 1 at 327, n. 63.

79. R. Stevens, *Law School* 81 (1983).

80. *Id.* at 203-204, fn. 63.

81. *Id.* at 81.

82. *Id.* at 195.

83. *Id.* at 195, 201-202, fn. 34.

84. *Id.* at 195.

85. *Id.* at 187, fn. 54.

86. *Id.* at 202, fn. 36.

87. There were only eight justices because Justice Benjamin Cardozo had died, leaving a vacancy. K. Hall, ed., *The Oxford Companion to the Supreme Court of the United States* 556 (1992).

88. *Wrighten v. Board of Trustees of the University of South Carolina*, 72 F. Supp. 948 (E.D.S.C., 1947)

89. Hall, *supra* n. 87 at 851.

90. See also the earlier case of *Sipuel v. Board of Regents of the University of Oklahoma*, 332 U.S. 631 (1948).

91. R. Leflar, *The First 100 Years* 276 (1972).

92. *Ibid.*

93. R. Leflar, *Legal Education in Arkansas*, 16 ARK. L. REV. 191, 208 (1962).

94. *Ibid.*, n. 67.

95. G. Nichols, in R. Leflar, *The First 100 Years*, *supra* at 277.

96. *Id.* at 278.

97. *Ibid.*

98. *Ibid.*

99. *Id.* at 279.

100. *Ibid.*

101. *Ibid.*

102. Leflar, *supra* n. 93 at 208.

103. Nichols, *supra* n. 95 at 276, 279.

104. *Id.* at 280.

105. *Id.* at 280.

106. *Id.* at 280-281. After the presentation, he asked Bill Smith if he agreed with Leflar, and the answer was that he did.

107. Leflar, *supra* n. 93 at 208-209.

108. *Id.* at 209.

109. Nichols, *supra* at 282.

110. *Id.* at 283.

111. *Ibid.*; Leflar, *supra* n. 93 at 209, n. 69.

112. Nichols, *supra* n. 95 at 284; Leflar at 209.

113. Leflar, *supra* n. 93 at 209.

114. Interview with Robert A. Leflar, Oct. 2, 1992, p. 16.

115. Nichols, *supra* n. 95 at 278.

116. *Id.* at 276.

117. This material is taken from G. Segal, *Blacks in the Law* 202 (1983) and from *Who's Who in America* 370 (1983).

118. *Who's Who in America* 1707 (1997).

119. The material about Judge Howard is taken primarily from this article by Ms. Carter that appears on pp. 90-98 of *The Arkansas Lawyer* for July 1987, and from an article by attorney (and now Congressman) J. W. Dickey, Jr., "George Howard, Jr.: Associate Justice, Arkansas Supreme Court," *The Arkansas Lawyer* 158 (October, 1978), and from personal knowledge.

120. Part of this is taken from "Coming of Age: Women Lawyers in Arkansas, 1960-1984, *The Arkansas Lawyer* pp. 58-63 (April, 1985) by Annabelle Davis Clinton—now Justice Annabelle Imber of the Supreme Court of Arkansas—and part of it is from personal knowledge.

121. Judge Griffen was the subject of a "High Profile" feature article in the *Arkansas Democrat-Gazette*, p. 1-D, Sunday, October 18, 1998.

122. An article entitled "Reflections on Rodney Slater," by Judge Wendell L. Griffen, is in *The Arkansas Lawyer*, p. 24 (Spring, 1997).

Chapter VIII

WOMEN LAWYERS

Introduction and Background

Every year since its approval in 1991, the Margaret Brent Women Lawyers of Achievement Award is presented at the annual meeting of the American Bar Association by the ABA Commission on Women in the Profession. The award was named after Margaret Brent (1601-1671) of Maryland, who was the first woman lawyer in America. Margaret Brent came to the colonies and settled in St. Mary's Parish, Maryland, in 1638. A cousin of Lord Baltimore, she had letters from him directing Governor Calvert of Maryland to let her acquire land on more favorable terms than other settlers, and she amassed some of the largest real estate holdings in America. She also got herself appointed counsel to the Governor and was addressed in person and in court records as "Gentleman Margaret Brent." She was involved in 124 court cases over a period of eight years in Maryland. She eventually demanded a "vote and voyce" in the Maryland Assembly, which the Governor denied. This led to her eventual move to Westmoreland County, Virginia, where she resided for the rest of her life on an estate and in a manor house called "Peace."[1]

In an article appearing in the *Michigan Law Review* in 1967, a professor at Michigan states authoritatively: "In 1869 Belle A. Mansfield, reputedly the first female lawyer admitted to practice in the United States, was admitted to the state bar of Iowa."[2] It would seem that although Margaret Brent may have been the first woman lawyer "in America," America during her lifetime consisted of English colonies, while Belle Mansfield was the first to be admitted to the bar of a state. What is so striking is that it was two centuries between the time of these two women lawyers.

This and case law illustrate the difficulty that women had in getting admitted to the bar during the first century of this nation's history and beyond. It is probably not surprising. Few women were interested in practicing law, and law was clearly viewed in the 19th and early 20th centuries as a man's profession. Married women were not allowed to control their own property during that period, and it was not until the Married Women's Property Acts that this was changed. Women did not obtain the right to vote until the 20th Century when the suffragette movement culminated in success. Black people were freed from slavery although discrimination remained. But women continued to be second-class citizens until the 20th Century, and even then, remnants of the discrimination combined with fixed attitudes as to "women's work" or a "woman's place" remained well past the half-century mark.

According to the ABA, in addition to the admission to the bar of Iowa of Arabelle (Belle) Mansfield, also in 1869, Lemma Barkaloo became the first woman admitted to law school. She was admitted to Washington University in St. Louis. In 1870, Esther McQuigg Morris became the first woman judge; she was a justice of the peace in South Pass City, Wyoming. And in the same year, Ada H. Kepley became the first woman law school graduate at Union College of Law, which is now Northwestern University. In 1872, the first African-American woman was admitted to the bar, Charlotte E. Ray.[3]

The cause of women was set back, however, in 1873 when Illinois denied admission to Myra Bradwell. This was upheld by the United States Supreme Court in *Bradwell v. The State*.[4] In a short opinion for the Court, Justice Samuel F. Miller denied that the privileges and immunities clause of the Constitution had any bearing on the matter and held that the granting of a license to practice law was a matter reserved for the courts of the states. Justice Joseph P. Bradley, concurring, pointed out that the plaintiff was a married woman and then set out the culture and mores of the time:

[T]he civil law, as well as nature herself, has always recognized a wide difference in the respective spheres and destinies of man and woman. Man is, or should be, woman's protector and defender. The natural and proper timidity and delicacy which belongs to the female sex evidently unfits it for many of the occupations of civil life. The constitution of the family organization, which is founded in the divine ordinance, as well as in the nature of things, indicates the domestic sphere as that which properly belongs to the domain and functions of womanhood. The harmony, not to say identity, of interests and views which belong, or should belong, to the family institution is repugnant to the idea of a woman adopting a distinct and independent career from that of her husband. So firmly fixed was this sentiment in the founders of the common law that it became a maxim of that system of jurisprudence that a woman had no legal existence separate from her husband, who was regarded as her head and representative in the social state. . . [5]

Bradley goes on to say that the "paramount destiny and mission of woman are to fulfil [sic] the noble and benign offices of wife and mother." "This is the law of the Creator."[6]

The Wisconsin Supreme Court took a similar view in *Matter of Goodell*,[7] decided in 1875 and involving the application of Miss Levina Goodell. The Court opined:

There are many employments in life not unfit for female character. The profession of law is surely not one of these. The peculiar qualities of womanhood, its gentle graces, its quick sensibility, its tender suceptibility, its deli-

cacy, its emotional impulses, its subordination of hard reasoning to sympathetic feeling, are surely not qualifications
for forensic strife. Nature has tempered woman as little for
the juridical conflicts of the court room, as for the physical
conflicts of the battle field. Womanhood is moulded for
gentler and better things.

* * * It would be revolting to all female sense of the innocence and sanctity of their sex, shocking to man's reverence for womanhood and faith in woman, on which hinge
all the better affections and humanities of life, that woman
would be permitted to mix professionally in all the nastiness of the world which find its way into courts of justice. .
. . [The court then chronicles "unclean issues" that courts
adjudicate—rape, abortion, sodomy, incest, seduction, for-
nication, adultery, bastardy, legitimacy, prostitution, las-
civious cohabitation, obscene publications, etc.]

This is bad enough for men. We hold in too high reverence the sex without which, as is truly and beautifully
written, "le commencement de la vie est sans secours, le
milieu sans plasir, et le fin sans consolation," voluntarily to
commit it to such studies and such occupations. Reverence
for all womanhood would suffer in the public spectacle of
woman so instructed and engaged. . . .

Law, it seemed self-evident to some judges, was too mean and foul
a sport to be engaged in by the gentler sex.

Yet women gradually made progress during the late 19th century. Belva Lockwood obtained federal legislation opening the federal courts to women lawyers and was the first woman to argue a
case before the U.S. Supreme Court.[8] Moreover, some law schools
had begun admitting women, among them Washington University

in St. Louis, Iowa and Michigan, although Yale, Columbia and Harvard did not admit women until well into the 20th century.[9]

Since this chapter is devoted to Arkansas women lawyers, we will now turn to the situation in the "land of opportunity."

Arkansas Women Lawyers: the Early Days

Until 1917, women were not permitted to practice law in Arkansas. Act 88 of 1873 limited admission to males. This particularly affected three women who had studied law and wanted to practice. These three pioneers were Lizzie Dorman Fyler of Eureka Springs and Clara McDiarmid and Erle Chambers of Little Rock. Lizzie Fyler was a native of Massachusetts who had read law in a law office in what was then the typical way to become a lawyer in Arkansas. Clara McDiarmid was a native of Indiana who had studied law in Michigan and came to Arkansas from Kansas with her soldier husband. Erle Chambers had attended the University of Arkansas Law Department and was its first woman graduate in 1912 (the school then being located in Little Rock as discussed in the chapter on legal education).[10]

Lizzie Fyler applied for admission to the bar in 1882 despite the law and was denied. But in 1885, Judge J. M. Pittman of the Fourth District Circuit Court notified her that he would allow her to represent people in court under a constitutional provision that permits anyone to appear in court in person or by an attorney or next best friend. She participated in several cases but died later that year.[11]

Clara McDiarmid came to Arkansas in 1866 with her new husband who was in the federal army. They moved to Little Rock from Kansas and in Kansas she could vote and she could practice law possibly under some local arrangement.[12] In Arkansas, in 1888, she formed the Equal Suffrage Association and offered free legal advice to women.[13] She remained active in the women's movement and in women's associations until her death in 1899.

Erle Chambers began studying law while employed as a secretary at the Little Rock firm of Moore, Smith and Trieber. After graduating in 1912 from the Law Department of the University of Arkansas, she attended the University of Chicago Law School. She was named county probation officer in 1913 and remained in that position until 1917 when she began an affiliation with the Arkansas Tuberculosis Association that lasted until she died in 1941. She was elected to the state legislature in 1923, the first woman legislator, and served a two-year term in the House. She got a bill passed abolishing the husband's right of curtesy in the wife's estate, which, of course, is no longer the law.[14] Although, as stated, the law on women lawyers was changed in 1917, Erle Chambers never practiced law.

One advocate of changing the law to allow women attorneys was Minnie Rutherford Fuller of Fort Smith who said that female attorneys would soften "the hardening effects" of the court atmosphere in matters involving children, these hardening effects being "largely the fault of men attorneys . . . men clerks . . . and men juries."[15] She also argued that this was a matter of fundamental justice.

The bill to permit women to practice law had no significant opposition in the 1917 legislative session, and the bill was approved. In January 1918, Sarah Shields of Hope, a graduate of the University of Kentucky Law School, who had done post-graduate work at Cumberland School of Law, passed the newly instituted bar examination with a grade of 100 and became the first licensed woman lawyer in Arkansas.[16]

Considerable attention is given to these early women lawyers in Frances Mitchell Ross's law review article, *Reforming the Bar: Women and the Arkansas Legal Profession*, 20 UALR L.J. 869 (1998), and in her article, "100 Years of History: Arkansas Women in Law, A Record of the Past," *The Arkansas Lawyer* 178 (Oct. 1984), and in the article by Jacqueline S. Wright,"Women of the Law in Arkansas: 1918 to 1959," *The Arkansas Lawyer* 17 (Jan. 1985). Here, we will not go into that much detail but will simply draw upon those sources by summarizing or repeating some of their observations.

Jacqueline Wright's article points out that a number of these early women lawyers were from "law families where the practice is a tradition."[17] She cites Judge Elsijane Trimble Roy, of whom much more will be written subsequently, who followed in her father's footsteps; Nancy Daggett White of the Eastern Arkansas Daggetts, and her daughter, Ellen; Ethel Jacoway Hart, whose father was Chief Justice of the Arkansas Supreme Court; and Mariperle Houston Robertson, whose brother was a lawyer. Zonola Longstreth and Patricia Robinson practiced law with their fathers, and others with father-lawyers included Gladys Milham Wied, Erle Chambers, Mary Burt Nash, and Frances Holtzendorff. Others with lawyer brothers or uncles included Ann Arnold Hastings, Ruth Lindsey, Ruth Dexter Vines, Frances Shaw, and Rebecca Norton. Those with lawyer husbands included Ruth Husky Brunson, Dorothy Howard, Neva Talley-Morris, Lily Carmichael, Elizabeth Gregg Young Huckaby, Ruth Wassell Gibb, Mabel Mahony, Mary Burt Nash, Mary Bullion, Bernice Parker Kizer, and Marian Penix.[18] Aside from the family connections, Jacqueline Wright points out that many women enter the legal profession for economic reasons. "The percentage of women who attended law school in order to have a career with good remuneration exceeded that of the males by a statistically significant margin," she wrote, citing a 1967 study by the University of Michigan Law School.[19]

The articles by Frances Mitchell Ross emphasize the educational background of these early women lawyers. As discussed in the chapter on legal education, at the time women could be admitted to the bar, the only law school in Arkansas was the Arkansas Law School in Little Rock. It was no longer associated with the University of Arkansas, the use of the University's name having been banned after the 1913-1914 academic year. However, graduates in 1915 were considered by the University as graduates.[20] Consequently, a number of the women lawyers attended the Arkansas Law School, presided over by Dean John H. Carmichael, in those early years and even after the founding and accreditation of the University of Arkansas Law School in Fayetteville. Prior to the dissolution of the association with the University, the Arkansas Law School graduated Erle Chambers in 1912 and Katherine Burke in 1915.

One of these early women law graduates of the Arkansas Law School was Mollie Aurelle Burnside of El Dorado whose speech to the Arkansas Bar Convention in the 1930's is reported in the chapter on the organized bar. She was a 1920 graduate, and she co-founded Alpha Delta Epsilon along with Mary Blakeney, Virginia Darden Moose, William Mary James, and Helen G. Humphrey. After being admitted to the bar in 1921, Ms. Burnside obtained an LL.B. from Yale in 1925. She was state and regional director of the National Association of Women Lawyers (NAWL).[21]

Two women were enrolled in the 1919 graduating class, R. Lively and Grace Wallace. Lively was assistant editor of the law school yearbook, made the highest grades in the junior class, and was elected president of the school's "Goar Lyceum," a student public speaking and moot court forum. Wallace was junior editor of the yearbook, junior class president, and an officer of Goar Lyceum.[22]

Virginia Darden Moose, another of the co-founders of Alpha Delta Epsilon, the women's legal fraternity, was also senior class president and graduated in 1921. Upon graduation, she served five years as an assistant attorney general and then became chief deputy clerk of the United States District Court. She was the first president of the Arkansas Association of Women Lawyers when it was formed in 1938.[23]

A few women lawyers went to out of state law schools. As mentioned, after graduating from Arkansas Law School, Aurelle Burnside later obtained a law degree from Yale. Lois Dale graduated from Tulane Law School in 1920 and subsequently became the first woman to serve as county and probate judge, having been appointed by Governor Thomas McRae.[24] The first woman member of the Arkansas Bar Association was Isabel Klein in 1919.[25]

These early women were pioneers and probably did not foresee what was to happen later in terms of women in legal education, women in the legal profession, and women in positions of prominence in law firms, the courts and the bar association. Beginning in the late 1960's, enrollment of women began increasing steadily in the nation's law schools. This trend accelerated during the 1970's and 1980's. Today, the enrollment for 1998-99 in the University of Arkansas at Little Rock Law School is 202 women and 222 men—close to being evenly divided.[26] The percentage of women enrolled in the University of Arkansas Law School in Fayetteville is not quite as high but also over 40%. This explosion of women law students and women lawyers is in my view the most striking event in legal education and the profession in the last thirty years.

Transition to Modern Times

According to an article by Jacqueline S. Wright, approximately 150 women were admitted to the Bar of Arkansas up to 1959.[27] These women lawyers often had family connections and often practiced with fathers or other relatives as previously mentioned. Probably the best known woman lawyer to make this transition to the present was Judge Elsijane Trimble Roy.

Elsijane Trimble Roy

Judge Roy grew up in a family in which her father was a lawyer who became a U.S. District Judge, Thomas C. Trimble. He served on the bench from 1937 to 1956, part of it as Chief Judge for the Eastern District of Arkansas. Her paternal grandfather was active in his law firm in Lonoke, Trimble, Robinson & Trimble, until his late 80's, and her maternal grandfather was U.S. Marshal. Her uncle was the late Senator Joe T. Robinson, majority leader of the Senate under President Franklin D. Roosevelt.[28]

The only woman in her graduating class in Fayetteville, she graduated from the University and was admitted in 1939. From 1940 until the end of World War II, she was an associate with the Rose firm in Little Rock. When she married, she moved to Blytheville and was in practice with her husband in Reid, Evrard and Roy and later with him in Roy & Roy. She was appointed in 1966 by Governor Orval E. Faubus as Circuit Court Judge, the first woman to be a Circuit Judge. At the time of her appointment she had been working as a law clerk to Justice Frank Holt on the Supreme Court. Judge Roy had campaigned for one of Faubus' opponents in the 1960 gubernatorial campaign and when she talked with the Governor about the appointment, she said, "Well, aren't you sort of brave? You don't even know me." She added, "No one could have been more shocked when Governor Faubus called me."[29]

Judge Roy commented about this in 1985 for the article by Ruth Williams, saying: "On the one side, I have an appointment from Orval Faubus and on the other, one from Win Rockefeller and who could have two more divergent governors appoint you to positions." Rockefeller appointed her in 1967 to the Constitutional Revision Study Commission.

After serving the appointed term as a state trial judge, she worked as an assistant attorney general and then as senior law clerk to U.S. District Judge Paul X. Williams.[30] In 1975, Governor David Pryor appointed her to the Arkansas Supreme Court, becoming the first woman ever to serve on the Court. A short time later, in 1977, by appointment of President Jimmy Carter, she became the first woman to serve as a U.S. District Judge in Arkansas. Her commission was for both the Eastern and Western Districts, and she was only the sixth woman federal district judge in the United States. She was the first woman federal judge in the Eighth Circuit. Shortly before she was appointed, she took two senior female law students to lunch and told them the world was opening to them, that she liked her job, that Judge Williams wanted her to stay as long as he was in that position, and so she was "going to stay and don't expect to do any great things."[31] The next week she was appointed.

The judge's son, Jimmy, is a successful lawyer in Springdale and she enjoys visiting with him and with her grandchildren.

No woman lawyer in the history of Arkansas has been more of a trail blazer for other women than Judge Roy. Her experience and her years of careful, well-researched, scholarly service opened the doors for the other, younger women who will subsequently be discussed. A summary of her many achievements up until 1976 is compiled in *The Arkansas Lawyer* 22-24 (Jan. 1976).

Arkansas Supreme Court and Court of Appeals Judges

When the Arkansas Court of Appeals was created in 1979, six judges were appointed to it by Governor Bill Clinton and one was the late Marian Penix of Jonesboro. She served through 1980 and then returned to law practice in Jonesboro with her husband, Bill Penix.[32] Marian Penix also served as part-time U.S. Magistrate in Jonesboro, a position that her husband assumed after her death.

Judge Judith Rogers has served in judicial positions for quite some time and has been on the Court of Appeals since 1989. She was the first woman elected to that court. Previously, she had served as Chancery Judge in Little Rock, having been elected to that court in 1982. Before that, she had served as a Pulaski County Juvenile Judge beginning in 1977 after having built a successful law practice.[33]

Annabelle Clinton Imber was the first woman to be elected to the Arkansas Supreme Court. She is a relatively new Associate Justice, having taken office on January 1, 1997. Prior to that time, she had been elected and had served several years as Chancery and Probate Judge for Pulaski and Perry Counties. Before that, she had served as an appointed Circuit Judge for the same district. She was a member of the Wright, Lindsey & Jennings law firm before becoming a judge.[34]

Although Judith Rogers and Annabelle Clinton Imber were both elected judges who have served at both the trial and appellate levels, Arkansas' first elected woman trial judge was Bernice Lichty Kizer of Fort Smith who was elected in 1974.[35]

By 1997, there were three women judges on the expanded twelve-judge Court of Appeals. In addition to Judith Rogers, they were Andree L. Roaf and Margaret Meads. Judge Roaf's career is discussed in the chapter on lawyers of African-American descent. Both Judge Meads and Judge Roaf are graduates of the UALR Law School as is Justice Imber.[36]

State Circuit and Chancery Judges

Women lawyers have increasingly been elected to judicial office. Judge Ellen B. Brantley has had a distinguished career as a Chancery and Probate Judge in Little Rock and before that as a law professor at UALR after serving previously on the Fayetteville faculty. Judge Robin Mays and Judge Alice Gray serve as Chancery and Probate Judges. Judge Mary Spencer McGowan is both a Circuit and Chancery Court Judge. Judge Joyce Williams Warren and

Judge Rita Gruber serve the Chancery Court Juvenile Division. That is in Pulaski County alone. There are numerous other women state court judges.

The Federal Courts

The only women to serve as U.S. District Judges in Arkansas are Judge Roy and Judge Susan Webber Wright, who was appointed by President George Bush when Judge Roy took senior status. Judge Wright replaced Judge Stephen Reasoner as Chief Judge of the Eastern District after his term was completed in the summer of 1998. She is the first woman Chief Judge and has been serving on the bench since May 1990.

Judge Wright was the first woman Editor-in-Chief of the *Arkansas Law Review* and when she graduated in 1975 from the University of Arkansas Law School, she worked as a law clerk for Judge J. Smith Henley of the U.S. Court of Appeals for the Eighth Circuit. She became Assistant Dean and Assistant Professor of Law at the University of Arkansas at Little Rock School of Law in 1976, and at the time she was appointed by President Bush in late 1989, she was a full Professor. She came, as did so many of the women lawyers, from a family of lawyers in Texarkana. Thomas E. Webber, her father, was a lawyer as were her grandfather, great-grandfather and great uncle. She was also especially close to Philip G. Alston, Judge Henley's career law clerk, and Judge Henley. She has gained extensive notoriety in recent years due to her being the trial judge, first of all, in the school desegregation case involving the three school districts in Pulaski County—a case assigned to her shortly after she became a federal judge—and more recently, the case of *Paula Corbin Jones v. William Jefferson Clinton and Danny Ferguson.*

Although serving in a prosecutorial capacity, another former member of the UALR law faculty is U.S. District Attorney Paula

Casey. Her office has been involved in a large number of cases involving drugs and was involved in a high profile investigation of a number of state legislators. Another interesting case was the one involving the admission to the United States of two Chinese women. These latter cases are ongoing at this writing. Paula Casey has an able Assistant U.S. Attorney in Sandra W. Cherry who is very active in the Arkansas Bar Association, having served as an officer and who is currently contemplating a race for President of the Bar.

Beverly Stites has served as a U.S. Magistrate in Fort Smith and before her marriage to Judge William R. Wilson, Cathy Compton was a U.S. Magistrate in El Dorado. However, the Western District has never had any Article 3 judges who were women.

Women Bar Leaders and Some Leading Practitioners

As mentioned in the chapter on the organized bar, the late Neva Talley-Morris was very active in the American Bar Association and served as Chair of the ABA Family Law Section. She was the first woman to be elected Chair of an ABA Section. She was also President of the Arkansas Association of Women Lawyers, the National Women Lawyers Foundation, and the National Association of Women Lawyers. She was also active in the Arkansas Bar Association and headed a number of committees. A Fellow of the American Academy of Matrimonial Lawyers, she also chaired the Arkansas Council on Children and Youth. She was clearly a trail blazer for women.[37]

Carolyn Witherspoon was the first woman to be elected President of the Arkansas Bar Association and also the first woman to head the Pulaski County Bar Association. She also was President of the Arkansas Association of Women Lawyers, and headed the William R. Overton Inn of Court. She is a partner in her own law firm and a successful practitioner.[38] She is also a delegate from the Arkansas Bar Association to the American Bar House of Delegates.

Sandra Wilson Cherry will be the second woman lawyer to serve as President of the Arkansas Bar in 2001-2002. She has been Assistant U.S. Attorney for many years currently serving in 2000 under Paula Casey.

The best known Arkansas woman lawyer nationally is obviously Hillary Rodham Clinton, the First Lady (now U.S. Senator, New York). She and President Clinton were students together at Yale Law School, and about a year after he became a member of the University of Arkansas law faculty, she joined him in Fayetteville as a law faculty member. They were married not long after that. She was a partner in the Rose Law Firm at the time of his election as President.

Patty Lueken has been President of the Arkansas Association of Women Lawyers and President of the Pulaski County Bar Association. She is also active in both the Arkansas and American Bar Associations. She was honored at the Annual Meeting of the American Bar in San Francisco in 1997 by the General Practice, Solo and Small Firm Section for her service to the Bar as an outstanding solo practitioner.

Jacqueline S. Wright recently retired as head Librarian of the Supreme Court Library. After a stint as a law clerk for Judge Elsijane Trimble Roy and Chief Justice John A. Fogleman, she replaced Ruth Lindsey as Supreme Court Librarian. Ruth Lindsey was a long-term librarian, and both served the Bar faithfully and well. Jacqueline Wright's book on appellate procedure has been widely used and is a service to the Bar.

Another librarian with a long history of service to the Bar was the late Ruth H. Brunson, who was the Director of the combined UALR Law School Library and the Pulaski County Law Library. She was the first law librarian at UALR beginning in 1965, and she built and managed the library until she retired and was replaced by Lynn Foster. Late in her career she received awards from the Arkansas Bar, Pulaski County Bar, and the law school.[39]

There are many other prominent Arkansas women lawyers who could be mentioned. M. Jane Dickey, a partner in the Rose Law Firm, has served as President of the National Association of Bond Lawyers and is a Fellow of the American College of Bond Counsel. Betty Dickey, who is not related to Jane, served for a number of years as Prosecuting Attorney in Pine Bluff, but was defeated in a race for Attorney General by Mark Pryor, the son of former Senator David Pryor. Other women lawyers are leading members of law firms all over the state, including the larger law firms in Little Rock.

For a rather conservative state, the "glass ceiling" referred to by women lawyers in the past seems largely to have been lifted.

Notes

1. This is taken from a short publication of the American Bar Association which excerpted its material from K. Morello, *The Invisible Bar* 3-7 (1986).
2. White, "Women in the Law," 65 MICH. L. REV. 1051 (1967), citing Thomas, *Women Lawyers in the United States* at vii (1957).
3. "Milestones in the History of Women Lawyers" ABA brochure for annual meeting, Aug. 3, 1997.
4. 83 U.S. 130 (1873).
5. 83 U.S. at 141.
6. *Ibid.*
7. 39 Wis. 232 (1875).
8. F. Ross, "Reforming the Bar: Women and the Arkansas Legal Profession," 20 UALR L.J. 869, 871 (1998), citing K. Morello, *The Invisible Bar, The Woman Lawyer in America: 1638 to the Present* 35 (1986).

9. F. Ross, *supra* at 872.

10. This material is found in greater depth in F. Ross, *supra*, 20 UALR L.J. 869, 874 *et seq.* (1998), and in F. Ross,"100 Years of History: Arkansas Women in Law, A Record of the Past," 18 *The Arkansas Lawyer* 178-179 (1984).

11. *Ibid.*

12. F. Ross, *supra*, 20 UALR L.J. at 875.

13. Ibid.

14. *Id.* at 876.

15. *Id.* at 877.

16. *Ibid.*

17. J. Wright, "Women of the Law in Arkansas: 1918 to 1959," *The Arkansas Lawyer* 17 (Jan. 1985).

18. *Id.* at 17-18.

19. *Id.* at 19.

20. R. Wright, *A Brief History of Legal Education in Arkansas*, 20 UALR L.J. 836 (1998).

21. F. Ross, "100 Years of History: Arkansas Women in Law," *The Arkansas Lawyer* 182 (Oct. 1984).

22. F. Ross, *Reforming the Bar: Women and the Arkansas Legal Profession*, 20 UALR L.J. 878-879 (1998).

23. *Id.* at 880.

24. Ross, *supra* n. 21 at 182 (Oct. 1984).

25. Ross, *supra* n. 22 at 880.

26. This is taken from UALR records.

27. J. Wright, "Women of the Law in Arkansas: 1918 to 1959," *The Arkansas Lawyer*, 17 (Jan. 1985).

28. See generally, R. Williams, "Breaking the Barriers," a profile of Judge Roy, in *The Arkansas Lawyer*, 21 (Jan. 1985).

29. *Ibid.*

30. *Id.* at 21-22.

31. *Id.* at 22-23.

32. M. Gitelman and B. Penix, "Before Central High . . . Brewer v. Hoxie School Distict," *The Arkansas Lawyer* 16, 17 (Fall, 1997).

33. A. Clinton, "Coming of Age: Women Lawyers in Arkansas, 1960-1984, *The Arkansas Lawyer* 58-59 (April, 1985), and Ross, *supra* n. 22 at 887.

34. See generally, "Profiles: The New Judges, Supreme and Appellate," *The Arkansas Lawyer* 14-15 (Spring, 1997).

35. A. Clinton, *supra* n. 33 at 58.

36. See *supra* n. 34 at 14-15.

37. Most of this is found in *Who's Who in the South and Southwest* 995 (1969-70) and in Ross, *supra* n. 22 at 882. Also, refer to the chapter on the organized bar.

38. See Ross, *supra* n. 22 at 889, and S. DeWitt, "President's Profile: Serving from Within, Carolyn Witherspoon," 29 *The Arkansas Lawyer* 22-28 (1995).

39. See generally, "Ruth Husky Brunson: Building from a Dream to Accreditation," *The Arkansas Lawyer* 24 (Jan. 1985).

Chapter IX

REMINISCENCES OF LAWYERS

One of the things that was done in the preparation of this book was to interview some of the prominent lawyers and judges about the past and about themselves. In that manner was gathered not only information about themselves but their thoughts on days gone by, along with their recollections of other lawyers, judges and court cases. In these two chapters on reminiscences of lawyers and judges, it is difficult to categorize them as has been done. All of the judges had a career as a lawyer before becoming a judge. A few of the judges were academics rather than practicing lawyers before becoming a judge. No attempt has been made to sort out the academics from the lawyer or judge categories. Because he had such an influence on both lawyers and judges, and on Arkansas law for that matter, although he was an academic, we will start with Robert A. Leflar.

Leflar has already been written about extensively in the chapter on legal education. He remembered vividly that he tore down the railing separating the black students from the white students at the law school. He recalled that when Governor Sid McMath appointed him to the Arkansas Supreme Court in the summer of 1949, he and George Rose Smith "were the two youngsters on the court, and we more or less worked together."[1]

Even at his advanced age, he remembered a great deal about people. He regarded Julian Waterman, the first Dean of the law school in Fayetteville, as "one of the truly great men that I have known in Arkansas or anywhere else."[2] Leflar's family was poor, and he had to be self-supporting. After he received his B.A. degree from the U of A, he taught school at Stuttgart and at John Brown

University in Siloam Springs to earn enough money to go to Harvard Law School. During the summer following his first year, he spent his time briefing second and third year casebooks so that he could earn money at Harvard tutoring first or second-year students.[3] The great Roscoe Pound was Dean at Harvard, and he also regarded Dean Pound as "a great man."[4] He took Pound's course in Jurisprudence as a third-year student—by permission of Pound—since it was a graduate course, and he read Pound's multivolume set on that subject which he viewed as "central to the development of modern American law."[5] He regarded Samuel Williston who taught Contracts as "probably the best teacher I had."[6] He regarded Zechariah Chaffee, the Equity expert, Joseph Warren and Eugene (Bull) Warren as good teachers. "Bull" Warren was the model for the law professor in "Paper Chase," although he taught Property rather than Contracts. He thought less of Joseph H. Beale who taught Conflict of Laws.[7]

Leflar recalled the story about Rex Perkins, a well-known, excellent trial lawyer in Fayetteville, and Dr. Frank Rigall. Dr. Rigall graduated from medical school in Canada and was a member of the Royal College of Surgeons, but he was refused admission to the Washington County Medical Society. He brought suit, and the medical society hired Rex Perkins to defend the case. The court ruled that since the society was voluntary in nature, it did not have to admit him. Perkins was bird hunting one day near Prairie Grove where Dr. Rigall practiced medicine. He had a heart attack, and when he awakened, there was Dr. Rigall staring down at him. He had apparently given him some medication and revived him. Dr. Rigall said, "Now is there anything else I might do for you." (He had a clinic with a few hospital rooms in Prairie Grove.) Rex Perkins replied, "Yes, take me to the Washington General Hospital."[8]

He remembered fondly Bill Putman, E. J. Ball, Dan B. Dobbs, Sid McMath, Henry Woods and others. He said that while he was in law school, J. Smith Henley was particularly close. He thought highly of U. S. District Judge John Miller. He had known Bill Clinton since high school and was probably responsible, he said, for getting him on the faculty. Moreover, in a faculty meeting sometime later, when the need for a woman faculty member was being discussed, Bill Clinton "proceeded to tell us about this wonderful woman [Hillary Rodham], who was at the head of her class in every school that she had been in, and that at this time she was doing graduate work at the head of her class at the Yale Law School. Well, he sold us on the idea. . ., and I think the fact that Bill was here was a persuasive fact in inducing her to accept."[9]

Leflar recalled Judge Henry Woods and former Governor Sid McMath. Both of them were interviewed also.

* * * *

Sid McMath, Judge Woods' longtime law partner, described Hot Springs immediately after World War II before and after he was elected prosecuting attorney:

Hot Springs was a health resort back in those days, and it had wide open gambling. You talk about casinos; they had them back then, and of course, it was illegal. It was a Mecca for gamblers who came to Hot Springs. They would check their weapons in at the police station and go about their business. Even different mobs would come down there, and they were like the old Indians: They would bury the hatchet during the time they were in Hot Springs. Then too, it was a Mecca for divorces [because of our] ninety day divorce law. Old people came there seeking restorative benefits from the waters. ... Since the gambling was illegal, they had to control everything. They controlled the elections to begin with. And the [election] judges and clerks would be people from the various bookies and gambling casinos and houses of prostitution, and so [Mayor Leo] McLaughlin, who was the boss over there, could tell you in advance how many votes anybody was going to get. Of course, they bought them. We had the poll tax back then, and the administration would buy up blocks of poll tax receipts and just vote them on election day. If they needed any votes when they closed the polls, they would just cross mark the ballots for what they needed. In controlling the election, they controlled the courts, prosecuting attorney, the judges, the marshals, and the mayor's office, of course. If you had a case that the administration had an interest in, they would select the jury and you could tell pretty well how it was going to end. That was a situation that we wanted to rectify and did rectify. ... I ran for prosecuting attorney in the primary in 1946. We had a GI ticket. We had somebody for every office, but I was the only one elected in the primary. I was elected because the district included Montgomery County and I got enough votes in Montgomery County to offset what they stole in the second ward in Hot Springs. When I was elected, we started a poll tax drive and all the other candidates who had been defeated ran as independents. They were elected, and I served as prosecuting attorney over there for a couple of years, and then ran for Governor and served as Governor for a couple of terms.[10]

Of course, while serving as prosecuting attorney, he succeeded in cleaning up the corruption in Hot Springs to a large degree, although the illegal casinos were not finally eradicated until Governor Winthrop Rockefeller did it in the late 'sixties.

Governor McMath described his first big case, also described by Judge Woods, in Forrest City against the Ben Hogan Construction Company. He described in detail how they obtained facts from the state trooper who investigated the accident, from the emergency room nurse and doctor who treated the decedent (and refuted the idea that alcohol was involved), and from a truck driver who corrected the report as to the speed the car was going. They went to the accident scene where, remembering the highway department's requirements, they found that the company did not refill the side they had been rebuilding before excavating on the other side. "The lesson that I learned from that was, and I tell the young lawyers, is get the facts. Don't take the face value of any police report or any other government document. If it's a serious case from the standpoint of injuries, don't turn it down just because the police report looks bad. Get the facts."[11]

He remembered fondly the first big admiralty case that was tried in Arkansas in which they received a million dollar verdict. It has been described by Judge Woods previously. "Judge [Oren] Harris was the judge, and, of course, Judge Harris was an outstanding individual, a great congressman, tremendous person, a good judge."[12] He remembered with pleasure the jury argument in which John Shepherd of St. Louis objected several times to his argument, contending McMath was going outside the facts of the case. Finally, after about the third objection, Judge Harris said, "Mr. Shepherd, don't interrupt the Governor when he's talking."[13] John Shepherd liked to tell the story, and some time later, Shepherd awakened him at about 3 o'clock in the morning to tell him that he was representing a plaintiff and had gotten a million dollar verdict.[14]

He was trying one case in Berryville before Judge Maupin Cummings, and was obtaining testimony from one witness that the opposing attorney did not like. The defense attorney "was a real stomping country lawyer," and in a recess he instructed the witness what he wanted him to say. When court resumed,

[H]e put him on the stand and he says, "now you are a little
hard of hearing, aren't you?" In a loud voice, the witness
says, "yeah." "You were in Korea, weren't you, and got shell
shocked, didn't you?" "Yeah." "And what were you doing
out there [about 3 or 4 a.m.] in the morning when you saw
this accident involving Joe here." "Looking for my dogs."
And he went ahead and told this story that was favorable to
the defendant's case.

[On cross-examination] I got as far away from the witness as I could and still be in the courtroom, and I asked
him in a loud voice, "You were out looking for your dogs."
"Yeah." And I said in a real low voice, "What kind of dogs
do you have?" He said, "black and tan."[15]

Sid recalled his experiences with other lawyers. "We've always
had a great relationship with the Wright firm. Of course, we used
to try a lot of cases against Alston [Jennings, Sr.]. Alston is a tremendous trial lawyer, a great trial lawyer, a tremendous person."[16]
He recalled a case that they won against him in Montgomery
County. They were visiting, and "Alston said you know I used to
worry about losing a lawsuit. It would just grieve me to no end.
One night, I was tossing and turning, worrying about losing a
lawsuit, and the thought occurred to me that it's not going to cost
me a dollar. I won't have to pay a penny of it, so why worry about
it?"[17] He described the late Bob Lindsey as "a prince of a guy."[18]

Of Boyd Tackett he said he "was a tremendous lawyer. He was
really an outstanding trial lawyer; he was rough; he was mean. He
defended McLaughlin when I tried McLaughlin." He recalled
their days in law school together during the depression when Sid
worked in the kitchen in Hill Hall and his room was just above the
kitchen. "Boyd would come to my room at meal time, and I would
hand him up his food through the window, and he would com-
plain sometimes because I didn't give him dessert."[19]

He liked John Lookadoo of Arkadelphia. "He was a judge with good sense, and [as a lawyer] he was very persuasive with the jury." "Of course, McLaughlin was a colorful lawyer, a tremendous advocate in the courtroom and had great jury appeal." Lamar Smeed in Camden was called "the white mule lawyer" because he could always produce a "white mule witness" when he needed one.[20]

Of his experiences in politics, he recalled in 1948 when he was in the run-off for Governor with Jack Holt, Sr., who was being supported by "Uncle Mac" Mackrell. Hamilton Moses of AP&L came to see him, and he was trying to decide which one to support. "Finally he got up to leave, and he made a remark that did not register on me at that time. He said, 'Well, it doesn't make any difference which one of you win, you ain't going to get haint done anyway.'"[21] He later learned about the constitutional provision that requires a 3/4ths vote of both the Senate and the House to pass any revenue measure other than the sales tax. "And I learned that the Arkansas Power and Light Company had more than a quarter of the House and the Senate on their payroll. One Senator who was not a lawyer was on their payroll as a lineman."[22] He criticized that provision and the low severance tax.

He recalled his statement that one of the worst things he did was build a road to Huntsville that let Orval Faubus out. "Of course, our principal problem at that time was to build roads. Get out of the mud and dust. We had twelve counties across the northern part of Arkansas that didn't have a single hard surface road. There weren't many people up there, and they had no political influence. Orval was good with the country delegations, the county delegations coming in. And told me, after I was elected, that he would like to have a paying job. So I brought him down, and he worked in the Governor's office, and his primary job was to meet with the delegations on road work."[23]

In discussing the state of the legal profession today, McMath believed that the cordiality and friendly relationships among lawyers has declined. "[T]here was more of a friendly relationship between foes. More cordiality than there is today. ... I think judges will tell you that the amiability between lawyers is not the same as it once was. . . And one reason you know is the advertising, and the competition for business and so forth. The law profession is becoming more materialistic, more of a trade than a profession. Which is sad."[24]

He decried the extensive professional advertising and related activities. "Of course, back in our time a lawyer would be considered a shyster if he advertised. And he wouldn't run a case. A lawyer, now, doesn't make any bones about it, about running cases. They watch the papers and the police reports and contact people who are involved in accidents."[25]

Sid McMath and Henry Woods did not have to do anything of that sort. Their reputation established them as the best personal injury lawyers of their time.

* * * *

J. Gaston Williamson had a different practice than that of McMath, Leatherman & Woods. His grandfather, James Gaston Williamson (for whom he is named), was the founder of the Williamson & Williamson Law Firm in Monticello. He had been the younger partner of an older lawyer, a Judge Wells, who died around the end of the 19th Century. His two sons, Lamar and Adrian Williamson, eventually came into the firm with him. Lamar was born in 1887, and Gaston, his son, was born in 1914; and both in their time were Presidents of the Arkansas Bar Association. The firm had a fine reputation in Southeast Arkansas. Due the litigation in the 1920's, '30's and '40's over titles pertaining to timber rights along the Mississippi and Arkansas Rivers, Lamar Williamson specialized to a large extent in riparian water rights law with respect to accretion and avulsion. Many of the landowners involved in this litigation were large lumber companies.

The principal opposing lawyers in these accretion lawsuits were another well-known, old Arkansas law firm, the Daggetts of Marianna. In those days, when public accomodations were not what they are today, the opposing lawyers would stay in the home of one of their opponents when in town on a case. They were opponents in court, but good friends otherwise.[26] Adrian Williamson specialized in wills, probate, estate planning and real estate law, unlike his brother, and was involved with the drafting of the Arkansas Probate Code of 1949. Back in that period of time, most litigation was civil litigation. There were relatively few divorce cases. The federal government was not as active because of fewer regulations and so most litigation was state court civil litigation. Adrian Williamson represented Southern Lumber Company in Warren and used to litigate against DuVal Purkins. William S. Arnold was a young attorney who was just getting started in Hamburg and Crossett back in that time period.

Gaston Williamson graduated in 1935 from the law school in Fayetteville, won a Rhodes scholarship and spent three years at Oxford, practiced law briefly in Monticello and was called to army duty during World War II. After the war, he worked for a couple of years in a Wall Street law firm practicing tax law and taking courses in tax at N.Y.U. He became a member of the Rose firm in 1948. The Rose firm was located at that time in a little white building on the site of the present Arkansas Bar Center. The firm had five partners, and he was the only associate. The partners were Harry Dobyns, Webster Dobyns, Archie House, William Nash, and Jack Barron. They would hold periodic firm meetings and briefly discuss the cases they had.[27]

When he returned to Arkansas, the only other tax lawyer in Little Rock and in the state was E. Charles Eichenbaum. The Rose firm at that time did most of the bond work in the state, but

the Friday firm became a major competitor for the bond law prac-
tice during the Faubus years in the late '50's and the '60's.[28] The
Bar was much smaller in those days and relationships more cordial.
He expressed it this way:

> I think there has been a change in attitude of lawyers. I
> think instead of a profession, we now have a business. To
> me, it is no longer a profession in the sense that a profes-
> sion generally implied back in those days. The competition
> was tough back then, but it was not a "dog-eat-dog" sort of
> thing, and it was a friendly competition, and you didn't
> carry any grudges, and you could battle each other in court
> and still remain friends. There was just not this mercenary
> attitude that you have now because now it's just a business,
> just a big business. The firms have gotten much bigger.
> The incomes have gotten much larger, and its just a differ-
> ent attitude in the whole practice of law. We don't seem to
> take the same pride in being a lawyer, and in the profes-
> sion, and protecting the reputation of the profession. I
> think the breakdown in morals in the law practice is the
> same as the breakdown in morals generally.[29]

He did not view advertising as "the main culprit"; it's a "moral
thing" that advertising "has only emphasized."[30]

In reminiscing about cases, Gaston recalled that his first case
and his last one were criminal cases, which is rather unusual for a
tax specialist. In the first case, his client was a black man accused of
stealing a pig. The day after he was found innocent, he came to
Gaston's office and offered to give him half of the pig as his fee.
The last one was a habeas corpus situation in which Judge Elsijane
Roy had appointed him to serve. Relying primarily on a young
woman associate who had some criminal case experience, they suc-

ceeded in getting him off at both the district and circuit level on the basis of double jeopardy.[31]

Among judges, he remembered Justice Carroll D. Wood fondly. He expressed admiration for former Chief Justice Griffin Smith. He thought a lot of Judge McHaney, the father of James McHaney and Ed "Buddy" McHaney. Among federal judges, he praised Judge John Miller, Judge Harry Lemley, Judge Smith Henley and Judge Gordon Young.[32]

In his own firm, he praised Harry Meek as "a wonderful fellow," but one who could not take criticism well and who twice "actually got into fist fights with opposing counsel." "He was a hell of a fine corporate lawyer and banking lawyer." "He helped write the commercial code and banking laws." If he was chair of a committee, he did most of the work because he did not know how to delegate. "He also had a tremendous sense of humor, and he was very much in demand as an after-dinner speaker." "He would deliver his speech in a dry Will Rogers style of speaking."[33] Archie House was just the opposite type of character as far as personality was concerned. "Everybody loved Archie" who was a "loveable, personal friend of everybody." "He was the sort that could battle like hell in court and then go have several drinks after the session with his opponent and still remain very close." He specialized in insurance law and did a great deal of bond work.[34]

Jack Barron "was a fine trial lawyer" who particularly excelled at cross-examination of witnesses. "He would put his witness perfectly at ease and make him think that they were real good friends, and the first thing you knew, he would have him making some very damaging admissions." "Bill Nash was a scholarly type of lawyer" who wasn't "a very personable type and didn't have too much of a sense of humor." One time, he came to his office late one evening and found two persons who were not married and who cleaned the offices having sex on his couch. The next morning he reported this "when all of the partners of the firm gathered to discuss the serious affairs of the firm." He "reported this in a grave tone with sharp accounts," and "when he finished he looked around and everyone was just staring at him." He did not understand their reaction and said, "Well, anyone who would do that would steal," and everyone burst into laughter "and kidded Bill ever after about his serious views on life."[35]

* * * *

Gaston Williamson's contemporary in tax law after World War II was E. Charles Eichenbaum.[36] Charlie grew up in Pulaski Heights which was then an incorporated village with one school in 1910. He went to college and law school at Washington University in St. Louis and worked for the *St. Louis Post Dispatch* where he became acquainted with the great publisher, Joseph Pulitzer.

The first law office he ever visited was that of Cohn & Clayton. Morris Cohn "was a highly respected member of the bar, well-known as an appellate lawyer and through an outstanding personality, had many clients in financial and mercantile areas of the city and state." Powell Clayton had been the governor, "frequently referred to as the 'Carpetbagger Governor.' " He was, however, a rather quiet individual.[37] This was about 1915 when, as a boy, he came into contact "with two very significant members of the bar."[38]

Another event that spurred his interest in becoming a lawyer was when he observed Senator Joe T. Robinson defend his friend, A. B. Banks of Fordyce, in a Pulaski County courtroom. This was during the Depression and Mr. Banks' insurance company had failed. "I remember Senator Robinson entering the courtroom, and he was wearing a linen suit, and I remember him taking off that coat and throwing it down on the counsel table and turning to the jury as if challenging them to dispute anything that he said to them. That day, if no other, he demonstrated to me that he was a lion above others on the plain."[39] He recalled others whom he regarded highly. "I can remember trials in which Frank Pace demonstrated an articulate command of the subject matter. He was the Dean of the plaintiff's bar in that period in which he served, particularly in the early '30's."[40] "I thought then and I think now that there never was in Arkansas a more astute lawyer for the defense" than R. E. Wiley. He had a "gravelly sort of voice, but [had] a determined, persistent type of questioning which resulted in uncovering every relevant factor in the examination." "I can remember Mr. Charles Coleman arguing cases before the Supreme Court of Arkansas, arguing them with scholarly distinction, a fervor, a mentality which commanded the respect of those on the bench."[41]

Charlie Eichenbaum had a "great relationship" with Joe House, who was the older brother of Archie House, and was in practice with Hamilton Moses. He hoped to become an associate in that firm. However, Willis Holmes became a partner, and Moses informed House that they were going to take Raymond Roddy as associate. However, "Mr. House saw that some work came my way for which I was very grateful."[42] Not long after that, Moses became full-time President of Arkansas Power & Light. In those days, "it was an unusual situation for there to be more than two or three lawyers, no matter how far up the ladder the law firm appeared to be."[43] He also recalled in that period around 1928 and the early thirties, the firm of Buzbee, Pugh & Harrison. Mr. Pugh was what we would call today a "rainmaker" for the firm through his extensive holdings. Buzbee was "a hard-hitting trial lawyer" who did not take ordinary trials. The ordinary trials were usually handled by Harrison, a very good insurance trial lawyer. Ultimately, they took in Ed Wright who had returned to Little Rock from law school about 1927, and he began to take some of the trial work. He "was a marvel at the organization of a law firm which fact was obviously demonstrated in the success of Wright, Lindsey & Jennings."[44]

He recalled the sad state of things during the Depression at the beginning of his law practice:

In Arkansas [the Depression] really began earlier. It began in the late '20's. In 1927 and 1928, agricultural markets
fell and property values declined. Improvement district
bonds sold for five and ten cents on the dollar. I remember
distinguished people of the community, people who were
looked up to, standing on the corners on Main Street sell-
ing apples. During that period, I did a lot of trial work. I
probably tried more cases in that first five years than in any
ten to fifteen year period thereafter. I traveled all through
the state, and at one time, I thought I had been in almost
every county, certainly every judicial district. I recall one occasion, I believe in Monticello, when the judge who was
offering the prayer turned to the jury and asked them to
have mercy and pity on that stranger in their midst. I [also]
remember how difficult it was in transportation in those
days. I can recall a matter in Arkansas County where I had
to go to on behalf of my client, the casualty company, and I
had to ride a mule into the area where the accident had occurred and determine the availability of witnesses. Of
course, these deprivations were nothing compared to those
which were engaged in by our earlier members of the bar
and bench.[45]

From his association with Lloyd Taylor in the 1930's, Charlie got
to know his father, retired Judge Felix Taylor, who had served as
Circuit Judge of the First Judicial District. "He would tell me of
how when he was a Circuit Judge, he forded the rivers in flood
time when the ferries were not working, how he swam his horse
through those flood waters with only two books in his saddle
bag—Blackstone's *Commentaries* and Saxon's *Instructions to the
Jury*. When the water was extremely high and the horse fractious,

he held the books in one hand over his head in order that pages would not stick together."[46]

Mr. Eichenbaum recalled some other law firms that were formed in Little Rock or were continuations of others. Moore and Turner, he said, eventually became Moore, Chowning & Burrow. Donham, Fulk & Mehaffy was the forerunner of Mehaffy, Smith & Williams, which became Smith, Williams, Friday & Bowen, and is today Friday, Eldredge & Clark. Of Pat Mehaffy, who became a Judge on the Eighth Circuit Court of Appeals, he said: "Pat started practicing at the same time I did. I suppose we were considered 'young rebels.' We organized the Junior Bar. Of course, we had some help, but Pat and I worked very hard on that. I have always been interested in Bar Association work." He recalled when Bill Smith came up to be Secretary to the Governor and described the Friday firm as "a very fine, distinguished law firm."[47] He then got to the Rose firm, stating that when he first knew them, there were four lawyers although one was relatively inactive. "It was Rose, Hemingway, Cantrell & Loughborough. Mr. Hemingway was a rather patrician sort, not a hail-fellow-well-met." He described Cantrell as a "fine desk lawyer" and Loughborough as "a gifted advocate, personable, community-oriented, and by far the most highly regarded of the three." "Mr. George Rose was interested in art, in music and in the beautiful things of life. About that time, Archie House was exceedingly active as the young associate in that firm, later became partner and really in later years was looked to as the spokesman for the group. A few years after I returned [from law school], a young man by the name of George Rose Smith became their associate, a very studious, scholarly and highly regarded young lawyer, later of course to ascend the bench and serve the longest period of any Supreme Court Justice in the history of our State."[48] (He digressed to refer to the Arkansas Supreme Court as having been comprised of "outstanding scholars and gentlemen" in the 75 years he had known it. Judges, including trial judges and some federal judges, have already been discussed to some degree, but more of that will follow later.)

There was one classification of lawyers that Charles Eichenbaum referred to as "Courthouse row lawyers." That row extended from Markham and Spring back to the alley behind the old Federal Building. Eight or nine offices were there and, at times, two or three lawyers occupied one of the offices. The Pulaski County jail was at the bottom of Spring Street along LaHarpe up until sometime in the 1970's. This was convenient because these lawyers practiced a great deal of criminal law. "I don't want you to have the impression that I am critical of the ability of those lawyers," he said. "They were some of the most able trial lawyers in the state."

Charlie Eichenbaum built up a substantial bankruptcy practice during the 1930's and a substantial tax practice after that. His firm developed a general corporate practice—although he once tried a court martial case at the request of President Truman. He had a successful law practice for many years with the very able Leonard Scott and W. S. Miller and was very active in both the Arkansas Bar and the American Bar. One of the last positions he held was Chair of the Senior Lawyers Division of the American Bar Association. He was a credit to Arkansas and the legal profession.

* * * *

Now, to some prominent members of the Bar, keeping in mind the quotation from Ecclesiasticus at the beginning of this book that many whose names were less well known served the profession and the public admirably.

Phillip Carroll, one of the senior partners in the Rose firm, recalls two events from his early life that he will, understandably, never forget. One involved a "bachelor woman," Lilly Mae McBride, who lived across the street from him with two brothers, a sister and their mother. Phil saw her brother, Danny, lying on the McBride lawn covered with blood and calling for help. Whereupon, Lilly Mae came out of the house, leveled a revolver at Danny and emptied it into him. At the murder trial, young Phil was qualified to testify, although under ten, after it was established that he knew the meaning and obligation of an oath. Lilly Mae was represented by John P. Woods of Fort Smith, "a very fine and very distinguished lawyer." The prosecuting attorney was Harold Harper and his deputy was one of the Gutensohns, names well-known among the Fort Smith Bar. After a mistrial, Lilly Mae was convicted but ended up in the state mental asylum. She had allegedly compiled a "death list" of people she was going to get even with, and Phil was number two on the list, just after the Presbyterian minister. Another unforgettable incident for Phil was being taken prisoner by the Germans in a battle near the Battle of the Bulge in 1944 in France. He was sent with other prisoners on a crowded train with no facilities, after walking many miles in bitter cold, to a prison camp in eastern Germany and was eventually released by the Russians.

After law school, he went in with the Rose firm in 1950, and his friend, Jack Deacon, was a recent associate. During the Korean War, he was called up, promoted to 2d lieutenant and was about to be shipped to the front when Jack, who had also been called up, got him assigned to the Pentagon where Jack was located. He viewed Jack as saving his life because the life span of a 2nd lieutenant in Korea was very short on average.[49]

Phil remembered his early days with the Rose firm in which he worked principally with Archie House. Archie House redlined everything he wrote, and it seemed that he could never satisfy him with his composition. (That is an interesting point about one who is a lifetime member and former President of the National Conference of Commissioners on Uniform State Laws, and whose job is to write laws to be adopted by the states.) He also remembers the scholarly, meek and mild Harry Meek having a fight with Dave

324 A HISTORY AND REMINISCENCES OF THE BAR OF ARKANSAS

Panich in the hall of the federal courts building over a remark made by Panich that suggested Harry Meek was a liar. (Dave Panich was appointed the Bankruptcy Trustee in numerous cases by the Bankruptcy Judge, Arnold Adams.) Archie House was an amateur boxer, and one day in the old Rose firm building at 314 West Markham, he came to fisticuffs with Carl Langston during a deposition and began chasing him around the conference table. Phil and others had to pull Archie off and calm him down.[50] He remembered also a faked fight between Dale Price and Bill Arnold of Texarkana while serving on the Supreme Court Committee on Jury Instructions. They had prearranged the stunt at a cocktail party the previous evening, but the other members and the chairman, Judge Paul Wolfe of Fort Smith, did not know it was faked. These two were always arguing the plaintiff's side (Dale Price) or the defendant's side (Bill Arnold), but on this occasion tempers were rising, they turned red in the face, then they were shouting, and then Bill walked down to the other end of the table and hit Dale. They got into a fist fight and wrestling match; Judge Wolfe, stunned, was pounding his gavel. Finally, both of them collapsed into laughter at having suckered the others with their performance.[51]

* * * *

Maurice Mitchell today heads one of the largest firms in Arkansas, Mitchell, Williams, Selig, Gates & Woodyard. He has served as President of the Pulaski County Bar and Secretary-Treasurer of the Arkansas Bar. After graduation from the University of Arkansas and Washington & Lee Law School, he went with Bailey & Warren for a short time and then held attorney positions with the IRS, the state Revenue Department, and then went into private practice, eventually forming the firm of Spitzberg, Mitchell & Hays with Henry Spitzberg and Steele Hays (which for a time included Tom Bonner and bore his name also). In the 1970's the firm expanded and in the early 1980's, there was a steady expansion when Dick Williams' firm was merged, and after having seventeen lawyers in 1981, it has grown to almost fifty lawyers.

Maurice talked some about judges that he had a high regard for, two of them being Murray O. Reed and Frank Dodge. Judge Reed struck down some printing contracts that Harry Parkin had with the State when he was appointed the Chairman of the Highway Commission. Maurice Mitchell had not supported Judge Reed, and he represented those trying to cancel the contracts. Judge Reed came under some intense pressure from Governor Faubus and others to uphold the contracts, but he did not let that interfere with his decision. He also mentioned Neil Bollinger as being a good Judge. He also had a particular regard and respect for Justice George Rose Smith. In addition, he also had favorable remarks about Justices Frank Smith, Darrell Hickman and Lyle Brown, and about trial Judges Guy Amsler, whom he viewed as one of the best, Mitchell Cockrill, and Warren Wood. He agreed with Winslow Drummond that Judge W. J. Waggoner from Lonoke was probably the worst, and he thought Judge Dexter Bush of Texarkana was pretty bad also.

He also recalled participating with Bob Shults and Ed Lester in trying to keep the schools open during the Central High crisis in 1957 and '58. He lost clients over that.[52]

Over the years, Maurice Mitchell has been quite active in Democratic Party politics, not as a candidate, but as a supporter of certain politicians and as a fund-raiser. However, his actions have manifested the better instincts of one who is politically involved, that is, to support those whom you think will perform effectively and admirably for the public. In his professional life, he has exemplified what hard work and dedication can achieve. That last remark applies also to his partner, Richard A. Williams, who went from a large firm (Wright, Lindsey & Jennings) to small firm practice and then began building with Maurice another large firm. Much could be said about so many members of this firm, such as Ed Dillon, an expert on utility law, who was a senior partner in the former firm of House, Holmes & Jewell before its untimely demise. Ed is one of the brightest of the bright and a superb advocate going back to law school days when he and Phil Carroll teamed to win numerous advocacy competitions.

* * * *

A prominent lawyer who both practiced law and was active in politics over several decades is Judge William J. Smith. Bill Smith was born in 1908 and admitted to practice in January 1937. He received his law degree in the same year from Cumberland Law School. In 1939, the legislature enacted the Worker's Compensation Act, and he was appointed to the Commission in 1940, from which he resigned when our country entered World War II in order to serve in the armed forces. He was reappointed after the war. He was appointed in 1940 to the Commission by Governor Carl E. Bailey whom he had supported previously, but he favored Homer M. Adkins in Governor Bailey's final gubernatorial campaign. Bailey was appointing people who would serve in the Adkins administration, choosing three from a longer list submitted by Adkins. Bill Smith was on the list.[53]

Prior to that, he had served as an investigator and arbitrator for one of the railroad labor unions. He lived in Texarkana and during the 1930's, he took the bar examination and tied for the high score. Some time after that, the labor union put him in charge of all arbitrations in the lower one-third of the United States, west of the Mississippi and south of the Union Pacific Railroad, which at that time was principally limited to the northwest. He performed some work during the administration of Governor Marion Futrell and lobbied for a workman's compensation law, as it was originally called. It was finally approved by the voters on a referendum on November 5, 1940, during Governor Bailey's administration. One of the things he did during his time on the Commission was to give a job as a referee to Francis Cherry, later to be elected governor. He also learned a lot by hearing lawyers argue the cases.

Ben Laney was elected governor after the war, but Judge Smith supported Bill Terry's father who was also a candidate. Subsequently, Governor Laney asked him to be his Executive Secretary, an offer he declined because he had not supported Laney. At the urging of Ned Stewart in Texarkana, where his parents lived, Smith agreed to help Governor Laney during a special legislative session. During that period of time, he wrote the Revenue Stabilization Act and otherwise spent full time on the Laney program even though he was still on the Commission. (He simply did not handle Commission cases during that time period.) Frank Storey and Julian Hogan were involved in the Revenue Stabilization Act formulation also.

Of all the things he did, and there were many, the drafting and passage of the Revenue Stabilization Act during Governor "Business Ben" Laney's administration is probably the most important as far as state government is concerned. Judge Smith's older brother was vice-president of Dun & Bradstreet, and he and his associates traveled to New York and met with the state insurance commissioner, a meeting presumably arranged by his brother. They had paid off outstanding bonds, as well as a debt that went back to the Civil War. Arkansas had suffered from financial problems prior to that, but the new act created a sound fiscal base. The result was that Arkansas was placed back on the approved list with respect to securities. Every school, county, city, and improvement district that might issue bonds could sell their securities with decent interest rates. In addition to the Revenue Stabilization Act, the Laney administration through Bill Smith and the others consolidated fourteen or fifteen boards and commissions and created a Resources and Development Commission.

This is an oversimplification, but the Revenue Stabilization Act essentially creates three categories along with some sub-categories. The "A" category is essential funding for state agencies and instrumentalities. It is solid money that will be received. The "B" category is appropriations that may be provided for, usually in part, but usually not fully. There is a formula for the allocation of these funds. The "C" category usually represents "appropriations" that are desirable but are unlikely to be funded because that category will not be reached until the "B" category is funded. To provide funding for the "C" category, there would have to be a gross underestimation of state revenue, and so, it is for the most part a wish list.

For all of his public service, Judge Smith nevertheless took time to form with Pat Mehaffy the firm of Mehaffy, Smith & Williams. John Williams had been practicing law in Marianna with the Daggett law firm and had been a deputy prosecuting attorney, which as previously mentioned was important to Mehaffy. During this period, he was involved in several political campaigns, including the election of J. L. (Bex) Shaver of Wynne as Lt. Governor. He was involved in reorganizing the Young Democrats along with Sid McMath and Nathan Gordon. However, in the gubernatorial election that Sid won, he worked for his friend, Jack Holt, Sr. When Governor McMath was defeated for a third term by Francis Cherry, Bill Smith went to work for Governor Cherry as legislative liaison and was able to get a package of bills through the legislature that Cherry's inexperienced staff could not get passed. Governor Cherry, however, only lasted one term. A former Chancery Judge, he was politically naive and seemed to many to be a stuffed shirt. Then, came the Orval Faubus era in the 1950's. When Bill Smith became legal advisor for Governor Faubus, he took a leave of absence from the law firm. As for Faubus, "he knew more about the state government than any governor I've known."[54] He devoted a great deal of time to going around with Faubus, organizing for the legislative session, talking to legislators, writing bills, and "working professionally on legislation." He was working on getting money released for highway contracts, *i.e.* the state had more contracts than it could pay for, when the desegregation of Central High boiled over. Griffin Smith, son of the Chief Justice, filed a lawsuit in connection with the desegregation order. This was the time when Faubus testified that violence would occur, according to his information, if the order were carried out. School Superintendent Virgil Blossom testified to the contrary. The federal district judge did not lift the order, and Governor Faubus called out the National Guard after going on statewide television to announce what he was doing and his reasons.

Bill Smith urged Faubus not to call out the National Guard until violence had occurred. Faubus insisted that there would be violence. "He said, Bill, you're telling me not to call out the Guard until after the violence. You think that I'm the Governor with the responsibility of keeping peace, [and I'm just] sitting here and letting somebody get killed."[55] Faubus, he is convinced, believed that there would be violence. Smith also talked to Virgil Blossom, the school superintendent, who had sent his wife out of town and put his daughter in school in Jonesboro. Both Blossom and Faubus had received telephone calls threatening their lives. Of course, eventually President Eisenhower sent in the 101st Airborne troops from Fort Campbell, Kentucky, and federalized the Arkansas National Guard to take them out of the picture.

This entire episode cast a stain on Little Rock and the state that has endured. Only now, over forty years later, is there attempted reconciliation with Central High being declared a national historic building and a mini-museum and visitors' center being created across the street in an old gasoline station building. But as an issue of the *Arkansas Times* on September 19, 1997, indicated, the old arguments are still being voiced. In that issue is an article by Harry S. Ashmore, who was Editor of the *Arkansas Gazette* during the crisis and later won a Pulitzer Prize for his editorials, expressing his point of view, and former state Supreme Court Justice Jim Johnson, an ardent opponent of integration, expressing the other side.[56] Johnson played an active role in all of this, according to Ashmore. Ashmore quotes an interview with Roy Reed, in which Johnson said: "We were dedicated to hustling him [Faubus]. Our people were phoning him from all over the state. Orval hid out, but our people got to him. There wasn't any caravan [of armed men from around the state coming to Central High to prevent integration]. But we made Orval believe it."[57] It was small wonder, if that is true, that Faubus believed that there would be violence and that he must act to prevent it. But the business and professional men and women who opposed Faubus' actions in connection with Central High never believed that, nor did the vast majority of the media. They believed that Faubus acted for his own purely political purposes. He spent the rest of his life, particularly after he left office, trying to refute their thesis. As Roy Reed stated in *Faubus: The Life and Times of an American Prodigal*: "The real betrayal by Orval Faubus was one that haunted him the last third of his life, all through the untiring revisionism, the endless pleading and explaining to justify the past to the future. It was the betrayal of his talent."[58] There is no attempt here to delve in depth into the Central High crisis; in fact, Roy Reed has done it admirably and at length in his book. The intent here is simply to take it up peripherally as it affected Bill Smith as well as other Arkansas lawyers—Archie House, the school board's attorney, who urged that the desegregation plan be put into effect without delay; Richard C. Butler, who argued all the way to the Supreme Court seeking a delay in implementation; Wayne Upton, a school board member and a partner in the Wright firm; Edwin Dunaway, who was involved around the fringes in supporting integration and opposing the closing of the school; Jim Johnson, who was a bitter opponent of integration; Sid McMath and Henry Woods, who attempted to deal with the crisis and sought to devise ways to protect the black students; Claude Carpenter, a Faubus aide; Congressman Brooks Hays, whose political career would be ended as a result of his attempt to reconcile the dispute; U. S. District Judge John E. Miller; U. S. District Judge Harry Lemley; Chancellor Murray O. Reed; and many others in addition to Bill Smith.

The Central High episode obscures an otherwise productive and progressive governorship under Faubus aided by Bill Smith. The school teachers received the largest pay increases that they had ever received. State employees were put on social security and their own retirement plan. The tax structure was altered to increase state income. The Justice Building was built. The courtroom was added later, and they had to have a special Supreme Court to approve the bond issue.[59]

During the pre-Central Faubus period, he supervised the completion of the University Medical Center. He signed legislation raising unemployment compensation and extending the period of eligibility. He secured a law requiring utilities to wait 120 days before collecting higher rates after applying for them. The publicity and parks department was created to promote tourism. He opened two new state parks, Queen Wilhelmina and Mount Magazine. Property reassessment to equalize property taxes statewide was passed. A systematic effort was made to industrialize the state, and Winthrop Rockefeller was named head of the Arkansas Industrial Development Commission. Practically all of this was done before the Central High crisis.[60]

During his long life, Bill Smith served, in addition to what has been stated, as a member of the first Legislative Council, the first Capitol Grounds Commission, as Associate Justice of the Supreme Court, as Chairman of the Arkansas Bar Executive Council, as Chairman of the National Foundation March of Dimes Campaign, as Secretary-Treasurer of the Arkansas Young Democrats, as Secretary-Treasurer of the Democratic State Committee, as State Chairman on the Committee to legalize voting machines (Amendment 50), as a Fellow in the American College of Trial Lawyers, on the Board of Governors and Executive Committee of the State Fair and Livestock Exposition, as a Chairman of the Board of Fifty for the Future, as President of the Little Rock Chamber of Commerce, as Chairman of the Federal Home Loan Bank of Little Rock, as State Co-Chairman of the Arkansas Heart Association, as Professor of Medical Jurisprudence at the University School of Medicine, and in numerous other capacities. He has been a man who has dedicated most of his life to public service and has been someone who can get things done.

Bill Smith's retired partner, William L. Terry, recalls his grandfather and father, who were both in Congress and active in the legal profession in Arkansas during the 20th Century. His grandfather, William L. Terry, was a graduate of Trinity College, the predecessor of Duke University, and came here from North Carolina in the late 19th Century. He was city attorney, a state senator, was president pro tem of the state senate, and served in Congress for ten years around 1890 to 1900. He was opposed once for Congress by Jeff Davis (who served three times as governor), but Davis withdrew after a disappointing showing at the convention held in his home county. David D. Terry was elected to Congress in 1933 in a special election that resulted when Heartsill Ragon was appointed to the federal bench. (This was the father of the Heartsill Ragon who was Arkansas Bar President some years later.) His opponents were Brooks Hays and Sam Roark. He served in Congress for almost ten years, but was defeated in a race for the U. S. Senate by John McClellan in 1942. After that, he served as Director of Water, Flood Control and Soil Conservation for the state under Governors Laney and McMath. He was always working for flood control on the Arkansas River, and the Terry Lock and Dam is named for him.[61]

* * * *

Louis L. Ramsay, Jr., and Paul Young both came to Pine Bluff from other towns—Louis from Fordyce and Paul from Malvern. They personify, to a large extent, the law practice in the Pine Bluff area during the last half of the 20th Century. Both are very fine gentlemen, and both have served as president of the Arkansas Bar Association. The firm of Bridges, Young & Matthews is over one-hundred years old, and the firm of Coleman, Gantt & Ramsay will be ninety years old in 2001. W. F. Coleman and Nicholas Gantt formed the firm in 1911. Mr. Gantt had previously been in the Bridges firm. Louis's firm has produced four presidents of the Arkansas Bar Association, Coleman, Gantt, Ramsay and E. Harley Cox, Jr.

Although both are graduates of the U of A Law School, Louis almost did not attend college in Fayetteville. Paul (Bear) Bryant was a native of Moro Bottom in Dallas County, was a high school star at Fordyce, and was an outstanding football player at Alabama. He was an assistant coach on the staff of Coach Frank Thomas at Alabama when Louis starred as quarterback for the Fordyce Redbugs. Bear recruited him for Alabama, and he agreed to come, but Coach Fred Thomson of Arkansas told him that he would help him get through law school financially when his eligibility for football was finished. Being a lawyer was Louis' goal in life and had been for a long time. Consequently, when Coach Thomson and Assistant Coach Gene Lambert came to his house and recruited him, he notified Alabama that he was going to Arkansas. They went to Fayetteville, and after a night at the coach's house, he went to a room in Hill Hall, which he did not like. So, he caught a bus for Tuscaloosa, although in the meantime, his parents had shipped his trunk to Fayetteville. When he got to Alabama, Bear told him to go to the field house and register; they planned for him to be a teacher or a coach after football, and that was not what he had in mind. After much prayerful thought and a telephone conversation with his mother, he packed his suitcase, wrote a note thanking Bear, and took a bus back to Fayetteville. It was the most important decision he ever made. He later reconciled with Bear who told him that that turned out to be the right decision for him as did Bear's ultimately becoming head coach at Alabama.[62]

Commenting on outstanding or memorable lawyers over the years in Pine Bluff, Paul Young named Frank Bridges, Jr., and his father, Jay Dickey (father of the Congressman), the Williamson law firm in Monticello, the Daggetts in Marianna, Jimason Daggett, Steve Matthews, David Solomon in Helena and Maurice Reinberger and Reggie Eilbott. Both Paul and Louis mentioned Reinberger and Eilbott. Reggie learned a lot from Maurice and developed into a fine trial lawyer. Reggie had most of the criminal defense practice, and his clients were devoted to Reggie; they felt that he "had put the protective arm around them," according to Louis. Mr. Coleman, addressing the jury in the 2-4-D cases that were tried in Pine Bluff and were either the first or among the first such cases in the nation, referred to "my friend, Gordon Young, wrapped in the protective arms of the Arkansas Power & Light Company for so many years." Gordon Young, of course, was a partner in Bridges, Young & Matthews and later became a federal district judge, serving for ten years prior to his death. His wife, Elizabeth Young, later Huckaby, was a lawyer and a legend at the numerous Arkansas Bar and Federal Eighth Circuit functions she attended, often called upon to sing "Sweet Bird" and other songs.

In addition to the outstanding lawyers mentioned by Paul Young, Louis Ramsay also mentioned the late Jeff Starling, who died in his 40's of cancer, Arthur Triplett,[63] John Harris Jones,

Frank Bridges, Henry Gregory, Ed Wright of Little Rock, James B. Sharp of Brinkley, William S. Arnold of Crossett, Herschel Friday, Heartsill Ragon, and John Fogleman.

As for outstanding judges, Paul Young mentioned Henry Smith, Carleton Harris, Tom Eisele, and John Miller. Louis Ramsay added Oren Harris, Elisjane Trimble Roy, mentioning also the same ones as Paul Young. One outstanding judge before their time in Pine Bluff was Judge T. G. Parham.

Louis Ramsay served as President of the Arkansas Bar Association and also of the Arkansas Bankers Association. His receiving so many honors reminded him of a story told him by the late DuVal Purkins of Warren, the Bar's Lawyer-Citizen one year, about an occurrence that he had. A man came up to him and said, "Aren't you Judge Purkins, or at least, you used to be our judge. You also used to be our state representative." And he named several positions Purkins had held in the past. The man then said, "You ain't nothin' now, are you?"

One of the high points of Louis' career was serving on the University of Arkansas Board of Trustees (and as its Chairman for a time). He served on the UALR Board, he said, before he was named to the U of A Board at a time when it was decided that the UA Board should expand its membership on a statewide basis. There were three presidents during his tenure—Drs. Mullins, Bishop and Martin. The UA System was being put in place during those years—UALR, UAPB, UA-Monticello—and there were growing pains. He had a great interest in the law school. The other members would say, "Don't fool with the law school or athletic department because that's Louis's domain."

Louis Ramsay concluded his remarks by saying, "My life has been blessed because I have been able to practice law." Even when he was President of Simmons Bank, he did not leave his firm. And Arkansas, and particularly the Bar, have been blessed because Louis did not choose to play football for the Crimson Tide. He has had a distinguished career not only in law but in public service, and Arkansas has been the beneficiary.

* * * *

John C. Deacon of Jonesboro was in law school in Fayetteville with many fine lawyers who have made great contributions to the Arkansas Bar: Robert L. Jones of Fort Smith (who, like Jack, has served as President of the Association, as has his son), Edward Lester, James (Deacon) Sharp of Brinkley (another past state bar president), William A. Eldredge, and Phil Carroll (yet another past president), to mention only a few. After graduation from law school in 1948, he picked up his Bar license in Little Rock (—in those days, graduates of the U of A Law School were admitted without passing an examination—), and drove to Jonesboro where his wife, Doreen Barrett Deacon, went into labor and delivered their oldest child. Edward L. Wright, who was then President of the Pulaski County Bar, called him and offered him a part-time job as legal aid attorney for $75 per month. It helped pay for the office he opened in the Pyramid Life building, where he paid $25 monthly rent and $10 for an answering service. He later gave Sam Laser his outer office to use as his office. When George Rose Smith went to the Supreme Court, Harry Meek offered him an associate's position with the Rose firm, where he stayed until January 1950, when he was called up because of the Korean War. After returning, he joined Joe Barrett, his father-in-law, in Jonesboro in 1952, and that was the beginning of Barrett & Deacon. Joe Barrett was a very fine lawyer who won the first Outstanding Lawyer award presented by the Arkansas Bar Association. He imbued in Jack the idea that you have to give something back to the profession. Jack started with the Arkansas Bar Association's Junior Bar and the Junior Bar of the American Bar, and he has never slowed down. In 1967, he was appointed a Commissioner to the National

Conference of Commissioners on Uniform State Laws (NCCUSL), a very prestigious organization that drafts uniform acts for adoption by the states. He later became President of NCCUSL as Mr. Barrett had been before him. He is now a lifetime Commissioner. He was elected a delegate to the American Bar House of Delegates and later served as State Delegate. He has been President of the Arkansas Bar Association, and he has served twice on the American Bar Board of Governors. He was an officer of the General Practice Section of the ABA and would have become Chair, but he resigned to go on the Board of Governors. He has more recently served as Chair of the ABA Senior Lawyers Division and as President of the American Bar Foundation.

Joe Barrett was also President of the Arkansas Bar Association and in the House of Delegates of the American Bar Association. He became Chair of the International Law Section of the ABA, even though he never had an international law case. It was an intellectual interest with him. He went to the International Law Conference at the Hague and to the Hague Peace Conference. He believed that international events and law affected all of us, including small town lawyers. He was a fine all-around lawyer who dealt mostly with probate, wills, trusts, and property work.

Other lawyers from Jonesboro that Jack thought were outstanding included Charles Frierson, David Walker, and Herbert McAdams, who became primarily a banker. Herbert McAdams was innovative. When he bought the Lake City Bank, he moved it to Jonesboro and merged with Citizens Bank. Because branch banking was illegal then, and because bank buildings had to be connected, he built a tunnel under the street to physically connect the two banks that were across the street from each other.

Outside of Jonesboro, he mentioned as fine lawyers, John Fogleman and Jim Hale (who always called him, "Smilin' Jack") as a good team, and another good team he mentioned were Bruce Ivy and Jim Hyatt. He mentioned Bill Kirsch in Paragould, and Ed

Wright and Herschel Friday in Little Rock. He had special mentions for Sid McMath and Henry Woods. When he tried a case with them, he felt like he had been put through a ringer on a washing machine. "Sid was a fine orator and there was no better book lawyer than Henry Woods. They were great gentlemen. The two most important lawyers I knew in Arkansas were Ed Wright and Sid McMath. Great lawyers, fine lawyers. Henry Woods has been a good lawyer and has made a fine judge. Tom Eisele has been a splendid judge, a great intellect. Another great federal judge that we lost prematurely was Bill Overton."

On state trial judges, Jack Deacon said that Charles W. Light of Paragould was one of the finest, possessed of great intellect and fairness. He was "the best circuit judge I have seen." He also mentioned Judge Gerald Pearson and Judge Olan Parker. A young judge with great promise, he thinks, is Judge John Fogleman of West Memphis, Julian Fogleman's son. As for the Supreme Court, "George Rose Smith jumps out at you," and he mentioned Chief Justice Griffin Smith, who had a newspaper background and wrote good opinions. Chief Justice Jack Holt, Jr., he thought, did well. Also, Robert Brown and David Newbern were viewed as having outstanding intellects. He was very fond of Chief Justice Carleton Harris, who could decide cases practically on the facts alone. He recalled a case he had with J. L. (Bex) Shaver on the other side representing the plaintiff against his client, the Cotton Belt Railroad. Bex admitted the flashing lights were on at the crossing and the train's whistle was blowing, but he argued that the train's operator was still negligent. Chief Justice Harris asked him what else could the railroad have done. Bex said that they could have had a flagman out in the road. Judge Harris said that if the sun was in the driver's eyes, as Bex contended, he would have run the flagman down. Bex later told Jack that as much money as the railroad had, they were bound to be negligent.

The changes in the profession that Jack Deacon has most noticed over the years have been the dramatic increase in the number of women lawyers and women law students, the size of the larger law firms, and the increasing complexity of the law. On women lawyers, he praised the late Marian Penix who served on the Court of Appeals with distinction. Today, some of the best lawyers are women lawyers, he said, citing Lucinda McDaniel. Judge Henry Woods told him about her, saying that he had just judged a moot court competition and that she "just put it all over" the male lawyers. Henry said Jack needed to hire her, and after looking at a tape of the moot court, he did. On the other points, the increasing complexity of the law may account for the large firms in Little Rock. When Jack entered practice, there were only about six lawyers each at the Rose firm, the Wright firm, and the Mehaffy firm.

He told several stories about lawyers. In another case of Bex Shaver's, the opposing counsel called a witness who was testifying about what God had told her. Bex objected on the basis of hearsay. Another version is that Bex did not object but began interrogating the witness about what God had told her. But Bex' good friend, Chancellor Ford Smith, said, "Mr. Shaver, you know that would be hearsay." Bex Shaver was a great raconteur.

In another case, John Daggett was cross-examining a witness who claimed to have seen a train wreck. Daggett kept getting farther and farther away from the witness stand. "Now," he said, "tell me how far away that train was." "I don't know, Mr. Daggett, how far away is you from me in this room?"[64]

Jack Deacon has enjoyed his professional work outside of the law practice, and it is essential to the legal profession that it have leaders such as Jack devoting their time, thought and energy to professional issues. There are not many who have done more of that than Jack Deacon.

* * * *

Oscar Fendler is also located in northeast Arkansas, as is Jack. He is 90 years old and has been in law practice continuously since the early 1930's except for several years as an officer in the Navy during World War II. He could have taken a job in Washington, D. C., after graduating from Harvard Law School, which he attended after graduating from the University of Arkansas, but it was the Depression, and his parents needed to educate two brothers. He could have done better in Washington. The first year in practice, after returning to Mississippi County, he made $240 for the entire year. Most of the work he did was for Cecil Shane, an established lawyer who practiced in an adjacent office, and who would become his father-in-law. He did collection work for Shane's clients, but you couldn't collect because they did not have any money. They would come around occasionally and pay him a few dollars. Cecil Shane also paid him a little money to write instructions and briefs and brief witnesses. Oscar used Shane's law books because he did not have any.

When Oscar Fendler took the bar, there was no centralized exam. The circuit judges appointed someone to give, supervise and grade the exam. The person doing this for him and for others in the area was Felix Taylor, a retired circuit judge. The applicants went to his house in Corning where they would take the exam, spend the night, and be fed by the Taylors. Oscar typed his exam on an old Underwood typewriter, and when he laid a sheet down, the other applicants would pass it around and copy his answers. They all passed, but they made different scores. Judge Taylor certified them to the Circuit Court, and it in turn certified them to the Supreme Court, and it issued a certificate admitting them. Then, they could use that admission to be admitted to the federal courts.

In his early, pre-Harvard years, Oscar lived and grew up in Manila near Blytheville. They had a mayor's court and justice of the peace courts which were largely "a travesty." The judges of these inferior courts would hold court in a porch swing or inside in the parlor if it were cold. Oscar handled some misdemeanors and minor civil cases even though they didn't pay him. The lawyers were considerate. Most of them had gone to law school at Ole Miss or Vanderbilt or Cumberland; none had gone to Fayetteville because it took three days to get there. Some had gone to Judge Carmichael's school in Little Rock. In 1919-21 approximately, Oscar started into politics in Manila when he was 13 or 14, and he regularly voted despite his age. He had influence in Manila because he was in with a group that ran the town. He was a voting official because he was the only one who could read and write. He would sit up all night with the voting officials and fill out the forms, and he started drinking with them when he was 17. They would be sure their candidates won in Manila; they won every time. He recalls them "as corrupt a bunch of sons of bitches as you ever did see."

In his early days of the Depression, law practice was hard. When representing a bankrupt, Oscar would fill out the papers and have trouble getting $100 for the filing fee and his fee. But he would not file the papers unless they paid over the money. He would try to collect money, but he had to get a judgment and use garnishments, attachments and writs of execution to collect. They didn't write many wills because people didn't have any money. They did not ask for retainer fees in advance in those days. Once he went into partnership with Cecil Shane, he got some good cases working for insurance companies. Also, Shane turned over to him the representation of Lee Wilson and Company, a large plantation with all kinds of cases, and Oscar tried 95% of those cases.

On lawyers, he viewed Bruce Ivy of Osceola as the best trial lawyer over there. He spoke well of Senator Caraway, Charles Frierson, Sr. and Jr., Roy Penix, Bill Kirsch, and Maurice Cathey. In Cross County, James Robertson and the Killoughs were men-

342 A HISTORY AND REMINISCENCES OF THE BAR OF ARKANSAS

tioned. In Marion, Frank Smith was an outstanding lawyer and good Supreme Court Justice, and there was Cecil Nance, Sr. He mentioned other good lawyers he remembered—Walter Pope from Pocahontas, Harry Ponder from Newport or Walnut Ridge, Ed Westbrooke. Sr. and Jr. from Jonesboro, and Francis Cherry (later governor) who was both a good lawyer and chancery judge. Outside of northeast Arkansas from the early days, he praised Joe House from Little Rock and Joe T. Robinson, as well as U. M. Rose, Harry Meek, and Archie House as outstanding lawyers.

In addition to those named previously, one of the best judges northeast Arkansas ever had, in Fendler's opinion, was Marion Futrell who later became governor.

In the old days, judges would travel the circuit, and they had to go by steamboat on the St. Francis River sometimes. You did not hear much about corruption in those days.

Among the presidents of the Arkansas Bar Association, he was particularly complementary of U. M. Rose, based on what he had heard about him. "He was one of the best lawyers in America. He was considered a legal brain by lawyers in New York City and Chicago." Then, he discussed other Bar Presidents. He had heard "exceedingly nice things" about Henry Caldwell. Allen Hughes had been a judge in Memphis and was one of the best. He had written a book on mortgages that was authority in both Arkansas and Tennessee. Joseph Stayton wrote a text on procedure, and he was highly thought of. Joe House was one of the most brilliant lawyers we ever had. (He digressed to refer to someone who was never president of the bar, Hamilton Moses, referring to him as "the Bill Clinton of his time, all things to all men, and he didn't turn down any women.") N. W. Norton had the reputation of being a good lawyer, but was eccentric and got off on tangents, but he did some of the best work the bar ever had done. Ashley Cockrill was a superior lawyer in Arkansas. Charlie Coleman was a gentleman and a good lawyer. Jake Trieber was "the meanest g__d___ judge in the history of the state. He would scare the s___ out of you. Senator T. H. Caraway hated his guts, and in one case, when he got to the back of the courtroom, he said, 'Go to hell, you son of a bitch' in a loud voice.'" Thomas McRae was a fine man, but he was strictly a politician. J. H. Carmichael was shallow. Loughborough was brilliant, knew the law, but nobody liked him. G. D. Walker from Fayetteville was a good lawyer. C. E. Daggett was real congenial, knew the law, "but was not interested in the problems of other lawyers." S. H. Mann, "Burke's daddy, had a good reputation." George B. Pugh, Merrick Moore, and T. D. Wynne had good reputations. T. C. Trimble had a good mind and was a fine man and made a fine judge, "but his daughter is much smarter than he was." Harry P. Daily was a fine man and a "damned good lawyer," and they began to do something for the Arkansas Bar about then. Daily and Woods were both fine men. Paul Jones and Robert Wylie were "sticks in the mud," although good lawyers. Walter Riddick was brilliant, went on the Eighth Circuit, "but did not do much for the bar." Abe Collins got Oscar working for the integration of the bar. He was a fine country lawyer who cared about improving the bar. Bat Harrison was a fine lawyer and a good after-dinner speaker. Nick Gantt was a gentleman and "a fine man who tried to get us interested in young lawyers." Henry Moore was a fine lawyer.[65] Joe Barrett was president while Oscar was in the Navy, but they supported him. Oscar did not care for Lamar Williamson.[66] He worshipped Archie House, whom he called a brilliant lawyer and a very good friend. Cecil Warner was viewed by him as an excellent lawyer. He thought that Terrell Marshall worked hard for the bar and was an excellent president. J. L. (Bex) Shaver was viewed as "the best raconteur I ever knew." He viewed Shields Goodwin as a "sweet man who ran with the big shots." He died in office, and "John Fogleman was Chairman of his Executive Committee and ran his administration" resulting in "a lot of good." He had a high opinion of Eugene Matthews. "Then came Ed

Wright and John Fogleman again." Will Mitchell "did a great job when he was President" and provided "the basis for the Arkansas Bar Foundation." Heartsill Ragon "was excellent," and "I followed Heartsill. I cannot remember that I accomplished much. I left most of the work to my Chairman of the Executive Committee, Bruce Bullion." He did not comment on bar presidents after that time.[67]

Whatever one might think of his evaluation of some of the bar presidents, Oscar Fendler has lived a long, fascinating life and has had the opportunity to view and interact with some of the leading lawyers of the Arkansas and American Bar during the 20th Century. He has devoted much of his life to professional service, and we are in his debt.

* * * *

Reference has repeatedly been made during this chapter to Edward L. Wright and Herschel H. Friday, Jr. In terms of service to the profession and to various worthwhile civic endeavors, they were dominant figures whose careers spanned the period from the 1930's (Ed Wright) and 1940's (Herschel Friday) up to the time of their deaths. As Louis Ramsay said, "Ed Wright was one of the outstanding leaders I have known. I have associated with him so much in bar work as well as in cases."[68] Jack Deacon said that the two most important lawyers he knew in Arkansas were Ed Wright and Sid McMath.[69] He "loved" Ed Wright, who was "thoughtful" and "didn't speak unless he had something [important] to say." This trait carried him far in the American Bar Association, and he was in his time probably the most influential member of that organization, which he served as President in 1970-71. Clearly, he was the epitome of the American lawyer in that time frame.[70]

Herschel Friday was described accurately by Louis Ramsay:

Herschel had a talent that few people have. He had a wonderful legal mind. He had the ability to move along with people without offending them. You could be on the other side of a case, but he never became irritated with you. He was able to keep a relationship with lawyers and business people better than anyone I have ever known. But he was still able to build an outstanding law firm. Herschel could work with anyone. He would explain things to the legislature, and there was a good chance that [the legislation] would be passed. He was a gentleman, courteous, thoughtful.[71]

Herschel Friday served longer in the American Bar House of Delegates than anyone in history—roughly about thirty years. He was, of course, President of the Arkansas Bar, and he was President of the American Bar Foundation. He was a member of the American College of Trial Lawyers, the American Law Institute, the American College of Probate Counsel, and other professional organizations. While Louis believes "it was a tragedy when he was not selected for the Supreme Court" of the United States, he thinks it worked out in retrospect for the better. Bill Smith advanced the same thought. He was able to do so much in society and for his firm that he would not otherwise have been able to do. He was generous to his profession and to charity. For example, the largest courtroom at the UALR Law School is named after him, and his full-length painting hangs inside at the entrance, and he was so generous to the Arkansas Children's Hospital that part of it is dedicated to him. He could have been President of the American Bar had he sought the position.

These men are followed today in the American Bar by the recent President, Philip S. Anderson, who is Ed Wright's son in law. After graduation from the U of A Law School, where he was Editor-in-Chief of the *Law Review*, he associated with Wright,

Lindsey & Jennings. In more recent years, he and W. J. Williams left that firm to form Williams & Anderson, which is one of the larger firms in Little Rock. Phil is a Fellow of the American Law Institute and of the American Bar Foundation. Phil served as President of the Arkansas Bar Foundation, in the American Bar House of Delegates for many years, as Chair of the ABA House of Delegates, on the ABA Board of Governors and more recently (1998-99) as President. During his year as ABA President, he attempted to deal with the ongoing problem of law firms being taken over by the large CPA firms—something that has happened in Europe and poses an increasing concern in the United States. Also, he had a particular interest in CEELI, the ABA program to aid the legal and political restructuring of the countries of Eastern Europe, and also assistance to China in the reform of its legal system. He had a distinguished career as ABA President, and he continues his professional service today.

These are people who have done well in representing Arkansas, and in whom Arkansas can take pride.

* * * *

Charles Norton of Forrest City was an irascible character and yet he had a fine reputation as a lawyer. His son, Nat, was a thoughtful and scholarly man with an inventive mind.

One day, Mr. Charlie told a story about N. W. Norton, his father, who had served in the early part of the 20th Century as President of the Arkansas Bar Association. He returned to the office after a trying morning arguing a point with a lawyer he did not particularly like. When asked about what the man had argued, he said, "He talked for half an hour and generally subtracted from the sum total of human knowledge."

Next door to the Norton office was the law firm of Mann and McCulloch who were friendly rivals. Richard B. McCulloch, Sr.

was a distinguished and very ethical lawyer. One time, an order or judgment was entered in favor of a client of a young opposing lawyer and an error shortchanged his client. Mr. McCulloch told him to draw up a new document correcting the error, *nunc pro tunc.* Law was more genteel in those days. Although the notice provisions for depositions were essentially the same as today, no one gave notice and instead made the arrangements orally with the opposing attorney. Court sessions were not as heated as now, and there was less nastiness between the opposing counsel. Of course, this was not invariably true, but much of the bickering and lack of professionalism that goes on today was absent.

One time in either St. Francis County or a nearby county in a criminal case, the defendant was charged with murder and his attorney had argued that the revolver that was supposed to be the lethal weapon would not shoot. He had tested it, and it wouldn't fire. So before his closing argument, he slipped the gun out of the exhibits lying on the table and put it inside his coat after inserting a cartridge. When he reached his peroration, he said something like, "And I say the defendant is an innocent man because this gun won't even fire." He withdrew the gun as he was talking, pointed it in the air and pulled the trigger. "Bang" went the gun and the bullet tore into the courthouse ceiling. The jury was not out long, and the defense attorney was probably held in contempt.

On another occasion, a personal injury and products liability case, the plaintiff was injured when an old ceiling fan plunged to the floor in a high ceiling store while the fan was running, and one of the blades flew loose. The defense claimed, among other things, that the fan would not lose a blade in such a manner. So, a similar fan was hoisted in the courtroom by pulleys to the proper height, turned on and then released. When it crashed to the floor and released its broken blades, lawyers had to climb on top of chairs and tables.

Many personal injury cases were filed by the late Harold Sharpe. One young lawyer settled two such cases with Lawyer Sharp in which Allstate was the insurer. For some time after that, whenever the lawyer bumped into Harold, he cupped his hands and held them together as in the advertisement, "You're in good hands with Allstate." He had every reason to feel that way personally.

An insurance defense case in which Harold Sharpe was also involved was so suspicious with regard to the facts that the defense lawyer checked with the company to make sure that it actually happened. In that case, the defendant was drunk, driving down the wrong side of the street in West Memphis, ran a red light and collided with a Baptist preacher and his wife who were returning from a Youth for Christ rally. The police were right at hand because they were pursuing the insured at the time. When asked why he was driving so fast considering his condition, he said he was hurrying to the liquor store to get another bottle to take back to the Plantation Inn where he was with a woman who was not his wife. At that time, comparative negligence was relatively new law replacing the old contributory negligence system and its defenses. But some older lawyers were uncertain as to whether all of the old defenses were gone. The defense lawyer asserted the old last clear chance doctrine because the minister could have avoided the accident by swerving into an adjacent parking lot. (Of course, if he had tried the case, he would have had to admit negligence and deal with damages because, fortunately, the preacher and his wife were not badly hurt.) After the case settled, Harold asked why he asserted the last clear chance rule, and he responded that it was the last clear chance he had to make a defense.

* * * *

This chapter and others have featured many, although not all, of the leaders of the Bar. However, there are other Bar leaders that should be mentioned as outstanding lawyers and as leaders in their communities. They are the people who are vital to their locales and to the legal profession. Mention has been made of Clint Huey before in connection with his activities in the state Bar and as President or Chair of the Arkansas Bar Foundation. Clint has been District Governor of Lions International and Arkansas President of ABOTA (American Board of Trial Advocates), an organization of able, experienced trial lawyers which Gordon Rather of Little Rock served as national President. Clint is an outstanding trial lawyer and parent and has served the small town of Warren in many civic and professional ways.

David Solomon, who has been mentioned several times before, is active in the American Bar Association and is a Fellow of the American Bar Foundation. He has served the state Bar in many ways also, and the same is true of his home town of Helena.

Bill Penix of Jonesboro has represented all kinds of clients in all kinds of cases. He is retired now, but as a storefront lawyer, along with his father, Roy Penix, and his late wife, Judge Marian Penix, he may be truly said to have represented the masses in a tradition worthy of what we think the American lawyer should be. Whether it be a school integration case (Hoxie) or putting aside temporarily his strong Democratic Party background to represent the Republican Party at the invitation of Governor Winthrop Rockefeller, he has had a diverse career.

Michael G. Thompson of New Orleans, Senior Vice President and Counsel of Entergy, formerly of Friday, Eldredge & Clark of Little Rock, also a member of ABOTA, before his elevation to the rarefied air of the executive suite, tried cases all over Arkansas of various and sundry kinds. He toiled, for example, on what was known as the Epstein case for years in Chicot County until that long experience ended in the early 1990's. When it started, a predecessor attorney of his was Bill Bowen, prior to his banking career, which shows how long it lasted. That case led to the state Supreme Court adopting a limitation on the size of briefs. Mike is a true professional and first-class lawyer as is his non-practicing spouse, "Judge" Suzanne Thompson.

Ray Baxter of Benton, a good country lawyer and a country good lawyer, is a superb advocate. Mike Mitchell, Bob Cearley, Win Drummond, Chip Welch, Herb Rule, and Bill Allen of Little Rock, are thorough professionals and know how to try a case. Bob Fussell is a superb Bankruptcy Judge who saved Fairfield Communities. The late Walter Niblock and Tom Pearson, Jr., of Fayetteville, have or had different types of skills. Walter had an instinct about cases and generally knew what to expect in a case. Tom has a unique way of looking at cases and careful insight and angles in connection with a case. The late Bill Putman of Fayetteville and Sid Davis, Bill Bassett and Tilden P. (Chip) Wright are excellent lawyers there, and the same can be said for Jim Cypert, Jim Blair and Jim Roy of Springdale. In Texarkana, Judge John Stroud was an excellent practicing attorney before he became an excellent judge. Nick Patton, LeRoy Autrey, and Ned Stewart, Jr., are others that come to mind. And, of course, there are Bob Compton and Bill Prewett in El Dorado, both fine lawyers, and Charlie Roscopf in Helena, and a host of lawyers in Fort Smith including Doug Smith, Brad Jesson, Bob Jones, III, and Ed Bethell, and many others in historically one of the strongest bars in Arkansas.

This has only touched the surface.

You have to conclude that this state has been very fortunate to have a group of lawyers such as our profession has had, and, despite the elective system, to have had a generally strong bench. Younger lawyers just coming along would do well to draw from the experience of those who have become respected members of the Bar. This is true of ones struggling to develop a practice as well as those who have had great success.[72] The temptation to cut corners to make a quick buck, or to forget your primary responsibility to your client and your concommitant duty to the court and the profession is one that should be avoided at all costs. Respect is something that is earned in the legal profession by performance and by conduct.

Those who offer these remarks or decry the practices of a few in recent years do so because the legal profession should remain a profession and not a business in which ethics are ignored or winked at. The increasing willingness of the Arkansas courts, particularly the Supreme Court, to enforce ethical standards and discipline violators is an encouraging indication that professional standards will be maintained. As the law expands like the universe, so must the ethical requirements expand also.

Notes

1. Interview with Robert A. Leflar, Oct. 2, 1992, p. 19.
2. *Id.* at 1.
3. *Id.* at 2.
4. *Id.* at 2-3.
5. *Id.* at 3.
6. *Id.* at 4.
7. *Id.* at 4-5.
8. *Id.* at 13.
9. *Id.* at 22.
10. Interview with Sid McMath, Nov. 30, 1993, pp. 1-2.
11. *Id.* at 4-5.
12. *Id.* at 5.
13. *Id.* at 7.
14. *Ibid.*
15. *Id.* at 8.
16. *Id.* at 10.
17. *Id.* at 11.

18. *Ibid.*
19. *Id.* at 10.
20. *Ibid.*
21. *Id.* at 11.
22. *Ibid.*
23. *Id.* at 13.
24. *Id.* at 9.
25. *Id.* at 8.
26. Interview with J. Gaston Williamson, Dec. 2, 1993, p. 2.
27. *Id.* at 3-5.
28. *Id.* at 5-6.
29. *Id.* at 6-7.
30. *Id.* at 7.
31. *Id.* at 8-9.
32. *Id.* at 9.
33. *Id.* at 10.
34. *Ibid.*
35. *Id.* at 11-12.
36. I interviewed Charles Eichenbaum for about two hours one day, and I got up to the 1950's. I intended to finish the interview later, but Charlie was stricken and died before I could do it.
37. Interview with E. Charles Eichenbaum, pp. 2-3.
38. *Id.* at 3.
39. *Id.* at 4-5.
40. *Id.* at 5.
41. *Ibid.* Note: Charles Coleman was a Little Rock attorney. His twin brother was W. F. Coleman, a partner in Coleman, Gantt & Ramsay of Pine Bluff.
42. *Id.* at 6.
43. *Ibid.*
44. *Id.* at 7.
45. *Id.* at 8.
46. *Ibid.*

47. *Id.* at 9-10.

48. *Id.* at 9-10.

49. All of the foregoing in this and the preceding paragraph is taken from an Interview with Phillip Carroll, December 2, 1993, pp. 1-2, 4.

50. *Id.* at 5-6.

51. *Id.* at 12.

52. The preceding paragraphs are from Interview, H. Maurice Mitchell, May 12, 1994.

53. The foregoing and the following are from an Interview with William J. Smith, April 19, 1994.

54. *Id.* at 14.

55. *Id.* at 15.

56. *Arkansas Times*, pp. 19-21, Sept. 19, 1997.

57. *Id.* at 20.

58. R. Reed, *Faubus* 368-369 (1997).

59. The Special Supreme Court consisted of Edward L. Wright, J. L. (Bex) Shaver, Ned A. Stewart, and other bar leaders.

60. See generally, R. Reed, *supra* at 138-140.

61. The foregoing is from Interview, William L. Terry, April 19, 1994.

62. Wally Hall, sports editor of the *Arkansas Democrat-Gazette*, has written that when Alabama begins searching for a new head coach, they go to the cemetery and pray at Bear's grave, and after three days when it appears that he still isn't available, they start the search.

63. He once placed an advertisement in the newspaper stating that he would no longer be responsible for any debts incurred by his wife in connection with the engagement and marriage of his daughter. Louis did not tell me that; I know that.

64. The foregoing is taken from an Interview with John C. Deacon on June 15, 1995.

65. He died in office or shortly before—author's comment.

66. He was the only person that I interviewed who did not.

67. The foregoing is taken from an Interview with Oscar Fendler in 1995 and a letter dated January 24, 1995 from Oscar Fendler to the author.

68. Interview with Louis L. Ramsay, Jr., *supra*.

69. Interview with John C. Deacon, *supra*.

70. His ideas changed with time. In the mid-1950's, a woman who had finished first in her law class in Fayetteville and had been an editor of the *Law Review* as well as a Phi Beta Kappa applied to the Wright firm, and received back a letter from Ed saying in effect that the firm was not ready for women lawyers. On the other hand, in the mid-1970's, he sought to hire Susan Webber, who had been the first woman Editor-in-Chief of the *Law Review*, telling her that he liked her because she thought like a man.

71. Interview, *supra*.

Chapter X

REMINISCENCES OF JUDGES

As stated at the beginning of the last chapter on lawyers' reminiscences and recollections, all of the judges discussed in this chapter had careers, usually as a practicing lawyer, before they became a
judge. In some cases, it was a long career practicing law or in academia. We begin with U.S. District Judge Henry Woods who had a
long career in private practice with Sid McMath and Leland Leatherman before being appointed to the bench. As mentioned previously, one of the great teams in tort practice was Sid and Henry.
Most of what he discusses is about private practice.

Henry Woods left his law practice in Texarkana to manage the
McMath gubernatorial campaign in May 1948. After success at the
polls, he stayed on as Executive Secretary to the Governor. When
McMath went out of office in 1953, Leland Leatherman (with
whom Sid had practiced in Hot Springs) came over, and they
formed McMath, Leatherman & Woods. Judge Woods recalled
some of the early, and at that time, large, verdicts that he and Sid
McMath recovered. They obtained a judgment at Helena that was
the first one over $100,000 in the state. They recovered $100,000
for the man and $125,000 for his wife. He mentioned that Alston
Jennings had recovered a $100,000 verdict several months earlier,
but the one at Helena was the first to top that figure.[1] He said it
was also a memorable case because it was either the first or second
recovery in the United States by a wife for loss of consortium. The
Supreme Court substantially reduced the amount of recovery.

Of course, McMath and Woods specialized in plaintiff's personal injury litigation and did very well. In the late 1950's they recovered a large verdict in Forrest City which Judge Woods recalled
to be $150,000 and which he thought to be the largest verdict in the

state down to that time.[2] The recovery was against the highway contractor, Ben Hogan Construction Company, who apparently in building the highway "cut the slab down on both sides" greatly narrowing the main highway from Forrest City to Memphis.[3] In 1969, in Pine Bluff, they recovered a million dollar verdict under the Jones Act for a boy who had been rendered a quadriplegic. At that time there was no reported million dollar verdict that had been sustained in the federal courts. When John Shepherd of St. Louis, the defense attorney, filed a motion to reduce the award because there were no million dollar cases that had been sustained in federal court, Woods knew about a case in Florida where the jury had rendered such a verdict that was on appeal. The following Monday it was affirmed, and he obtained a copy of it. That was really the first case involving a million dollar verdict, and that was viewed as enormous in 1969. Since then, times have changed.

That was the case in which Judge Oren Harris admonished John Shepherd, a fine trial lawyer and later President of the American Bar Association, for interrupting Governor McMath when he was "explaining" the law and the facts to the jury.[4]

One of the biggest cases the two were involved in was the explosion at the Titan rocket silo about 40 or 50 miles northeast of Little Rock that killed 53 people. They recovered about $4,000,000 for the families of those who were killed.[5] That was an agreed settlement that they negotiated with the Justice Department. On other trial lawyers that he recalled, "I would say technically Alston Jennings was as good as any, really an outstanding trial lawyer." He said that he could usually settle cases with Bob Lindsey, but "Alston didn't; Alston was a litigator . . .[who] just wanted to beat you."[6] Also: "One of the cleverest and one of the toughest defense lawyers I ever had anything to do with was Sam Laser. He always put on this act of not being prepared and the little [expletive deleted] was prepared down to the nth degree." "I tell you a very good litigator that I tried a number of cases against was Buddy Sutton. I thought he was the best over there at that firm, really. Although they have some good lawyers over there, Buddy was exceptional."

In other parts of the state after mentioning Louis Ramsay and Jack Deacon favorably, he turned to Boyd Tackett:

> I had one case where if Judge [John] Miller had been on the bench, he would have stopped the trial and sent Boyd home and told him not to come back until he was sober. Old Boyd was just stumbling drunk the whole trial. Paul X [Williams] just let him go. But Boyd had much raw talent, and if he had prepared well and stuck to business and laid off the booze, he was virtually unbeatable down there in Southwest Arkansas, particularly in the rural counties down there. He was tough because he understood the psychology of those people down there, and he just had a tremendous amount of raw native ability. I think he was as tough to deal with in that part of the state as any lawyer I ever saw.[7]

In connection with Boyd Tackett, several lawyers and judges recalled the story about a prominent out-of-state lawyer calling a lawyer acquaintance about hiring a good trial lawyer in Southwest Arkansas. "Who is the best trial lawyer in Southwest Arkansas?" he asked. He was told that it was Boyd Tackett when he was sober. That bothered him and he asked about the second best. He was told that was Boyd Tackett when he was drunk.

Judge Woods was appointed to the U. S. District Court by President Jimmy Carter in 1980. During his years on the bench, he maintained his scholarly writing, including his nationally used treatise on comparative law. He recalled fondly his work with the jury instructions committee on the model rules. One was a story about a faked fight involving Dale Price. Dale, of course, was a plaintiff's lawyer and Bill Arnold of Texarkana represented insurance companies. Dale flew into him, "and really it frightened old Paul Wolfe to death." Judge Wolfe was the chairman. "Old Paul rushed in there to separate them and Dale said [to Bill] 'you S.O.B. you've been opposing me and representing those damned insurance companies and I ain't going to take it anymore.' Everybody thought the fight was real, but it was cooked up."[8]

* * * *

In the interview with Charles Eichenbaum in the preceding chapter, he described U. S. District Judge Jacob Trieber as a legal scholar who "ran his courtroom like a military bootcamp, incurring great dissatisfaction, but the fact that he was generally almost always correct in his legal determinations brought credit to the federal bench." One time, "there was a lawyer who was rattling some silver coins in his pocket, and Judge Trieber said, 'Step up to the bench,' and he stepped up and the judge said, 'What do you have in your pocket?' He said, 'I have two quarters, judge,' and the judge said, 'Well, I'll fine you twenty-five cents, and now you rattle the one that's left.' "[9]

He regarded Justice Carroll D. Wood, with whom he had "a particular relationship" as "almost mentor, as well as Justice."[10] He had a high regard for Chancellor John Martineau and Chancellor Frank Dodge. "There was no finer analyst of fact and disposer of conflicts than Frank Dodge."[11]

* * * *

The oldest judge or former judge interviewed was former Associate Justice Sam Robinson.[12] He went on the Supreme Court on January 1, 1951, and prior to that had served five years as Prosecuting Attorney in Pulaski County and had been in private practice. He was almost 100 years old at the time of the interview. His professors at the old Arkansas Law School in Little Rock included a number of judges that he regarded highly—Judge J. H. Carmichael, the Dean; Judge T. N. Robinson, the secretary; Judge John W. Wade (who handled criminal cases and taught criminal law); Judge Archie House; and Judge Martineau, previously mentioned.[13] Chancellor Martineau later became Governor and still later, U. S. District Judge.

Justice Robinson also mentioned federal Judge Trieber, whom Mr. Eichenbaum had discussed. He said he spoke with a decidedly German accent having not come to this country until he was about sixteen years old. His "w's" would come out as "z's." A trial lawyer whom he referred to as "Colonel Murphy" was trying a case in front of Judge Trieber when the judge said, "Zell, that's not the law." Most lawyers were intimidated by Judge Trieber, but not Colonel Murphy. He tore a page out of a book of the judge's and said, "Well, if that's not the law, then you ought not to have it in your book."[14] Apparently, in the early 20th century, some U. S. Senators tried cases (as mentioned previously in connection with Senator Joe T. Robinson). Senator T. H. Caraway was trying a case before Judge Trieber, and although his background was as a prosecuting attorney in northeast Arkansas, he was defending the case. When it came time for a witness to identify the defendant, he was looking all over the courtroom, even though the man was sitting at the counsel table. Judge Trieber suggested that he look at the lawyers and maybe he would see him. This angered Caraway who said he might also see him up on the bench.[15] (Of course, that is not something that should be recommended procedure. Anyone other than a U. S. Senator probably would have been held in contempt.)

Judge Robinson said that when he went on the Supreme Court, the other members were Chief Justice Griffin Smith, Justice Ed McFaddin, Justice George Rose Smith, Justice J. Seaborn Holt, Justice Minor Milwee and Justice Paul Ward. In his autobiography, he does not say much about the Supreme Court "because there's just not much to tell." "[T]he cases are assigned to the judges by the clerk. . . , and there is practically no small talk, no socializing. . ., no putting your feet on the desk and just shooting the bull."[16] He described it as all work and as a job you had to work on at night as well as during the daytime.[17]

* * * *

One of the hardest workers the Court ever had was Justice John Fogleman who became Chief Justice before he retired. Judge Fogleman was from an old East Arkansas family in Crittenden County. The family came there before Arkansas was a state. Like his partner, Jim Hale, John was an outstanding trial lawyer, and his brother, Julian Fogleman, now heads his old firm. Elton Rieves and John Mac Smith were a prominent competing firm. When the interstates were being built in Arkansas, John Fogleman represented many landowners in Eastern Arkansas whose land was taken by the highway department, and he did quite well in those cases in recovering damages. He did well enough, in fact, to enable him to run for the Supreme Court. Well known to the Arkansas Bar by virtue of his reputation as a trial lawyer and by reason of his having served as Arkansas bar president, his slogan was "Ask Your Lawyer." (That is what a great many people do anyway in our system of election of judges; so it was a good and successful slogan.)

When Judge Fogleman went on the Court, there were only three incumbent justices remaining—Carleton Harris, who served as Chief Justice longer than anyone; George Rose Smith, who served on the Court longer than anyone else; and Paul Ward. (Frank Holt and Jim Johnson had resigned to run unsuccessfully for Governor. Frank Holt later was re-elected to the Court.)[18]

Before Judge Fogleman was elected to the Court, he had served in various capacities connected with the Court. He had served three years on the State Board of Law Examiners and then as Chair of the Arkansas Judiciary Commission which had been created by the legislature to make a study of the judicial system. That interest and involvement prompted him to seek election to the Court.[19]

In discussing the quality of judges who had served on the Supreme Court, Judge Fogleman mentioned several that he regarded as the best or among the best: George Rose Smith, Ed F. McFaddin, Frank G. Smith, and he said that Frank Smith thought that B. B. Battle was the greatest justice in the history of the Court.[20] He also mentioned Carleton Harris as a great Chief Justice. (Judge Thomas O. Butt of Fayetteville, who has served as Chancellor longer than anyone else, named George Rose Smith, Ed McFaddin and John Fogleman as the three foremost.)[21]

Many of the recommendations of the 1965 Judiciary Commission report were adopted, one of the most important being the creation of an administrative office of the courts. Because of potential opposition from trial judges to appointment of a court administrator, they called it the Judicial Department and originally called the chief administrator the Executive Secretary. For many years, Dick Huie of Arkadelphia, a former judge, held that position. He was diplomatic in his approach, and Judge Fogleman advised him that he was going to have to make trial judges realize that the office was created to help them in their work and not "something to cram a lot down their throats." That is the way he ran it and that is why it succeeded.[22] This has been a truly significant agency exercising its general superintending authority over all inferior courts as provided in Article VII, section 4 of the Arkansas Constitution.

The former Chief Justice said that his "greatest disappointment" was despite "a unanimous recommendation of that commission that the merit selection of judges" was never adopted. Merit selection was also approved by a citizens' conference of leading citizens. As recently as 1991, although the state Senate approved putting that proposal to the voters, it failed by two votes to gain submission in the House as a constitutional amendment to be voted on by the people.[23]

In discussing outstanding trial judges in Eastern Arkansas, the first one Judge Fogleman mentioned was Charles Light of Paragould who "was born to be a Circuit Judge."[24] He also mentioned as outstanding judges, Neil Killough, Marion Futrell, Leon Smith, Elmo Taylor, and W. J. Driver. He told this story about lawyer Virgil Greene who was trying a case in Osceola against Bruce Ivy:

> Bruce paced up and down in front of the jury, but he put a glass of water on the counsel table, and when he thought he made a point, he would run over to the table and take a sip out of this glass of water. And every time Bruce would take a drink out of that glass, Virgil would fill it up again. Bruce finished his argument after taking a lot out of his glass, and Virgil got up and started out his argument by saying: A great many of you people know that I have traveled a great deal in my life, and I have seen some of the ancient wonders of the world, and I have seen many of the modern wonders, but I had to come to Osceola, Arkansas, to see a windmill run by water.[25]

Aside from being an energetic leader of the bench and bar of Arkansas, John A. Fogleman was one of the best justices the Arkansas Supreme Court has ever had. He fit in well with George Rose Smith, Carleton Harris and his other contemporaries on the court. Despite his insistence that George Rose Smith was the scholar on the court (although the statement is true as far as it goes), his opinions were also scholarly with numerous citations. They complemented each other quite well in the sense that Justice Smith's opinions were short, concise and thoughtful, and Justice Fogleman often wrote much longer opinions. His opinions were filled with law, however, and served lawyers well as precedent in the years that followed. His main object, he once told me, was not to mess up the law. Although he wrote a few opinions that I did not agree with, he hit the nail on the head almost all of the time, and he had a good reason without exception for what he said. You cannot do any better than that.

* * * *

The senior trial judge in the 20th Century was Judge Tom Butt of Fayetteville who died May 20, 2000. He had been Chancery and Probate Judge in Northwest Arkansas since January 1, 1951, which means he would have served half a century on that date in 2001. When asked to evaluate trial lawyers, Judge Butt said that Rex Perkins "was the finest trial lawyer I ever knew, except for my father, Mr. F. O. Butt of Eureka Springs. Rex Perkins was a consummate trial lawyer, he had all of the tools, he was quick, he was sharp, and he could read his witness and read the jury, and he had a good sense of humor."[26] He recalled "dramatic battles" between Perkins and Ted Coxey, a prosecuting attorney who was also "a fine trial lawyer and an excellent prosecutor." Other fine trial lawyers he mentioned included Vol T. Lindsey of Bentonville who was "a perfectionist" who "prepared his cases in minute detail"; A. L. Smith of Siloam Springs who also was a "perfectionist"; Lon Garrett of Huntsville who was a "home-grown, self-trained" lawyer; Hosea Leathers and Ernest Simpson in Carroll County. "Hosea had a wonderful sense of humor and a sassy, keen, cutting wit," and he and Ernest Simpson had many "epic battles" in the old courthouse in Berryville.[27] In more recent years, "Bill Putman was Rex Perkins' equal in my judgement."[28] "Bill was more of a student of the law than Rex was. Rex had an instinctive feel for the law."[29]

As a trial judge, Judge Butt has attempted to follow precedent. "Although there are many times when I have felt what I perceive to be the established law was wrong, I was obligated to follow the precedents. I never did feel comfortable with trying to establish new law. When I was a younger judge, I used to take cases home with me. I worried and fretted whether I did right or wrong. I've long since quit that; there is no profit in it. I shoot my best stick at the trial level, and I leave it to the appellate court to tell whether I was right or wrong."[30]

Asked to name other good trial judges in Arkansas, he listed Leon Smith from Northeast Arkansas ("a very careful and competent judge"); Guy Amsler of Little Rock (who "didn't project the notion of being studious or an academician, but he very seldom got reversed"); and Maupin Cummings of Fayetteville ("a fine judge" who "also had an instinct for what was right about things").[31] He also remembered Lee Seamster as a fine judge. He regarded U. S. District Judge John Miller as "probably the best trial judge that Arkansas ever saw, state or federal. He worked hard and was rarely reversed. He also was a craftsman; he paid attention to his business, and I never heard anybody speak ill of Judge Miller as a judge."[32] (Before appointment to the federal bench, Judge Miller served as U. S. Senator and before that, in the U. S. House of Representatives.) Of Judge J. Smith Henley, after saying he was a good judge, and that he always had "the warmest feelings and best respect for Smith Henley," he told this story about when Smith was appointed:

My father wrote to the Attorney General and the two senators, John McClellan and Bill Fulbright, and said "I have become aware in recent months that the administration is looking for someone to appoint as federal judge in the Eastern District." He said "you have a fairly young judge right under your nose in the Attorney General's office who in my judgement would make a fine federal judge. I've known him since he was a boy. I knew his parents before him, and he's a good lawyer and would make a good judge." I have no idea whether my father's letter had any influence at all. Of course, he was appointed. Smith was a good judge; he called the shots the way he saw them.[33]

He was friendly with Judge Paul X Williams also, and he gave him this advice when he became a federal judge:

> I said you and my brother, John, were the closest of friends, and I have inherited his regard for you, and I only ask one thing. Don't let yourself get so stuffed up with pride about being a federal judge that you forget that the common folks are still around. There have been instances in the past where federal judges will set cases, and they don't give a damn whether the lawyers have a case in state court or not. Remember you were a state judge, and the same lawyers are going to be practicing before you as a federal judge as they did as chancellor.[34]

Commenting on state Supreme Court justices, as previously mentioned, he listed Ed McFaddin, George Rose Smith and John Fogleman as the best. "I just believe and still believe that those three, they're the kind of appellate court judges that I would like for all of our courts to have all of the time. It happens that both John Fogleman and George Rose, I have regarded as two of the finest men and best friends I ever had. They are of a little bit different turn, but they make a wonderful balance on the court, and Ed McFaddin is pretty much the same way."[35]

Judge Butt had some good stories about courtroom events in divorce cases. One concerned the legendary Rex Perkins as counsel for the wife and Charles Davis of Springdale for the husband. Charlie had been asking questions which had to do with the infidelity of the plaintiff wife. Rex Perkins got up and said:

> Now, Mrs. Blank, my good friend, Mr. Davis, has been asking you several questions and what he's really getting down to, he's trying to lay the notion that you have been

sleeping around with somebody and then going back to your husband since you filed this divorce case. Now, you tell the truth about this matter. And she said, "Yes, Mr. Perkins, I have." With that, Rex went back to the counsel table, folded up his case file, and said, "That's all, goodbye," and he walked out of the courtroom.[36]

In another divorce case, his brother, John Butt, was the Chancellor in Huntsville, and Tom Butt was then practicing law. The case involved the fact that the defendant had been dallying with another woman who was not his wife. Unlike most of these situations, there was an "eyeball" witness who was testifying:

> "Well, did you see her with the husband?" "Yes, I saw him." "Where was it?" "Well, it was behind the old school house." "Well, what did you see?" "Well, the car was parked and they were in the back seat." "Well, go on, what did you see?" "Well, well, they was just a-going at it." "What do you mean they were going at it?" He looked up and said, "Judge, can I say what they were doing?" The Chancellor said, "Yes, but if you are going to say what I think you are going to say, just refer to it as intercourse." The witness said, "yes sir, they were having intercourse." On cross-examination, he went through the same routine. "What was it you said that you saw?" And he looked up at the judge and said, "Judge, what was that fancy word for [deleted] you used?"[37]

Judge Butt suggested that the last story be edited. The judge was skeptical about law reform. One young lawyer had a case before him representing a fellow lawyer, Tom Pearson, Jr., against a man with an Italian name from Dallas who had played in the line for the Pittsburgh Steelers. The key was to get him into court under the (then new) long-arm statute. Bill Putman very eloquently presented the ex-pro's case and argued against the legality of the Arkansas long-arm statute. Judge Butt did not like the statute and thought it did not relate to anything that he had learned about court jurisdiction. But he upheld it. Then, he spent several minutes chewing the young lawyer out in connection with that statute. The lawyer was at that time a Commissioner on Uniform State Laws, and the judge might have thought that he had something to do with its drafting. The true "culprit" was Bob Leflar. But the lawyer had won a case that was later settled, and that was the important thing. This illustrates something about Judge Butt—the legislative presumption was that the statute was valid, and Bill Putman had not given him any constitutional reason to declare otherwise. He would follow the law whether he liked it or not.

In my view, he is one of the finest trial judges that Arkansas has ever had. In addition to that, he fits to perfection the concept of a gentleman and a scholar.

When Judge Butt retired on the occasion of his 83rd birthday in March, 2000, the Supreme Court of Arkansas entered an order on March 28 expressing gratitude for his "life and good works" and "the eloquency, wit, decorum, and nobility that distinguished his conduct and his court."[38]

* * * *

Throughout this discourse, we keep coming to the name of George Rose Smith. You find it not only in this chapter but in the chapter on the organized bar. George Rose Smith died in the early morning of the day I was scheduled to interview him, but in addition to knowing him since the 1950's and knowing his good friends, such as Judge Fogleman, I did conduct a lengthy interview with his wife, Peg Newton Smith.[39] Moreover, much has been written about him in various publications. There are few "legends," but he was one. Another legend, much discussed previously, was his grandfather, U. M. Rose, the founder of the organized bar in Arkansas.

Judge Smith practiced law for a number of years with the Rose law firm after graduating from the University of Arkansas Law School in 1933. The firm was named for his grandfather, and George B. Rose, his uncle, was one of the senior partners. After election to the Arkansas Supreme Court in the late 1940's, he served on the Court for 38 years before retiring on January 1, 1987. His term was the longest of any judge in the history of the Court, exceeding that of Justice Frank Smith by one year. He was "the architect, chief implementor and overseer of the system by which the Supreme Court assigns and decides its cases."[40] He became a nationally recognized authority on the appellate decision process, wrote law review articles on the subject, and lectured for years at the American Academy of Judicial Education. Former Clerk Dona Williams said that he had a mechanical mind in which he would identify the problem and come up with the simplest solution in solving problems within the system.[41] He was devoted to the dignity and integrity of the Supreme Court as an institution and to its traditions. His friend and former Chancellor, the late Bruce Bullion, said, "George Rose Smith is highly moral and ethical in every inch of his body and faithfulness and loyalty to the office he holds are total."[42] That compliment came about naturally. His father and grandfather were Presbyterian ministers. His uncle served as president of Davidson College and Washington & Lee.

He never liked campaigning, and he insisted that "the real politician in the family" was his wife, Peg, who is charming and vivacious by nature. He had only two contested elections, and in the second one against Attorney General Tom Gentry in 1962, he received what former Justice Edwin Dunaway described as the largest endorsement ad by lawyers in history.[43] After that election he became a supporter of the "Missouri Plan" for judicial selection and appointment as opposed to the election of judges. Within the

Court, he developed the practice of circulating written opinions prior to any conference of the justices rather than the boring and tedious practice of having them read their opinions to the others, and he also developed the practice of editing what his colleagues wrote and correcting misspelled words (which did not set well with Chief Justice Griffin Smith). He also worked to perfect the Supreme Court rules. In writing about opinion writing, he drew from Dean John H. Wigmore, Karl Llewellyn, U. S. Supreme Court Justice Benjamin Cardozo, Justice Frank Smith of Arkansas, Webster's New International Dictionary (2nd edition), and the Uniform System of Citations employed by law reviews.[44]

Although scholarly and rather quiet by nature, Judge Smith had a keen sense of humor that manifested itself on two occasions in April Fool's Day opinions. The first was *Poisson v. d'Avril* (reproduced in a law review article in 22 *Arkansas Law Review* 741 (1971) written by a fellow using assumed names.[45] (If you eliminate the "v" for versus, poisson d'Avril in French means fish of April and is used by the French in the same manner as we use "April's Fool.") His opinion was concerned with a repealer in a legislative act that repealed "all laws and parts of laws" and did not include the customary modifying clause limiting them to laws inconsistent with the act. The opinion stated that the omnibus repealer referred only to statutory law and did not affect the common law which remained "unmonkeyed with." The other case, *Catt v. State*, published by West Publishing Company at 691 S.W.2d 120 (1985), because presumably they did not get the joke, involved twin brothers, Kilkenny Catt and Gallico Catt, who received inconsistent jury verdicts for fraud and cocaine possession. What people may not know is that one of the mid-Atlantic states later cited *Catt* as authority for some point of law.

The tendency to want to polish his cases may have come from the fact that he made up crossword puzzles that were published in *The New York Times*. According to his wife, Peg, he was constantly polishing his crossword puzzles.[46] One puzzle was rejected by the newspaper because they said it was too difficult to solve.

The Smiths would make many trips to Mt. Nebo near Dardanelle. The origin of that was his grandfather, U. M. Rose, and several other men who built summer homes on Mt. Nebo and developed it as a type of resort in the 1880's. (Recall that U. M. Rose and other Southern lawyers founded the American Bar Association at Saratoga Springs, New York, where they vacationed in the summer to get away from the hot Southern summers. Mt. Nebo was a closer-to-home attempt to create a similar retreat.) These homes were not vacation cottages but were large Victorian houses with sleeping porches and water towers. The families of these men would move up there in the summer because it was much cooler, particularly at night, and they would stay there, some taking servants with them. The men would come up on Friday and return to Little Rock on Monday. Judge Smith spent summers up there in the Rose house that has long since been sold and has deteriorated somewhat. But Mt. Nebo was a part of his childhood, and later, they would go up there in groups, Bill Moorhead and his wife from Stuttgart (—Bill was his first law clerk—), Judge Jim Chesnutt and his wife from Hot Springs, Richard Allin and his wife, and others. They would rent cottages because the Rose house was no longer owned by the family. They took their child, Laurie, there when she was little so that she could have some of the same experiences he had.[47]

He had other hobbies that he pursued such as his golf ball collection. He began it when he used to jog around the old Riverdale Country Club golf course, and he would collect lost balls. He said he recognized lost balls because "when they stopped rolling, they were lost."[48] Then there were the raccoons that would come up around his house to be fed about dark each evening—an enormous amount of raccoons. For twenty-five years, Judge Smith designed Christmas cards doing things no raccoon could or would ever do. One, for example, had a raccoon distributing Christmas gifts. He spent a great deal of time deciding how to get raccoons to do what he wanted them to do as if they were humans and acted as humans would.

Justice Robert L. Brown in his article, "George Rose Smith" in *The Arkansas Lawyer* at p. 23 (Jan. 1987), compiled a list of his sayings from time to time over the years. Only a few are reproduced here. To a new Justice, he said, "New judges dissent." To Justice Darrell Hickman, who liked to talk, he said, "You have the right to remain silent." When a very late opinion was submitted by a colleague: "Better never than late." On a new history book about the Civil War: "It's an unbiased history from a Southern point of view." When Webster Hubbell was sworn in, he apologized for the robe saying that it "may not be a good fit because Little Rock Tent and Awning was not able to make a robe in such a short time."[49] He asked Justice John Purtle one time, "Are you going to commit another dissent." And finally, he listed the methods of settling judicial disputes at conferences: "(a) dueling, (b) fisticuffs, (c) flouncing from the room, (d) profanity, (e) standing oration (shouting optional), (f) calm and detached reasoning."

He obviously chose the last one. He was a legend on the Court who will not be forgotten.

* * * *

This book has not concentrated that much on judges who are still actively engaged in their careers except for some women judges and African-American judges. Suffice it to say that there are those on the Supreme Court and Court of Appeals who are making history as they continue to serve. John Stroud has served both on the Court of Appeals and the Supreme Court and has contributed his time and talent to the bench as well as to the Bar. He has, in fact, won more awards for meritorious service to the Bar than any other person, according to a pronouncement at a recent state bar convention. A fellow Texarkanian, Alex Sanderson, was a brilliant trial judge, and he presided over the long-running *Festinger v. Angel* case that lasted over fifteen years in Lake Village and involved numerous lawyers and appeals.

The careers of several federal judges who have served in recent years should be considered, all but one of whom is still serving. Richard Sheppard Arnold has had an outstanding judicial career, first at the District Court level and then on the Circuit Court of Appeals for the Eighth Circuit. In the latter capacity, and while Chief Judge, he came very close to being appointed to the U. S. Supreme Court by President Bill Clinton. He was among the finalists and apparently was not appointed for health reasons (although one never knows in these situations). Judge Arnold was recently honored by the American Bar Association, through its Standing Committee on Federal Judicial Improvements, by being presented the Meador-Rosenberg Award for outstanding service to the judiciary and the legal profession. The award was presented at a dinner of the Board of Governors, presided over by ABA President Philip S. Anderson of Little Rock, at the 1999 Annual Meeting in Atlanta. This award has been rarely presented. Another award that he received in 1999 is the seventeenth annual Edward J. Devitt Distinguished Service to Justice Award.

After graduating first in his class at Yale, Richard Arnold entered the Harvard Law School where he also graduated first in his class. He then served as a law clerk to Justice William J. Brennan, Jr., of the U. S. Supreme Court. That background would normally take a person into teaching at a prominent law school, but instead it took him back to Texarkana to the family law practice following three years with Covington & Burling in Washington. After unsuccessful races for Congress, he was appointed U. S. District Judge for the Eastern and Western Districts in 1978 and to the Circuit Court of Appeals in 1980.[50] On January 7, 1992, Judge Arnold succeeded Judge Donald P. Lay as Chief Judge. In a symposium paying tribute to Judge Lay in volume 18 of the *William Mitchell Law Review* at page 561 (1992), Judge Arnold expressed his own favorable feelings about Judge Lay and in so doing revealed some things about his own character. Much more is revealed, however, in a symposium about him the following year in 78 *Minnesota Law Review* 1-59 (Nov. 1993). Participants included Justice Brennan, John P. Frank, Judge A. Leon Higginbotham, Judge Lay, and Judge Patricia M. Wald.

In that symposium, which is too long to summarize adequately, Justice Brennan praised Arnold as a "courageous and stalwart supporter of individual rights" and as a consistent protector of "the First Amendment guarantees of freedom of the press and freedom of speech, even in cases in which the protected expression was controversial, distasteful, or hateful."[51] John P. Frank and Judge Higginbotham wrote about his early childhood in Texarkana, about his clerkship experience with Justice Brennan and about his subsequent days in Arkansas and in the federal courts. He learned that Justice Brennan, for example, did not agree much with Professor Henry Hart of Harvard, a Frankfurter protege, and Brennan also did not agree with some Harvard viewpoints on constitutional law that had also found support at Yale.[52] "What Arnold learned from Brennan is the need to articulate the *reason* for his decision" and when there is "clear authority" that governs, "there is virtually no need for an opinion."[53] Moreover, by 1967, "he had overtly added Justice [Hugo] Black to his pantheon of intellectual heroes, and to this day, insofar as he has any model for his opinions, he deliberately follows Black's style of concise clarity."[54] They also write extensively of his decisions protecting the rights of women, a matter explored extensively by Judge Wald.[55] Judge Wald stated: "The decisions of Judge Arnold . . . have on the whole been distinctly sympathetic to women's claims of discrimination in the workplace and in school."[56]

Justice Brennan related, in closing, one of Arnold's great achievements on behalf of all federal judges in the United States.

374 A HISTORY AND REMINISCENCES OF THE BAR OF ARKANSAS

The judiciary is at the mercy of the Congress for its budget, and Congress in recent years has not regarded the judiciary with favor. In Brennan's words:

> A tribute to Judge Arnold cannot confine itself to his jurisprudential achievements. Judge Donald Lay pays fitting homage to his successor's contributions to the administration of the federal judiciary, most especially Judge Arnold's heroic efforts as the chairman of the Budget Committee of the Judicial Conference. The unfortunate fact is that the wheels of justice too often turn slowly and always at great expense. Judge Arnold has played a prominent role in ensuring that the Third Branch is provided with the resources necessary to enable us to fulfill our vital mission of efficiently resolving legal disputes, fairly enforcing the laws, and vigorously safeguarding our most cherished rights and freedoms.[57]

Richard S. Arnold and his brother, Morris S. Arnold, are the latest in a distinguished Arkansas family to serve the legal profession. The Arnold firm has existed in Texarkana for well over a century. Previous discussion has referred to their forebears in the chapter on the organized bar.

When Morris Sheppard Arnold was appointed to sit with his brother, Richard, on the U. S. Court of Appeals for the Eighth Circuit, that was a first for the American federal judiciary. Brothers had not served together before on a federal court of appeals. Because both are special and yet different, we will now turn to Morris S. (Buzz) Arnold. (Buzz's colorful nickname was bestowed on him by his step-grandfather, the late Senator Tom Connally of Texas, when he was about six months old. It was taken from a character in Dickens' *Pickwick Papers* named Serjeant Buzz Fuzz.) Buzz is about five years younger than Richard, and although he recalls dropping a brick on Richard's head during childhood one day in the sandbox, "both agree that it did no permanent damage."[58]

They are different in that their lives took different courses in several aspects. Buzz Arnold became in his earlier life a distinguished academician, about which more will be said. Richard went from law practice, after his ventures in politics, to the federal bench. Richard was a Democrat, and his federal judicial appointments came from Democrats. Buzz was a Republican, on the other hand, and served for a time as Chair of the Arkansas Republican Party, and his appointments came from Republicans.

They were also different in that Buzz did not exactly track his father and his brother in matriculating at Phillips Exeter Academy for prep school, Yale for college, and Harvard for law school. He graduated from Exeter with a classical diploma in 1959, attended Yale for two years, and then decided to study engineering at the University of Arkansas, from which he received a B.S.E.E. degree in 1965. He was selected for Tau Beta Pi, the engineering honorary equivalent of Phi Beta Kappa, in his junior year. He then entered law school in Fayetteville graduating in 1968 at the top of his class and having served as Editor-in-Chief and Notes Editor of the *Arkansas Law Review*. After a short time practicing law with the Arnold firm in Texarkana, he entered Harvard Law School and received the LL.M. degree in 1969 and later an S.J.D. from Harvard in 1971. In the interim between the two degrees, he was a Teaching Fellow and received the Knox Fellowship from Harvard for study at the University of London. His doctoral dissertation was published by the Ames Foundation.[59]

Obviously suited for an academic career, he began teaching law at Indiana University in 1971. In 1977, he became Associate Dean of the University of Pennsylvania Law School, also holding professorial rank on the law faculty, and became a Vice-President of the University. While at Penn, he was a Visiting Professor at Stanford Law School and taught in summer sessions at Michigan and Texas.

In 1978, he was a Visiting Fellow Commoner at Trinity College, Cambridge University, and was a member of the law faculty. In 1981, he was appointed Ben J. Altheimer Distinguished Professor of Law at the University of Arkansas at Little Rock, and a short time later became State Chairman of the Republican Party.

At the time he was under consideration for appointment as U. S. District Judge for the Western District of Arkansas in 1985, he accepted an appointment as Dean of the Indiana University Law School with the understanding that he would leave if the appointment came through. After only a few months it did, and he became a federal judge situated in Fort Smith. Approximately seven and a half years later, he was appointed to the U. S. Court of Appeals for the Eighth Circuit and moved back to Little Rock.

Since becoming an appeals court judge, with the court centered in St. Louis, he has continued periodically to teach legal history at Washington University in St. Louis. He is a prolific writer, having produced a number of books and many articles on the subjects of English legal history and Arkansas legal and governmental history. (Some of the latter material has been cited extensively in the early parts of this book.) Suffice it to say that although his job is as a judge, he was a scholar before that and will probably always remain a scholar first and foremost. However, that is a good thing particularly in an appellate judge. As such, he brings that strong background of learning in the law to any judicial panel on which he sits.

Another federal judge of the latter half of the 20th century who, like the Arnolds, has been mentioned previously and who shares a place in the history of Arkansas is J. Smith Henley of Harrison. He was a product of North Arkansas and the Ozarks and the University of Arkansas. The only experience he had in the East was not at Harvard, but in the Justice Department and the Federal Communications Commission. He was a Republican from his birth to his death and exercised considerable influence in that party. In one case in which there was a dispute over whether Ronald May, a distinguished senior partner in Wright, Lindsey & Jennings of Little Rock, was a Republican or not, the comment was made that more trust could be put in Smith Henley's determination that he was than in the records of the party itself.

Smith Henley was born in St. Joe in 1917 and graduated from the University of Arkansas Law School in 1941. He practiced law in Arkansas and served as a part-time bankruptcy referee in the Western District in the early 1940's. In 1954, he became Associate General Counsel for the F.C.C. under the Eisenhower administration, and after that, was Director of the Office of Administrative Procedure in the Justice Department. In 1957, of course, the integration situation in Little Rock was explosive, and there was a vacancy on the federal district court. At first consulted about potential candidates, he learned from an aide to Acting Attorney General William Rogers that he would not be further consulted because he was under consideration. On Washington's birthday, 1958, President Eisenhower nominated him to the federal district bench. By that time Eisenhower had sent federal troops to Little Rock, a second federal judgeship vacancy had occurred, and there was apprehension locally about having two Eisenhower appointees on the federal bench. In October 1958, he was appointed district judge under a special recess appointment, and in September 1959, after Gordon E. Young had been nominated to the other vacancy, both appointments were confirmed by the Senate. From October 31, 1958, until his assumption of office as Circuit Judge for the Eighth Circuit on March 24, 1975, he served as Chief Judge of the Eastern District.

Judge Harry J. Lemley originally had the Little Rock school case and attempted to delay implementation of the integration plan for two years while passions cooled. He was reversed in the Court of Appeals in a 6-1 *en banc* opinion which was affirmed by the U. S. Supreme Court.[60] Eventually, Judge Henley got the case and nursed it along until he was able to declare a unitary school system shortly before his service began on the Court of Appeals. The case resurfaced in the late 1980's when the Little Rock School District brought suit against the North Little Rock and Pulaski County School Districts, and it was assigned to Judge Henry Woods. After Judge Woods recused in 1990, the case was assigned to newly appointed Judge Susan Webber Wright, a former law clerk of Judge Henley's, and it remains in her court as of this writing, although the parties are following an agreed-upon plan and the Little Rock School District hopes to achieve unitary status and compliance by 2001.[61]

Aside from Judge Henley's school rulings,[62] there is his monumental ruling in holding the entire prison system unconstitutional.[63] Another outstanding federal district judge, a contemporary of Judge Henley's, Senior Judge G. Thomas Eisele wrote: "Judge Henley was tolerant of human frailties, but he was not tolerant of any abuse of official power. He supported honest, effective law enforcement officers, but he rightly held them to a high standard. He was the first, or one of the first, judges to hold an entire state penal system unconstitutional. His words describing the essence of the massive poblems he confronted still resonate almost thirty years later:"

> For the ordinary convict a sentence to the Arkansas Penitentiary today amounts to a banishment from civilized society to a dark and evil world completely alien to the free world, a world that is administered by criminals under unwritten rules and customs completely foreign to free world culture.[64]

In this "dark and evil world," such contraptions as the "Tucker Telephone" were employed to punish or gain information from the prisoners. The Tucker telephone was an old 1930's or 1920's style of telephone in which you wound a handle to cause it to function. (You also talked into a receiver at the front of the telephone and held a hearing piece to your ear that was connected by a covered wire to the telephone.) The Tucker telephone had been rigged so that it operated off of a battery and had wires that could be attached to the testicles or genitalia of a prisoner. When the handle was wound, the result was to give the prisoner a very painful shock in a very sensitive place.[65] This was only one example of prison life at that time.

Judge Henley was not a judicial activist, as Judge Eisele points out. He cited a newspaper feature article that quoted Judge Henley as follows: "In a field of social change I think it is wise for trial courts to hang back just a little because so many times legislation is needed, buildings have to be built. It takes a little time."[66] His objective was "to bring the citizenry along as he moved to enforce the Constitution and insure the equal rights of all of the inhabitants of this land. He was very successful in this regard."[67]

Judge Eisele tells a story about a trial in Judge Henley's court that he says might be apocryphal, but I think not. It seems that in a case involving moonshine whiskey, the government had neglected to obtain an expert witness to testify that the bottle offered in evidence was in fact moonshine. Judge Henley had been born and grew up in St. Joe, Searcy County, in the heart of the Ozarks, and he directed that the bottle be handed to him. He smelled the contents, took a swig of it, pronounced it to be moonshine and admitted it into evidence. The Court of Appeals reversed him on the ground that there was no expert witness. He was indignant and opined, "How would you find a person who, by training and experience, could be a better expert on moonshine than I am?"[68]

One time, a number of judges from the Eighth Circuit went to Canada to hunt Canadian geese. Although invited, Henley declined. He received a call one evening from the Canadian Mounties who had arrested and taken into custody these judges for exceeding their limits in shooting geese. They claimed to be American judges and wanted him to vouch for them, according to the Mounties. At first, he said that they sounded like dangerous characters, but eventually he relented and identified them for the Mounties.[69]

One product of Philip Graham Alston, Judge Henley's senior career law clerk, that gained considerable behind-the-scenes notoriety was *The Miller County Fulminator*. According to Judge Richard S. Arnold, *The Fulminator* came out daily, was a page long, contained Philip's "humorous and trenchant commentary on the events of the day, social and political, and it was anything but bland and impartial."[70] According to Judge Arnold, the circulation of *The Fulminator* at its peak was around eight,[71] although it was actually more than that as a result of people duplicating it and passing it on to others. It did not use actual names, but nicknames the author developed for various friends and political figures:

> Governor (as he then was) Dale Bumpers was the Earnest Young Man. The United States Attorney, W. H. Dillahunty, was El Supremo—the name perhaps reflecting the importance Mr. Alston placed on law enforcement. A certain United States Bankruptcy Judge was Little Fuzz. The Youngest Fulminatee was none other than Susan Webber Wright, now Chief Judge of the United States District Court for the Eastern District of Arkansas, and a former Henley law clerk. (I had a nickname too, but I choose not to reveal it.) The author himself was Titius Proudfoot, and the Judge for whom he worked was Justinian S. Blackstone.[72]

As Judge Arnold points out, the publication could not have continued without Judge Henley's acquiescence in it, and although judicial work is serious and must be disinterested, judges still must have a sense of humor and demonstrate their humanity in order to retain their balance.[73]

Judge Morris S. Arnold summed up Judge Henley this way, and it is probably a good way to conclude this discussion:

> I would not want these affectionate reminiscences to leave the impression that Judge Henley was not serious about his work. Far from it. Judge Henley, it is true, was not serious about himself, that is, he was not in the least bit self-important; but when it came to deciding cases, there was no one on the court more serious about getting it right than Smith was. He was tenacious. . . . That was because he was devoted to the judicial enterprise and to the proposition that every case deserved his best and most careful attention. He never gave up and the quality of his work remained extraordinarily high, right up to the end.[74]

The position that opened on the Court of Appeals for Judge Henley came about because Judge Pat Mehaffy of Little Rock took senior status in August 1974. Judge Mehaffy was appointed by President John F. Kennedy to the Eighth Circuit in 1963 to succeed Judge Joseph W. Woodrough of Nebraska, who had retired in 1961. At that time, there were no judges from Arkansas on the Court of Appeals. U. S. District Judge John E. Miller of Fort Smith, one of the finest judges Arkansas ever had, sought the job in 1961, as he had done earlier and unsuccessfully in 1954. Judge Miller was 73 years old by then, and in 1962 at a judicial conference, he was told by Attorney General Robert F. Kennedy that he was too old.[75] After that, the leading candidates were Edward L. Wright, Robert A. Leflar, and Pat Mehaffy. The appointment went to Pat Mehaffy, who attended Hendrix College and the University of Arkansas and graduated from the Arkansas Law School in Little Rock in 1927. After graduation, from 1929 to 1940, he served as assistant attorney general, chief deputy prosecuting attorney and then prosecuting attorney. He formed what was to be one of Little

Rock's most prominent firms, Mehaffy, Smith & Williams, with William J. Smith and John Williams. That firm grew to become Smith, Williams, Friday & Bowen and now is Friday, Eldredge & Clark. In 1973, Judge Mehaffy became Chief Judge of the Eighth Circuit.[76] While a practicing attorney, before going on the bench, Judge Mehaffy required each new associate in his firm to spend a year with the prosecuting attorney's office in Pulaski County to learn how to try a case. Robert V. Light and William Terry were two who had that experience. His orientation was directed toward the basic, nuts and bolts, practical approach to law.

Judge Mehaffy was the first Arkansas appointment to the Circuit Court of Appeals since Walter G. Riddick, who came from a prominent Little Rock family and served on the Court from 1942 until his death in 1953. Walter Riddick graduated from Washington & Lee and was a graduate of the Arkansas Law School at a time when it was the Law Department of the University of Arkansas. He had practiced law in Little Rock for 33 years when he was appointed to the Eighth Circuit. He was with the Missouri Pacific Railroad law department, then served in World War I, and then entered a firm that included Senator Joseph T. Robinson, later to be the Democratic vice-presidential nominee and in the 1930's, Senate Majority Leader. He excelled in practice, developed a large general business practice, and was elected Democratic National Committeeman in 1940. Senator Hattie Caraway wrote the Attorney General pleading for an Arkansas appointment and arguing that "Arkansas has never had a member on the Bench of this Circuit since it was organized." She said she excepted "a Carpetbagger, who was given a temporary appointment after the Civil War."[77] Although there was competition from other states and although Judge John E. Miller, a former U. S. Senator, and Congressman Clyde T. Ellis were also interested in the job and sought to characterize Riddick as a corporation lawyer, he was nonetheless nominated by President

Franklin D. Roosevelt in December 1941, and that was confirmed in 1942.[78]

Senator Caraway's description of Judge Henry C. Caldwell as a "carpetbagger" was hardly fair. Caldwell served the Eighth Circuit with distinction for thirteen years—hardly a temporary appointment—and served as Chief Judge.[79] He contributed extensively to the law of Arkansas even though he came from Iowa. He was a Union officer during the Civil War, and according to his great-great-grand nephew, writing for the Historical Society of the Eighth Circuit:

> He took the keys of surrender from Little Rock, then protected Arkansas from the Carpetbaggers. He was also a national figure who fought usury, and struggled to support the rights of minorities, the right to collectively bargain, and a common sense justice system. Two Presidents considered him for Chief Justice of the U. S. Supreme Court. Every major party tried to get him into the White House. Uriah Rose suggested that a statute be built of Clay [Judge Caldwell].[80]

Actually, Henry Clay Caldwell was born in Virginia—that part that later became West Virginia—and when he came to Arkansas, he liked it and stayed.

We have today a very fine federal bench in addition to the ones I have previously talked about in the Eastern District, Judges G. Thomas Eisele, Judge Stephen Reasoner, and Judge James Moody. (There is previous discussion of Judges Howard, Roy, Wilson, Woods and Wright, either in this chapter or in previous chapters.) In the Western District, we have Chief Judge Jimm Hendren, former Chief Judge Frank Waters, and Judges Harry Barnes and Robert Dawson. All of these are able judges. All of them added greatly to their capabilities in the private practice of the law, practicing with capable partners and associates and gaining a wealth of experience. Judge Harry Barnes was one of the most respected state trial judges in Arkansas even before he went on the federal bench, conducting court in the southern part of the Western District. That niche had gone unfilled since the retirement of Judge Oren Harris.

Of these judges, Judge Reasoner was referred to in law school as "Lord Coke" by one professor due to his fondness for the old common law. He frequently said, "the old law is the best law," but this had no adverse effect on his service as Editor-in-Chief of the *Arkansas Law Review* nor did it permeate his opinions on the bench.

Judge H. Franklin Waters of the Western District, who has been on the federal bench since 1981, and served as Chief Judge for much of that time, recently took senior status. An undergraduate of the University of Arkansas, he received his law degree from St. Louis University and worked for some years as a corporate attorney with Ralston-Purina. After that, he became a partner in Crouch, Blair, Cypert & Waters of Springdale and practiced there for fourteen years before he went on the bench. A decisive, no-nonsense judge, he has been thought of very highly by the practicing bar all of his career and is viewed as a first-rate trial judge. His decisiveness was brought home when he enjoined Warren Carpenter from filing frivolous lawsuits against a large number of defendants including Governor Bill Clinton and Judge Susan Webber Wright, among others. When Carpenter pursued these types of cases outside Arkansas in such venues as Memphis and Kansas City, Judge Waters issued a nationwide injunction against him. He also fined the plaintiff along the way. Carpenter was later placed in a federal institution.

Although he served only a few years on the bench because of a fatal illness, Judge William R. Overton had one of the highest profile cases in Arkansas in the early 1980's. The legislature passed a law requiring the teaching of "creation science" in the public schools. Creation science was the assertion of fundamentalist Christians that Darwin's theory of evolution was erroneous and that God created the earth and humans without any evolutionary process. Fortunately, the trial was not surrounded by the circus-like atmosphere of the Scopes trial in Tennessee in the early 20th Century. Judge Overton, in a well-reasoned opinion, declared the law unconstitutional as an effort to inject religion into the public school curriculum, and the Court of Appeals and Supreme Court affirmed.[81]

This discussion of federal judges concludes with Judge G. Thomas Eisele, who is now a Senior District Judge, but who has been one of the finest of Arkansas' trial judges during the last three decades of the 20th Century. A native of Hot Springs, Judge Eisele received his bachelor's degree from Washington University, and his LL.B. from Harvard Law School in 1950, followed a year later by an LL.M. from Harvard. He had extensive practice experience before going on the bench in 1970, serving as an associate with Wooten, Land & Matthews in Hot Springs for one year, then as Assistant U. S. Attorney, then with Owens, McHaney, Lofton & McHaney in Little Rock for several years, and finally in solo private practice. For sixteen years, he served as Chief Judge of the Eastern District. He took senior status in the early 1990's. Publicly spirited, he was an advisor to Governor Winthrop Rockefeller in the late 1960's, was a delegate to the 1969-70 state constitutional convention, and served on the Board of Trustees of the University of Arkansas. Moreover, he was honored by the national trial lawyers along the way as the outstanding trial judge in America. He had his share of tough cases along the way. When Judge Henley went to the Eighth Circuit in the mid-1970's, he inherited the prison case; and he had some tough cases relating to capital punishment, among numerous others. In all of this, he is universally looked upon as one of our finest judges, possessed of a superb mind and judicial temperament.

Some extensive discussion of state Supreme Court justices has previously been provided. Probably no member of our Supreme Court in history has had a more diverse, distinguished career in public service than Ray Thornton. He has served as Attorney General, as Congressman from two different congressional districts, as President of Arkansas State University, and as President of the University of Arkansas, prior to being elected an Associate Justice of the Supreme Court. David Newbern, who recently retired, had a substantial academic career in Fayetteville as a law professor prior to going on the Court of Appeals and then a few years later on the Supreme Court. Donald Corbin practiced law in Lewisville and Stamps for many years and represented Lafayette County in the General Assembly before being elected to the Supreme Court. Recently re-elected, he is one of the longest serving members of the Court today. Tom Glaze had an outstanding career as an attorney and worked considerably in public interest matters, serving as head of the Election Research Council, as an attorney for legal aid, and as assistant and then deputy Attorney General. He served as Chancery Judge, on the Court of Appeals and went on the Supreme Court in 1987. The Chief Justice, W. H. (Dub) Arnold, was in private practice in Arkadelphia for many years, and served for some years as a Chancellor and Probate Judge before being recently elected to the Court. Robert L. Brown, previously mentioned, began practice with Chowning, Mitchell, Hamilton & Burrow in Little Rock, was a deputy prosecuting attorney, served as a legal or legislative assistant to Governor and then Senator Dale Bumpers and later as an administrative assistant to Congressman Jim Guy Tucker, and then practiced law for thirteen years in Little Rock before being elected to the Court. Justice Annabelle Clinton Imber is discussed in the chapter on women lawyers.

* * * *

Conclusion

Despite the elective system of state judges, Arkansas has had good fortune in its judges, both state and federal. There have been some exceptions to that conclusion, but not many. Many judges have served long years in office, as is common in the federal courts, but applies in Arkansas to state judges also. Unless a judge is controversial, the people have tended to elect him or her over and over again.

A life of a person is not very long, even for those who live a very full life. So, it is perhaps well to close with thoughts expressed in a book published over thirty years ago:

> This book . . . is an urge to respond to the here and now and the immediate future just beyond. How well we climb our own hills will determine whether the hills to come after that will be momentous or not for those who follow us. Our chapter is written for today, but tomorrow will in large measure live by it. What we do will remain after us, in that moment when we pass "out of history into history and the awful responsibility of Time."[82]

Notes

1. Interview with Henry Woods, March 17, 1994, at p. 2.
2. *Id.* at 3.
3. *Ibid.*
4. *Id.* at 4-5.
5. *Id.* at 6.
6. *Id.* at 7.
7. *Ibid.*
8. *Id.* at 21.
9. *Id.* at 12.

10. *Id.* at 11.

11. *Id.* at 13.

12. Interview of March 2, 1993.

13. *Id.* at 1.

14. *Id.* at 4.

15. *Id.* at 4-5.

16. *Id.* at 7.

17. See generally, Justice Robinson's autobiography which he wrote shortly before he died.

18. All of the foregoing is from the interview with John A. Fogleman, March 19, 1993, pp. 1-10.

19. Interview, *id.* at 11-12.

20. *Id.* at p. 11.

21. Interview with Judge Tom Butt, Oct. 4, 1992, p. 11.

22. Fogleman Interview, *supra*, at 12.

23. *Ibid.*

24. *Id.* at 16.

25. *Id.* at 17-18.

26. Interview with Judge Tom Butt, October 4, 1992, pp. 1-2. I might add that, having lived in Fayetteville for a good many years as a student and later as a member of the law faculty, I had heard of the legendary Rex Perkins long before Judge Butt zeroed in on him, and I have included at least one Rex Perkins story in this material involving Dr. Frank Rigall.

27. *Id.* at 2-3.

28. *Id.* at 3.

29. *Ibid.*

30. *Ibid.*

31. *Id.* at 4-5.

32. *Id.* at 8-9.

33. *Id.* at p. 10.

34. *Id.* at p. 10.

35. *Id.* at p. 11.

36. *Id.* at p. 12.

37. *Id.* at p. 15.

38. 14 S.W.3d, number 2 at Ct. R-6 (March 28, 2000).

39. Interview with Mrs. George Rose Smith, February 26, 1993.

40. Brown, "George Rose Smith," *The Arkansas Lawyer*, Jan. 1987, pp. 17-18, by Justice Robert L. Brown.

41. *Id.* at 18.

42. *Ibid.*

43. *Id.* at 21.

44. *Id.* at 20-21.

45. The alleged authors were Jasper Bogus McClodd and Pepe LePeu. The article on legislative and judicial dynamism in Arkansas does not appear on my resume.

46. Interview with Mrs. Peg Newton Smith, Feb. 26, 1993, pp. 1-2.

47. Interview with Peg Smith, *supra*, at pp. 7-8.

48. *Id.* at p. 9.

49. Of course, Hubbell was an all-SWC tackle for the Razorbacks and was very large.

50. Prior to that, he was a delegate to the Constitutional Convention of 1970 and was a member of the University of Arkansas Board of Trustees during a short period in the 1970's.

51. Brennan, *Preface*, 78 MINN. L. REV. 1-2 (1993), with citations.

52. Frank and Higginbotham, *A Brief Biography of Judge Richard S. Arnold*, 78 MINN. L. REV. 5, 8 (1993). "In short, Arnold learned to question what had been the Harvard point of view during his law school and law review years."

53. *Id.* at 11.

54. *Id.* at 13.

55. In *Dodson v. Arkansas Activities Association*, 468 F. Supp. 394 (E.D. Ark. 1979), he struck down high school women's half-court basketball and opined that they do not have the same experience as boys nor the same access to college scholarships.

56. Wald, *Judge Arnold and Individual Rights*, 78 MINN. L. REV. 35, 48 (1993).

57. Brennan, *supra* at 3; and see also, Lay, *supra* at 26-27.

58. Frank and Higginbotham, *supra* at 6.

59. Much of the foregoing comes from his biography which appears in 18 WILLIAM MITCHELL LAW REVIEW at 553 (1992).

60. *Aaron v. Cooper*, 257 F.2d 33 (1958), and *Cooper v. Aaron*, 358 U. S. 1 (1958).

61. Much of the foregoing bibliographical material on Judge Henley is taken from Judicial Conference of the United States, *A History of the United States Court of Appeals for the Eighth Circuit*, pp. 78-81 (1977). Some is taken from personal knowledge.

62. These are compiled in footnote 1 in S. Wright, *The Judge from St. Joe*, 52 ARK. L. REV. 308 (1999).

63. *Holt v. Sarver*, 309 F. Supp. 362 (E.D. Ark. 1970).

64. *Holt v. Sarver*, 309 F. Supp. 362 at 381 (E.D. Ark. (1970). The foregoing quotation from that case and from Judge Eisele is taken from Eisele, *A Tribute to Judge J. Smith Henley*, 52 ARK. L. REV. 305, 306 (1999).

65. When I taught one year at the University of Cincinnati College of Law as a Visiting Distinguished Professor in the early 1980's, a group of students who had been taking a seminar in Civil Liberties came to my office to ask me to explain what the Tucker telephone was. The group included some young women. I explained it in much the same way after apologizing for any graphic language that I might have to use.

66. Eisele, *supra* at 306, quoting from Patrict Henry, "Judge Who Reformed Prison System Dies," *Arkansas Democrat-Gazette*, p. B-1 (Oct. 20, 1997).

67. Eisele, *supra* at 307.

68. *Ibid.* This same story was told to me by Judge J. Smith Henley.

69. As told by Judge J. Smith Henley to the author.

70. R. Arnold, *Judge J. Smith Henley: A Personal Reminiscence*, 52 ARK. L. REV. 300, 303 (1999).
71. *Ibid.*
72. *Ibid.*
73. Copies of *The Fulminator* may be found in the Arkansas Supreme Court Library, having been compiled by Supreme Court Librarian Jacqueline S. Wright.
74. M. Arnold, *A Tribute to Judge J. Smith Henley*, 52 ARK. L. REV. 297, 299 (1999).
75. Judicial Conference of the United States, "A History of the United States Court of Appeals for the Eighth Circuit," pp. 74-75 (1977).
76. *Ibid.*
77. *Id.* at 60. The foregoing about Judge Riddick is from the same source.
78. *Id.* at 60-61.
79. *Ibid.*
80. Roeder, "Henry Clay Caldwell: The Early Years," v. 6, p. 1, *Historical Society News* (1997).
81. *McLean v. Arkansas Board of Education*, 529 F. Supp. 1255 (E.D. Ark. 1982).
82. R. Wright, *The Law of Airspace* 420 (1967), with the last quote being from Robert Penn Warren, *All the King's Men* 464 (1953).

INDEX

(References are to pages)

Bonner, Tom, 325

Boone, Joe L., 143

Boswell, Ted, 138

Bott, George, 127

Bowen, J. H., 145

Bowen, William H., 128, 131, 218, 232-234, 238, 350

Bowie, Jim, 43

Boyce, Edward, 176

Boyce, Sam H., 188

Boyce, Wayne, 160, 161, 167

Boyett, Comer, 138

Bradley, Joseph P., Justice, 291

Bradshaw, D. E., 92

Bradwell, Myra, 290

Brantley, Ellen B., Judge, 177, 188, 300

Branton, Wiley A., 274, 276, 277, 279

Branton, Wiley A., Jr., Judge, 277, 282

Brennan, William J., Justice, 372, 373, 374

Brent, Margaret, 289

Cherry, Sandra Wilson, 173, 175, 176, 187, 189, 194, 302, 303

Chesnutt, Jim, Judge, 370

Civil War, 65-76
    Condition disruptive, 75-76
    Regional differences, 65
    Seat of capital moved, 68
    Slaves in state, 66
    Wealth of state, 66

Civiletti, Benjamin R., 179

Claiborne, W. C. C., Territorial Governor, 6

Clark, Tom C., Justice, 125, 150

Claycomb, H. Murray, 193

Clayton, Powell, Governor, 79, 257, 318

Cleburne, Patrick Ronayne, General, 68

Clendenin, J. J., 71

Client Security Fund, 153, 183

Clinton, Bill, Governor and President, 153, 167, 182, 232, 234, 303, 309, 342, 372, 384

Clinton, Hillary Rodham, 153, 182, 189, 303, 309

Cocke, John W., 22

Cockrill, Ashley, 104, 342

Cockrill, Howard, 137

Gerstaecker, Friedrich, 44
  Description of early Arkansas courts, 44-46

Gibb, Ruth Wassell, 295

Gibbs, Mifflin W., 255, 256-260, 262, 263, 268, 269

Gilbert, Martin, 171

Gilbert, Victoria V., 129

Gill, John P., 155, 159, 164, 173, 182

Gill, Marion, 141

Gill, Marjem Jackson, 164

Gingerich, James D., 184

Gitchel, W. Dent, 218, 235, 237

Gitelman, Morton, 214, 215, 218

Givens, Art, 224

Glaze, Thomas A., Justice, 147, 190, 386

Glover, David M. (Mac), 170, 172, 176, 178, 188

Goar, Frank M., 207-208

Goldberg, Arthur, Justice, 149

Goldner, Charles W., Jr., 234, 238

Goodell, Levina, 291

Huie, C. R., Judge, 145, 162-163, 361

Hughes, Allen, 98, 342

Hughes, Charles Evans, Chief Justice, 271

Hughes, Sarah F., Judge, 138

Humphrey, Helen G., 296

Humphrey, Marion A., Judge, 282

Humphreys, T. H., 104

Hunt, Eugene, 181

Hunt, Silas, 269, 274, 276

Hussman, Walter, 141

Hyatt, Jim, 337

Imber, Annabelle Clinton, Justice, 166, 167, 170, 171, 189, 190, 300, 386

Inheritance Act of 1969, 149

Integrated (unified) bar, 107, 110, 111, 148, 149, 150, 343

IOLTA, 170, 172, 174, 175, 176-177, 178

Isgrig, Fred A., 264

Ishmael, Randall W., 166, 173, 188

Ivy, Bruce, 337, 362

Morse, Joshua M., III, 227

Moses, Hamilton, 313, 319, 342

Mouser, Rosalind M., 178, 182

Mullins, David W., U. of A. President, 219, 335

Mullins, M. Eugene, 236

Murphey, Arthur G., Jr., 234

Murphy, George W., 264

Murphy, Isaac, 67

Murrah, Albert P., Chief Judge, 129

Nance, Cecil B., Sr., 342

Nash, William, 122, 210, 315, 317

Neal, Olly, Judge, 188, 190, 280, 281

Nelson, Sheffield, 169, 224

Neuhoff, Ralph R., 128

Newbern, David, Justice, 166, 176, 190, 214, 338, 386

Newton, Thomas W., 18

Niblock, Walter, 141, 160, 167, 350

Nichols, Guerdon D., 272, 273, 276